ANOREXIA NERVOSA

A Monograph of the National Institute of Child Health and Human Development

Anorexia Nervosa

A Monograph of the National Institute of Child Health and Human Development

Edited by

Robert A. Vigersky, M.D.
Reproduction Research Branch
National Institute of Child Health and Human Development
National Institutes of Health
Bethesda, Maryland

Raven Press ▪ New York

Raven Press, 1140 Avenue of the Americas, New York, New York 10036

Made in the United States of America

International Standard Book Number 0–89004–185–7
Library of Congress Catalog Card Number 76–57005

Preface

Anorexia nervosa is a disorder of unknown etiology which has recently enjoyed the investigative attention of physicians and basic scientists. It is of interest: to psychiatrists because of its psychologic and perceptual abnormalities; to endocrinologists because of its hypothalamic–pituitary–end organ dysfunction; to gynecologists because it frequently presents as secondary amenorrhea; to pediatricians because it often occurs in preteenagers and it appears to be a reversal of puberty; and to internists of varied subspecialties because of its protean manifestations and complications. For basic scientists, it serves as a model for the study of the effects of malnutrition, for the investigation of neurogenic amines, and for the understanding of factors such as critical body mass and hypothalamic function. Finally, it presents a major therapeutic challenge that has yet to be successfully met.

These considerations, added to the apparent increasing incidence of the disorder, inspired the convening of the first multidisciplinary conference on anorexia nervosa held on October 13–15, 1976 at the National Institutes of Health, Bethesda, Maryland. This conference not only provided a platform for the presentation of the chapters included in this volume, but, more importantly, provided a forum for an exciting and productive interchange of ideas, methods, philosophies, and speculations between scientists of vastly different backgrounds.

Robert A. Vigersky

Acknowledgments

It would be impossible to acknowledge all those people who provided assistance in the development, organization, and administration of this conference. However, credit for the scientific, administrative, and financial support of this conference must first be given to the National Institute of Child Health and Human Development, the Institute's Scientific Director, Dr. James Sidbury, and its Administration Officer, Mr. John Smart. The additional financial support of the National Institute of Mental Health and the aide of its Scientific Director, Dr. Robert Cohen, and its Chief of the Adult Psychiatry Branch, Dr. William Bunney must also be acknowledged. Most important, however, was the invaluable inspirational and intellectual guidance of Dr. D. Lynn Loriaux. Finally, the secretarial assistance of Ms. Mary Flanagan and Mrs. Jane Santymire was crucial in bringing the conference and book to fruition.

Contents

Contributors

Stewart Agras, M.D.
Department of Psychiatry and Behavioral Sciences
Stanford University School of Medicine
Stanford, California 94305

Arnold E. Andersen, M.D.
The Johns Hopkins Hospital
Henry Phipps Clinic
Baltimore, Maryland 21205

Lester Baker, M.D.
Philadelphia Child Guidance Center
34th Street and Civic Center Boulevard
Philadelphia, Pennsylvania 19104

J. Baulu, M.S.
Neurobehavioral Laboratory
Yale University School of Medicine
333 Cedar Street
New Haven, Connecticut 06510

C. J. Beardwood, M.D.
Academic Department of Psychiatry
Royal Free Hospital
London, NW3 2QG England

Robert M. Boyar, M.D.
Department of Internal Medicine
Texas Southwestern Medical School
5323 Harry Hines Boulevard
Dallas, Texas 75235

H. Leon Bradlow, M.D.
Institute for Steroid Research
Montefiore Hospital and Medical Center
111 East 210th Street
Bronx, New York 10467

Gregory M. Brown, M.D., Ph.D.
Clarke Institute of Psychiatry
250 College Street
Toronto, Canada M5T 1R8

Hilde Bruch, M.D.
Baylor College of Medicine
Texas Medical Center
Houston, Texas 77030

Kenneth Burman, M.D.
Walter Reed Army Medical Center
Washington, D.C. 20012

Regina Casper, M.D.
Illinois State Psychiatric Institute
1601 W. Taylor Street
Chicago, Illinois 60612

Lee Combrinck-Graham, M.D.
Philadelphia Child Guidance Center
34th Street and Civic Center Road
Philadelphia, Pennsylvania 19104

Donald Coscina, Ph.D.
Clarke Institute of Psychiatry
250 College Street
Toronto, Canada M5T 1R8

A. H. Crisp, M.D.
Academic Department of Psychiatry
St. George's Hospital Medical School
Blackshaw Road
London, England SW17 OQT

John Davis, M.D.
Illinois State Psychiatric Institute
1601 W. Taylor Street
Chicago, Illinois 60612

V. DeSouza, B.A.
The Royal Free Hospital
Pond Street
Hampstead
London, England NW3 2QG

Yin-Ying Djuh, B.A.
Kyle Metabolic Unit
Walter Reed Army Medical Center
Washington, D.C. 20012

Elke Eckert, M.D.
University Hospitals
University of Minnesota
Box 393
Mayo Memorial Building
Minneapolis, Minnesota 55455

Philip Felig, M.D.
Yale University School of Medicine
333 Cedar Street
New Haven, Connecticut 06510

Marshall Folstein, M.D.
The Johns Hopkins University
School of Medicine
Baltimore, Maryland 21205

Hans Fries, M.D.
University Hospital
750–14 Uppsala, Sweden

Rose E. Frisch, Ph.D.
Harvard Center for Population Studies
9 Bow Street
Cambridge, Massachusetts 02138

Paul E. Garfinkel, M.D.
Clarke Institute of Psychiatry
250 College Street
Toronto, Canada M5T 1R8

David Garner, Ph.D.
Mental Health Clinic
Toronto East General Hospital
833 Coxwell Avenue
Toronto, Canada M4C 3E8

Solomon C. Goldberg, Ph.D.
National Institute of Mental Health
5600 Fisher's Lane
Rockville, Maryland 20852

Richard S. Green, M.D.
Long Island Jewish-Hillside Medical Center
P.O. Box 38
Glen Oaks, New York 11004

Katherine Halmi, M.D.
Department of Psychiatry
University of Iowa
500 Newton Road
Iowa City, Iowa 52242

Britta Harding, B.A.
Academic Department of Psychiatry
St. George's Hospital Medical School
Blackshaw Road
London SW17 OQT England

Y. H. Huang, Ph.D.
Neurobehavioral Laboratory
Yale University School of Medicine
333 Cedar Street
New Haven, Connecticut 06510

Nikolai Jeuniewic, M.D.
Clarke Institute of Psychiatry
250 College Street
Toronto, Canada MST 1R8

Ann Johanson, M.D.
Department of Pediatrics
University of Virginia Medical School
Charlottesville, Virginia 22901

R. S. Kalucy, M.B.
Academic Department of Psychiatry
St. George's Hospital Medical School
Blackshaw Road
London SW17 OQT England

Jack Katz, M.D.
Department of Psychiatry
Montefiore Hospital and Medical Center
Bronx, New York 10467

Norman J. Knorr, M.D.
Department of Psychiatry
University of Virginia Medical School
Charlottesville, Virginia 22901

J. H. Lacey, M.B.
Academic Department of Psychiatry
St. George's Hospital Medical School
Blackshaw Road
London SW17 OQT England

Ronald Liebman, M.D.
Philadelphia Child Guidance Center
34th Street and Civic Center Boulevard
Philadelphia, Pennsylvania 19104

D. Lynn Loriaux, M.D., Ph.D.
National Institute of Child
Health and Human Development
Building 10, Room 10B-09
Bethesda, Maryland 20014

J. W. Mass, M.D.
Neurobehavioral Laboratory
Yale University School of Medicine
333 Cedar Street
New Haven, Connecticut 06510

Paul R. McHugh, M.D.
The Johns Hopkins Hospital
550 N. Broadway
Baltimore, Maryland 21205

Salvador Minuchin, M.D.
Philadelphia Child Guidance Center
34th Street and Civic Center Boulevard
Philadelphia, Pennsylvania 19104

Harvey Moldofsky, M.D.
Clarke Institute of Psychiatry
250 College Street
Toronto, Canada M5T 1R8

Timothy H. Moran, B.S.
Department of Psychiatry and
Behavioral Sciences
Johns Hopkins University
School of Medicine
Baltimore, Maryland 21205

Seoras Morrison, M.D.
Laboratory of Pathophysiology
National Cancer Institute
National Institutes of Health
Bethesda, Maryland 20014

Thomas Moshang, Jr., M.D.
Hahnemann Medical College and
Hospital
230 N. Broad Street
Philadelphia, Pennsylvania 19102

Herbert L. Needleman, M.D.
Children's Hospital Medical Center
300 Longwood Avenue
Boston, Massachusetts 02115

Sven J. Nillius, M.D.
University Hospital
750–14
Uppsala, Sweden

Ghanshyam N. Pandey, Ph.D.
Biological Research Laboratory
Illinois State Psychiatric Institute
Chicago, Illinois 60612

Michael Pertchuk, M.D.
Center for Behavioral Medicine
Department of Psychiatry
University of Pennsylvania
Philadelphia, Pennsylvania 19104

John H. Rau, Ph.D.
Department of Psychology
Long Island Jewish-Hillside Medical
Center
Glen Oaks, New York 11004

D. Eugene Redmond, Jr., M.D.
Neurobehavioral Laboratory
Yale University School of Medicine
34 Park Street
New Haven, Connecticut 06510

Bernice Rosman, Ph.D.
Philadelphia Child Guidance Center
34th Street and Civic Center Boulevard
Philadelphia, Pennsylvania 19104

Gerald F. Russell, M.D.
The Royal Free Hospital
Pond Street
Hampstead, London NW3 2QG,
England

Barry M. Sherman, M.D.
University of Iowa Hospital
Iowa City, Iowa 52242

Joseph A. Silverman, M.D.
Babies Hospital
The Children's Medical and Surgical
Center of New York
Columbia Presbyterian Medical Center
630 W. 168th Street
New York, New York 10032

D. R. Snyder, Ph.D.
Neurobehavioral Laboratory
Yale University School of Medicine
333 Cedar Street
New Haven, Connecticut 06510

Harvey C. Stancer, M.D., Ph.D.
Clarke Institute of Psychiatry
250 College Street
Toronto, Canada MST 1R8

Daniel Strum, M.D.
Kyle Metabolic Unit
Walter Reed Army Medical Center
Washington, D.C. 20012

Robert D. Utiger, M.D.
Department of Medicine
The University of Pennsylvania
The School of Medicine
Philadelphia, Pennsylvania 19104

Apostolas G. Vagenakis, M.D.
University of Massachusetts
Medical Center
55 Lake Avenue North
Worcester, Massachusetts 01605

Robert A. Vigersky, M.D.
Reproduction Research Branch
National Institute of Child Health
and Human Development
National Institutes of Health
Bethesda, Maryland 20014

Deborah Waber, Ph.D.
Department of Psychiatry
Children's Hospital Medical Center
300 Longwood Avenue
Boston, Massachusetts 02115

Anthony Wakeling, M.D.
The Royal Free Hospital
Pond Street
Hampstead, London NW3 2QG,
England

Michelle P. Warren, M.D.
The Roosevelt Hospital
428 W. 59th Street
New York, New York 10019

Leonard Wartofsky, M.D.
Kyle Metabolic Unit
Walter Reed Army Medical Center
Washington, D.C. 20012

Joellen Werne, M.D.
560 Oxford Avenue, Suite 6
Palo Alto, California 94025

Leif Wide, M.D.
Department of Clinical Chemistry
University Hospital,
S-750 14
Uppsala, Sweden

Frances D. Wright, B.S.
Kyle Metabolic Unit
Walter Reed Army Medical Center
Washington, D.C. 20012

Anorexia Nervosa, edited by
R. A. Vigersky. Raven Press,
New York © 1977.

Psychological Antecedents of Anorexia Nervosa

Hilde Bruch

Department of Psychiatry, Baylor College of Medicine, Houston, Texas 77030

INTRODUCTION

Anorexia nervosa is an illness with a rather sudden onset in seemingly healthy adolescent girls, who are described as having been perfect children, obedient, hard working, excelling academically, admired by their teachers, and often the confidants of their parents. What supposedly precipitates this severe illness are trivial remarks or commonplace events. The question offers itself, why are the youngsters so unprepared to meet the challenge of adolescence—namely, the need to grow beyond the immediate family and to engage in relationships with members of their own age group; and what are the antecedents in their thinking and behavior that make them withdraw to their own bodies and choose the road of starvation?

Study of the life histories of many patients with anorexia nervosa has shown that this excessive concern with the body and its size and the rigid control over eating are late symptoms, representing a desperate fight against feeling enslaved and exploited, not permitted or competent to lead lives of their own. In this blind search for a sense of identity and selfhood, they will not accept anything that their parents, or the world around them, have to offer; they would rather starve than continue a life of accommodation. The trouble is that this effort is in many ways a futile struggle because changing their body size cannot provide what they want to achieve or compensate for the deficits in the overall development.

This view of anorexia nervosa as a struggle for a self-respecting identity developed gradually from contact with many patients who were seen in extensive psychotherapy (1). An effort was made to identify the psychological issues and faulty adaptive patterns that at a crucial period in their life had resulted in the impasse from which they tried to escape through self-starvation.

To reconstruct and define the underlying psychological problems and issues is not easy because hunger has such a dramatic effect on the physiological and psychological functioning. The somatic consequences of starvation are well known; they are called the classic symptoms of anorexia nervosa. The enormous psychological changes due to hunger have often been confused with the underlying psychological problems instead of being identified as consequences of the nutritional deficiency. In speaking of the enormous behavior changes, parents often state that their daughter seems to act like a different person. In some respects this is a correct observation; she suffers now from the hunger disease in the literal sense of the word.

Much of what has been described as "anorectic behavior" resembles in many respects what has been observed in ordinary starving people who are also tormented by a continuous preoccupation with food. Many features which are described in elaborate psychodynamic formulations as characteristic of anorexia nervosa—such as narcissistic self-absorption, regression to earlier levels of mental functioning, splitting of the ego, and fragmented and psychotic-like thinking—are also observed in other victims of famine and must be considered to be consequences of the hunger experience.

Marked individual differences are observed in the severity of these symptoms, depending on the pre-illness personality, the damaging effect of increasing isolation, and the severity of the starvation. Anorexia nervosa patients are very reluctant to give direct information about the psychic effects of starvation; what I have learned about it was revealed only during later phases of therapy. Denial of illness is characteristic of anorexia. This may be negativistic refusal to communicate but also it may express disturbed perception and abnormal interpretation of experiences. To give just one example: hyperacuity and hypersensitivity to various sensory stimuli during the acute starvation phase are often handled with great secrecy, or they may be cherished as mysterious signs of specialness. A meaningful therapeutic exploration of the underlying and initiating factors can be accomplished only after the worst emaciation has been corrected. I have come to the conclusion that the starvation effect on the psyche is to a large extent responsible for the drawn out course of the illness, sustaining it in many ways and making recognition and resolution of the underlying psychological issues so difficult.

FAMILY INTERACTION

Family relationships also undergo marked changes. There are few conditions that provoke so much concern, but also frustration, rage, and anger, as the spectacle of a starving child refusing food. Life in the quiet, smooth-running, "happy" homes now seems to degenerate into constant arguments and open fighting. A struggle for power is now out in the open; in many ways this is an exaggeration of what was formerly only implied. Characteristically, patients with anorexia nervosa have been well cared for as children, were well fed and well dressed, and were exposed to the best educational and cultural opportunities. The parents may be described as overprotective, overconcerned, and overambitious. They overvalue their children and expect obedience and superior performance in return. As long as the children comply, they fulfill the parents' dreams of their own ideals by growing and behaving exactly as the parents had planned and expected. With approaching adolescence conditions change and the child starts to make justified claims for independence; this is unacceptable to the parents and the illness begins as an expression of this struggle that is not being acknowledged.

The parents' need to be in control, only implied as long as the child was overconforming, now comes into the open and is expressed in dictatorial efforts to force the child to eat and attempts to make her go back to her former behavior. Resolution of these acute conflicts is a precondition for effective treatment; long-range recovery requires change of the old patterns of family interaction. In conjoint family sessions, parents appear impervious to the emotional needs and reactions of the patients, in the past as well as in the present, and they focus on weight loss as the only difficulty, or they stress the nuisance value of the illness.

The families look stable, with few broken marriages, and the parents emphasize the happiness of their homes. Underlying the apparent marital harmony, deep disillusionment between partners can be recognized during extended contact. Each partner is convinced that he or she is an unusually good parent, with secret competition about who is bringing the greater sacrifice, and each parent expects confirmation and loyalty from this, the perfect child (3). Often a mother needs this child to feel complete and as proof of her own perfection. The fathers, despite social and financial success which is often considerable, feel in some sense "second best." They are enormously preoccupied with outer appearances, admire fitness and beauty, and expect proper behavior and measurable achievement from their children. Many are exceedingly weight conscious, some weighing themselves every single day, even expecting this of other members of the family.

The family constellation may be of psychological importance. Two-thirds of the families have no sons, daughters only. In other families, the anorexic girl was the youngest with two or three older brothers, thus feeling under pressure to keep up with the boys. The age of the parents may also be a factor of some psychological significance. In my last 50 cases, although many of the daughters were first-born, the average age of the fathers at the time of the birth of the child was 38 years, with 55 as the highest age. The mothers' ages were above 30, with 43 years as the oldest. Whatever the individual characteristics of such parents, their age implies well-established, well-functioning, and set-in-its-ways homes. Concepts of "special achievement" and "only outstanding is good enough" are built-in in such families, although this is rarely openly expressed. When talking with parents who have had no previous psychiatric contact, it is not unusual to hear frank statements that "she is the supreme disappointment of our life."

HUNGER AWARENESS AND INDIVIDUATION

Such families fail to transmit an adequate sense of competence and self-value to a child whose feelings of worth and importance may derive from being needed by each parent. The illness represents an effort to escape from this overdemanding role and to establish a sense of identity. Since their goal is a life of absolute perfection, their concepts of being significant and worthwhile are quite unrealistic. Avoidance of fatness, which all mention as the driving motive, is part of this search for perfection.

The means of attaining this goal is severe restriction of the food intake. This they do not describe as deliberate refusal, but as not needing to eat, not feeling hungry, or feeling full after only a few bites. What looks like a failure of appetite is basically the fear of having no control over their eating. The fear of not being in control, not only of the eating function, is a basic issue underlying the anorexia nervosa syndrome. This is expressed in their clinging dependency on the home, accompanied by open rejection of everything that comes from the parents, and the inability to make decisions.

To illustrate how parental attitudes are related to a child's failure to develop a sense of self-directed identity, I have constructed a model of child development with a dual emphasis. Two forms of behavior need to be differentiated from birth on, that *initiated* in the individual and that *in response* to external stimuli. For healthy development, appropriate *responses to clues* originating in the child are as essential as *stimulation* from the environment. According to former assumptions of development, the child was conceived as rather undifferentiated, molded mainly by the ministrations of the environment. There has been a shift in our view of the infant; the emphasis is increasingly on the infant's own individual contributions to his development from his birth on. In reconstructions of the early development of anorexia nervosa patients, the outstanding findings are deficits in confirmation of child-initiated clues. In these families, growth and development are not conceived of as the child's accomplishments but as those of the parents.

The confusion in hunger awareness, the deep fear of having no inner control, can be related directly to the early experiences. These children were well cared for in every physical detail, but everything was done according to the mother's decisions and feelings, not according to the child's demands. A mother who is sensitively attuned to her child's expression of need offers food when he shows signs of nutritional distress, and thus the child learns to recognize "hunger" as a distinct sensation. If a mother's reactions are inappropriate or contradictory—be they neglectful, oversolicitous, or inhibiting—the child fails to learn to differentiate between being hungry and other sources of discomfort, and he grows up without discriminating awareness of his bodily sensations or a sense of control over them. This type of superimposition can be recognized with great regularity in the developmental histories of patients with anorexia nervosa and in the ongoing transactions of such families. It not only results in serious intrapsychic disturbances in confusion about hunger, but it also deprives the child of feeling that she is living her own life. Instead, she feels she is the property of her parents, feeling helpless under the influence of internal urges and external demands without inner guideposts.

The pubertal growth spurt with its greater nutritional needs is frightening to these patients. They become panicky if they gain some extra weight. This coincides with the general dissatisfaction about feeling enslaved and exploited, not developing as individuals in their own right. They expect that by being slimmer they will be more competent and deserving of respect.

CONCEPTUAL DEVIATIONS

Disturbed hunger awareness, the frightened feeling of not being in control, is only a small fraction of the disturbances in conceptualization that can be related to faulty transactional patterns and excessive accommodation. Long before the illness becomes manifest, these youngsters, suffering from a lack of autonomy, had difficulties with decision-making. Instead of being recognized as abnormal overconformity, this was praised by the parents, and also teachers, as special goodness. They had always done what they had been drilled to do, and they had never dared to test their own capacities. These shortcomings become dramatically apparent with adolescence. Subtle expressions were present throughout childhood but were overlooked.

As treatment progresses beyond the obsession with food and weight, these girls become capable of looking at their early development in objective terms; then they no longer claim defensively that everything was right, or are so preoccupied with blaming others that they remember only rage, frustration, and disappointment. During this new self-evaluation, it becomes apparent that throughout childhood they had, in a way, "marched to a different drummer," a drummer who kept them tied to the values and convictions of early thinking.

We have learned from Piaget and Inhelder (2) that the capacity to think, the conceptual development, goes through definite phases that partly are innate but need interaction with an encouraging environment for appropriate development. Experiences are organized through the processes of *assimilation* and *accommodation*. Both adaptive processes are essential, but the potentially anorexic youngsters function more with the accommodating mode, assimilating little as truly their own. They continue to function with the morality and style of thinking of early childhood, that of preconceptual and concrete operations; Piaget called this the period of egocentricity. The next step to formal operations, the ability to perform new abstract thinking and evaluations that is characteristic of adolescent development, is deficient or completely absent in them.

The discovery of real defects in conceptualization came as a surprise. Patients with anorexia nervosa usually excel in their school performance, and this has been interpreted as indicating great giftedness and intelligence. Not uncommonly, the excellent academic achievements are the result of great effort, which becomes even greater after they become ill. Sometimes it comes as a shocking surprise that performance on college aptitude tests or other evaluations of general ability falls below what the excellent school grades suggested. As a group these patients are what one might call academic overachievers.

A much more serious indication of a disharmonious development is found in their everyday thinking and their rigid interpretation of human relationships, and in their self-evaluation and self-concept. A symptom that has been puzzling for a long time is a nearly delusional disturbance in their "body image"—they are unable to "see" themselves and the severe emaciation realistically. This distortion must be viewed as part of misperceptions on a much wider scale. Although they have absorbed an enormous amount of knowledge from their teachers and from reading, their everyday conceptual development seems to be arrested at an early level.

During the collaborative reevaluation of their development, the early roots of their cognitive egocentricity can be recognized. These girls describe themselves as having always been driven to be good, to live by the rules, and as having made every effort never to arouse criticism or discontent in their parents or teachers. A few parents are aware of the literal mindedness of their children, their continued childish interpretations of life situations; most glory in having such conforming and obedient children.

It has been recognized for a long time that these youngsters skip the classic period of resistance early in life; they continue to function with the morality of a young child, remaining convinced of the absolute rightness of the grown-ups and of their own obligation to be obedient. Asking them if they ever misbehaved or to describe the worst thing they ever did is deeply disturbing to them. Following their own inclinations or expressing desires of their own is outside the range of consideration, it has never occurred to them. This overcompliance extends to minute details in everyday living. They accept presents of their parents' choosing, what they are "supposed" to get, and will not dare to express wishes of their own, even if they are aware of wanting something else. Even during the brittle fight about their right to be as skinny as they want to be, they feel they are not doing anything unusual. On the contrary, since society praises slenderness, they feel they have earned and deserve praise, awe, and respect for the thinness they have accomplished.

The same overcompliant adapting to others is expressed in their friendship patterns. One girl described a series of friendships, only one friend at a time. She had strong feelings for each girl and developed different interests and a different personality with each new friend. She felt that she was a blank who had to go along with what others enjoyed. The idea that she had something of her own individuality to contribute to a friendship never occurred to her.

This is a common pattern for girls with anorexia nervosa, each time the friendship ending without any particular reason except their getting out of step. Others take care of the newcomers in the school, the lame ducks, who are otherwise handicapped and have no established friendship group. Over and over they repeat the painful and disappointing experience that the lame duck friend gains a position in one of the groups and leaves them behind. If they have one particular friend, they are invariably in the role of the follower.

If one looks for it, one finds with great regularity that they become socially isolated during the year preceding the illness; some will explain that they have withdrawn from their former friends, others feel they are being excluded. These youngsters are excessively concerned with the prestige rating of various cliques and complain that they have always been on the fringe, not truly belonging to any group. With their rigid, judgmental attitude, they begin to complain that the others are too childish, too superficial, too much interested in boys, or in other ways not living up to the ideal of perfection according to which they themselves function and also demand from others. The new ways of acting and thinking that are characteristic for adolescence are strange and frightening to them. The illness becomes manifest when they are completely out of step with their age group. This is probably the most obvious expression of their failure to make the change from concrete operations to abstract thinking, which involves the new capacity to make independent propositions and deductions.

Unsatisfying overcompliance is also apparent in their attitude toward work and school; doing what is expected remains for them the dominant theme. Even when there is some expression of independent thinking, even originality, the inner experience is that of conforming. One girl was quite imaginative in writing short stories, but she reacted to praise by her teacher with the feeling that she was lucky she had a teacher who liked the way she wrote; the idea that she had made a genuine contribution was outside her range of thinking. After her illness began, she felt she had lost her imagination, that she no longer could write. When she received a high grade, she thought that the teacher had felt sorry for her.

There are many individual differences in how the literal-minded, concrete style of thinking expresses itself. An important feature is the rigidity with which these youngsters cling to their early convictions and notions, and they conduct their life with a distorted sense of reality. They defend with vigor and secret superiority the absolute rightness of their early convictions.

I would like to give just one example of how such rigid early childhood convictions overshadow the whole development. This girl was born as the fourth daughter of parents who were in their 40s. The older sisters married when she was quite young, and the one next to her in age went away to boarding school. So she grew up as an only child in a well-functioning, sophisticated, and well-meaning household. There were memories of being bewildered when these grown women (her sisters) visited and acted as though they belonged; she was very concerned about their good opinion. She vividly remembered one sentence that was often used: "Isn't she spoiled?" Although this was said jokingly and with affection, she came to the conclusion that being spoiled was a shameful attribute of a child and she devoted her life to not being "spoiled."

She never expressed a wish for anything, materially or otherwise, and she accepted gifts and privileges—only because she did not know how to refuse them—without feeling justified to receive them. Since her well-to-do parents were deeply devoted to her, she received many gifts, each one arousing in her the obligation to prove she was worthy of it. A few gifts were reassuring that they were really meant for her: her father's profession involved foreign travel, and she accepted with love and gratitude dolls he brought home in his briefcase; they were proof that he had thought of her while abroad. Most other gifts were to her an expression of her parents' goodness, of their doing the right thing, because it made them feel good to be generous and to show they cared for her.

This fear of giving the image of being "spoiled" resulted in an extraordinarily stingy attitude toward herself. She was always rather frugal in what she permitted herself and was exceedingly modest in the way she dressed, although she had daydreams of being dressed with elegance in striking good style. Still more stringent was her attitude toward food; even before the actual weight loss occurred, she felt it was wrong to "eat food for enjoyment." During treatment she came to understand the extent to which she had overaccommodated herself to what she felt others had wanted, that she had denied herself expressing her own wishes and feelings. She realized that she "could no longer maintain the enormous discrepancy of superior intellectual achievement, while having the body of a child." Even when she "wanted" to gain, her own stinginess, her frightened refusal to indulge herself in any way, interfered with the now honest desire to gain weight. She clung to her basic rule of not being "spoiled," not permitting herself to buy anything but the cheapest brand of any food or preparing fresh food when there were any leftovers in the refrigerator. She spent hours in comparative shopping to find a brand cheaper than the one in a store more accessible. To make things convenient for herself or to eat more interesting or tasty food would be "spoiling herself" and thus violate a basic childhood rule.

The relationship to her parents had been dominated by the conviction that she had to prevent ever deserving blame or criticism or ever doing anything that might arouse their disapproval. The great strain of her childhood was to figure out what they wanted her to do, what they would encourage, what they would honestly permit her. She was aware that they wanted to be kind and considerate, but she was under continuous strain to outguess them. She developed a kind of double-track thinking so that she never confronted them with the dilemma of being asked permission for something of which she was not sure that they would honestly approve.

This type of exceedingly narrow-minded good behavior, reflecting the moral judgment of a very young child, is characteristic of the thinking of all these girls, even those with occasional episodes of angry disagreement or disobedience.

APPLICATION TO TREATMENT

Anorexia nervosa is a much more complex disorder than dieting out of hand. Underlying it are serious developmental defects. These youngsters seriously misinterpret their biological functioning and social role, and they attempt to correct this by changing their body size. They interpret fashion's demand to be thin in an exaggerated concrete way. They truly believe that they can achieve respect and very special recognition through excessive thinness. Their concept of "specialness" is a direct continuation of unrealistic childish thinking that only the most conspicuous success makes them feel that they fulfill what is expected of them.

For effective treatment, these underlying problems must be recognized and corrected. These patients need help in their search for autonomy and self-directed identity. To accomplish this, the underlying problems in the family interaction need to be resolved. These youngsters have not been recognized as individuals in their own right, but they have been treated as something to complement the parents' needs. Therapy must be directed toward evoking awareness of impulses, feelings, and needs that originate within themselves. This can be accomplished through a therapist's alert and consistent, affirming or correcting, responses to any self-initiated behavior and expression. As they gain self-confidence and become more competent in living as self-directed individuals, they become ready to reevaluate their overrigid, moralistic value system. This step is not easy, since they have clung with enormous tenacity to these erroneous convictions.

Treatment is further complicated by the fact that hunger itself has such a far-reaching distorting influence on their thinking. Correction of the abnormal nutritional state is therefore essential. The question is how to accomplish this without doing psychic damage. All too often in a simple-minded approach weight increase is enforced, and this is considered a cure which, of course, cannot last. Fear of being overpowered by others underlies the whole syndrome and this needs to be acknowledged. Once these frightened youngsters perceive that the therapist understands their deeper problems, they are more ready to listen to explanations that many of their painful, obsessive thoughts are caused by the starvation itself, the effect of altered biochemical processes. With this understanding, they will permit a gradual refeeding, as an active step of their own, and not feel tricked by behavioristic routines.

REFERENCES

1. Bruch, H. (1973): *Eating Disorders: Obesity, Anorexia Nervosa and the Person Within.* Basic Books, New York.
2. Inhelder, B., and Piaget, J. (1955): *The Growth of Logical Thinking from Childhood to Adolescence: An Essay on the Construction of Formal Operational Structures.* Basic Books, New York.
3. Selvini, M. P. (1974): *Self-Starvation: From the Intrapsychic to the Transpersonal Approach to Anorexia Nervosa.* Chaucer Publishing Co., Ltd., London.

Anorexia Nervosa, edited by
R. A. Vigersky. Raven Press,
New York © 1977.

Atypical Anorexia Nervosa

Arnold E. Andersen

*Henry Phipps Psychiatric Clinic, The Johns Hopkins Hospital,
Baltimore, Maryland 21205*

INTRODUCTION

The purpose of this chapter is to examine the clinical usefulness and conceptual implications of the diagnostic category of atypical anorexia nervosa. The clinical cases discussed have been selected from 66 patients seen at the Clinical Center of the National Institutes of Health, and 7 at Johns Hopkins Hospital, Department of Psychiatry. The criteria of Feighner et al. (3) have been used exclusively for the diagnosis of anorexia nervosa since they were published. These criteria are listed in Table 1.

It may be helpful to review the stages through which the understanding and classification of a disease generally progresses (4). Initially, most diseases are described as syndromes, that is, collections of symptoms, which serve the twofold functions of all diagnoses: prognosis and treatment. For example, the syndromes of congestive heart failure and temporal lobe epilepsy have been recognized as clinical entities for many years. A further stage in the understanding of a disorder arrives when an underlying tissue abnormality is discovered. For example, temporal lobe epilepsy may be associated with a neoplasm, a cortical scar, or other neural pathologic lesions. The final stage in the understanding of a disorder is reached when a cause and a mechanism for the disease are known. For example, the syndrome of renal failure may be demonstrated in some patients to be the sequel of a streptococcal infection, mediated by an immunological mechanism. In summary, the three stages through which disease understanding and classification progress are the stages of defining the syndrome, recognizing a tissue abnormality, and understanding the cause and mechanism.

Most psychiatric disorders today exist as syndromes. The evidence for the specific neurochemical basis of even the more clearly defined syndromes such as the manic-depressive disorder remains indirect. Anorexia nervosa is defined as a syndrome whose symptoms are clinically and empirically derived. The symptoms are clinically derived in contrast to those disorders with biochemical or pathological definitions. The symptoms are empirically derived from empirical, statistical evidence, rather than derived rationally from a known mechanism or causative factor.

TABLE 1. *Feighner criteria for anorexia nervosa*

Anorexia nervosa. For a diagnosis of anorexia nervosa, A through E are required.

A. Age of onset prior to 25.

B. Anorexia with accompanying weight loss of at least 25% of original body weight.

C. A distorted, implacable attitude toward eating, food, or weight that overrides hunger, admonitions, reassurance, and threats: e.g., (1) denial of illness with a failure to recognize nutritional needs; (2) apparent enjoyment in losing weight with overt manifestation that food refusal is a pleasurable indulgence; (3) a desired body image of extreme thinness with overt evidence that it is rewarding to the patient to achieve and maintain this state; and (4) unusual hoarding or handling of food.

D. No known medical illness that could account for the anorexia and weight loss.

E. No other known psychiatric disorder with particular reference to primary affective disorders, schizophrenia, obsessive-compulsive and phobic neurosis. (The assumption is made that even though it may appear phobic or obsessional, food refusal alone is not sufficient to qualify for obsessive-compulsive or phobic disease.)

F. At least two of the following manifestations: (1) amenorrhea, (2) lanugo, (3) bradycardia (persistent resting pulse of 60 or less), (4) periods of overactivity, (5) episodes of bulimia, (6) vomiting (may be self-induced).

Data from ref. 3.

Even though definitions of anorexia nervosa may appear to vary among different investigators, these definitions are all syndrome definitions of one variety or another. There is simply a different relative weight given in the different definitions to the various symptoms characteristic of anorexia nervosa. For example, some investigators (2) stress a psychological symptom such as weight phobia as crucial to the diagnosis, but this symptom is considered a defining characteristic only when associated with amenorrhea and weight loss. Other investigators (1) emphasize a psychodynamic theme, such as the pursuit of thinness or control issues. But again, these become defining characteristics only when associated with weight loss and amenorrhea. In short, all definitions of anorexia nervosa are syndromic definitions.

It may be helpful to look at the clinical implications of the syndrome stage of disease classification as it applies to anorexia nervosa. Using the Feighner criteria as the syndrome definition of anorexia nervosa, investigators have seen a variety of disorders of weight and feeding behavior which do not strictly fit these criteria and yet have much in common with classic anorexia nervosa. In this group of patients the clinical usefulness and conceptual implications of the category of atypical anorexia nervosa will be examined.

CASE STUDIES

If we consider separately whether a patient's *presentation* is typical or atypical, and whether a patient's *syndrome* is typical or atypical, four logical categories result (Table 2). By "presentation" is meant the patient's

TABLE 2. *Categories of anorexia nervosa*

Clinical features	Conceptual implication
Typical presentation, typical syndrome	Classic patient
Atypical presentation, typical syndrome (type 1 atypical)	Problem of recognition
Typical presentation, atypical syndrome A. Quantitatively atypical: mild or incomplete B. qualitatively atypical (type 2 atypical)	Problem of classification
Atypical presentation, atypical syndrome (type 3 atypical)	Problem of weight loss of unknown origin

age at onset of weight loss and the mode of initiating weight loss. By "syndrome" is meant the patient's symptoms: attitudes and behavior toward food, weight, activity and sexuality, and the presence of physical factors such as amenorrhea and weight loss.

Typical Presentation of a Typical Syndrome

The first category is the typical presentation of a typical syndrome: the classic patient. The classic patient is an adolescent girl without psychiatric or medical disorder preceding weight loss, who initiates her weight loss by dieting, and who pursues lower and lower weights, often with pleasure in each pound lost. She is morbidly afraid of gaining weight, may induce vomiting, develops amenorrhea, and denies thinness and illness even when severely emaciated. She is preoccupied with food, likes to cook for others, and knows caloric information in detail. Most clinicians would recognize this as anorexia nervosa and treat the patient accordingly.

Type 1 Atypical Anorexia Nervosa

A second logical category is the atypical presentation of the typical syndrome: the problem of recognition. For convenience, this may be called type 1 atypical anorexia nervosa. Consider the following case. H. was a 53-year-old married white female admitted to NIH for evaluation of a 22-year history of weight loss. At age 31, after the birth of her second child, she began to deprive herself of food, declining gradually from 130 lb to her admission weight of 49 lb. She denied any attempt at dieting, however. Even at 49 lb she believed she was not too thin, and often limited herself to lettuce and coffee. She was a good cook, urging others to eat heartily. She was physically very active. She had amenorrhea for 22 years and lacked sexual interest throughout her marriage. On mental state examination, she had no signs of schizophrenia, affective disorder, or obsessional illness. She said she did not eat because she "might be too full to enjoy [her] next meal." She had resisted weight gain in several previous hospitalizations. She had no medical disease to account for her weight loss.

The patient's self-imposed food restriction, denial of extreme thinness, resistance to weight gain, immersion in food preparation activities, amenorrhea, sexual disinterest, and sustained physical overactivity are common findings in anorexia nervosa. Her age of onset was greater than that allowed in the Feighner criteria, and the mode of onset, provoked by childbirth, without dieting, is unusual. In every other way except her presentation, she had typical features of anorexia nervosa.

The clinical problem here was one of recognition. Once recognized as having a typical syndrome of anorexia nervosa, such a patient can be treated appropriately and investigations for obscure medical disorders discontinued. The recognition problem which arises from the atypical presentation of a typical syndrome results from one aspect of the syndromic approach to diagnosis: the exclusionary criteria. The Feighner criteria exclude patients greater than 25 years of age. The purpose of exclusionary criteria in a syndromic definition is to aid in the recognition of a syndrome by focusing the clinician on the expected clinical territory. The exclusionary criteria are not the heart of the syndrome, however. They are not defining characteristics, but only a statistical, empirical statement of experience. Therefore, there arises a clinical problem of recognition of typical syndromes presenting atypically if such criteria are seen as defining criteria rather than as exclusionary criteria to be disregarded when appropriate. The conceptual implication of this class of patients, of whom several have been seen, is that a relatively stereotyped syndrome can be provoked by a variety of means and at different ages. Once provoked, the syndrome has a predictable sequence of events and an autonomy which is enduring.

Type 2 Atypical Anorexia Nervosa

A second logical category of atypical patients is the group which has a typical presentation, but an atypical syndrome: the problem of classification. This may be called type 2 atypical anorexia nervosa. This category of patients comprises individuals in the 12- to 25-year age range who lose weight as a result of dieting, but who have an atypical syndrome. The syndrome may be atypical *quantitatively* or *qualitatively*.

QUANTITATIVELY ATYPICAL SYNDROMES

If we consider first those patients with the typical presentation but a quantitatively atypical syndrome, they may be seen to be quantitatively atypical in that they have either mild syndromes or incomplete syndromes.

Mild Syndrome

Most clinicians with experience in the treatment of anorexia nervosa have seen adolescent girls who initiate weight loss by dieting, who become morbidly afraid of weight gain, develop amenorrhea, but never develop the 25% weight loss required by the syndrome definition. Consider the following case. T. was an 18-year-old single white female admitted to NIH for evaluation of weight loss and amenorrhea. Two years prior to admission, the patient began to diet to improve her appearance. She decreased her weight from 115 lb to a low of 85 lb (height, 5 feet 3 inches), with resulting amenorrhea. She was not preoccupied with food and did not induce vomiting. She took pleasure in weight loss, however. She spontaneously increased her weight to 104 lb, but then decreased it back to 95 lb, which she considered her best weight even though it was below the ideal for her height and was associated with amenorrhea. She was moderately but not severely anxious about gaining too much weight.

There is no clinical problem in recognizing or treating this patient's disorder, even though her stable weight is not 25% below her initial weight, and she is only moderately anxious about gaining too much weight. There is no conceptual problem with this group of patients either. The existence of this class of patients results naturally from the fact that when a defining characteristic of a syndrome is a smoothly varying function, the designation of a particular point as a threshold point must be arbitrary, albeit useful. The weight loss required for fulfillment of the Feighner criteria is a loss of 25% of body weight, rather than 24%. Statistical significance is defined as occurring at a probability of less than 0.05 rather than at less than 0.06. This convention of designating a point along a line of continual variation is necessary for technical classification but can, and should, be cheerfully ignored by clinicians in treating mild cases of anorexia nervosa.

Incomplete Syndrome

In addition to individuals who present typically but with a syndrome which is quantitatively atypical by being mild, there are patients who present typically, but with a syndrome which is quantitatively atypical because it is incomplete. For example, a patient may have only one of the six characteristics listed in requirement F of the Feighner criteria. The syndrome definition requires two of the six characteristics to be present. Although such a patient would not meet the strict syndrome classification of anorexia nervosa, the clinician should respond, as with mild cases, with appropriate treatment of the quantitatively incomplete syndrome, which nonetheless can be appreciated as being essentially that of anorexia nervosa.

QUALITATIVELY ATYPICAL SYNDROMES

In contrast to patients who present typically, but with quantitatively atypical syndromes, there are those who present typically in regard to age of onset and mode of initiating weight loss, but who differ qualitatively from the syndrome definition. For example, B. was a 19-year-old single white male admitted to NIH for evaluation of weight loss of 47 lb. Fifteen months prior to admission, at a weight of 140 lb, the patient began to diet because he felt his weight was not well distributed. Specifically, he felt his stomach protruded over his belt and his thighs spread out too much when sitting down. He decreased his food intake, reaching a minimum weight of 93 lb. During his weight loss, he was preoccupied with thoughts of food and of calories. He increased his physical activity. He rated himself, however, as being very thin, and desired weight gain to his former weight if his added weight were muscle mass and not adipose tissue. At NIH, after gaining 2 lb, he measured his biceps to see if the added weight had increased his muscle size in order to decide whether to keep or discard the 2-lb weight gain. While tests involving intravenous administration of fluids were in progress, he was noted to be doing pushups.

This patient had a typical presentation of weight loss secondary to dieting during adolescence. He specifically had a morbid fear of adipose tissue, however, and not of weight gain in general. He put on and took off weight in accord with whether it increased his muscle mass or the fat around his stomach, the former acceptable, the latter not. In other ways, however, he had the typical attitude toward food and calories found in anorexia nervosa patients. Although others would disagree, we consider all males who otherwise fulfill the Feighner criteria as being in a qualitatively atypical category.

The classification problem of a patient with a qualitatively atypical syndrome is unresolved, and perhaps is best approached clinically by giving whatever classification is most appropriate to the patient's most prominent symptoms. Since this category of patients differs qualitatively from the actual defining characteristics of the syndrome, its presence reflects the empirical rather than rationally derived understanding of anorexia nervosa.

Type 3 Atypical Anorexia Nervosa

The last logical category of atypical anorexia nervosa is the atypical presentation of an atypical syndrome: the problem of weight loss of unknown origin, or type 3 atypical anorexia nervosa. Although this category might appear to strain the limits of clinical usefulness, there does exist a group of patients with disorders of weight loss, without adequate medical or psychiatric explanation, who present atypically with an atypical syndrome, but who nonetheless overlap more with anorexia nervosa than with any other diagnosis. Consider the following two cases.

N. was a 24-year-old single white female admitted to NIH for evaluation of the loss of 37% of her body weight. The patient was 5 feet 2 inches tall and weighed 100 lb throughout adolescence. At age 20 she began to lose weight without dieting. Her weight decreased to 63 lb but was not a source of concern to her. "To be perfectly truthful, I don't worry about it." She was not preoccupied with food, did not fear weight gain, and showed no change in physical activity during her weight loss. She basically had appetite neglect, but had no diagnosable psychiatric or medical disorder.

C. was a 41-year-old married black female referred to the Phipps Psychiatric Clinic of Johns Hopkins Hospital for diagnosis and treatment of weight loss of 2 years' duration, which began after the birth of her second child. She thought she remembered hearing a comment about that time that she appeared fat. She began to diet, gradually restricting her food intake until she weighed 84 lb. In the hospital she resisted weight gain, hid her food, induced vomiting, and added padding and weights to her body when weighed. She also was noted to have clear evidence of Addison's disease. Addison's disease was presumed to be the cause of her weight and appetite disorder and was adequately treated. She persisted, however, after complete correction of the endocrinological problem, to refuse to eat, to dispose of food secretly, and to add weights to her body when weighed by staff.

Here we are dealing with the limits of our knowledge. The first case illustrates appetite neglect of a profound degree, similar to that found in anorexia nervosa, but without fear of weight gain, desire for weight loss, pleasure in weight loss, or preoccupation with food. The patient had no diagnosable psychiatric or medical disorder. The second patient illustrates an atypical presentation (in an older age group, and shortly after childbirth) of an atypical syndrome (in association with Addison's disease).

This category of atypical presentation of an atypical syndrome is probably a heterogeneous group of disorders, some patients having "true" anorexia nervosa, and some with other disorders of different medical or psychiatric origin. In the absence of a defining tissue abnormality or a rational explanation of cause and mechanism, these disorders are perhaps best considered to be weight disorders of unknown origin, to be classified as wheat or tares at a later date when the nature of anorexia nervosa is more fully understood. Meanwhile, because of the absence of satisfactory medical or psychiatric explanation for these disorders, it is clinically useful to approach these patients as *formes frustes* of anorexia nervosa, and to encourage weight gain as the treatment of choice, all the while searching with special diligence, even more so than in a typical presentation of a typical syndrome, for a medical or psychiatric disorder which could better explain the weight loss.

CONCLUSION

The syndrome method of definition of a disorder has strengths and weaknesses. The strengths include the fact that, although the basic mechanism and cause are not known, a syndrome can be both validly and reliably diagnosed. The validity of the syndrome approach to anorexia nervosa is supported by the finding that none of the more than 30 cases at NIH diagnosed as having anorexia nervosa by the Feighner criteria has been later found to have any other disorder, medical or psychiatric, to account for the weight loss. Also, in those cases in which the weight loss initially improved and then later recurred, the clinical picture of the second episode was the same as that of the first.

The syndrome of anorexia nervosa can be reliably, as well as validly, diagnosed. If the syndrome criteria are adhered to, the same observer at different points in time, or different observers at the same point in time, agree on the diagnosis.

Perhaps the greatest strength of the syndrome method of diagnosis is that it allows for the collection of a group of patients which can be investigated to determine the next level of understanding: the discovery of the pathological features, cause, and mechanism of the disorder. Syndrome methods of diagnosis are therefore methods of convention, methods which are essentially arbitrary but nonetheless necessary, valid, reliable, and useful in the absence of a more basic understanding of the nature of the illness.

The syndrome method of diagnosis of anorexia nervosa stands mute and agnostic to a basic question underlying this volume: Is anorexia nervosa a *process* or a *reaction?* Is it a biological event gone awry, leading to a stereotyped set of symptoms and behaviors, or is it a psychologically understandable reaction of a vulnerable and conflicted individual to a difficult set of circumstances which provoke the typical features of anorexia nervosa? Evidence exists for both viewpoints, that of process and that of reaction, and often exists in the same individual, suggesting a possible continuum of inversely proportional biological and psychological vulnerabilities in different patients who appear to have the same syndrome. The syndrome definition does not speak to this crucial issue of process versus reaction because by its nature this method states it does not know the answer. The method says only that a collection of symptoms can be validly and reliably diagnosed.

In summary, the diagnosis of anorexia nervosa employs the syndrome method. This method has strengths and weaknesses. The syndrome method also leads to several classes of atypical syndromes of anorexia nervosa which may have some clinical utility. The syndrome stage of diagnosis is the first stage in the search for the cause and mechanism of this intriguing disorder.

REFERENCES

1. Bruch, H. (1973): *Eating Disorders,* p. 267. Basic Books, New York.
2. Crisp, A. H. (1974): Primary anorexia nervosa or adolescent weight phobia. *Practitioner,* 212:525–535.

3. Feighner, J. P., Robins, E., Guze, S. B., Woodruff, R. A., Jr., Winokur, G., and Munoz, R. (1972): Diagnostic criteria for use in psychiatric research. *Arch. Gen. Psychiatry,* 26:57–63.
4. McHugh, P. R. (1975): Psychologic illness in medical practice. In: *Textbook of Medicine, Vol. 1, 14th Ed.,* edited by P. B. Beeson and W. McDermott, p. 562. W. B. Saunders Co., Philadelphia.

Anorexia Nervosa, edited by
R. A. Vigersky. Raven Press,
New York © 1977.

Analogue Scale Measurement of the Symptoms of Patients Suffering from Anorexia Nervosa

*M. F. Folstein, **A. Wakeling, and **V. DeSouza

**General Hospital Psychiatry Division, The Johns Hopkins Hospital, Baltimore, Maryland 21205; and **The Royal Free Hospital, Hampstead, London, NW3 2QG, U.K.*

INTRODUCTION

Patients suffering from anorexia nervosa are recognized by the mental symptoms of fear of fatness and distortion of body size; the behavioral signs of self-starvation and weight loss; and the pathophysiological state marked by amenorrhea. In addition, patients report several distressing inner states including abnormalities of hunger, satiety, mood, and sexual feelings (2–4,9,10,12,13). The quantitation of inner states such as these can now be accomplished by the use of analogue scales. This method was introduced in the 1920s but only recently was demonstrated to be a reliable, valid, and practical method for patient use (1,5–8,11). We have applied this method to patients with anorexia nervosa and will demonstrate that the patients' inner states of hunger, fullness, anxiety, and sexual excitement can be quantitated and related to conditions of weight gain and meal ingestion. The analogue method also makes possible a rough comparison of the reports among the inner states of patients suffering from anorexia nervosa, the reports of depressed patients, and the reports of student nurses.

SAMPLE

The patients were attending the Royal Free Hospital Outpatient Department or were hospitalized there for the treatment of anorexia nervosa. Diagnostic criteria were a fear of becoming fat, self-starvation resulting in substantial weight loss, and secondary amenorrhea. The sample included 38 patients with anorexia nervosa, 52 nurses, and 38 depressed female patients requiring antidepressant medication. Eight of the patients with anorexia nervosa were tested before and after treatment and weight gain.

PROCEDURE

All subjects reported at 10 A.M. after an overnight fast. They were weighed and a venipuncture was performed. They were then instructed to fill out analogue scales (Table 1). They reported their inner state by marking a 100-mm line bounded by "not at all" or "extremely" and a descriptive word or phrase. Thus, the score of the first item indicated the subject's rating of hunger along a continuum from "not at all hungry" to "extremely hungry" on a 100-mm line. The item was scored by measuring with a ruler from "not at all hungry" to the patient's mark. The items were arranged so that "not at all" and "extremely" were alternated from side to side on the page. Thus, response set was minimized. The content of items included adjectives referring to hunger, sex, thirst, mood, and body size. The same 36 scales were completed before and twice immediately after a standard meal

TABLE 1. *Sample analogue scale used in evaluating patients with anorexia nervosa*

Age ______ LMP ______ Date ______ Time ______ Ht: ______ Wt: ______

1. Please note the way you feel in terms of dimensions given below.
2. Note your feelings as they are at the moment.
3. Mark clearly perpendicularly across any part of each line *toward* the dimension which best describes how you feel at this moment. You may mark any part of the line.

Extremely hungry	______________________	Not at all hungry
Not at all fat	______________________	Extremely fat
Extremely blown out	______________________	Not at all blown out
Not at all thirsty	______________________	Extremely thirsty

of two packages of Carnation Instant Breakfast® in 400 cc of whole milk (approximately 460 kcal). Reliability of the scales in each diagnostic group was obtained by correlation of the second and third sets of scales. Validity was documented by correlation of items with each other and with the Zung Scales of Anxiety and Depression. Analysis of variance and then selected t-tests were used for a comparison of the differences among groups.

RESULTS

Changes in the Inner State After Treatment and Weight Gain

With this method we have quantitated changes in the patients' inner experiences after treatment and weight gain. The reliability and validity of the scales were acceptable as in previous studies. After weight gain anorexic patients reported feeling less unwell and more hungry before eating (Table 2). The change in hunger after eating was also related to treatment and weight gain: patients with anorexia nervosa report the normal experience of decreasing hunger and increasing fullness after a meal only when they are treated and have gained weight (Tables 2 through 4).

Before treatment and weight gain, they report nausea after the same standard meal. This unpleasant experience following a high-carbohydrate meal is no longer reported after weight gain. Thus, treatment and gain of weight affect the feeling of hunger before eating and feelings of fullness and nausea after eating. The state of hunger in patients with anorexia nervosa depends on their body weight.

TABLE 2. *Pre-meal and post-meal (460 kcal) scales: effects of weight gain in 8 patients*

	41 kg		52 kg		
	Pre-meal	Post-meal	Pre-meal	Post-meal	p
Hunger	25[a]	29	50	34	0.05
Unwell	36	—	2	—	0.005
Nausea	13	40	1	8	0.05

[a] Values in millimeters.

TABLE 3. *Report of "full stomach" after 460-kcal meal*

	Anorexia nervosa <45 kg	Anorexia nervosa >45 kg	Nurses
	$N = 9$	$N = 21$	$N = 13$
Pre-meal	35[c]	31	14
Post-meal	53	53[a]	53[b]

[a] $p < 0.01$.
[b] $p < 0.005$.
[c] Values in millimeters.

TABLE 4. *Post-meal change in full stomach*

	Increase post-meal (%)	No change or decrease post-meal (%)
Anorexia nervosa <45 kg	50	50
Anorexia nervosa >45 kg	78	22

Persistent Morbid Features of the Inner State after Weight Gain

After treatment and weight gain, anorexic patients could still be distinguished from comparison groups of nurses and depressed patients by the analogue scale method. Anorexic patients reported more fullness before

TABLE 5. *Pre-meal scales (mm)*

Inner feeling	Anorexia nervosa 51 kg ($N = 26$)	Nurses 60 kg ($N = 31$)	t^a
Unhappy	41	24	2.13
Guilty	39	12	3.50
Anxious	60	36	2.96
Sexually excited	24	42	2.62
Hungry	38	53	1.87
Thirsty	53	65	1.55
Depressed	38	24	1.79
Interested in sex	49	59	1.60
Sexually attracted by opposite sex	48	60	1.78

[a] $p < 0.05$ if $t > 2.00$.

TABLE 6. *Pre-meal scales (mm)*

Inner feeling	Anorexia neurosa >45 kg ($N = 26$)	Depressed patients ($N = 38$)	t^a
Unhappy	41	63	2.78
Guilty	39	55	3.89
Depressed	38	58	2.32
Self-confident	53	29	3.27
Tense	37	67	3.95

[a] $p < 0.05$ for all.

eating than nurses. In addition, these patients felt significantly more unhappy, guilty, and anxious than nursing students. This finding is in accord with the clinical impression that anorexic patients need psychiatric management of their emotional state during and after weight gain.

Several trends in the data are notable. These patients reported a reduction in the experience of several motivational states (Table 5). Even after weight gain the patients reported feeling less hungry, thirsty, and sexually excited than the nurses. Although more dysphoric than nurses, anorexics were less dysphoric than nonanorexic patients diagnosed as depressed (Table 6).

DISCUSSION

Patients with anorexia nervosa suffer a variety of psychiatric symptoms. The analogue scale method allows us to quantitate aspects of their suffering and to study them scientifically. The patients' inner states can be studied as can the abnormal behavior and abnormal physiology of the condition.

Even though treatment was not complete, the patients' weights were still less than the weights of nurses, and their menstruation had not yet returned. We were able to demonstrate some relief of the symptoms of anorexic patients. They felt less unwell, and they again experienced the normal aspects of the inner state associated with eating. But even after 20 lb of weight gain, they remained anxious and unhappy.

Claims for complete cure must demonstrate relief of the distressing symptoms of disturbed moods, sexual feelings, and the experiences around eating, as well as the return of body weight and menstruation. Demonstration of patients' recovery from these disturbances can now be accomplished by the use of the analogue scale.

REFERENCES

1. Aitken, R. C. B. (1969): Measurement of feelings using visual analogue scales. *Proc. R. Soc. Med.,* 62:989–993.
2. Bruch, H. (1973): *Eating Disorders.* Basic Books, New York.
3. Crisp, A. H. (1967): Anorexia nervosa. *Hosp. Med.,* 1:713–718.
4. Dally, P. J. (1969): *Anorexia Nervosa.* Heineman, London.
5. Folstein, M., and Luria, R. (1973): Reliability, validity and clinical application of the visual analogue mood scale. *Psychol. Med.,* 3:479–486.
6. Freyd, M. (1923): The graphic rating scale. *J. Educ. Psychol.,* 14:83–102.
7. Garfinkel, P. E. (1974): Perception of hunger and satiety in anorexia nervosa. *Psychol. Med.,* 4:309–315.
8. Hayes, M. H. S., and Patterson, D. G. (1921): Experimental development of the graphic rating method. *Psychol. Bull.,* 18:98–99.
9. Janet, P. (1965): *The Major Symptoms of Hysteria* (1906), pp. 228–243. Hafner Publishing Co., London.
10. Kay, D. W., and Leigh, D. A. (1954): The natural history, treatment and prognosis of anorexia nervosa based on a study of 38 patients. *J. Ment. Sci.,* 100:411–431.
11. Robinson, R., McHugh, P. R., and Folstein, M. F. (1975): Measurement of appetite disturbances in psychiatric disorders. *J. Psychiatr. Res.,* 12:59–68.
12. Russell, G., and Beardwood, C. J. (1968): The feeding disorders with particular reference to anorexia nervosa and its associated gonadatrophin changes. In: *Endocrines and Human Behaviour,* edited by R. P. Michael. Oxford University Press, London.
13. Russell, G. F. M. (1970): Anorexia nervosa's identity as an illness and its treatment. *Mod. Trends Psychol. Med.,* 2:131–164.

Anorexia Nervosa, edited by
R. A. Vigersky. Raven Press,
New York © 1977.

Measurement of Body Image in Anorexia Nervosa

*David M. Garner and **Paul E. Garfinkel

**Mental Health Clinic, Toronto East General Hospital, Toronto, Ontario, Canada, M4C 3E8; and **Clarke Institute of Psychiatry and University of Toronto, Toronto, Ontario, Canada, M5T 1R8*

Body image refers to the mental image that a person has of the physical appearance of his body (6,22). It is also said to include the attitudes and feelings of the individual to his body (12). The concept of body image evolved from neurological observations of patients who reported the phantom-limb phenomenon (11). This work provided support for the fact that one's body image is not necessarily consistent with one's anatomical appearance (12).

Although of interest to clinical psychiatry for many years (11,15), the issue of body image has actually been of relatively recent concern in the study of eating disorders. This interest stems from independent clinical study of individuals with anorexia nervosa and obesity. In anorexia nervosa, disturbed body image is often inferred from the patient's lack of concern over her extreme thinness (1,13,16,17). In a clinical report Gottheil et al. (10) claimed to have successfully treated one anorexic patient's denial of thinness by repeatedly showing her motion pictures of her emaciated body. Bruch (1) has considered realistic body image to be of sufficient importance to constitute "a precondition for recovery in anorexia nervosa" (p. 90).

The construct of body image as applied to obese patients has often been conceptualized as primarily attitudinal in nature. Using self-drawings, Gottesfeld (9) found evidence of "negative body cathexis" with "super-obese patients." With a similar measure Nathan and Pisula (14) found the human figure drawings of 15 obese adolescents to be primitive and lacking age-appropriate features. Stunkard and Mendelson (21) described body image disturbances based on the attitudes of obese patients to exposure to their images in a mirror. Stunkard (20) has suggested that body image disturbance is a relatively stable phenomenon which develops in the neurotic adolescent who internalizes other peoples' derogatory appraisal of his body.

Other measures have involved the visual perception of one's self and an estimation of one's size. Shipman and Sohlkhah (18), using a distorting mirror technique, claimed that obese women "substantially overestimated" their body size. A more sophisticated method was employed by Glucksman and Hirsch (7), who used a distorting photograph technique and found that six obese patients, during a weight reduction program, showed overestimation in body size in comparison with four controls. Employing the same method with larger groups, Garner et al. (5) found an overestimation tendency in approximately one-half of the juvenile-onset obese ($N = 16$) and anorexia nervosa ($N = 18$) subjects tested. This was in contrast to an underestimation tendency in three non-eating disorder control groups. Of importance, overestimation was found to be associated with independent measures of psychopathology. Patients with anorexia nervosa who overestimated their body sizes were found to be more neurotic, extroverted, and external in their perception of locus of control. On clinical follow-up of the anorexic subjects, overestimation was strongly predictive of poor prognosis (4).

As Slade and Russell (19) have observed, most tests, including the distorting photograph technique, assume a general factor of body image; that is, distortion will be of the same magnitude for all parts of the body. Using a caliper device to assess specific body regions (face, chest, waist, and hips), they found that anorexic subjects overestimated body widths and that self-perception was more accurate as weight was restored. More recently, Crisp and Kalucy (2), using a similar technique, reported this overestimation tendency to be displayed also by nonanorexic controls. However, in contrast to that of controls, the overestimation by anorexic subjects was markedly increased by the ingestion of a meal with a high carbohydrate connotation. The inability of Slade and Russell's (19) apparatus to differentiate eating disorder from non-eating disorder group was confirmed by Garner et al. (5), who found overestimation of all bodily regions by all five groups tested. In contrast, Fries (3) has reported that the caliper device differentiated between anorexic subjects and an older group of normal weight controls. Crisp and Kalucy (2) have offered a possible explanation for these discrepant results with Slade and Russell's measure. Self-estimation with this technique may be systematically influenced by age; that is, overestimation of body regions may decrease with increasing age. The above two studies which did distinguish anorexic from control groups employed older controls not matched to the anorexic subjects. In a preliminary report, Goldberg et al. (8) found the Slade and Russell caliper device capable of predicting in-hospital weight gain for 44 anorexic subjects. However, in their study, estimation of body widths was conducted in a well-lit room rather than in a darkened room as used by earlier investigators.

The conflicting findings with the Slade and Russell caliper technique and the results with the global measure of body size (5) indicate the necessity for critical assessment of the reliability and validity of currently popular operational measures of "body image." This may be facilitated by rigorous methodological uniformity which would ensure the comparability of findings among studies. An initial step in understanding body image as a construct and its relationship to anorexia nervosa could come from a design employing multiple assessments with convergent measures. A multiple-measure strategy would yield valuable data on the interrelationship between measures, in addition to comparisons of their respective abilities to predict clinical outcome. Also, determination of what constitutes a "normal" body image would require testing a larger series of people without eating disorders with the recently advanced measures.

There appears to be good support for the hypothesis that body size perception is meaningfully related to anorexia nervosa, in spite of the inconsistent sensitivity of some operational measures of "body image." As yet unresolved are questions regarding the origin and stability overtime of these self-perceptual disturbances. It is also not known how these misperceptions may be modified with treatment. Prospective investigations using objective indices of body perception will further clarify the role of body image in anorexia nervosa.

REFERENCES

1. Bruch, H. (1973): *Eating Disorders.* Basic Books, New York.
2. Crisp, A. H., and Kalucy, R. S. (1974): Aspects of the perceptual disorder in anorexia nervosa. *Br. J. Med. Psychol.,* 47:349–361.
3. Fries, H. (1976): Secondary amenorrhea and early recognition of anorexia nervosa. Presented at the National Institute of Child Health and Human Development and National Institute of Mental Health Conference on Anorexia Nervosa, Bethesda, Maryland, October 13–15.
4. Garfinkel, P. E., Moldofsky, H., and Garner, D. M. (1976): Outcome of anorexia nervosa: Significance of clinical features, body image and behaviour modification. Presented at the National Institute of Child Health and Human Development and National Institute of Mental Health Conference on Anorexia Nervosa, Bethesda, Maryland, October 13–15.
5. Garner, D. M., Garfinkel, P. E., Stancer, H. C., and Moldofsky, H. (1976): Body image disturbances in anorexia nervosa and obesity. *Psychosom. Med.,* 38:327–336.
6. Glucksman, M. L. (1972): Psychiatric observations on obesity. *Adv. Psychosom. Med.,* 7:194–216.
7. Glucksman, M. L., and Hirsch, J. (1969): The response of obese patients to weight reduction. III. The perception of body size. *Psychosom. Med.,* 31:1–7.
8. Goldberg, S. C., Halmi, K. A., Casper, R., Eckert, E., and Davis, J. M. (1976): Pretreatment predictors of weight gain in anorexia nervosa. Presented at the National Institute of Child Health and Human Development and National Institute of Mental Health Conference on Anorexia Nervosa, Bethesda, Maryland, October 13–15.
9. Gottesfeld, H. (1962): Body and self-cathexis of super-obese patients. *J. Psychosom. Res.,* 6:177–183.
10. Gottheil, E., Backup, C. E., and Cornelison, F. S., Jr. (1969): Denial and self-image confrontation in a case of anorexia nervosa. *J. Nerv. Ment. Dis.,* 148:238–50.
11. Head, H. (1920): *Studies in Neurology.* Oxford, London.
12. Kolb, L. C. (1959): Disturbances of the body image. In: *American Handbook of Psychiatry,* edited by S. Arieti. Basic Books, New York.
13. Meyer, J. E. (1971): Anorexia nervosa of adolescence, the central syndrome of the anorexia group. *Br. J. Psychiatry,* 118:539–542.
14. Nathan, S., and Pisula, D. (1970): Psychological observations of obese adolescents during starvation treatment. *J. Child Psychiatry,* 9:722–740.
15. Schilder, P. (1935): *Image and Appearance of Human Body.* Kagan, Paul, Trench, Trubner & Co., London.

16. Selvini, M. P. (1970): Anorexia nervosa. In: *The World Biennial of Psychiatry and Psychotherapy,* edited by S. Arieti. Basic Books, New York.
17. Selvini, M. P. (1974): *Anorexia Nervosa.* Chaucer Publishing Co., London.
18. Shipman, W., and Sohlkhah, N. (1967): Body distortion in obese women. *Psychosom. Med.,* 29:540 (abstract).
19. Slade, P. D., and Russell, G. F. M. (1973): Awareness of body dimension in anorexia nervosa: Cross-sectional and longitudinal studies. *Psychol. Med.,* 3:188–199.
20. Stunkard, A. J. (1976): *The Pain of Obesity.* Bull Publishing Co., Palo Alto, California.
21. Stunkard, A., and Mendelson, M. (1967): Obesity and the body image: characteristics of disturbances in the body image of some obese persons. *Am. J. Psychiatry,* 123:1296–1300.
22. Traub, A. C., and Orbach, J. (1964): Psychological studies of body-image: The adjustable body-distorting mirror. *Arch. Gen. Psychiatry,* 11:53–66.

Anorexia Nervosa, edited by
R. A. Vigersky. Raven Press,
New York © 1977.

Pretreatment Predictors of Weight Change in Anorexia Nervosa

*Solomon C. Goldberg, **Katherine A. Halmi, ***Regina Casper, †Elke Eckert, and ***John M. Davis

**Psychopharmacology Research Branch, National Institute of Mental Health, Rockville, Md. 20852; **Department of Psychiatry, University of Iowa, Iowa City, Iowa 52240; ***Illinois State Psychiatric Institute, Chicago, Ill. 60612; and †Department of Psychiatry, University of Minnesota, Minneapolis, Minn. 55455*

INTRODUCTION

This report is based on the same 44 female anorexia nervosa patients described in Chapter 6. On being admitted to the study, patients were assessed with a wide variety of measures during a 7-day pretreatment period, after which they received treatment in the hospital for 35 days.

The purpose of this preliminary report, based on approximately one-third of the total expected sample, is to search for relationships between weight gain and a wide variety of pretreatment characteristics exhibited by the patients. To the extent that we can identify variables other than our treatments that are related to weight change, we shall be able to sensitize our ultimate treatment comparisons by holding constant these variables. Moreover, examination of these predictors of weight change is expected to illuminate some of the dynamics of the recovery process in anorexia nervosa patients.

METHOD

Sample and Procedure

Eligibility of patients for the study is described in detail in Chapter 6.

After a patient's eligibility for study was ascertained, the patient was observed prior to treatment for 7 days. On the eighth day of hospitalization the patient was assigned to study treatment (drug or placebo and behavior modification or its absence) on which she remained for the next 35 days. Details of treatment procedure will not be given here since treatment results are not presented.

MEASURES

Measure of Outcome

Weight change was taken as that change in body weight between the last day of pretreatment and the final (35th) day of treatment.

Predictor Battery

On the fifth day of pretreatment the following assessments were made. These form the basis of our putative predictor battery.

1. Slade Anorectic Behavior Scale (10). This scale requires the nurses to observe the presence or absence of specific anorectic behaviors in the patients on the ward. The behaviors are scored in the following categories: (a) unusual food habits, e.g., begins eating by cutting food into small pieces, disposes of food out of windows; (b) vomiting; (c) purgative abuse; and (d) hyperactivity, e.g., is as active and industrious as possible.

Scoring is based on the average of two nurses' ratings.

2. The Raskin Mood Scale (9) is a list of 52 adjectives describing one's mood. The scale concerning the patient's mood is completed by the patient and by two nurses. This scale has undergone considerable prior research, and factor analysis has produced the following categories: depression, friendliness, anxiety, guilt, hostility, activity, fatigue, well-being, cognitive function, and carefree mood.

3. The Hopkins Symptom Check List (HSCL) (3) is composed of 61 signs and symptoms concerning the patient and is completed by the patient and by two nurses. The HSCL provides six factor scores entitled (a) somatization, (b) depression, (c) obsessive-compulsive symptoms, (d) interpersonal sensitivity, (e) anxiety, and (f) sleep disturbance. Norms are available for normals and for several patient groups.

4. Anorectic Attitude Scale. This new scale, completed by the patient, is composed of 63 attitude statements presumed to be typical of anorectic patients. The items were grouped with the aid of factor analysis into eight categories entitled (a) denial of illness, (b) loss of appetite, (c) interpersonal control, (d) thin body ideal, (e) hypothermia, (f) hyperactivity, (g) psychosexual immaturity, and (h) independence seeking.

5. Interpersonal Manipulativeness Scale is a new scale of 15 items by means of which the nurse describes the patient's inclination to test limits and manipulate the staff. The scale is a modification of one by Davis, Janowsky, and El-Yousef (2), who found this behavior in manic patients. A total score is computed as the sum of the 15 items.

6. Slade Perceptual Distortion Task. This procedure devised by Slade and Russell (11) requires the patient to indicate when the distance between two movable markers is equivalent to (a) the width of her waist at its nar-

rowest point, (b) the width of her hips at their widest point, (c) the width of her chest between axillae, (d) the width of her face between the zygomas, (e) the depth of her body at its greatest point below the waist, (f) the length of her right foot, (g) the length of her right arm from axilla to fingertips and, (h) a control block of wood 250 mm in length. Scoring is the quotient of perceived distance over actual, multiplied by 100 to remove the decimal. Slade has found anorectics to overestimate widths compared with normals, and that overestimation of width is reduced as the patient regains weight.

7. The Situational Discomfort Scale consists of 20 items describing various aspects of food and eating, e.g., being told to eat everything on the plate. The patient is asked to indicate the extent to which she is bothered by this from "not at all" to "very bothered." The expectation is that those who are bothered less will gain more weight. Scoring was taken as the sum of the 20 items.

8. The Psychiatric Rating Scale for Anorexia Nervosa contains 14 items describing different global characteristics of anorectic patients, e.g., "thin body ideal, desire for physical activity, depressed mood, etc." Psychiatrists rate the patient on the basis of a brief interview.

RESULTS

Pretreatment Levels

Table 1 shows the means and standard deviations of the measures that were significantly related to weight change. For reasons of brevity, those measures that were not significant are omitted from Table 1. Although these data are presented only for reference purposes, some interesting highlights are worth pointing out.

In the Slade Anorectic Behavior Scale there is seemingly a higher level of hyperactivity (1.43) than there is of unusual food handling (1.22). This pattern is the same as described by Dr. Halmi concerning the family's description of the patient's behavior just prior to hospitalization. It is surprising because the disorder is defined in terms of food habits. Patients may be hyperactive, but they are not required to be to qualify for the diagnosis.

The Hopkins Symptom Check List as self-rated does have norms, and, as we will see in Dr. Halmi's chapter, the patients report significantly more pathology than normals and particularly on depression and sleep disturbance. The nurses' ratings parallel the self-ratings in profile, but the nurses see fewer pathological features in the patients than the patients see in themselves.

The Anorectic Attitude Scale shows relatively high scores on loss of appetite, thin body ideal, hypothermia, and hyperactivity, with a low point on interpersonal control.

TABLE 1. *Pretreatment variables used as predictors of weight change in 44 patients with anorexia nervosa*

Scale	Mean	SD
Slade Anorectic Behavior Scale		
(Not present = 1; present = 2)		
Unusual food handling	1.22	0.13
Vomiting	1.07	0.20
Purgative abuse	1.00	0.00
Hyperactive	1.43	0.30
Anorectic Attitude Scale (self-rating)		
(Not at all = 1; a little bit = 2; quite a bit = 3; extremely = 4)		
Denial of illness	1.81	0.76
Loss of appetite	2.52	0.65
Interpersonal control	1.53	0.71
Thin body ideal	2.70	1.00
Hypothermia	2.77	1.08
Hyperactivity	2.85	0.70
Psychosexual immaturity	1.90	0.60
Independence seeking	1.80	0.66
Hopkins Symptom Check List (self-rating)		
(Not at all = 1; a little bit = 2; quite a bit = 3; extremely = 4)		
Somatization	1.53	0.49
Depression	2.08	0.74
Obsessive-compulsive	1.73	0.69
Interpersonal sensitivity	1.83	0.79
Anxiety	1.73	0.73
Sleep disturbance	2.10	0.95
Slade Body Image Distortion Test		
Foot length	93.75	12.83
Face width	131.00	32.10
Chest width	120.53	41.77
Waist width	130.01	38.19
Hip width	105.87	25.80
Arm length	83.83	11.22
Body depth	145.37	48.62
Block of wood	98.77	11.31
Psychiatric Rating Scale		
(Absent = 1; nearly absent = 2; mild = 3; moderate = 4; substantial = 5; severe = 6; most extreme = 7)		
Denial	4.63	1.40
Fear of fat	5.45	1.21
Thin ideal	5.34	1.20
Loss of appetite	3.65	1.36
Selective appetite	4.86	1.19
Fear of becoming compulsive eater	4.95	1.16
Desire for activity	4.70	1.29
Desire to control	4.29	1.44
Manipulative	4.09	1.51
Depressed	3.89	1.22
Obsessive	4.06	1.02
Immature	4.66	1.43
Purgatives and diuretics	2.32	1.41
Exaggerated cheerfulness	2.89	1.22

The Slade Body Image Distortion Test shows that patients overestimate body widths, underestimate body lengths, but neither over- nor underestimate the length of a control block of wood 250 mm in length. These results confirm the earlier findings of Slade and Russell, but an age-matched normal control group is required for proper interpretation.

Pretreatment Predictors of Weight Change

Table 2 presents the intercorrelations of weight change with its statistically significant predictors. Because of different scoring directions, the direction of relationship cannot be determined from the table. The following is a summary of results from this table.

Greater weight gain is associated with:

1. A greater degree of hyperactivity and exercising as observed by two nurses on the ward. (This result is counter to common expectation.)
2. A lesser degree of denial of the seriousness of her illness, as indicated on an attitude scale by the patient. She would agree with the statement, "There was nothing really wrong with me that a few days' rest couldn't cure."
3. A greater expression of hunger and appetite as indicated on a self-rated attitude scale. For example, "I feel hungry by the time mealtime comes around."
4. A lesser degree of psychosexual immaturity as self-rated by the patient. For instance, the patient would disagree with the statement, "Sex appeal in men is vastly overrated."
5. A lesser tendency to overestimate the actual size of one's body parts (face width, chest width, waist width, hip width, body depth, foot length, and arm length) but not a control block of wood.
6. Greater appetite as rated from an interview by the treating psychiatrist.
7. Less sleep disturbance as self-rated.

Interestingly, although these predictors are experimentally independent in the sense of using different raters (nurses' observations, patient self-ratings, objective performance tests, and psychiatric ratings), they are moderately intercorrelated. Thus self-rated denial is associated with loss of appetite which might be interpreted as a denial of appetite. Even psychosexual immaturity is correlated with denial and loss of appetite.

In turn, the tendency to overestimate body size is associated mainly with low appetite but also with denial and psychosexual immaturity.

The psychiatric rating of loss of appetite is associated with loss of appetite as self-rated, less hyperactivity, more denial, more psychosexual immaturity, and a modest tendency to overestimate one's body size.

Only the nurses' observations of hyperactivity correlate with other pre-

TABLE 2. *Pretreatment predictors of weight change* ($N = 44$; $r_{0.05} = 0.295$)

	2	3	4	5	6	7	8	9	10	11	12	13	14
1. Weight gain	.353	−.364	−.364	−.322	−.406	−.313	−.400	−.566	−.549	−.305	−.589	−.395	−.322
2. Activity		−.166	−.174	.064	−.229	−.211	−.093	−.211	−.162	−.325	−.193	−.297	.031
3. Denial			.670	.602	.118	.279	.187	.454	.452	.031	.454	.314	.576
4. Hunger				.577	.292	.446	.448	.478	.556	.056	.534	.509	.555
5. Psychosexual immaturity					.146	.315	.366	.505	.531	.080	.560	.292	.509
6. Foot length						.652	.596	.488	.384	.464	.346	.212	.002
7. Face width							.482	.494	.468	.169	.409	.256	.095
8. Chest width								.691	.625	.230	.623	.279	.337
9. Waist width									.853	.188	.842	.352	.403
10. Hip width										.157	.827	.398	.450
11. Arm length											.112	.054	.095
12. Body depth												.499	.476
13. Appetite													.171
14. Sleep disturbance													

TABLE 3. *Pretreatment versus social history predictors* ($N = 44$; $r_{0.05} = 0.295$)

	Wt. loss from norm	Precipitants	Hypothermia	Mother's age at patient's birth	Complications in pregnancy	Emphasis on food in childhood	Premorbid hyperactivity	Premorbid ritualistic	Complications of delivery
Hyperactivity on ward	.071	−.200	.071	.141	−.212	−.075	−.131	−.371	.262
Denial of illness	.259	.176	.019	−.109	.332	−.046	.254	−.049	−.413
Appetite (self-rating)	.290	.069	.030	.050	.236	.148	.328	.009	−.350
Psychosexual immaturity	.342	.029	.019	−.096	.101	.051	.218	.138	−.289
Overestimation of foot length	.203	−.101	−.100	−.263	.009	.101	.390	.295	−.123
Overestimation of face width	.133	−.153	−.084	−.109	.021	−.046	.407	.119	−.095
Overestimation of chest width	.368	−.029	−.141	−.189	−.043	.115	.279	.061	−.177
Overestimation of waist width	.411	.196	−.020	−.226	.193	.035	.517	.253	−.511
Overestimation of hip width	.456	.058	.025	−.246	.274	−.003	.613	.128	−.563
Overestimation of arm length	.062	.159	−.041	−.141	−.164	−.167	.006	.305	.150
Overestimation of body depth	.421	.269	−.080	−.239	.361	.079	.394	.213	−.607
Appetite (psychiatric rating)	.124	.100	−.133	−.142	.294	.213	.164	.209	−.405
Sleep disturbance (self-rating)	.221	.181	−.012	−.096	.237	.008	.107	−.116	−.327

dictors in a direction counter to common expectation. Hyperactivity is associated with the tendency to underestimate arm length and with the psychiatric rating of little loss of appetite.

Interrelations of Pretreatment and Social History Predictors

Table 3 presents the intercorrelations among the significant pretreatment predictors and the social and psychiatric history predictors of weight change presented in Chapter 6.

Extent of weight loss from a normal standard weight on entering the study is associated with psychosexual immaturity and approaches significance with denial and loss of appetite. Those with a greater emaciation on entering the study are less mature, deny their illness, and profess a greater loss of appetite.

Greater weight loss is also related to overestimation of chest width, waist width, hip width, and body depth. The more emaciated patients are those who have the most exaggerated feeling that their body is oversized. Greater premorbid hyperactivity is associated with greater loss of appetite, greater overestimation of foot length, face width, waist width, hip width, and body depth.

Greater premorbid ritualistic behavior is associated with less hyperactivity on the ward and greater overestimation of foot length and arm length.

Birth and delivery complications are associated with more denial of illness, greater loss of appetite (self-rated), overestimation of waist width, hip width, and body depth, greater loss of appetite as rated by the psychiatrist, and more sleep disturbance as self-rated.

Pregnancy complications are associated with denial of illness, overestimation of body depth, and greater loss of appetite according to the psychiatrist.

The pretreatment predictors were not significantly related to precipitants of the disorder, hypothermia, mother's age at patient's birth, or undue emphasis on food in childhood.

DISCUSSION

A number of variables have been identified in prior studies which distinguish anorexia nervosa patients from normals or from those in other psychiatric categories. These variables may or may not be the same as those associated with improvement in anorexia nervosa. The present chapter is concerned with the latter set of variables.

Our most interesting result is with the variable entitled denial of illness. Patients state on self-report form, for example, "there was nothing wrong with me that a few days' rest couldn't cure." Denial has been reported in a number of papers (7,8,11,12) as being characteristic of anorexia nervosa. Now we are able to show that the degree of denial manifested by the patient prior to treatment is correlated with weight change during 35 days of treatment in hospital.

Another aspect of the self-report scale is the expression of appetite, e.g., "I feel hungry by the time mealtime comes around." Patients who agree with that statement tend to gain more weight and this too seems reasonable. Anorexia nervosa has been considered a misnomer for the disorder because many patients do not have a loss of appetite but rather starve themselves in the face of extreme hunger. What is interesting is that the expression of loss of appetite is associated in turn with the expression of denial of illness. The implication is that patients who profess a loss of appetite are either denying it or failing to recognize it. The further implication is that stimulation of appetite by drugs or other means would probably not succeed in inducing greater food intake or weight gain since patients already have an appetite which is, through some unknown mechanism, being denied.

A third aspect of the self-report scale concerns psychosexual immaturity. Patients who agree with such statements as "Sex appeal in men is vastly overrated" tend to gain less weight. The dimension of psychosexual immaturity has also been recognized by other investigators as a feature of the disorder. What is of further interest is that the most immature patients tend to deny their illness and their hunger.

The strongest predictors of weight change are based on a size estimation procedure devised by Slade, who had his patients indicate when the distance between two markers was equal to the width or length of various parts of their body (face, chest, waist, arm, etc.). One of his findings was that patients reduce their distortions of body image as they regain weight, which suggests that those who overestimate their body width more would regain less weight. Our results confirm this hypothesis, but unexpectedly we find the same relationship to weight gain with overestimation of length (foot and arm) as well as width. Of further interest, overestimators tend to deny their illness.

Another of Slade's results is that the tendency to overestimate body width diminishes as the patients regain their weight. Thus a more accurate body perceptual ability is regained with weight. Denial may be regarded as a lack of insight and in our study is highly correlated with overestimating of body parts. Often this denial or lack of insight is the focus of psychotherapy with the expectation that greater insight will bring about a concomitant increase in weight. Slade and Russell, by treating the emaciation, indirectly decreased the amount of overestimation of body parts by the patients. One may speculate from the correlations found in our study that their patients concomitantly obtained greater insight or had a reduction of denial of their illness. The implication would be for early intervention for weight restoration before the patient comes to accept her emaciated state as "natural."

Unrelated to denial in any way is our result showing hyperactivity on the ward to be associated with greater weight gain. This is a surprising result because hyperactivity is a well-documented characteristic of anorexia nervosa, and ordinarily one expects a low level of disease to be associated with better outcome. At present, we have no explanation.

The relationship of the pretreatment with the social and psychiatric history predictors is particularly interesting. The evidence is that degree of weight loss, premorbid hyperactivity, and pregnancy and delivery complications are not only related to each other but in turn are related to denial of illness, loss of appetite, psychosexual immaturity, distortion of body image, and sleep disturbance. From the pretreatment predictors alone one could not say whether the pattern indicated an "earlier versus later stage" of the same illness with the implication that patients in the earlier stage (e.g., nondeniers) could eventually enter a later stage. The correlations of the pretreatment predictors with pregnancy and delivery complications would argue strongly against the "early versus late stage" hypothesis and instead would invoke the notion of there being both more and less severe forms of the disorder, the more severe form affecting those with a greater number of pregnancy and birth difficulties.

Halmi and Goldberg (5) have published age-specific norms for body image distortion in normal adolescent girls. Their results indicate a sharp reduction in body image distortion between ages 10 and 11 and a more gradual decline thereafter to age 18. These results are interpreted as a maturational development and would not be inconsistent with the suggestion of organicity in our present results with patients.

A note of caution should be voiced about all our results in that they are based on only the first third of our sample. What is desired for any of these results is a replication in different clinical settings. When our sample of 112 is completed, we will have the opportunity to test whether any result is found equally in all three institutions participating in the study. The results presented today have not undergone this replication process and must therefore be considered tentative.

A few comments should be made about the fact that a number of predictors found in other prognostic studies were not found here.

Other predictors of long-term outcome found variously by Theander (12), Halmi, Brodland, and Loney (4), Morgan and Russell (8), Halmi and Larson (6), and Kalucy, Crisp, and Harding (7) are (a) age at onset; (b) duration of illness; (c) a history of vomiting, laxative abuse, psychosomatic complaints, and depressive and obsessive-compulsive manifestations; and (d) social class.

Most of these studies used a more complex follow-up criterion of community adjustment, of which weight maintenance was only a part. It is possible that our nonconfirmation of those results is partly a function of using a somewhat different measure of outcome since some of the predictors might be indicating an aspect of community adjustment not contained in weight gain. Moreover, evidence is provided by Bean, Myers, and Pepper (1) that higher social class is associated with better community adjustment in normals. What is necessary is a comparison of patient adjustment with normals at the same social class level before one can implicate social class as a prognostic factor in anorexia nervosa.

ACKNOWLEDGMENT

This research was supported by NIMH grants MH-26218, MH-26310, and MH-26409.

REFERENCES

1. Bean, L. L., Myers, J. K., and Pepper, M. P. (1964): Social class and schizophrenia: a ten year follow up. In: *Blue-Collar World, Studies of the American Worker,* edited by A. B. Shostak and W. Gomberg. Prentice-Hall, Englewood Cliffs, N.J.
2. Davis, J. M., Janowsky, D., and El-Yousef (1976): The effect of drug treatment on interpersonal styles of manic patients. Presented at meetings of Collegium Internationale Neuro-Psychopharmacologicum, Quebec City.
3. Derogatis, L. R., Lipman, R. S., Rickels, K., Uhlenhuth, E. H., and Covi, L. (1974): The Hopkins Symptom Checklist (HSCL): a measure of primary symptom dimensions. In: *Psychological Measurements in Psychopharmacology: Modern Problems in Pharmacopsychiatry, Vol. 7,* edited by P. Pichot, pp. 79–110. Karger, Basel.
4. Halmi, K., Brodland, G., and Loney, J. (1973): Prognosis in anorexia nervosa. *Ann. Intern. Med.,* 78:907–909.
5. Halmi, K., and Goldberg, S. C. (1977): Perceptual distortion of body image in adolescent girls. *Psycholog. Med.,* (*in press*).
6. Halmi, K., and Larson, L. (1977): Behavior therapy in anorexia nervosa. *Adolescent Psychiatry* (*in press*).
7. Kalucy, R. S., Crisp, A. H., and Harding, B. (1975): A study of 56 families with anorexia nervosa. Presented at 2nd Congress, International College of Psychosomatic Medicine, Rome.
8. Morgan, H. G., and Russell, G. F. M. (1975): Value of family background and clinical features as predictors of long-term outcome in anorexia nervosa: four year follow up study of 41 patients. *Psychol. Med.,* 5:355–371.
9. Schulterbrandt, J., Raskin, A., and Reatig, N. (1974): Further replication of factors of psychopathology in the interview, ward behavior and self reported ratings of hospitalized depressed patients. *Psychol. Rep.,* 34:23–32.
10. Slade, P. D. (1973): A short anorexic behavior scale. *Br. J. Psychiatry,* 122:83–85.
11. Slade, P. D., and Russell, G. F. M. (1973): Awareness of body dimensions in anorexia nervosa: cross-sectional and longitudinal studies. *Psychol. Med.,* 3:188–199.
12. Theander, S. (1970): Anorexia nervosa, a psychiatric investigation of 94 female patients. *Acta Psychiatr. Scand.* [*Suppl.*], 214.

Anorexia Nervosa, edited by
R. A. Vigersky. Raven Press,
New York © 1977.

Pretreatment Evaluation in Anorexia Nervosa

*Katherine A. Halmi, **Solomon C. Goldberg, ***Elke Eckert, †Regina Casper, and †John M. Davis

**Department of Psychiatry, University of Iowa, Iowa City, Iowa 52242; **Psychopharmacology Research Branch, NIMH, Rockville, Md. 20852; ***Department of Psychiatry, University of Minnesota, Minneapolis, Minn. 55455; and †Illinois State Psychiatric Institute, Chicago, Ill. 60612*

INTRODUCTION

In a multicenter collaborative treatment study on anorexia nervosa, 44 female anorexia nervosa patients were systematically assessed by a variety of measures during a 7-day pretreatment period. This is a preliminary report on the pretreatment evaluation based on approximately one-third of the total expected sample for the treatment study.

METHODOLOGY

The structured psychiatric and social interview was conducted by a social worker with the patient's family and the patient. This interview was designed to cover clinical characteristics of the patients just prior to hospitalization including: (a) behavior typical of anorexia nervosa and sexual attitudes, (b) mental status, (c) menstrual history, and (d) previous medical history and premorbid personality. Information concerning demographic features and medical and psychiatric illness in the patient's family was also obtained. Included in the social-psychiatric history was the Slade Anorectic Behavior Scale (11), which covers such items as vomiting, purgative abuse, aberrant food handling, and hyperactivity. In addition to the structured interview, a variety of other measures were used to assess the patients during the 7-day pretreatment period. One of those reported on in this study is the Hopkins Symptom Check List (SCL), a self-report symptom inventory which has undergone extensive research dating from pre-World War II (4).

In order to participate in the study the patient had to be female and meet the criteria in Table 1. Independent agreement on diagnosis was made by two psychiatrists before the patient was accepted into the study. The patients were weighed on the day of admission and thereafter every morning in the same hospital gown prior to breakfast and after voiding.

On the seventh day of pretreatment the patients were randomly assigned

TABLE 1. *Criteria for diagnosis of anorexia nervosa*

1. Patients had to be between the ages of 10 and 40 and had to have had the onset of their illness between the ages of 10 and 30 years.
2. Patients had to have lost at least 25% of their original body weight and/or be 15% below a normal weight for their age and height (normal weights were obtained from the Metropolitan Life Insurance Policy Scales and the Iowa Growth Charts for Children).
3. Patients had to demonstrate a distorted attitude and behavior toward eating, food, or weight which was represented by any one of the following:
   a. Denial of illness with a failure to recognize nutritional needs
   b. Apparent enjoyment in losing weight
   c. A desired body image of extreme thinness
   d. Unusual hoarding or handling of food
4. Patients had to have at least one of the following manifestations:
   a. Lanugo (persistence of downy pelage)
   b. Bradycardia (persistent resting pulse of 60 or less)
   c. Hypothermia (<36.1°C)
   d. Periods of overactivity
   e. Episodes of bulimia (compulsive overeating)
   f. Vomiting (may be self induced)
5. Patients had to have amenorrhea of at least 3 months' duration unless illness occurred before onset of menses.
6. There must have been no known medical illness that could account for the anorexia and weight loss.
7. Patients had to have no other known psychiatric disorders which were excluded according to the Research Diagnostic Criteria (RDC) (13). If during but not prior to the present illness the patient met concurrently criteria 1–6 above and manifested depression or obsessive-compulsive neurosis, she was considered to have anorexia nervosa.

to one of the four programs: (a) cyproheptadine and behavior modification, (b) cyproheptadine and no behavior modification, (c) placebo and behavior modification, or (d) placebo and no behavior modification. After the random assignment, the patients were followed for 35 days and assessed periodically. Since we have obtained only one-third of the expected patient sample at this time, analysis of treatment results would obviously bias our study. Therefore, the first of our data analysis presented here is an investigation of variables on the pretreatment assessments that were significantly correlated with weight change irrespective of the type of therapy.

RESULTS

Although this study was not exclusive of any ethnic or social group and two of the treatment centers had large black populations, all the patients referred meeting the criteria of anorexia nervosa were Caucasian. There is not a single well-documented case in the literature of this illness occurring in a black. Table 2 gives a description of our patient sample. Note that most of them had been ill for approximately a year before they were admitted to the treatment study. It has been shown that a longer duration of the illness before treatment influences poor outcome (8). The family rating of the

TABLE 2. *Description of 44 patients with anorexia nervosa*

	Range	Mean	SD
Age at admission	12–36	20.18	5.38
Age at onset of illness	10–30	17.52	4.04
Months since onset of present illness	0–96	20.02[a]	21.28
Height on admission (cm)	145–174	159.80	5.96
Weight just prior to onset of present illness (kg)	26–87	51.18	11.73
Weight at admission (kg)	26–44	33.73	4.65
Desired weight for age and height (kg)	43–60	50.66	4.07
Weight change after 35 days (kg)	(−)4.0–(+)13.2	+4.62	3.64

[a] Median = 13.

patients' typical anorectic behavior just before treatment is shown in Table 3.

On the Slade scale (1 = no; 2 = yes), the mean (±SD) severity of hyperactivity (1.69 ± 0.33) was greater than that of strange food habits (1.39 ± 0.18) as noted by the family. Vomiting and purgative abuse were present in one-third of the patients and bulimic episodes in one-half. The frequency distribution of these behaviors was similar to that in other large patients series (6,16). Approximately one-half of the patients admitted to having a strong appetite. The association of this admission to outcome will be shown later. The behavior identified most frequently by the families was the anorectics' excessive cooking (present in almost 80%).

Information on the anorectics' sexual attitudes was obtained from the patients (Table 3). The preponderance of disinterest in sex, decreased sex interest since onset of illness, and the stronger expression by one-third of the patients of disgust with sex has been the subject of many previous speculations concerning anorexia nervosa (1,16). Identifiable social precipitants occurring with the onset of illness were noted in two-thirds of the patient sample (Table 3). This is associated with weight gain during treatment and is discussed later.

Personality characteristics of patients with anorexia nervosa have been frequently described but seldom assessed with objective personality testing. Smart et al. (12), using the Eysenck Personality Inventory and the Leyton Obsessional Inventory, found the anorectics to have a profile of highly neurotic, introverted persons with moderately severe obsessional features. In our sample specific behavioral symptoms were assessed with the SCL and compared with those of other neurotic patient groups and a control sample (Table 4). Note that on no factor listed do the controls reach a score as high as 1.2. In comparison, the anorectics score highly (in the direction of more pathological features) on all items except psychoticism. Their factor scores are in the same range with those of the anxious and depressed neurotics. Of special interest is the remarkable similarity between the

TABLE 3. *Anorectic behavior and attitudes just prior to hospitalization in 44 patients*

	f^a	%
Vomiting	15	34.1
Purgative abuse	17	38.6
Frequency of bulimia in current illness		
1. Never	23	52.3
2. Less than once a week	4	9.1
3. About once a week	6	13.6
4. Several times a week	7	15.9
5. At least every day	4	9.1
Appetite		
1. Has no appetite	24	54.5
2. Admits to strong appetite but is afraid of losing control	20	45.5
Cooks for others to excessive extent		
Yes	34	77.3
No	10	22.7
Decrease in sex interest since onset of illness		
Not at all	21	47.7
A bit	6	13.6
Quite a bit	9	20.5
Extremely	8	18.2
Patient disinterested in sex		
Not at all	16	36.4
A bit	15	34.1
Quite a bit	9	20.5
Extremely	4	9.1
Patient regards sex as disgusting		
Not at all	28	63.6
A bit	11	25.0
Quite a bit	3	6.8
Extremely	2	4.5
Compulsive stealing in present illness		
Yes	5	11.4
No	39	88.6
Precipitants to onset of illness	30	68.2

[a] f = frequency of occurrence.

families' ratings of the patients' symptoms (the anorectic scores prior to hospitalization) and the patients' ratings of their own symptoms (the anorectic scores on day 5 of pretreatment). The patients consider their most distressing symptoms to be those of sleep disturbance and depression. The families feel the symptoms most distressing to the patients are, first, the obsessive-compulsive ones, and, second, the depressive factors. The families give the highest scores to those items specific to anorectic behavior, i.e., "obsessive-compulsive behavior related to anorexia nervosa" and "industrious and controlling behavior."

A typical feature frequently observed in anorectic patients is their disinterest in and at times actual resistance to treatment (1). A total of 52% of

TABLE 4. *Comparison of anorectic patients with other patient groups and controls on the SCL*

SCL Factor	Anorectics prior to hospitalization ($N = 44$)	Anorectics day 5 of pretreatment	Anxious neurotics ($N = 1,435$)	Depressed neurotics ($N = 367$)	Oakland, Cal. normals ($N = 735$)
Obsessive-compulsive	2.25	1.73	1.95	2.30	1.16
Depression	2.08	2.08	2.04	2.62	1.14
Somatization	1.72	1.53	1.97	1.89	1.15
Anxiety	1.78	1.74	2.22	2.45	1.13
Interpersonal sensitivity	—	1.83	2.00	2.33	1.12
Age	20.20	20.20	37.00	35.60	38.20
Sleep disturbance	—	2.10	—	—	—
Paranoid	1.69	—	—	—	—
Psychoticism	1.26	—	—	—	—
Obsessive-compulsive related to anorexia nervosa	2.81	—	—	—	—
Industrious and controlling	2.72	—	—	—	—

1 = Not at all; 2 = a bit; 3 = quite a bit; 4 = extremely.

No

TABLE 5. *Menstrual history in 40 patients with anorexia nervosa*

	f^a	%
Regularity of menstrual cycles before onset of illness		
1. Fairly regular		
Same number days ± 3	22	50.0
2. Somewhat irregular		
Variation 4–10 days	3	6.8
3. Very irregular		
Variation > 10 days	15	34.1
Months amenorrhea occurred before illness		
1	1	2.3
2	1	2.3
5	1	2.3
12	1	2.3
18	1	2.3
36	3	6.8
Not applicable	36	81.8

[a] *f* = frequency of occurrence.

patients were actively in favor of hospitalization, but 23% were neutral, 20% were mildly opposed, and 5% strongly opposed. In 71% of patients another person was influential in causing the hospitalization.

The menstrual history of this patient sample is presented in Table 5. The mean ±SD menarchal age (12.8 ± 1.2 years) is almost identical to that found by Crisp (2) in 55 anorectics. Four patients (9%) never menstruated. One-half of the patients had fairly regular menstrual cycles before the onset of

No

TABLE 6. *Past medical history in 44 patients with anorexia nervosa*

	f^a	%
Term of pregnancy		
Premature (at least 2 weeks prior to date)	7	15.9
Full term	32	72.7
Postmature (at least 2 weeks after due date)	5	11.4
Complications in pregnancy		
None	36	81.8
One or more of the following: bleeding, toxemia, infection, blood type, hyperemesis	8	18.2
Complications in delivery		
None	31	70.5
One or more of the following: anoxia, prolonged labor, abnormal presentation, medication, forceps, medical illness	13	29.5
Medical status first year of life		
No serious illness	34	77.3
One of the following: anoxic spells, serious infections, concussions, convulsions, high fevers	10	22.7

[a] *f* = frequency of occurrence.

anorexia. In 23% amenorrhea occurred before and in 14% at the onset of anorexia nervosa before an appreciable amount of weight had been lost; 55% of patients had amenorrhea after the onset of anorexia nervosa. These findings are commensurate with previous studies (16). Other physical manifestations found on admission were lanugo hair in 34%, bradycardia in 48%, edema in 11%, and hypothermia in 41% of patients. The patients' past medical histories are outlined in Table 6. The mean ±SD mothers' and fathers' ages at time of patients' birth were 28.6 ± 4.8 and 31.8 ± 6.5 years. This is confirmatory with a previous study (16). Almost one-fifth of patients had complications in pregnancy, and close to one-third had delivery complications. The medical history after delivery and prior to the onset of anorexia nervosa is unremarkable. During this time feeding prob-

TABLE 7. *Premorbid personality and school performance in childhood in 44 patients with anorexia nervosa*

	Not at all		A bit		Quite a bit		Extremely	
Trait	f[a]	%	f	%	f	%	f	%
Shy or timid	10	22.7	18	40.9	13	29.5	3	6.8
Well-behaved	1	2.3	5	11.4	20	45.5	18	40.9
Anxious or nervous	26	59.1	12	27.3	5	11.4	1	2.3
Extroverted	16	36.4	16	36.4	9	20.5	3	6.8
Episodes of hyper-activity	35	79.5	6	13.6	2	4.5	1	2.3
Short attention span and distractability	37	84.1	5	11.4	1	2.3	1	2.3
Perfectionistic	8	18.2	9	20.5	18	40.9	9	20.5
Competitive and achieving	8	18.2	9	20.5	21	47.7	6	13.6
Ritualistic behavior (such as "things being in a specific order or place")	17	38.6	14	31.8	10	22.7	3	6.8
Phobias or fears of certain places, persons, or things	27	61.4	12	27.3	5	11.4	0	0
Bed wetting after age 4	42	95.5	1	2.3	1	2.3	0	0
Running away from home, truancy, or trouble with juvenile authorities	43	97.7	1	2.3	0	0	0	0
Kleptomania	44	100.0	0	0	0	0	0	0

School performance	Above average		Average		Below average	
	f	%	f	%	f	%
Grade school	28	63.6	14	31.8	2	4.5
High school	30	68.2	10	22.7	4	9.1

[a] f = frequency of occurrence.

lems were most prevalent in the first year of life (34% of patients) and during adolescence (54% of patients). There was no significant incidence of feeding problems between ages 1 and adolescence.

Predominant premorbid personality characteristics of the anorectics described by their parents are presented in Table 7. In summary, "very well behaved" typified 86%, perfectionistic 61%, and competitive and achieving 61%. Noticeably absent in their premorbid personality were hyperactivity—7%, short attention span—5%, and delinquent behavior—none. Their school performance was commensurate with their premorbid

TABLE 8. *Educational and occupational levels of the parents of 44 patients with anorexia nervosa*

	Mother		Father	
Educational level	*f*[a]	%	*f*	%
1. Completed postgraduate training	2	4.5	5	11.4
2. Some postgraduate training	0	0	3	6.8
3. Completed college, received 4-year academic degree	9	20.5	2	4.5
4. Attended college, but didn't receive 4-year academic degree	5	11.4	5	11.4
5. Completed high school; may have attended or completed trade school or other nonacademic training requiring high school completion	17	38.6	13	29.5
6. Attended high school	7	15.9	7	15.9
7. Completed grammar school (8th grade)	3	6.8	6	13.6
8. Attended grammar school	0	0	2	4.5
9. No schooling	1	2.3	1	2.3
Mean	4.68	100	4.79	100
SD	1.55		2.06	

	Father	
Occupational level	*f*	%
1. Higher executive, proprietor of large concern, major professional	6	13.6
2. Business manager of large concern, proprietor of medium-sized business, lesser professional	8	18.2
3. Administrative official, owner of small independent business, minor professional, owner of large firm	5	11.4
4. Clerical or sales worker, technician, owner of small business, owner of medium-sized farm	13	29.5
5. Skilled manual employee, owner of small farm	7	15.9
6. Machine operator, semiskilled employee, tenant farmer who owns little equipment	4	9.1
7. Unskilled employee, sharecropper	1	2.3
Mean	3.52	100
SD	1.62	

[a] *f* = frequency of occurrence.

TABLE 9. *Number of first-degree relatives (mother, father, sibs, and children) with gastrointestinal disorders*

	Relatives			
Disorder	0	1	2	3
Peptic ulcer	37	5	1	1
Ulcerative colitis	40	3	1	0
Gastritis	28	12	3	1
Irritable colon	34	8	2	0
Undiagnosed GI problems	40	3	1	0

personality (Table 7). Two-thirds had above-average performance in grade school and high school. These findings confirm those of other studies (1,5) and become of particular interest when correlated with the outcome factor of weight gain. In all, 48% of the patients cooked excessively before onset of illness. This behavior may be one of the best warning signs of anorexia nervosa.

The mean educational level of both mother and father was that of some college education (Table 8). Of special interest is the fact that both parents were at the same level. The mean occupational level of the fathers was between that of white collar workers and administrative personnel. We have not translated these findings into the Hollingshead social classes, but it is obvious from these data that social classes I and II would predominate. This is commensurate with findings in previous studies (8).

The specific illness of anorexia nervosa had been present in 3 of 88 (3.4%) parents and 4 of 130 (3.1%) siblings. This is a much more frequent occurrence than the latest prevalence figures, $^1/_{250}$ (0.4%), in the age group at risk (3). Frank obesity was present in 18% of the parents, 5.4% of siblings, and 15.9% of grandparents. Gastrointestinal disorders were not uncommon in the first-degree relatives (Table 9).

Only one patient in this sample of 44 had no sibling. The mean ±SD number of sibs was 2.9 ± 1.9. The distribution of patients in ordinal positions was not unusual: 25% of patients were the first child, 36% were second, 30% were third, 7% were fourth, and 2% were sixth. Only 3 of 44 parents were divorced. This remarkably low figure of broken homes has been reported previously (16).

All the social and psychiatric history variables just described were correlated with weight change and with each other. Those variables that significantly correlated with weight change are presented in Table 10. The direction of the correlation cannot be determined from the table since various scales had different scoring directions. In summary, a greater weight gain is associated with: (a) a smaller amount of weight loss from a normal target weight, (b) presence of precipitants to onset of illness, (c)

TABLE 10. *Social history predictors of weight change* (N = *44;* $r_{0.05} = 0.295$)

	2	3	4	5	6	7	8	9	10
1. Weight gain	−.295	−.328	−.439	.462	−.340	−.303	.365	.479	−.309
2. Weight loss from norm		.064	.316	−.434	.265	.254	.028	.002	−.168
3. Precipitants to illness			.184	−.246	−.010	.120	.027	−.044	.046
4. Complications in pregnancy				−.863	.235	.074	−.272	−.206	.149
5. Complications in delivery					−.496	−.139	.090	.221	−.129
6. Premorbid hyperactivity						.121	.118	−.091	.022
7. Premorbid ritualistic behavior							−.029	−.042	.076
8. Admission hypothermia								.419	−.380
9. Mother's age at patient's birth									−.275
10. Premorbid emphasis on eating									

fewer complications in pregnancy, (d) fewer complications in delivery, (e) a lower frequency of hyperactivity during childhood, (f) less frequent ritualistic behavior in childhood, (g) presence of hypothermia, (h) a higher mother's age at patient's birth, and (i) undue emphasis on eating in childhood.

As expected, delivery and pregnancy complications correlate highly in the same direction and both correlate significantly with a greater amount of weight loss from a normal target weight. Complications in delivery are correlated with a greater frequency of hyperactivity in childhood.

DISCUSSION

Contrary to our expectation that a greater weight gain would occur in those patients most severely emaciated, we found just the opposite. The weight change was measured as total gain or loss over a 6-week period. Those patients who required a longer hospitalization for rehabilitation received it but not on this study protocol. Thus at the end of the treatment study period patients were at varying percentages from their target weight. Actually, the weight change over a 6-week period is more reflective of the patients' rates of weight change. Therefore, the most emaciated and hence the most seriously ill patients had the slowest weight gain.

Those patients who had clearly evident external stress occurring with the onset of anorexia nervosa had a greater weight gain during the treatment study. An obvious implication would be that those patients who develop the illness without a noxious environmental stress have a continuing or more severe pathological process which predisposes them to a worse outcome. Those patients responding to an environmental stress with change (illness) have a less-serious underlying biological process. The well-known "process" and "non-process" subgroups in schizophrenia (14) are the precedence for this concept.

Complications in pregnancy and delivery increase the susceptibility to minimal cerebral damage, and this in turn can generate a predisposition to tolerate and recover from illness poorly. Hence patients with prenatal complications would be expected to gain weight (improve) at a slower rate. The significant correlation of childhood hyperactivity and ritualistic behavior with delivery complications and a slower weight gain is not surprising. There is sufficient evidence in the literature (7,9,10,15) that prenatal and perinatal factors associated with damage to the nervous system increase the vulnerability of the individual to childhood behavior problems.

In this group of patients hypothermia was not associated with the degree of emaciation; however, it was associated with greater weight gain during treatment. It is possible that hypothermia is an effective hypothalamic adaptive response to conserve energy during the illness. Those patients who are unable to make this adaptive response have a greater degree of hypothalamic dysfunction and hence a slower recovery. To our knowledge there is no rational explanation as to why hypothermia, higher mother's age at patient's birth, and undue emphasis on eating in childhood correlate highly with each other and why the latter two items correlate with a greater weight change.

In this preliminary analysis a well-defined subgroup of anorexia nervosa is emerging. This subgroup has a slower rate of weight gain and is characterized by a history of pregnancy and delivery complications.

REFERENCES

1. Crisp, A. H. (1965): Clinical and therapeutic aspects of anorexia nervosa—a study of 30 cases. *J. Psychosom. Res.,* 9:67–78.
2. Crisp, A. H. (1970): Reported birth weights and growth weights in a group of patients with primary anorexia nervosa (weight phobia). *J. Psychosom. Res.,* 14:23–50.
3. Crisp, A. H., Palmer, R. L., and Kalucy, R. S. (1976): How common is anorexia nervosa? *Br. J. Psychiatry,* 128:549–554.
4. Derogatis, L. R., Lipman, R. S., Rickels, K., Uhlenhuth, E. H., and Covi, L. (1974): The Hopkins symptom check list (HSCL): A self-report symptom inventory. *Behav. Sci.,* 19:1–15.
5. Halmi, K. (1974): Anorexia nervosa: Demographic and clinical features in 94 cases. *Psychosom. Med.,* 36:18–26.
6. Halmi, K., Brodland, G., and Loney, J. (1973): Prognosis in anorexia nervosa. *Ann. Intern. Med.,* 78:907–909.
7. Hertzig, M. E., and Birch, H. G. (1966): Neurologic organization in psychiatrically disturbed adolescent girls. *Arch. Gen. Psychiatry,* 15:590–598.
8. Morgan, H. G., and Russell, G. F. N. (1975): Value of family background in clinical features as predictors of long term outcome in anorexia nervosa: Four year follow-up study of 41 patients. *Psychol. Med.,* 5:355–371.
9. Pasamanick, B., and Knobloch, H. (1960): Brain and behaviors: Brain damage and reproductive causality. *Am. J. Ortho. Psychiatry,* 30:298–305.
10. Pincus, J. H., and Glaser, G. H. (1966): Syndrome of minimal brain damage in childhood. *N. Engl. J. Med.,* 275:27–35.
11. Slade, P. D. (1973): A short anorexic behavior scale. *Br. J. Psychiatry,* 122:83–85.
12. Smart, D. E., Beumont, P. J. V., and George, G. C. W. (1976): Some personality characteristics of patients with anorexia nervosa. *Br. J. Psychiatry,* 128:57–60.
13. Spitzer, R. L., Endicott, J., and Robins, E. (1975): *Research Diagnostic Criteria (RDC)*

for a Selected Group of Functional Disorders, Ed. 2. Biometrics Research, New York State Psychiatric Institute, 722 W. 168th St., New York, New York 10032.
14. Stephens, J. H., and Astrup, C. (1963): Prognosis in "process" and "non-process" schizophrenia. *Am. J. Psychiatry,* 119:949–953.
15. Taft, L. T., and Goldfarb, W. (1964): Prenatal and perinatal factors in childhood schizophrenia. *Dev. Med. Child Neurol.,* 6:32–43.
16. Theander, S. (1970): Anorexia nervosa, a psychiatric investigation of 94 female patients. *Acta Psychiatr. Scand.,* 214:1–190.

Anorexia Nervosa, edited by
R. A. Vigersky. Raven Press,
New York © 1977.

The Long-Term Prognosis in Anorexia Nervosa: Some Factors Predictive of Outcome

A. H. Crisp, R. S. Kalucy, J. H. Lacey, and Britta Harding

Academic Department of Psychiatry, St. George's Hospital Medical School, London SW 17, England

INTRODUCTION

The diagnostic criteria for anorexia nervosa that we have used have been previously outlined (3,5). They are strict and are in accord with those used by others (1,18,26). Over the past 17 years, a series of 350 patients with primary anorexia nervosa has been extensively studied, usually before and during treatment. This chapter is based on several follow-up studies within this population. It also comments on the findings of other follow-up studies in which similar diagnostic criteria were used. These studies include those reported by Kay and Leigh (22), Meyer (23), Crisp (4), Thoma (33), Farquharson and Hyland (19), Seidensticker and Tzagournis (27), Dally (18), Theander (32), Morgan and Russell (24), and Stonehill and Crisp (31).

All our findings are hampered by several major problems.

1. The condition is common, now affecting approximately 1 in every 100 women aged 16 to 18 years who are still at school in and around London (15). The incidence is probably increasing and the nature of the morbidity may also be changing in relation to this.

2. Many people with the disorder avoid medical attention or correct diagnostic evaluation, even when their disability is severe. The differential diagnosis of the chronic case is one of the most complex clinical exercises in medicine.

3. We cannot be sure that population studies at different centers are comparable in every respect, although it is likely that units known to provide a major clinical service for anorexia nervosa attract the most severe cases and perhaps also patients with particular social attributes.

However, we can perhaps all agree that ultimate outcome can vary between spontaneous recovery and death (5), and that the illness may last from a few months to a lifetime (Fig. 1). Moreover, Morgan and Russell (24) found that, after a minimum follow-up period of 4 years, 40% of severely ill patients had made a good recovery in both biological and psychosocial terms. This is roughly in accord with most other workers' findings (40 to

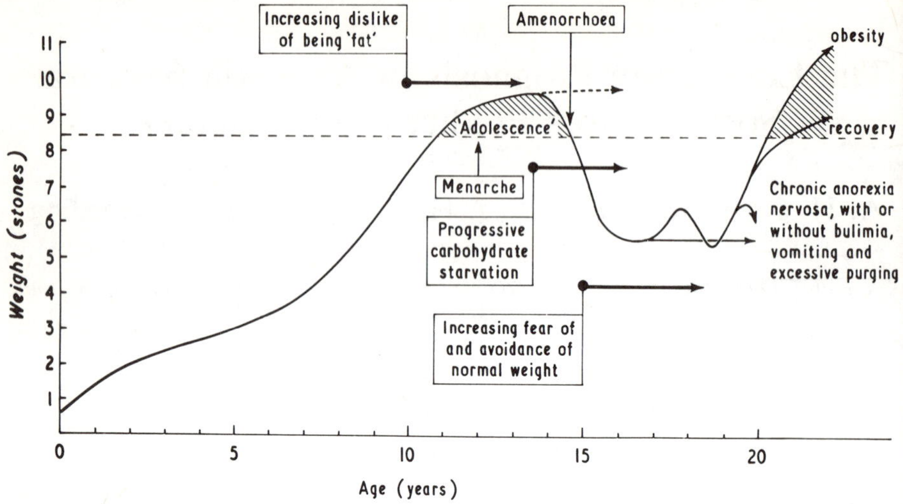

FIG. 1. Typical developments in the evolution of anorexia nervosa. The figure also displays the concept of pubertal weight threshold around which the disorder pivots in patho-psychobiological terms (4). (From ref. 5 with permission.)

60%) including our own (4,31). It is generally agreed that death from the condition ultimately occurs in at least 5% of anorexia nervosa patients who have been attending hospital clinics at one stage or another. It is almost always due either to an effect of the starvation-dehydration-hypokalemia syndrome or to a specific act of suicide. Death from intercurrent infection is rare and probably always was (7).

It is not known for certain whether treatment has any effect on the long-term course of the disorder. Many different therapeutic approaches have been advocated. Our own, rooted in the notion of the illness as a phobic avoidance posture pivoting around the pubertal weight threshold (3), has depended on a 'behavioral' technique for restoring weight to normal. This involves a mean weight gain of 20 kg. This part of the program is aimed at minimizing the patient's preoccupation with her own weight control, while allowing her gradually to reexperience a rekindling of the early pubertal process. This creates an opportunity for meaningful individual and family psychotherapy directed at the larger-order problems of psychosocial and emotional growth, differentiation, and control (5). The behavioral aspects of our approach also include specific social skills training and a behavioral approach to particular sexual problems as they emerge with the patient's weight gain. It is our view that our treatment does sometimes have an effect. If this is true for us and also for other clinical investigators, it creates further difficulties in identifying natural prognostic indicators.

FACTORS AFFECTING OUTCOME

Below are described some of the factors which have most clearly been found to be related to long-term outcome.

Gender

Anorexia nervosa is infrequent in males, although more common than is generally recognized (17). Problems in diagnosis arise since all males have amenorrhea and their attire masks their shape. In our series there are 27 males (8% of all anorectics) with the unequivocal primary anorexia nervosa/weight phobia syndrome. The common adolescent female desire to slim (20,25) contrasts with the prevalent male lack of concern with his shape or else his wish to be bigger and stronger. Only very obese males or those with major gender identity problems are likely to diet. These patients may then go on to develop anorexia nervosa. Moreover, overeating and vomiting is probably a more common feature among male than female anorectics. These factors may contribute to our observation that the prognosis is worse among the males in our own population. We would suggest that, in general, males are resistant to the development of anorexia nervosa and only develop it within the context of overwhelming psychopathology and/or premorbid massive obesity (*vide infra*).

Social Class

The disorder is commonest among social classes I and II (Registrar General's classification) (8,15,24). Working class families are resistant to anorexia nervosa whereas obesity is more common among them than in the professional and managerial classes (29). In our experience, patients with anorexia nervosa from social classes IV and V do less well. We are struck by the stark psychopathology, often of a clear sexual kind among such patients, who are thus more readily accessible to psychotherapy. Profound resistance frequently develops in the patient and the family at the prospect of change, and they often disengage rapidly from further significant psychotherapy. Furthermore, at 2-year follow-up, in a series of 56 consecutively treated families (21), patients from social classes IV and V have done significantly worse as a group.

Age of Onset

It is probable that late onset (e.g., in the third decade and later) is associated with poor outcome. This is the clear finding of Morgan and Russell (24) and Theander (32). However, there is no doubt that early-onset patients can also do poorly, especially if they have been obese in relation to rapid growth and early puberty. It is sometimes very difficult to determine age of onset in someone presenting in their twenties or thirties. If they have established a pattern of bulimia/vomiting/purging, secret or explicit, they will be likely to identify the onset of their problems as the time when they could no longer maintain an abstinence posture. The years of pathological abstinence from carbohydrate and perhaps irregular menses (including delayed menarche) during their early and mid-teens is forgotten or denied.

Family Nutritional Characteristics, Weight Control Patterns, and Attitudes Toward Shape

Patients often come from families in which there is weight disorder (obesity and/or sometimes anorexia nervosa), excessive involvement in some or other nurturent profession, or need to control normal weight by excessive exercise (6,21). Patients from families in which the life style is so limited and seemingly such a concrete influence in the patient's illness do particularly badly. We have found other families in which the parents reveal, using a standardized measure for indicating body widths (14), a desired body size for their daughters which is of anorectic proportions; this despite their expressed wish for their daughter to recover. Such parents sometimes also indicate similar aspirations and distortions with respect to their own body widths. We suspect that they carry a poor prognosis for the anorectic. We are now systematically investigating these parameters.

Patients' Premorbid Weight

A considerable number of patients were obese premorbidly (10,16), although they may now minimize this. The propensity for ultimate binge eating and vomiting to emerge as the dietetic pattern within the illness and also for the more profound perceptual disturbances concerning reported self-estimates of body widths occurs in this group. It is also characterized by a failure of gonadotropins to reestablish themselves immediately within the context of restoration of weight to normal (11). Our overall finding is that premorbid obesity confers a worse prognosis.

Marriage

Someone who marries another person with anorexia nervosa is likely to have very restricted and specific needs in life (5,7,9). For instance, he will have sought a perversely sexual (if the individual with the disorder displays persistent bulimia and vomiting as a means of weight control) or an asexual, but still infertile, partner. The marriage is thereby embedded in the powerful neurotic needs of both partners. Neither dares explore change.

Such marriage conveys a worse natural prognosis although we have had occasional success in treating such patients. Sometimes the marriage has broken down under the challenge of the patient's radically changed life style once her weight was normal and remained so. In two other instances we have been successful in treating such patients and their husbands, even after 20 years of illness. In both cases, although the marriage had been established during the illness, it nevertheless survived the patient's recovery. With these patients we had adopted our usual treatment program but with particular emphasis on marital therapy including behaviorally oriented sexual therapy. One of these patients, severely ill for 22 years, not only recovered but now has a child. Several of our recovered patients have children. Severely ill anorectics (bulimic/vomiting/purging types) become sexually active and conceive without prior menses during times of modest weight gain. Such pregnancies are followed by severe relapse.

Duration of Illness

It is our view that the disorder serves and indeed exists so as to divorce the individual from any meaningful biological maturity and growth and hence any effective peer relationships. Her peers grow steadily away from her and she becomes progressively isolated within her biologically immature, childlike, status. The longer she is ill the more difficult it is for her to contemplate and explore, through weight gain, the tasks of catching up with life again. Some investigators have claimed that it is almost impossible to alter the chronic nature of the illness (18) once it has been established for 10 years or more. Although we agree with Morgan and Russell (24) that chronicity confers a worse natural prognosis, we believe that such patients can recover and that treatment is still occasionally effective as described above. At the same time we believe that injudicious and major attempts merely to manipulate the weight of such patients can be damaging. Under such conditions a long-standing pattern of abstinence may give way to the more malignant pattern of bulimia, vomiting, and purging (especially if modified insulin treatment has been used), and the likelihood of suicide is enhanced (5). One of us has previously described a patient whose illness spontaneously remitted at the age of 42 years, having served to stifle her reproductive life and its implications since puberty (5). Chronicity, of course, is also associated more often with bulimia, vomiting, and purging (7,10), an unfavorable development in itself.

Personality

Others have emphasized the prognostic importance of premorbid personality (18). We have claimed instead that the illness arises as a response to problems of adolescent identity formation in someone with major psychological developmental defects and an absence of other defense mechanisms (5). It is thus not meaningful to claim that a premorbid personality has become established before illness onset. This is not to say that within the syndrome patients do not come to display a wide variety of more or less persistent behaviors, attitudes, and emotional stances related to their ongoing struggle over weight control. Their "personality" within the illness is in fact reduced to their total preoccupation and engagement with this struggle. It determines their manipulative behavior, their moments of despair and ecstasy, their dietary rituals, and their industry at school (5,7).

We suspect that prognostic indicators are to be found within the field of childhood behavior; this despite our view that the disorder in psychopathological terms is one of the meaning of postpubertal weight and not primarily the prepubertal symbolic significance of food and eating. Dally (18) has suggested that patients with premorbid obsessional traits do less well than those with hysterical styles of relating. Morgan and Russell (24) find that patients with childhood neurotic and/or behavior problems do badly. We would agree that undue rigidity in both the patient and the family is associated with poor prognosis. This may have been manifest in the patient's childhood in terms of obsessionality, undue compliance (carrying in our view a particularly poor prognosis), or acting out behavior sometimes associated in the immediate pre-illness phase with an ill-sustained and, to the patient, frightening phase of almost undifferentiated impulse-ridden behavior.

We (31) have recently examined psychiatric characteristics in a series of 42 patients in a 4- to 7-year follow-up. Our measurement instrument was the Middlesex Hospital Questionnaire (MHQ), a standardized self-rating inventory of six categories of psychoneurotic status—anxiety, phobic behavior, obsessionality, somatic complaint, depression, and hysteria—with scores ranging from 0 to 16 in each instance.

High levels of somatic complaint at the time of presentation carry a significantly worse prognosis 4 to 7 years later. However, there is no relationship between outcome at this stage and levels of anxiety, depression, or obsessionality at presentation, although, in the subgroup of vomiters, characterized at presentation by low obsessional scores, the outlook was worse. However, at follow-up, and with approximately 50% of the patients recovered in physical, social, and psychological terms from their anorexia nervosa, the group still displays significantly high levels of phobic anxiety but now with a social basis.

Family Psychopathology

There is some literature on the psychiatric morbidity and the specific psychopathology of families of patients with anorexia nervosa (2,5,7,9,10,21,22,28,33). We reported (13) a prospective study of measured aspects of the psychoneurotic status of the parents in a series of 22 consecutive anorectic patients, once again using the MHQ for this purpose. During the period of the patient's restoration of weight back to matched population mean levels, the parents became significantly more anxious and depressed despite their initial angry, helpless, and guilt-ridden presentations when they had sought help for their daughter. Such worsening in the parents' psychiatric status (severe anxiety in the mothers, major depression in the fathers) was not associated with a bad outcome for the patient and was often a fruitful phase within the family psychotherapy. It was particularly associated with a severely impaired marital relationship. This finding agreed with our clinical understanding of such patients' illnesses; namely that it often served, through regression, to lock the parental marriage or in other ways minimize conflict in one or both parents. The patient, now childlike, is no longer challenging the family stability as she had begun to do as an adolescent. At 6 months' follow-up, patients who were doing badly were characterized by parents whose initial presentation had included high levels of depression as measured by the MHQ, also a tendency to higher obsessionality in the mothers and significantly more somatic complaint, and a high degree of extroversion (hysteria scale) in the fathers (Fig. 2).

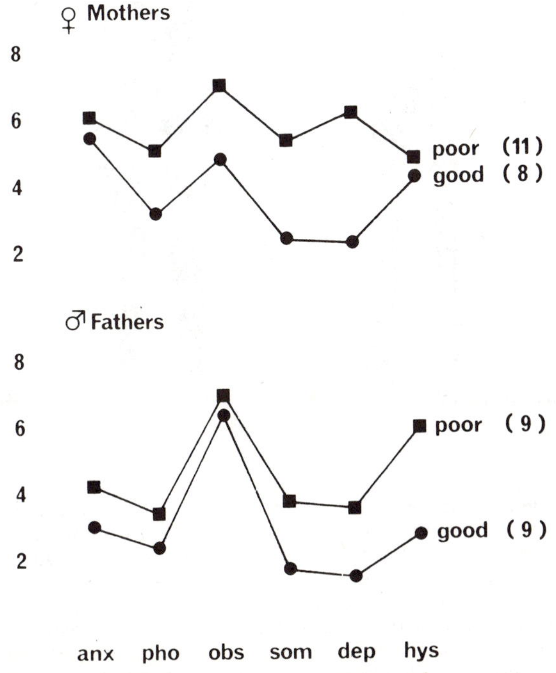

FIG. 2. Pretreatment MHQ profiles on the parents of 19 anorexia nervosa patients, classified according to outcome. (From ref. 13 with permission.)

Finally, the subgroup of vomiters was significantly worse at follow-up, and they, with their particular problems of impulse control, were characterized at presentation by high levels of obsessionality in their fathers.

Perceptual Characteristics and Changes

Slade and Russell (30) have shown that these patients characteristically report overestimates of their body widths. We (14) believe that this is a complexly determined phenomenon and that it is also shown by other nonanorectic women in their teens, as well as by obese subjects. We agree with Slade and Russell that the prognosis is probably better in those whose self-reported estimates are more or less accurate following restoration of weight, and also no longer influenced by an ordinary carbohydrate meal

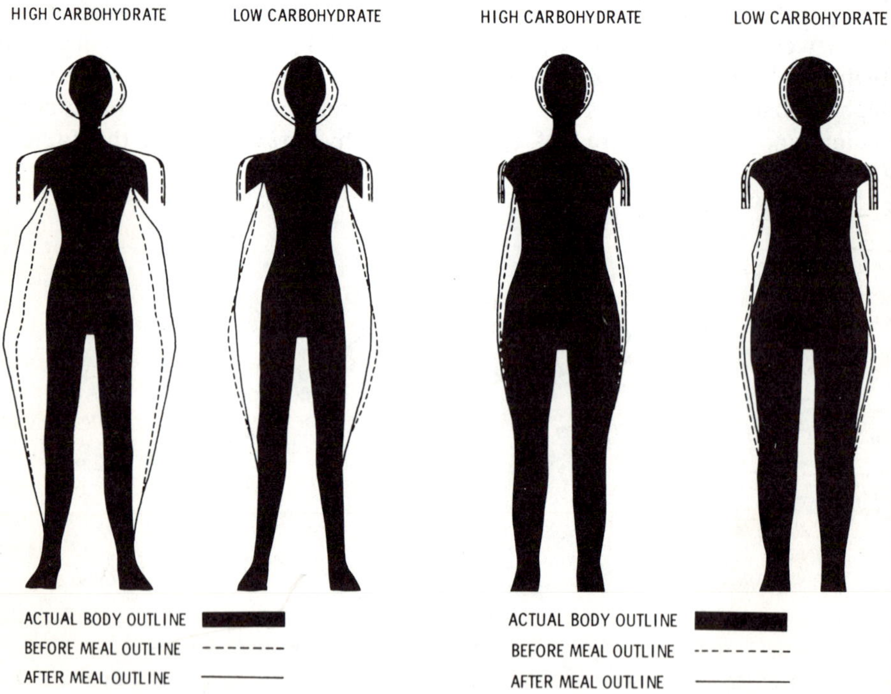

FIG. 3. Estimated versus actual body widths. **Left:** Two sets of outlines of an anorexia nervosa patient, aged 15 years, height 1.72 m, premorbid weight 56 kg, present weight 42.8 kg, target weight 58 kg. **Right:** Two outlines of the same patient recovered from anorexia nervosa. Black areas represent actual measured body dimensions; dotted outlines indicate pre-meal self-estimations of body widths; continuous outlines indicate self-estimations of body widths shortly after high- and low-carbohydrate isocaloric meals. The figures show (a) the characteristic gross overestimation of body width by an anorectic, (b) the specific and symbolic impact of carbohydrate on this process, (c) the restoration toward accuracy of these perceptions following recovery. (From ref. 14 with permission.)

(Fig. 3). As previously stated, gross overestimation of body widths is associated with premorbid obesity and with bulimia and vomiting.

Dietary Pattern

Persistent overeating and attendant vomiting and purging as the means of weight control is a chronic pattern significantly associated with premorbid obesity. Often there is a history of premorbidly voracious appetite and rapid growth, sometimes with a period of frighteningly poor premorbid impulse control since puberty. A particularly poorly differentiated sense of the self is often evident. The complications of hypokalemia, hyperinsulinemia, and related abnormalities lead to such clinical problems as epilepsy, cardiac conduction defects, and a greater risk of death (6,8,10), and the pattern is associated with greater psychiatric morbidity in the parents, especially the fathers. When these complications are present as a persistent feature, especially within a chronic (5 years +) course, they confer a worse prognosis.

Motivation for Treatment

Most anorectics are intensely ambivalent about the prospect of change and the need to surrender control of their diet and weight to others. Our own treatment approach (5,7) involves an initial 3-hr consultation with the patient and family in which we aim to identify the family psychopathology as well as the biological parameters of the disorder. We hope to engage the individual to become a genuine patient, contemplating the prospect of real change and maturation, so far only dealt with by avoidance. For this she will usually need to see that her parents are also prepared to explore and to submit to change. At the end of the interview a treatment contract is put to the patient and family and they are invited to accept or reject it given a few days' reflection. At this stage one can sometimes identify a determination within the patient to make a major effort to get over her illness. It is our impression that this carries a good prognosis.

In conclusion, it will be seen that our findings show some similarities with those of other workers. Where there are differences these may be due to (a) idiosyncratic characteristics of our respective patient groups, or (b) the impact of our particular treatment program with its emphasis on weight control combined with individual and family psychotherapy.

SUMMARY

Factors associated with poor outcome probably include (a) being male; (b) occupying social classes IV or V; (c) late onset of disease; (d) excessive weight disorder, concern over weight control, and preoccupation with body shape within the family; (e) premorbid obesity; (f) marriage; (g) long duration of illness; (h) excessive compliance or behavior disorder during childhood and excessive somatic complaint within the disorder; (i) high levels of depression in the parents at the time of presentation, obsessionality in the mothers, high somatic complaint and extrovert traits in the fathers; (j) continued misperception of body widths following restoration of weight to normal; (k) persistent overeating, vomiting, and purging as the established means of weight control; (l) poor motivation for treatment aimed at tackling the adolescent maturational problems underlying the disorder.

REFERENCES

1. Bruch, H. (1966): Anorexia nervosa and its differential diagnosis. *J. Nerv. Ment. Dis.*, 141:555–566.
2. Bruch, H. (1974): *Eating Disorders: Obesity, Anorexia Nervosa and the Person Within.* Routledge & Kegan Paul, London.
3. Crisp, A. H. (1965*a*): Clinical and therapeutic aspects of anorexia nervosa—a study of 30 cases. *J. Psychosom. Res.*, 9:67–78.
4. Crisp, A. H. (1965*b*): Some aspects of the evolution, presentation and follow-up of anorexia nervosa. *Proc. R. Soc. Med.*, 58:814–820.
5. Crisp, A. H. (1967*a*): Anorexia nervosa. *Hosp. Med.* 1 (May): 713–718.
6. Crisp, A. H. (1967*b*): The possible significance of some behavioral correlates of weight and carbohydrate intake. *J. Psychosom. Res.*, 11:117–131.
7. Crisp, A. H. (1970): Anorexia nervosa: "feeding disorder," "nervous malnutrition" or "weight phobia"? *World Rev. Nutr. Diet.*, 12:452–504.
8. Crisp, A. H. (1973): The nature of primary anorexia nervosa. *J. R. Coll. Surg. Edinb.*, 42:18–30.
9. Crisp, A. H. (1974): Primary anorexia nervosa or adolescent weight phobia. *Practitioner*, 212:525–535.
10. Crisp, A. H. (1975): Anorexia nervosa: Some psychobiological aspects of adolescent growth and their relevance. *Mod. Med.*, 20(10):26–32.
11. Crisp, A. H., Chen, C., MacKinnon, P. C. B., and Corker, C. S. (1973): Observations of gonadotrophic and ovarian hormone activity during recovery from anorexia nervosa. *Postgrad. Med. J.*, 49:584–590.
12. Crisp, A. H., Fenton, G. W., and Scotton, L. (1968): A controlled study of the EEG in anorexia nervosa. *Br. J. Psychiarty,* 114:1149–1160.
13. Crisp, A. H., Harding, B., and McGuinness, B. (1974): Anorexia nervosa. Psychoneurotic characteristics of parents: Relationship to prognosis. *J. Psychosom. Res.*, 18:167–173.
14. Crisp, A. H., and Kalucy, R. S. (1974): Aspects of the perceptual disorder in anorexia nervosa. *Br. J. Med. Psychol.*, 47:349–361.
15. Crisp, A. H., Palmer, R. L., and Kalucy, R. S. (1976): How common is anorexia nervosa? A prevalence study. *Br. J. Psychiatry,* 128:549–554.
16. Crisp, A. H., and Stonehill, E. (1971): Relation between aspects of nutritional disturbance and menstrual activity in primary anorexia nervosa. *Br. Med. J.*, 3:149–151.
17. Crisp, A. H., and Toms, D. A. (1972): Primary anorexia nervosa or weight phobia in the male: Report on 13 cases. *Br. Med. J.*, 1:334–338.
18. Dally, P. (1969): *Anorexia Nervosa.* Heinemann Medical Books, London.
19. Farquharson, R. F., and Hyland, H. H. (1966): Anorexia nervosa: The course of 15 patients treated from 20 to 30 years previously. *Can. Med. Assoc. J.*, 96:411–419.
20. Huenneman, R. L., Shapiro, L. R., Hampton, M. C., et al. (1966): A longitudinal study of gross body composition and body conformation and their association with food and activity in a teenage population. *Am. J. Clin. Nutr.*, 18:325–338.
21. Kalucy, R. S., Crisp, A. H., and Harding, B. (1977): A study of 56 families with anorexia nervosa. *Br. J. Med. Psychol.* (*in press*).

22. Kay, D. W. K., and Leigh, D. (1954): The natural history, treatment and prognosis of anorexia nervosa, based on a study of 38 patients. *J. Ment. Sci.,* 100:411–431.
23. Meyer, J. V. E. (1961): Das syndrom der anorexia nervosa. Katamnestische untersuchungen. *Arch. Psychiatr. Nervenkr.,* 202:31–59.
24. Morgan, H. G., and Russell, G. F. M. (1975): Value of family background and clinical features as predictors of long-term outcome in anorexia nervosa: Four-year follow-up study of 41 patients. *Psychol. Med.,* 5:355–371.
25. Nylander, I. (1971): The feeling of being fat and dieting in a school population. *Acta Sociomed. Scand.,* 3:17–26.
26. Russell, G. F. M. (1970): Anorexia nervosa: Its identity as an illness and its treatment in modern trends. In: *Psychological Medicine,* Vol. 2, edited by J. H. Price, pp. 131–164. Butterworth, London.
27. Seidensticker, J. F., and Tzagournis, M. (1968): Anorexia nervosa—clinical features and long term follow-up. *J. Chronic Dis.,* 21:361–367.
28. Selvini, M. P. (1974): *Self-starvation.* Human Context Books, London.
29. Silverstone, J. T. (1968): Psychosocial aspects of obesity. *Proc. R. Soc. Med.,* 61:371–375.
30. Slade, P. D., and Russell, G. F. M. (1973): Awareness of body dimensions in anorexia nervosa: Cross-sectional and longitudinal studies. *Psychol. Med.,* 3:188–199.
31. Stonehill, E., and Crisp, A. H. (1977): Psychoneurotic characteristics of patients with anorexia nervosa before and after treatment and at follow-up 4–7 years later. *J. Psychosom. Res. (in press).*
32. Theander, S. (1970): Anorexia nervosa. A psychiatric investigation of 94 female cases. *Acta Psychiatr. Scand.* [*Suppl.*], 214:1–194.
33. Thoma, H. (1967): *Anorexia Nervosa.* International Universities Press, New York.

Anorexia Nervosa, edited by
R. A. Vigersky. Raven Press,
New York © 1977.

An Examination of the Concept of Satiety in Hypothalamic Hyperphagia

Paul R. McHugh and Timothy H. Moran

Department of Psychiatry and Behavioral Sciences, The Johns Hopkins University School of Medicine, Baltimore, Maryland 21205

INTRODUCTION

Among the plausible explanatory hypotheses for anorexia nervosa is that which proposes the disorder to be a primary disruption of hypothalamic function. The relative stereotyped character of the illness and the demonstration of changes in feeding behavior, temperature control, and endocrine regulation produced by hypothalamic injury or stimulation are invoked to support this opinion. There is no evidence to refute it. However, neither is there much evidence to confirm it. Its survival may depend on our rudimentary knowledge of hypothalamic physiology and on the nonspecific, vague, heuristically feeble character of the hypothesis itself.

A more specific suggestion is that the patients are anorexic because the ventromedial region of the hypothalamus (VMH) is provoking satiety inappropriately in them. The main support for this suggestion rests on the assumption that the VMH harbors a satiety mechanism. This assumption is derived from the overeating produced by VMH lesions and the aphagia produced by VMH stimulation. These results and complementary results in the lateral hypothalamus have led to the concept of a "satiety center" in the VMH playing on a "feeding center" in the lateral hypothalamus, a concept that is something of a textbook orthodoxy.

The purpose of this chapter is to consider some operational definitions of satiety and then to review experiments intended to test the hypothesis that the VMH harbors a satiety center under such a definition. To anticipate, it is our opinion that the hypothesis does not survive such experiments and that knowledge of the particular role of the VMH in feeding is not yet sufficiently advanced to be confidently applied in anorexia nervosa.

In the search for the particular function disrupted by VMH lesions producing hyperphagia, the common assumption has been that in some way a satiety mechanism has been affected by these lesions so that the animal's capacity to monitor how much it eats by its sense of satisfaction is impaired. It thus eats to excess. But it is clear that the term *satiety* may be being employed in two ways. First as a term for a state of satisfaction after meal taking, that is, as the opposite of the state of hunger that precedes feeding; or second, satiety may be the designation of a dynamic process of inhibition on feeding that develops in a graded fashion as more and more food is ingested. It has been a hidden assumption that hypothalamic hyperphagia after VMH lesions is somehow due to a disturbance in the dynamic process of satiety. In fact, the only original evidence for any satiety problem is that the animals eat more in reaching a state of satiety, a result as easily explained by greater initial hunger as by a satiety disturbance. Only a failure of feeding to decline as nutrients are supplied could indicate a disorder of the dynamic process of satiety. Thomas and Mayer (3) and Panksepp (2) have sought such a disorder in the rat; we have sought it in the monkey (1). None of us has found it.

METHODS

To provoke hypothalamic hyperphagia in our experimental animal, the rhesus monkey, we developed a technique for hypothalamic disconnection. A knife-like device was inserted into the longitudinal fissure of the monkey while it was anesthetized, and with this knife a cut was made around the VMH. These cuts could completely isolate the VMH from all its neural connections, or partial cuts such as parasagittal incisions running along the fornix bundles in the hypothalamus could be made.

If bilateral parasagittal incisions running along the fornix bundles at the level of the median eminence were produced, all monkeys would increase their feeding and grow fat. The ventromedial region in such animals did not seem to change appreciably in its histological character. Four monkeys in the dynamic phase of hyperphagia were the hyperphagic subjects for our experiments and were compared with seven intact monkeys in our satiety tests.

All the rhesus monkeys were maintained in individual cages. The monkeys were trained to take their food in the form of Purina Monkey Chow® over a 3-hr period each day. They were maintained on this schedule 7 days a week. The monkeys also had implanted into their gastric lumen a chronic silastic cannula through which could be infused a variety of liquid preloads prior to the 3-hr feeding period. This cannula was held in place by investing the monkey in a leather jacket onto which was attached a stainless steel cable. After being brought through the skin of the animal, the intragastric cannula could be passed through the cable. The cable and the enclosed cannula were brought out of the cage and the cannula connected to an infusion pump. Monkeys restrained in their cage only by this vest and cable carrying the gastric cannula quickly adapted to their circumstances and ate and behaved as they had before implantation of the cannula.

In the experiments reported here, the monkeys were offered 600 g of monkey chow for 3 hr each day. Through the cannula, nutrient solutions or equal volumetric saline infusions were made into the stomach of the animal, 15 min prior to the onset of the feeding period. The eating of the animal was then calculated from the amount of food remaining in his tray after 3 hr.

RESULTS AND DISCUSSION

Figure 1 shows the effects on feeding of progressive increments of nutrient in the form of Carnation Instant Breakfast® provided intragastrically to intact monkeys and compared with the effects on feeding of equivolumetric saline infusions. There is a progressive reduction in the amount of chow eaten with increasing volumes of Carnation Instant Breakfast®. There is no significant change in feeding with increasing volumes of saline. This reduction of food eaten in response to an increment of nutrient exemplifies the process of satiety. It is a graded phenomenon related to nutrient and eventually capable of stopping all feeding completely, i.e., the sated state.

A similar experiment in monkeys with hypothalamic hyperphagia provoked by the VMH disconnection is shown in Fig. 2. These animals ate more than the intact animals as is evident by the greater quantity of food eaten with the saline controls. There is a decline in the amount of food eaten when Carnation Instant Breakfast® is provided in the infusions. It might seem that there is some resistance to the inhibition provoked by Carnation Instant Breakfast® as it appeared that more is eaten by these animals under these conditions than is eaten by the normal animal. However, to propose a distinction between hyperphagic animals and normal animals in their satiety,

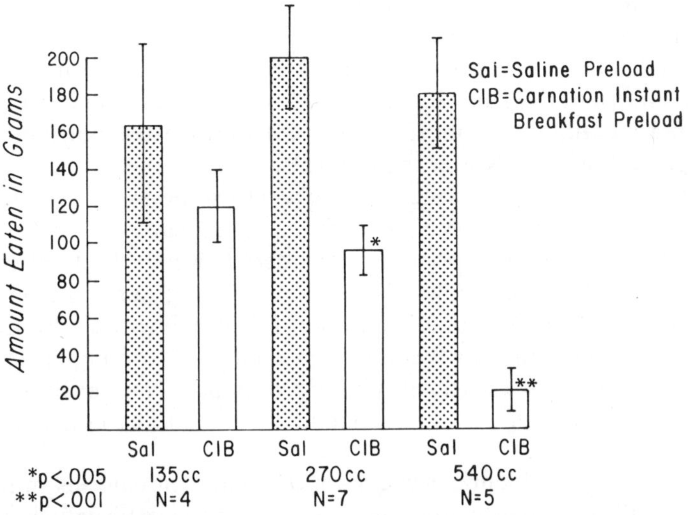

FIG. 1. Food consumed in 3-hr meal period by intact monkeys following intragastric preloads of Carnation Instant Breakfast® or isovolumetric saline.

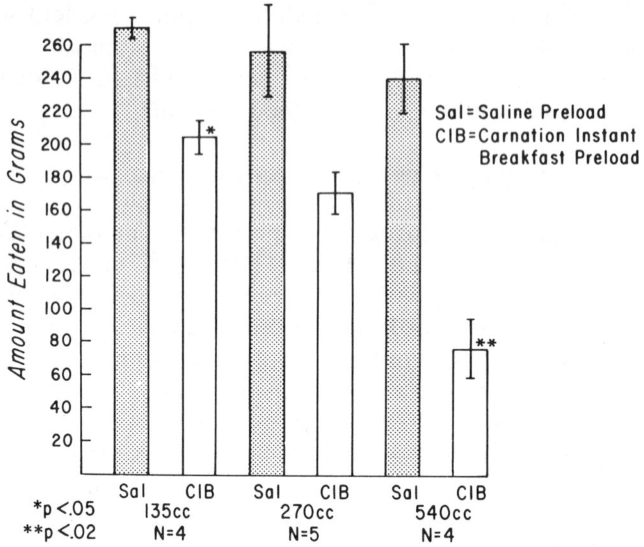

FIG. 2. Food consumed in 3-hr meal period by monkeys with hypothalamic hyperphagia following intragastric preloads of Carnation Instant Breakfast® or isovolumetric saline.

one must demonstrate a distinction not in the absolute amount of food eaten, but rather in the reduction in food eaten provoked by similar nutrient preloads. As shown in Fig. 3, the reduction in meal size produced by the nutrients is identical in the intact monkey and the hypothalamic hyperphagic monkey. Although the operated monkeys always eat more than the control animals, the reduction in meal size for each preload is identical in both sets of animals. There is no suggestion that the operated animals are less responsive to the nutrient than are the controls. Such a conclusion could be drawn only if the reduction in the meal provoked by intragastric nutrients was less in the operated animal than in the controls.

That the reduction in feeding must relate to some aspect of the nutrient character of the preload is indicated when, as in Table 1, the energy contents of the preloads and chow are considered. When the total energy intake of the hyperphagic animals is divided into that derived from the preloads through the gastric cannula and that taken deliberately by the animal in feeding, the reduction in feeding is just enough to compensate for the calories provided intragastrically in the preload. The result is that the animals regulate feeding so as to produce a constant and consistent energy intake.

We have found an identical accuracy of control of calories in intact animals (4). In these experiments we have used intragastric infusions of pure nutrients, either carbohydrates, fats, or proteins. In Fig. 4 is shown the reduction in food intake to the calories in the intragastric preload over 65

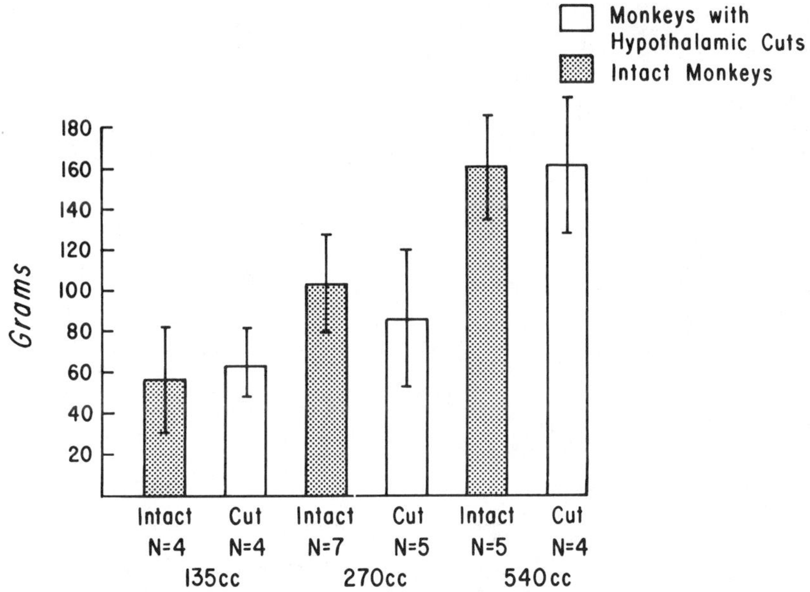

FIG. 3. The reduction in meal size provoked by nutrient preloads is the difference in the amount eaten following nutrient preloads and saline preloads.

experiments. The zero calorie preload represents a cellulose infusion. The linear reduction in food eaten with increasing calories permits an estimation of the calories that presumably should be in the chow if the monkey is controlling for calories. The inverse slope of this linear relationship is 4.22 cal/g. When we measured the nutrient calories by the oxygen bomb calorimeter, we found that Purina Monkey Chow® contained 4.21 cal/g. The impressive point is that the dynamic process of satiety functions in such a way as to enable an animal to control for the calories received with an accuracy comparable to a physical measurement. There appears to be no loss of this capacity in hyperphagic animals since there is no difference between the normal and the hyperphagic animal in this inhibitory effect.

TABLE 1. *Total energy intake (preload + meal) at different gastric preloads*

	kcal in preload			
	0	150	300	600
Hyperphagic monkeys ($N = 4$)	857 ± 31	879 ± 65	892 ± 72	813 ± 44
Intact controls ($N = 7$)	588 ± 43	540 ± 40	631 ± 31	664 ± 19[a]

[a] Significantly different from saline control ($p < 0.05$, matched-pair *t*-test, two-tailed). Note that preload calories exceed the control intake.

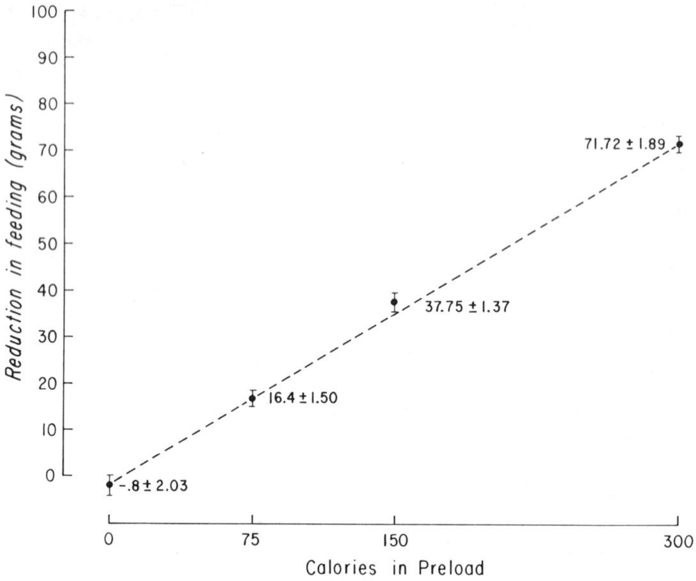

FIG. 4. Reduction in food intake from saline controls provoked by a variety of preloads (lipid, protein, carbohydrate, or mixed). The 0 preload is methylcellulose, a nonmetabolizable carbohydrate. There is a regular dose-response relationship to the calories in the preload.

Thus if satiety is defined as that inhibition on feeding produced by food itself, then by these experiments normal and VMH hyperphagic animals do not differ in satiety. Both sets of animals demonstrate a capacity for regulating feeding so as to control with great accuracy the energy they ingest. As there is no loss of this capacity in the hyperphagic animal, the deficit in satiety cannot explain the hyperphagia. VMH hyperphagia in our animals was produced by disconnecting the neural links from the VMH. Since satiety was retained unmodified as demonstrated by these experiments, the disconnected VMH cannot be indispensable for satiety unless its influence is exerted through a humoral path and thus survives the disconnection. But if this region exerts a nonneurally mediated satiety influence, the hyperphagia provoked by the disconnection would remain to be explained and it was this hyperphagia that started the satiety issue originally.

Thus, although hyperphagic monkeys eat more than intact animals, they appear to meter their intake just as accurately. The perennial question, Why does the hyperphagic animal eat more?, is not answered by proposing that it has lost the normal capacities to meter intake or modify feeding in relationship to calories already ingested. This is the function we wish to define as the satiety process, as it is that graded function leading eventually to full satiation. Although it is possible to say that an animal is only half-sated when another animal is full, it is incorrect without other information to attribute this to a disturbance in satiety. It may be only half-sated because it was originally more hungry.

Since our results do not support the idea that hyperphagia is caused by disruption of a satiety process or what the VMH is a crucial satiety center, it would appear that some traditional views of hypothalamic function in hunger and satiety would need revision. Likewise, if it is to be held that the hypothalamus is the neural center disrupted in anorexia nervosa, then the view that a VMH-generated satiety signal is the explanation for the anorexia cannot be supported. And, finally, if satiety must be suggested as a problem in anorexia nervosa, let it be directly investigated by seeking an exaggerated inhibition on feeding provoked by nutrients.

ACKNOWLEDGMENT

This research was supported by NIH grant RO1 AM 18554–01.

REFERENCES

1. McHugh, P. R., Gibbs, J., Falasco, J. D., Moran, T., and Smith, G. (1975): Inhibitions on feeding examined in rhesus monkeys with hypothalamic disconnexions. *Brain,* 98:441–454.
2. Panksepp, J. (1971): Is satiety mediated by the ventromedial hypothalamus? *Physiol. Behav.,* 7:381–384.
3. Thomas, D. W., and Mayer, J. (1968): Meal taking and regulation of food intake by normal and hypothalamic hyperphagic rats. *J. Comp. Physiol. Psychol.,* 66:642–653.
4. McHugh, P. R., Moran, T., and Barton, G. (1975): Satiety: A graded behavioral phenomenon regulating caloric intake. *Science,* 190:167–169.

Anorexia Nervosa, edited by
R. A. Vigersky. Raven Press,
New York © 1977.

Extrahypothalamic Controls of Feeding

S. D. Morrison

Laboratory of Pathophysiology, National Cancer Institute, Bethesda, Maryland 20014

A major impetus to the enormous amount of work done on the central hypothalamus in the last 25 or 30 years has been the conviction that this area embraces the predominant central control of feeding. However, there is justification for doubting this conviction and for proposing that much, and possibly the most important part, of the control of feeding is extrahypothalamic.

It has become obvious that much of the feeding effect from hypothalamic manipulation is extrahypothalamic in the sense that it originates in associated neural areas (such as the amygdala, globi pallidi, striatum) and that the hypothalamic involvement arises from division or stimulation of fibers of passage to or from these and other areas, rather than from effects of hypothalamic cell aggregates (6,10). However, "extrahypothalamic" is used here to refer to feeding controls that are unaffected by hypothalamic manipulation whatever the primary, functional, central site may be.

The intact normal rat shows feeding responses, either positive or negative, to a variety of independent stimuli, such as taste adulteration, change in caloric density of the diet, change in environmental temperature, exogenous insulin, and others. These responses reflect different feeding control mechanisms. Three of these are considered here: reduced caloric density, reduced environmental temperature, and administration of exogenous insulin. All of these induce increased food intake in the normal animal. Damage to the ventromedial hypothalamus that produces hyperphagia and obesity, or damage to the lateral hypothalamus that produces acute aphagia with later escape and persisting chronic feeding and drinking deficits, does not abolish or seriously impair the feeding responses to caloric dilution or to lowered environmental temperature (3,4). The same damage to the lateral hypothalamus almost totally abolishes the feeding response to exogenous insulin (4), and the reciprocal changes in electrical activity of the ventromedial and lateral areas that can be demonstrated in response to change in glucose utilization (1) also indicate hypothalamic mediation of glucogenic control. The response to degree of glucocytopenia, which is believed to be the basis of insulin-stimulated feeding, is the only feeding response that has been definitely shown to be mediated by the hypothalamus. The other two responses considered here appear, at the least, to be not exclusively mediated by the hypothalamus.

A way of examining this further is to find out which of these controls are impaired in disease-induced abnormalities of food intake, and the extent to which hypothalamic manipulation can block or modify the abnormality. An animal model of the disease is needed for this. Anorexia nervosa is peculiarly unhelpful in this respect, for there is no even approximate spontaneous animal model of it. However, the disease syndrome of cancer cachexia produces hypophagia and, eventually, aphagia. There are a variety of acceptable animal models of this syndrome that have been used to examine the problem.

Cancer cachexia is a very complex metabolic syndrome of many but not all cancers. It has been assessed as the most important single cause of death in cancer (7), and probably approximately two-thirds of the people who die of cancer are cachectic at death (19). Its definitive feature is progressive depletion of body tissue caused, predominantly, by progressive hypophagia: that is, food intake progressively fails to meet metabolic need. Most experimental tumors, whether transplanted or chemically induced, eventually produce a form of this syndrome in the host animal.

It has been proposed, from time to time, that the hypophagia of cancer cachexia is mediated by the hypothalamus, arising from cancer-induced dysfunction or from spurious stimulation of the hypothalamus (9,21). The little direct work on hypothalamic involvement in cancer cachexia is simply summarized. There is no involvement. Damage to either ventromedial or lateral hypothalamus that produces the well-established feeding abnormalities in otherwise normal animals does not block or substantially modify the development of cancer-induced cachexia and hypophagia (2,9,12). (The acute phase of lateral hypothalamic aphagia, of course, converts the hypophagia of cancer into the total aphagia of acute lateral hypothalamic damage, with correspondingly more rapid decay of the cancerous organism. But tumors growing in recovered rats that have chronic lateral hypothalamic damage produce the same pattern of development of hypophagia as seen in intact tumor-bearing animals.) The only even tenuous link so far established between cancerous hypophagia and experimental hypothalamic feeding effects is that both depress the diurnal cycles of feeding and drinking (16).

Sprague-Dawley rats growing the Walker 256 carcinoma invariably develop cachectic decay with hypophagia (Fig. 1a). In this tumor-bearing organism the feeding response to caloric dilution of food is progressively attenuated and eventually abolished (13,14) (Fig. 1b).

There are occasional (approximately 1 in 20) rats of this strain that do not show the normal hyperphagic response to caloric dilution. However, at least one strain of rat, the Buffalo, totally lacks this feeding control mechanism (15). When the Morris 5123 hepatoma grows in this strain it also

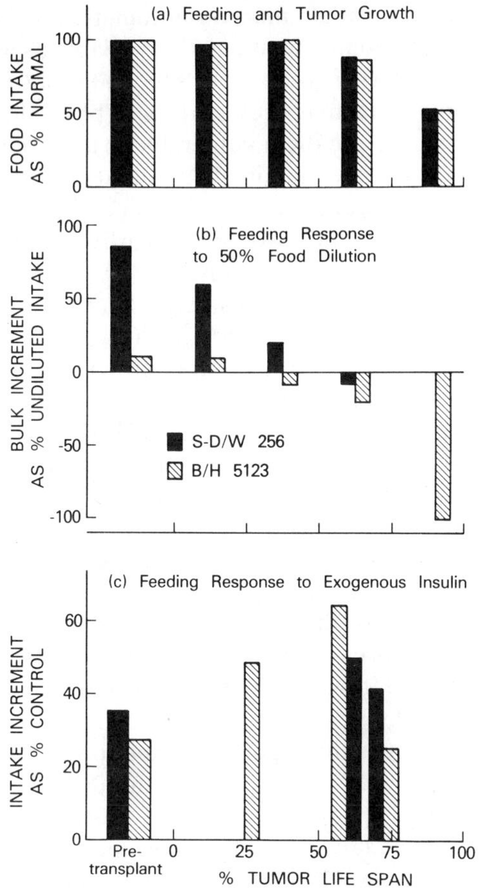

FIG. 1. The course of (a) decline of food intake, (b) deterioration of response to 50% caloric dilution of diet, and (c) response to exogenous insulin (1.5 U/100 g, protamine zinc insulin) of Sprague-Dawley rats growing Walker 256 (S-D/W256—*solid blocks*) and Buffalo rats growing Morris 5123 (B/H5123—*hatched blocks*) hepatoma. Growth of the tumors is expressed as fractions of life span of tumor (time from transplant to death of host from tumor). The absolute tumor life spans are: Walker 256, 30 days; Morris 5123, 50 days.

generates cachexia and hypophagia (Fig. 1a), and the feeding response to caloric dilution is pushed from zero (no response) to negative (reduced or zero food intake) (17) (Fig. 1b).

This strain difference in response to caloric dilution may have wide-reaching implications. In the total absence of one physiological control mechanism in the potentially available set of controls, the onus of feeding control is presumably thrown more onto those mechanisms that do exist. This may entail greater dependence on hypothalamic mechanisms if a non-hypothalamic control is absent, or it may entail greater dependence on learned feeding behaviors rather than on automatic physiological controls. On the assumption that people are at least as variable as are laboratory rats in their heritable characteristics, one can speculate that human individuals and, possibly, human strains may lack particular physiological mechanisms of control. This lack may make them vulnerable to a degree of dysfunction of the reduced set, for example, minimal hypothalamic dysfunction, which would ordinarily be totally compensated; or vulnerable to acquired, bizarre, learned feeding behaviors, which would ordinarily be suppressed by a full complement of physiological mechanisms.

In the two cancerous organisms considered here, overt hypophagia does not appear until the last third of tumor life (time from implant until the tumor kills the host) (Fig. 1a). But the impairment of response to caloric dilution starts almost immediately on transplant, in the first quarter of tumor life, long before there is any overt hypophagia (Fig. 1b).

The Sprague-Dawley/Walker 256 organism shows an approximately normal feeding response when environmental temperature is lowered from 25° to 5°C (20); in this organism and in the Buffalo/Morris hepatoma organism the normal responses to less-severe exposure (13° or 17°C) are significantly depressed (*unpublished work*). Again this depressed feeding response appears well before the cancerous hypophagia.

The feeding response to exogenous insulin, a response mediated by the hypothalamus, is not at all impaired by either of these tumors and may even be slightly enhanced (17) (Fig. 1c).

There are other changes in feeding behavior associated with lateral hypothalamic damage: increased food scattering (8,11), reduced efficiency of feeding (i.e., less food ingested per unit of time spent on feeding), and others. The tumor bearer, however, shows no increase in food scattering, and some tumor bearers show a progressive increase in feeding efficiency during the period of deterioration of feeding controls before the appearance of overt hypophagia (18). It seems possible that this represents a behavioral compensation for the loss of these feeding controls. Preliminary unpublished work indicates that although lateral hypothalamic damage reduces feeding efficiency, the tumor-induced increase in feeding efficiency is not mediated by the lateral hypothalamus as it also occurs in recovered laterals growing tumors.

The central point to be made here is that the feeding controls that are so far known to be impaired in cancer cachexia are those that are not mediated by the hypothalamus. On the other hand, a control that is known to be mediated by the hypothalamus (response to exogenous insulin) is not impaired by tumor growth. This particular anorexia/hypophagia appears to have no hypothalamic component. It is reasonable to wonder what, if any, pathological aberration of food intake does. It is certainly a sufficient caveat against dogmatic acceptance of a hypothalamic origin of all abnormal feeding.

In the absence of a suitable animal model, the experimental approach used here cannot be directly applied to anorexia nervosa. Also, responses to such stimuli as change in caloric density or in environmental temperature are much more difficult to demonstrate in man than in animals (5), largely because man is able to retain too many alternative options, such as putting on more clothes or insisting on alternative foods. However, examination of accessory characteristics such as coarseness of feeding, feeding efficiency, or reactivity to exteroceptive characteristics of food (taste, texture) might be adaptable to man to allow discrimination between hypothalamic and extrahypothalamic mechanisms.

REFERENCES

1. Anand, B. K. (1972): Experimental observations on anorexia. *Adv. Psychosom. Med.*, 7:243–256.
2. Baillie, P., Millar, F. K., and Pratt, A. W. (1965): Food and water intakes and Walker tumor growth in rats with hypothalamic lesions. *Am. J. Physiol.*, 209:293–300.
3. Carlisle, H. J., and Stellar, E. (1969): Caloric regulation and food preference in normal, hyperphagic and aphagic rats. *J. Comp. Physiol. Psychol.*, 69:107–114.
4. Epstein, A. N., and Teitelbaum, P. (1967): Specific loss of the hypoglycemic control of feeding in recovered lateral rats. *Am. J. Physiol.*, 213:1159–1167.
5. Garrow, J. S. (1974): *Energy Balance and Obesity in Man.* North Holland, Amsterdam.
6. Grossman, S. P. (1972): Neurophysiological aspects: extrahypothalamic factors in the regulation of food intake. *Adv. Psychosom. Med.*, 7:49–72.
7. Hardy, J. D. (1962): On the cause of death in cancer: systemic effects of non-endocrine tumors. *Surg. Clin. North Am.*, 42:305–334.
8. Kissileff, H. R. (1970): Free feeding in normal and "recovered lateral" rat monitored by a pellet-detecting eatometer. *Physiol. Behav.*, 5:163–174.
9. Liebelt, R. A., Gehring, G., Delmonte, L., Schuster, G., and Liebelt, A. G. (1974): Paraneoplastic syndromes in experimental animal model systems. *Ann. N.Y. Acad. Sci.*, 230:547–564.
10. Morgane, P. J., and Jacobs, H. L. (1969): Hunger and satiety. *World Rev. Nutr. Diet.*, 10:100–213.
11. Morrison, S. D. (1968*a*): The relationship of energy expenditure and spontaneous activity to the aphagia of rats with lesions in the lateral hypothalamus. *J. Physiol.* (*Lond.*), 197:325–343.
12. Morrison, S. D. (1968*b*): Effect of growth of a tumor on the regulation of water intake. *J. Natl. Cancer Inst.*, 41:1241–1248.
13. Morrison, S. D. (1972): Feeding response to changes in absorbable food fraction during growth of Walker 256 carcinosarcoma. *Cancer Res.*, 32:968–972.
14. Morrison, S. D. (1973*a*): Control of food intake during growth of a Walker 256 carcinosarcoma. *Cancer Res.*, 33:526–528.
15. Morrison, S. D. (1973*b*): Differences between rat strains in metabolic activity and in control systems. *Am. J. Physiol.*, 224:1305–1308.
16. Morrison, S. D. (1974): Diurnal distribution of motor activity and feeding during growth of tumors. *Cancer Res.*, 34:1632–1635.
17. Morrison, S. D. (1975): Origins of nutritional imbalance in cancer. *Cancer Res.*, 35:3339–3342.
18. Morrison, S. D. (1976*a*): Generation and compensation of the cancer cachectic process by spontaneous modification of feeding behavior. *Cancer Res.*, 36:228–233.
19. Morrison, S. D. (1976*b*): Control of food intake in cancer cachexia: a challenge and a tool. *Physiol. Behav.*, 17:705–714.
20. Stevenson, J. A. F., Box, B. M., and Wright, R. B. (1963): The effect of a cold environment on malignant anorexia. *Can. J. Biochem. Physiol.*, 41:531–532.
21. Theologides, A. (1974): The anorexia-cachexia syndrome: a new hypothesis. *Ann. N.Y. Acad. Sci.*, 230:14–22.

Anorexia Nervosa, edited by
R. A. Vigersky. Raven Press,
New York © 1977.

Norepinephrine and Satiety in Monkeys

D. E. Redmond, Jr., Y. H. Huang, J. Baulu, D. R. Snyder, and J. W. Maas

Neurobehavioral Laboratory, Yale University School of Medicine, New Haven, Connecticut 06510

INTRODUCTION

Our laboratory is engaged in detailed studies of the noradrenergic nucleus locus ceruleus in the brains of nonhuman primates. This nucleus provides the principal noradrenergic innervation of the ipsilateral cerebral cortex (16,20,42,68), the hippocampus (36,39,54,62,63,68), cingulate gyrus (36,54), and amygdala (54,63). It may also provide noradrenergic innervation to portions of the hypothalamus and other brain areas (13,36). Although extensive pharmacologic data links the catecholamines norepinephrine (NE) and dopamine (DA) to a variety of important mammalian behaviors, it has proven difficult on the basis of pharmacologic techniques alone, to identify physiologically specific sites of catecholamine action or to distinguish specific behavioral effects of NE from those of DA. Thus, we have turned to more anatomically based approaches which developed out of studies showing the highly specific noradrenergic activity associated with the l. ceruleus system.

Pharmacologic studies have suggested but not proven definable roles for NE and DA in the control of eating. NE injected into the hypothalamus of satiated rats elicits feeding (6,12,25,48). On the other hand, suppression of feeding has been observed after injections of L-norepinephrine and increased feeding after administration of an α-adrenergic antagonist, phentolamine (43). Dopamine has also been found both to support (15,45,67) and to suppress eating (4,5,11,14,40,56). It is therefore not clear in many pharmacologic studies whether NE or DA is responsible for appetite changes.

For many years brain lesions have been known to cause hyperphagia and obesity, but until recently little information relevant to specific neurochemical systems was provided. In 1888, Brown and Schaffer suggested a relationship between temporal lobe functions and food intake in the monkey (9). In 1901 Frohlich implicated the pituitary in a human case report of obesity associated with a pituitary tumor (17). Camus and Roussy (10) concluded that the hypothalamus might also be involved in obesity on the basis of autopsy material from patients with Frohlich's syndrome. In 1930

Smith (65) reported that lesions of the hypothalamus alone would result in obesity without involvement of the pituitary, beginning many years of studies focusing on the role of the hypothalamus in the control of eating. In 1940 using stereotaxic methodology, Hetherington and Ranson (30) further localized the "cause" of hypothalamic hyperphagia and obesity to specific lesions of the ventromedial nucleus (VMN).

Many lesions outside the hypothalamus have also been reported to change eating behavior (see 27). Most of these lesions do not provide information concerning the specific neurochemical systems involved, but lesions of a number of areas possibly involved with, or receiving NE innervation from the l. ceruleus, produce hyperphagia, e.g., the thalamus (60), frontal lobe (59), and amygdala (9,26,35). The fact that the lesions effective in producing hyperphagia in the region of the ventromedial hypothalamus were actually lateral, ventral, and caudal to it led to the hypothesis by Brobeck in 1946 that the "hypothalamic" hyperphagia was due to projections to or from the lower brainstem (7). Gold (23) and Ahlskog and Hoebel (1) have recently demonstrated that the "hypothalamic" hyperphagia is reproduced, in most respects, by lesions of the ventral noradrenergic bundle. These findings, along with the finding that lesions restricted to the VMN do not produce hyperphagia (33), would support a major role for norepinephrine outside the hypothalamus in the regulation of eating. The ventral noradrenergic bundle arises from cell groups in the medulla and pons, including cells in the "subcerulear" region (18,19,51). At least in the rodent, the ventral bundle does not appear to contain any contribution from the cells of the l. ceruleus. Lesions of the dorsal-rostral projections from the l. ceruleus do not produce hyperphagia in rats (1). Studies of lesions of the l. ceruleus in rats have shown normal eating behavior (3), as well as aphagia (2), and transient hypophagia (52). Hyperphagia has not been reported, although hyperdipsia has been reported in one study (52). We trust that a gross injustice is not done to an extensive and detailed body of literature to say that the net functional effect on eating of increasing or decreasing noradrenergic activity in the large but specific NE associated l. ceruleus system in the primate would be difficult to anticipate. (For recent reviews, see 24,50.)

METHODS

Seven adult female *Macaca arctoides* (speciosa) have been studied after bilateral lesions of the l. ceruleus along with four female control monkeys after sham operations. The monkeys were weighed once weekly, and food and water intake was recorded daily during most of the studies. Since the eating effects of the lesions were initially unexpected, the attention to parameters related to appetite and weight gain increased after the first animals studied. Initially, in some animals, food was limited to the standard ration for monkeys in our laboratory (50 Purina monkey chow biscuits =

268 g/day) which probably limited weight gain in these monkeys. Except as noted, subsequent animals received an excess of monkey chow, and intakes were determined from the number of biscuits remaining at the time of daily cage cleaning. The monkeys weighed 5.5 to 7.8 kg at the beginning of the study.

The l. ceruleus was identified by our technique (32) which depends upon the location of the motor nucleus of the trigeminal nerve and then upon the responses of single unit activities to different stimuli recorded at a particular position in relation to the motor nucleus. Lesions of the nuclei were made bilaterally by 3 to 4 placements of concentric electrodes and a constant current of 2 mA for 1 min at each site. The locations and extent of the lesions were verified histologically and biochemically as previously described (32).

RESULTS

All of the lesioned animals had destruction in the region of the l. ceruleus, with that being the principal structure in common destroyed in all of the monkeys (Fig. 1). NE and its principal metabolite 3-methoxy-4-hydroxyphenethyleneglycol (MHPG) concentrations were significantly lower in known l. ceruleus projection areas of the lesioned monkeys compared with controls (Table 1). All seven monkeys with bilateral l. ceruleus lesions had some degree of hyperphagia and hyperdipsia.* Food and water intake showed small increases immediately after the lesions compared with sham-operated controls. Body weights in the lesioned monkeys also showed significant increases within a few days of the lesions [6.49 ± 0.34 (SEM) kg mean weight of six monkeys before surgery compared with 7.31 kg ± 0.43 after surgery] but no significant changes occurred in the control monkeys (Fig. 2). Food and water intake and body weight continued to increase. In a competitive feeding situation for 5 weeks after lesions four monkeys studied gained a mean of 2.1 kg ± .43 SEM (paired $t = 4.9$, two-tailed $p < 0.02$) (Figs. 3A, 3B) compared with a mean loss of 0.31 kg ± 0.27 SEM (NS) for the controls. Two monkeys studied to sacrifice at 5 months showed continuing hyperphagia, hyperdipsia, and weight increases up to 208% of body weight at surgery (Figs. 4 and 5). In three monkeys studied the hyperdipsia was not diminished by a limitation of food intake to a prelesion normal level (Fig. 6).

The monkey studied for the longest period of time showed continued weight gain until the eighth month after bilateral destruction of the l. ceruleus

* One monkey was eliminated from some of the analyses because she was found at autopsy to have been pregnant during the latter part of the study. Two of the seven monkeys died at 8 and 17 days after surgery of causes apparently unrelated to eating. Both of these monkeys had hyperphagia, and one of them continued to eat voraciously in spite of an apparent paralytic ileus prior to death. These monkeys were also eliminated from the analyses of longer duration effects.

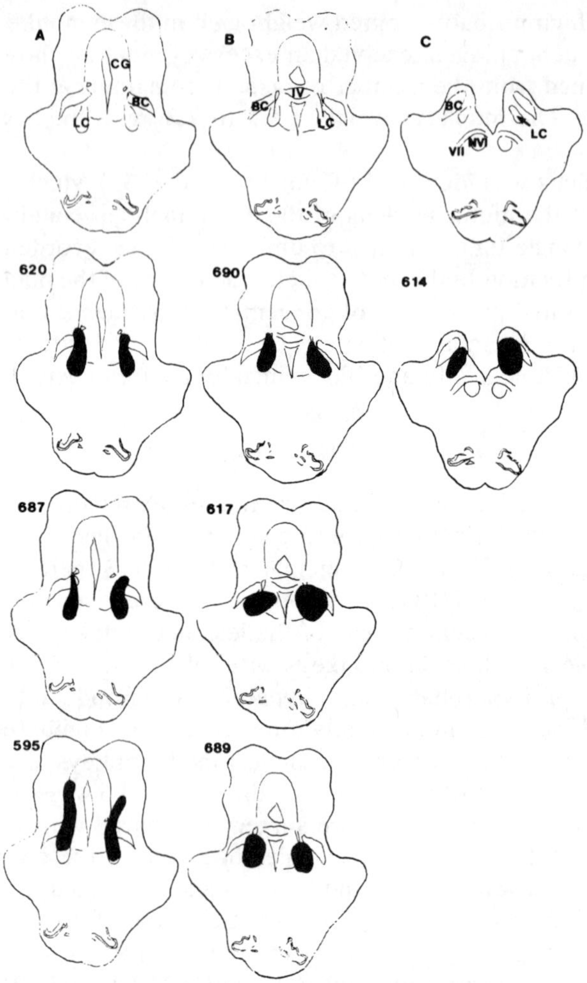

FIG. 1. Schematic representation of l. ceruleus-aimed lesions in seven monkeys traced from histological sections at the level of the greatest destruction. Structures at each level A, B, and C are identified as follows: LC = locus ceruleus; BC = brachium conjunctivum; IV = tract of cranial nerve IV; NVI = nucleus of cranial nerve VI; and VII = tract of cranial nerve VII; CG = central gray.

(Fig. 7). This was followed by weight loss, the physical appearance of illness, and death of causes not determinable by necropsy. Food and water intake showed continued increases in this monkey until 6 months after the second of the two unilateral lesions. After that time, food intake declined whereas water intake continued to increase until just before death. In spite of the decline in food intake, eating remained increased over that seen prior to the lesions (Fig. 7). The weight increases which occurred in this monkey after a unilateral l. ceruleus lesion suggest that bilateral lesions are not

TABLE 1. *NE and MHPG concentrations in specific brain regions approximately five months after bilateral destruction of the nucleus l. ceruleus in five monkeys compared with four control monkeys*

	Mean level (ng/g wet weight) ± SEM		
	LC lesions (5 monkeys)[a]		Controls (4 monkeys)
	ng/g	% control	ng/g
Cerebral cortex NE	12.3 ± 3.3	11	107.7 ± 7.2
Cingulate gyrus NE	4.2 ± 3.3	4	236.7 ± 11.6
Hippocampus NE	10.4 ± 7.8	11	93.8 ± 24.9
Cerebellum NE	20.0 ± 5.1	33	60.0 ± 4.2
Cerebral cortex MHPG	7.5 ± 2.0	42	17.8 ± 1.0

[a] Two animals died, preventing proper brain removal for biochemical analysis.

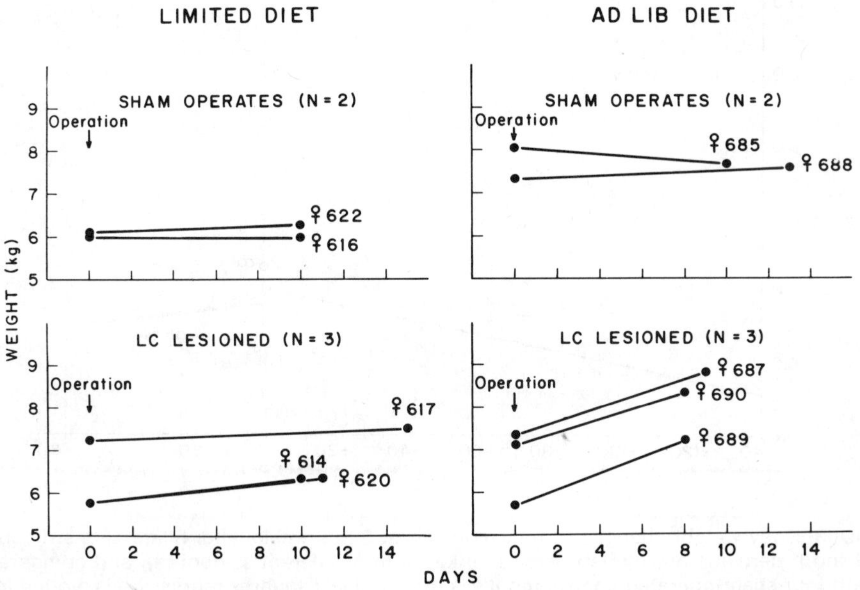

FIG. 2. Immediate effects of bilateral destruction of the l. ceruleus on body weight (8 to 15 days). Two sham-operated and three lesioned monkeys were fed limited diets during this period, and an equal number were fed a surplus of Purina monkey chow. All of the animals had unrestricted water. All of the lesioned animals which were kept on limited food showed small increases in weight in this period (NS). As expected, the lesioned monkeys on unlimited food gained more weight. All six lesioned monkeys gained weight during the period when analyzed together (paired $t = 3.12$, 2 tailed $p < 0.03$), while the sham-operated monkeys showed no change.

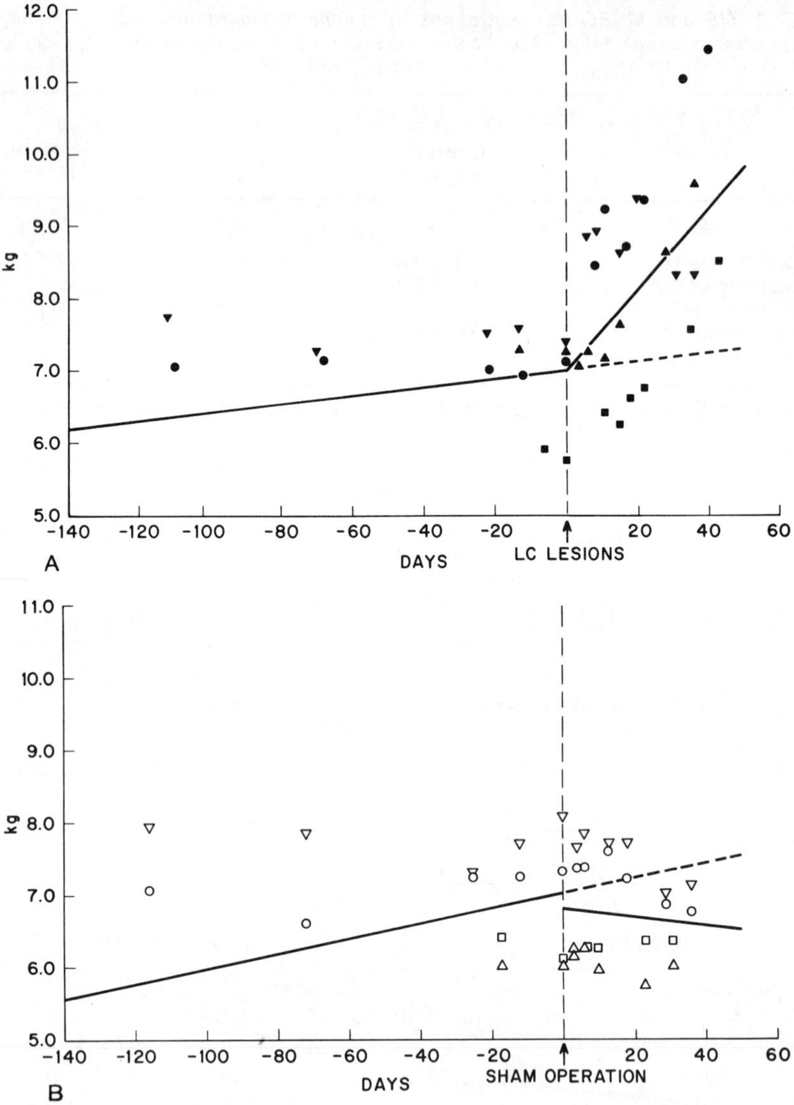

FIG. 3. Body weight changes of four monkeys at 5 to 6 weeks after bilateral destruction of the l. ceruleus are plotted, each monkey with a different symbol **(a),** and compared with four sham-operated control monkeys **(b).** The least squares regression is plotted for each group extending to initial weights on arrival at the laboratory from the importer (approximately 177 days before operation: points not shown), and projected (dotted line) through the study period. The least squares regressions are plotted for actual weight after operation and are significantly different from the slopes of projected weight only for the lesioned monkeys. Although the amounts of food provided in the initial days after surgery differed for one-half of each group, a surplus of food was provided for all of the animals in a social group for 18 days before the end of the period shown. Monkeys #614 and #689 died early in the study and were eliminated from this analysis. Both, however, showed weight gain prior to death (Fig. 2). One monkey (#595) had different experimental conditions and was also not included in this analysis.

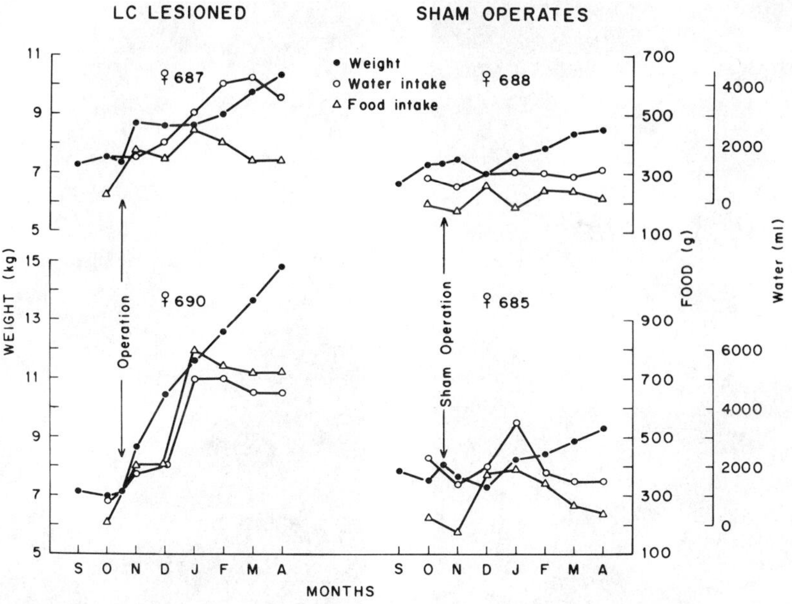

FIG. 4. Body weight, food, and water intake are shown for five months after bilateral destruction of the l. ceruleus in two monkeys and sham operations in two monkeys. These monkeys had identical feeding conditions throughout the study period, with a surplus of monkey chow and water always provided.

necessary to produce a partial syndrome of hyperphagia (Fig. 7) if the unilateral lesion is sufficiently complete. This increase occurred in spite of the fact that the monkey was on a limited diet.

Eating appeared to be an almost constant activity of the lesioned monkeys. These monkeys seldom were observed to stop eating and did not eat in specific meals which would allow the application of operational definitions of "satiety," such as the ratio of meal size to inter-meal interval. In time-sampled behavioral observations, the l. ceruleus-lesioned monkeys increased the percentage of time that they were eating or chewing food, whereas the control monkeys were unchanged (57). In nonsystematic observations, the lesioned monkeys were noted to sleep, but food and water continued to be ingested between 7 P.M. and 7 A.M. They stuffed themselves in some instances to the point of compromising ventilatory-capacity and producing marked abdominal distention (Fig. 8). Some monkeys consumed up to 1,070 g of food and 5,000 ml of water per day, a total of 40 to 50% of their body weight. This level of oral intake would indicate that not all of the initial rapid or total increased body weights were due to increased body tissue, but autopsies showed extensive increases in adipose tissue throughout the body.**

** In one of the more obese monkeys at death the pericardial fat weighed 66 g compared with 39 g for the heart itself. Little or no pericardial fat is normally found.

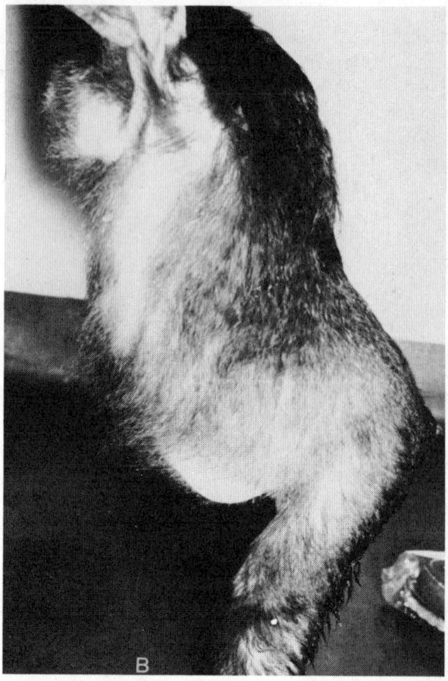

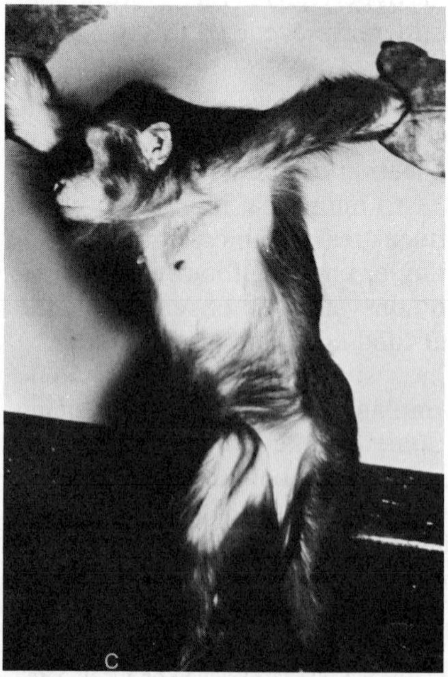

FIG. 5. Front **(a)** and side views **(b)** of obese 13.7 kg female monkey $7\frac{1}{2}$ months after bilateral lesions of the l. ceruleus, compared with a 7.4 kg normal control monkey **(c).** Both animals arrived from the importer on the same day, weighing 5.23 and 4.55 kg respectively.

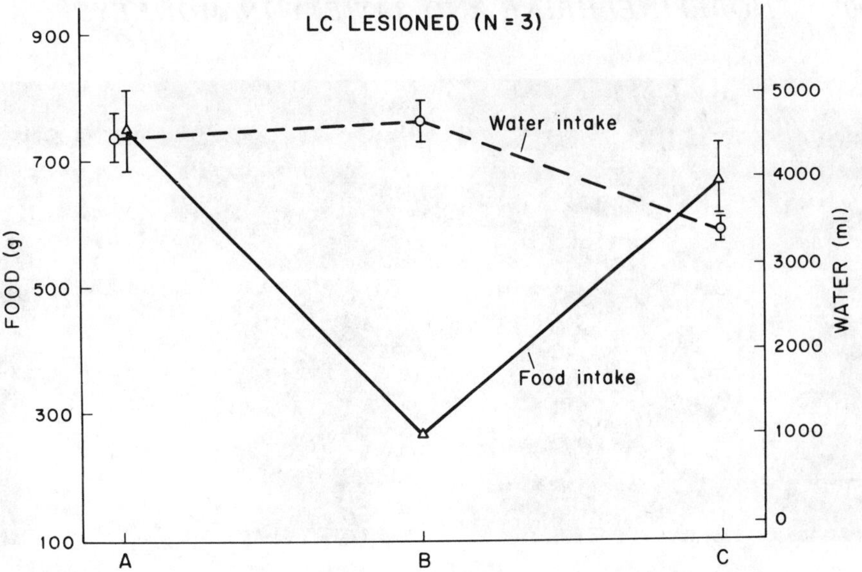

FIG. 6. Increased water intake in monkeys with bilateral destruction of the l. ceruleus was not affected by limitation of food to approximately 268 g monkey chow/day. Mean ± SEM daily food and water intake for 3 monkeys are shown for 3 one week periods. A = *ad lib.* food and water, B = food limited to 268 g/day with unlimited water, and C = *ad lib.* food and water.

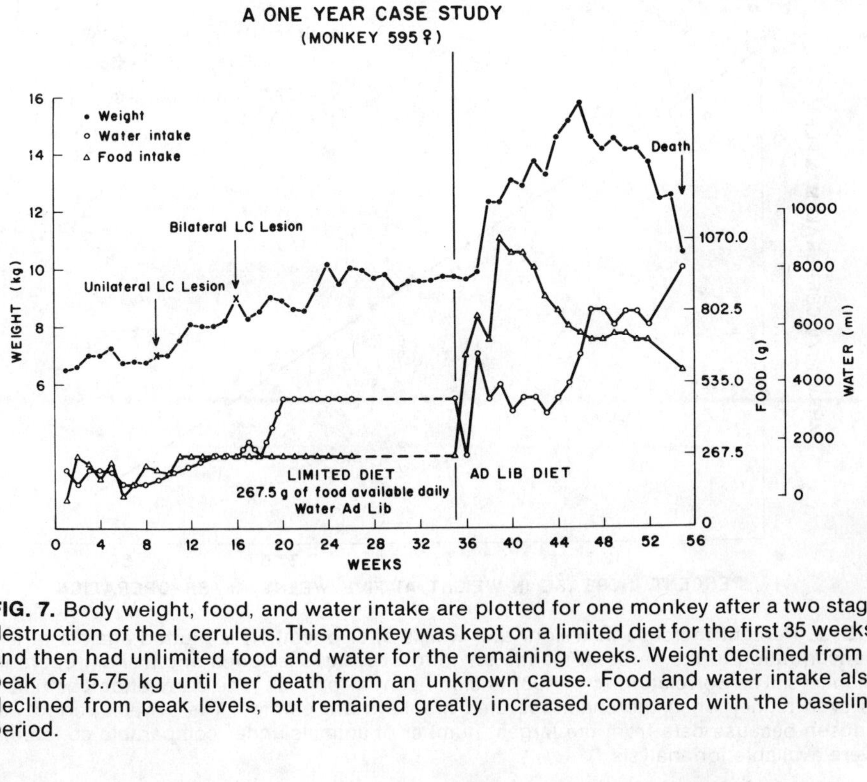

FIG. 7. Body weight, food, and water intake are plotted for one monkey after a two stage destruction of the l. ceruleus. This monkey was kept on a limited diet for the first 35 weeks, and then had unlimited food and water for the remaining weeks. Weight declined from a peak of 15.75 kg until her death from an unknown cause. Food and water intake also declined from peak levels, but remained greatly increased compared with the baseline period.

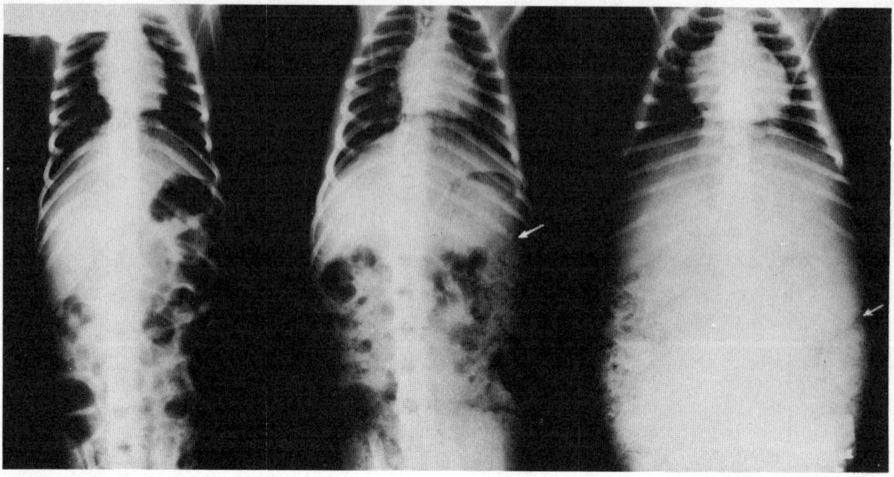

FIG. 8. X-rays of female #617 on arrival from importer on 12/12/74 weighing 5.0 kg; 8 days after bilateral l. ceruleus lesions (6/20/75) weighing 7.2 kg; and 36 days after the lesions (7/18/75) weighing 9.45 kg. The greater curvature of the stomach, where visible on the original X-ray, is marked by an arrow.

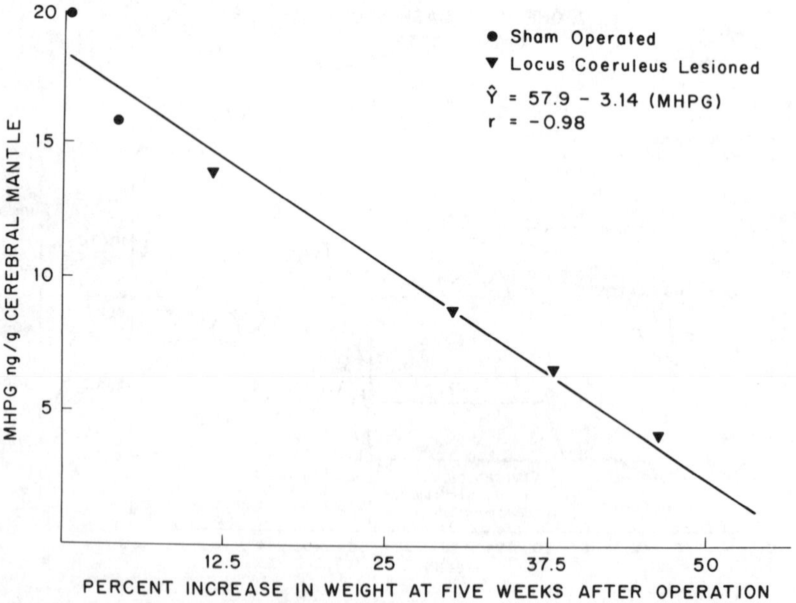

FIG. 9. Percent increase in weight at 5 weeks after operation is plotted against MHPG concentration in the cerebral mantle for four l. ceruleus-lesioned and 2 sham-operated monkeys. The correlation ($r = -.98$) is significant at $p < .01$. The correlation coefficient is even higher when the sham-operated monkeys are omitted. The 5-week period was chosen because data from the largest number of animals under comparable conditions were available for analysis.

A step-wise regression analysis identified MHPG in the cerebral cortex at sacrifice as correlating most closely ($r = -.98, p < 0.01$) with percentage weight gain at 5 weeks after the lesions, a time when data from the largest number of monkeys under similar conditions was available for analysis (Fig. 9).

DISCUSSION

The first question which must be considered in any study of brain lesions is whether the changes observed are in fact due to the physiologic function of the targeted area, or whether they are instead a result of damage to an adjacent area or to fibers of passage adjacent to or within the area. This latter explanation has recently been offered to explain the "myth of the ventromedial nucleus" (23) as the cause of the classical hyperphagia syndrome. This possibility must be considered in this study especially since hyperphagia has been reported after ventral noradrenergic bundle lesions (1,23), but not after lesions of the dorsal bundle which arises from the l. ceruleus (1), or from the l. ceruleus itself in rats (2,3,18,19). Lesions of the l. ceruleus which descend ventrally into the "subcerulear" region might affect this ventral system in the primate (21,22). On the basis of histological evidence, this did not occur in the present study. In fact, one animal with particularly large appetite increases (#595) had a somewhat dorsal and anterior lesion. Evidence of a relationship between the weight gain and the l. ceruleus lesioning is supported by the very high correlation ($r = -0.98$) between weight gain and cortical MHPG. If the lesions had variably missed the l. ceruleus to hit adjacent tracts or descend into the subcerulear-ventral system, this correlation, as a marker of changes in l. ceruleus function, could not have been so high unless MHPG depletion correlated with histologically-determined lesion size. It did not. The possibility that other tracts passing through the l. ceruleus might account for the behavioral changes is not supported by the presently available data. The nucleus is almost exclusively composed of NE-containing cell bodies in the primate (29). No changes in DA or serotonin have been reported after lesions of the l. ceruleus (37,69). The presence of a high statistical correlation of weight gain with MHPG in the cerebral cortex, however, should not be taken as evidence that the appetite effects are due to cortical mechanisms. We were unable to study the biochemistry of other possibly relevant areas with the same quantitative and statistical techniques. NE concentrations in several areas were below the assay sensitivity (5 ng/g tissue) hence preventing quantitative analysis of gradations that might have actually been present, nor were MHPG determinations possible in all of the areas studied. On the basis of previous studies the hypothalamus might be important primarily or secondarily, and concentrations of NE in the rat hypothalamus are slightly affected by l. ceruleus lesions (36). Biochemical analysis of hypothalamic tissue was not possible in this study, and a correlation of the extent of NE depletion in hypothalamus with weight gain could not be done.

The hyperphagia and hyperdipsia reported here appear to be quantitatively as great as any hyperphagia previously reported in monkeys after VMN lesions (28) or knife cuts (47).*** In terms of percent of body weight ingested daily (up to 50%), some of these monkeys appear to show as extreme as any hyperphagia yet reported. We have not as yet done the detailed studies necessary to characterize the hyperphagia as to "hunger" or "satiety," as so elegantly described in rhesus monkeys by McHugh and co-workers (46). If in a general way "satiety" refers to mechanisms to stop eating, these monkeys appear to have a "satiety" deficit. Extreme foodstuffing is the most obvious behavior after the lesions. The monkeys did not appear to eat rapidly, just continuously. There was insufficient evidence of a "dynamic" weight gain phase and a "plateau" phase as reported with the VMN syndrome in rats (7) and monkeys (28). Most of our monkeys were not studied long enough to make certain that weight gain would not "plateau." In fact intake did increase in several monkeys only up to a certain point. This point, however, 1.07 kg of chow and 6 to 8 kg of water daily, may represent some physical maximum volume that an adult monkey can ingest in one day, and not the action of a brain "satiety" center. If the "satiety" changes produced by various other lesions are merely a change in the "set-point" of a brain mechanism that still retains the capacity to inhibit eating (31), such a set-point was not clearly reached in this study. One monkey studied for one year showed increased weight and high food and water intake until the tenth month. The interpretation of the decline thereafter is made difficult by the fact that the monkey died of unknown causes at the end of the twelfth month and after a two months' decline in weight.

Hypothalamic hyperphagia is also accompanied by polydipsia which has been attributed entirely to the increased food intake (66). In fact, a relative "hypodipsia" has been reported due to a failure to increase water intake commensurate with the increases in food intake (49). The failure of water intake in the l. ceruleus monkeys (Fig. 6) to diminish when food intake was limited suggests that the hyperdipsia reported in this study is not secondary to increased food intake.

Many characteristics of the hyperphagia syndromes previously reported have not yet been systematically investigated in l. ceruleus-lesioned monkeys. Among these are stomach pre-loads (46), increasing or decreasing blood glucose (41,64), changes in steroid hormones (8,34,53,55) and "finickiness" to the adulteration of food (24,50).

The data presented here would suggest that a deficiency in the function of one or more projection areas of the l. ceruleus in primates is associated

---

*** McHugh and co-workers (47) report an intake of 342 ± 12 g food daily ($N = 3$) and Hamilton and Brobeck (28) report a mean intake of 350 g ($N = 2$) compared with a mean intake of 776 ± 179 g food intake daily ($N = 3$) in this study.

with a pronounced and persistent hyperphagia and hyperdipsia. It is puzzling that this syndrome was not previously seen in rats. Profound species differences are a possible explanation: appetite may be more influenced by cortical mechanisms in primates. Technical differences, however, also might have obscured the findings in rats. If stereotaxic coordinates and histologic classification are the bases for determining the completeness of l. ceruleus lesions, considerably more variability in the remaining functional NE will be present than in our monkeys and presumably more variability in weight gain (38). It is also possible that NE depletions in previous studies were not consistently as large as those reported here. A depletion of 80 to 90% on at least one side might be a threshold for actually eliciting the effects of NE deficits. Many rats have been studied for short periods during which, according to our results, food intake may be decreased compared with the period before lesions rather than with sham-operated control animals. Finally, it has been reported that male rats show only hyperdipsia in response to brain lesions which also produce hyperphagia and weight gain in females (61). If males were studied exclusively or if males were also included in experimental studies with females, changes in weight might be obscured in the females. For example, Osumi et al. (52) who reported hyperdipsia after l. ceruleus lesions, used only male rats, produced mean NE decrements of 64% of controls in the cortex (compared with 11% in this study), and studied them for only 7 to 10 days after the lesions. These considerations would suggest that careful studies of female rats for longer periods after 80 to 90% NE depletion in projection areas of the l. ceruleus might reveal profound hyperphagia as well as hyperdipsia. The effects of l. ceruleus lesions on ingestive behavior of male monkeys have not yet been studied.

The data reported here suggest that the net effect of diminishing the function of a major NE system in brain is to produce a gross hyperphagia and hyperdipsia in the female primate. It is not certain that the effects are entirely due to the absence of noradrenergic function, but the findings are consistent with pharmacologic evidence supporting the concept of an adrenergic "satiety" mechanism (43,44).

Several symptoms of anorexia nervosa suggest that increased activity of biological "satiety mechanisms" might be the cause of anorexia nervosa. Redmond, Swann, and Heninger recently hypothesized that hyperactivity of postsynaptic noradrenergic receptors might be associated with pathological satiation in humans (58). The clinical efficacy of α- or β-adrenergic antagonists in patients with anorexia nervosa would provide supporting evidence for this hypothesis.

ACKNOWLEDGMENTS

We would like to thank D. H. Landis, E. Wesloh, and G. Hu for biochemical analyses and skillful technical assistance. This work was supported by the following grants from the National Institute of Mental Health: MH 24607, MH 24393, and MH 25642.

REFERENCES

1. Ahlskog, J. E. and Hoebel, B. G. (1973): Overeating and obesity from damage to a noradrenergic system in the brain. *Science,* 182:166–168.
2. Amaral, D. G. and Foss, J. A. (1975): Locus ceruleus lesions and learning. *Science,* 188:377–388.
3. Anlezark, G. M., Crow, T. J., and Greenway, A. P. (1973): Impaired learning and decreased cortical norepinephrine after bilateral locus coeruleus lesions. *Science,* 181:682–694.
4. Baez, L. A. (1974): Role of catecholamines in the anorectic effects of amphetamine in rats. *Psychopharmacologia,* 35:91–98.
5. Barbeau, A., Mars, H., Gills, and Joffroy, L. (1971): Adverse clinical side effects of levodopa therapy. In: *Recent Advances in Parkinson's Disease,* edited by F. H. McDowell, C. H. Markham, pp. 204–237. F. A. Davis, Co., Philadelphia.
6. Booth, D. A. (1967): Localization of the adrenergic feeding system in the rat diencephalon. *Science,* 158:515–517.
7. Brobeck, J. R. (1946): Mechanisms of the development of obesity in animals with hypothalamic lesions. *Physiol. Rev.,* 26:541–559.
8. Brobeck, J. R., Wheatland, M. and Strominger, J. L. (1947): Variations in regulation of energy exchange associated with estrus, diestrus, and pseudopregnancy in rats. *Endocrinology,* 40:65–72.
9. Brown, S. and Schaffer, E. A. (1888): An investigation into the functions of the occipital and temporal lobes of the monkey's brain. *Philos. Trans. R. Soc. Lond.* [*Biol.*], 179:303–327.
10. Camus, J. and Roussy, G. (1913): Hypophysectomie et polyurie experimental *C. B. Soc. Biol. (Paris),* 75:483–486.
11. Cole, S. O. (1973): Hypothalamic feeding mechanisms and amphetamine anorexia. *Psychol. Bull.,* 79:13–20.
12. Coury, J. N. (1967): Neural correlates of food and water intake. *Science,* 156:1763–1765.
13. Dahlstrom, A. and Fuxe, K. (1964): Evidence for the existence of monoamine-containing neurons in the central nervous system. I. Demonstration of monoamines in the cell bodies of brain stem neurons. *Acta Physiol. Scand.,* 62:(Suppl 232) 1–55.
14. Ernst, E. M. (1967): Mode of action of apomorphine and dexamphetamine on gnawing compulsion in rats. *Psychopharmacologia,* 10:316–323.
15. Fibiger, H. C., Zis, A. P., and McGeer, E. G. (1973): Feeding and drinking deficits after 6-Hydroxydopamine administration in the rat: Similarities to the lateral hypothalamic syndrome. *Brain Res.,* 55:135–148.
16. Freedman, R., Foote, S. L. and Bloom, F. E. (1975): Histochemical characterization of neocortical projection of the nucleus locus coeruleus in the squirrel monkey. *J. Comp. Neurol.,* 164:209–232.
17. Frohlich, A. (1901): Ein Fall von Tumor der Hypophysis Cerebri ohne Akromegalie. *Wien Klin. Wochenschr.,* 15:883–886.
18. Fuxe, K. and Hokfelt, T. (1969): Catecholamines in the hypothalamus. In: *Frontiers in Neuroendocrinology,* edited by F. Ganong and L. Martini. Oxford University Press, New York.
19. Fuxe, K. (1965): Evidence for the existence of monoamine-containing neurons in the central nervous system: IV. Distribution of monoamine nerve terminals in the central nervous system. *Acta Physiol. Scand.* 64:(Suppl. 247) 37–85.
20. Fuxe, K., Hokfelt, T., and Ungerstedt, U. (1970): Morphological and functional aspects of central monoamine neurons. *Intern. Rev. Neurobiol.,* 13:93–126.
21. Garver, D. L. and Sladek, J. R., Jr. (1975): Monoamine distribution in primate brain: I. Catecholamine-containing parikarya in the brain stem of Macaca speciosa. *J. Comp. Neurol.,* 159:289–304.

22. Garver, D. L. and Sladek, J. R., Jr., (1977): Monoamine distribution in primate brain. III. Brainstem catecholaminergic pathways in Macaca speciosa. *Brain Res.* (*in press*).
23. Gold, R. M. (1973): Hypothalamic obesity: The myth of the ventromedial nucleus. *Science,* 182:488–490.
24. Grossman, S. P. (1975): Role of the hypothalamus in the regulation of food and water intake. *Psychol. Rev.,* 82:200–224.
25. Grossman, S. P. (1960): Eating or drinking elicited by direct adrenergic or cholinergic stimulation of hypothalamus. *Science,* 132:301–302.
26. Grossman, S. P. and Grossman, L. (1963): Food and water intake following lesions or electrical stimulation of the amygdala. *Am. J. Physiol.,* 205:761–765.
27. Grossman, S. P. (1972): Neurophysiologic aspects: Extrahypothalamic factors in the regulation of food intake. *Adv. Psychosom. Med.,* 7:49–72.
28. Hamilton, C. L. and Brobeck, J. R., (1964): Hypothalamic hyperphagia in the monkey. *J. Comp. Physiol. Psychol.,* 57:271–278.
29. Hubbard, J. E. and DiCarlo, V. (1973): Fluorescence histochemistry of monoamine-containing cell bodies in the brain stem of the squirrel monkey (Saimiri sciureus). 1. The Locus coeruleus. *J. Comp. Neurol.,* 147:5533–556.
30. Hetherington, A. W., and Ranson, S. W. (1940): Hypothalamic lesions and adiposity in the rat. *Anat. Rec.,* 78:149–172.
31. Hoebel, B. G. and Teitelbaum, P. (1966): Weight regulation by normal and hypothalamic hyperphagic rats. *J. Comp. Physiol. Psychol.,* 61:189–193.
32. Huang, Y. H., Redmond, D. E., Jr., Snyder, D. R. and Maas, J. W. (1975): In vivo location and destruction of the locus coeruleus in the stumptail macaque (*Macaca Arctoides*). *Brain Res.,* 100:157–162.
33. Joseph, S. A. and Knigge, J. M. (1968): Effects of VMH lesions in adult and newborn guinea pigs. *Neuroendocrinology,* 3:309–331.
34. Kennedy, G. C. and Mitra, J. (1963): Hypothalamic control of energy balance and the reproductive cycle in the rat. *J. Physiol.,* 166:395–407.
35. Kluver, H. and Bucy, P. C. (1939): Preliminary analysis of functions of the temporal lobes in monkeys. *Arch. Neurol. Psychiat.,* 42:979–1000.
36. Kobavashi, R. M., Palkovitz, M., Jacobowitz, D. M. and Kopin, I. (1975): Biochemical mapping of the noradrenergic projection from the locus coeruleus. *Neurology,* 25:223–233.
37. Kostowski, W., Samanin, R., Boreggi, S. R., Marc, V., Garattini, S., and Valzelli, L. (1974): Biochemical aspects of the interaction between midbrain raphe and locus coeruleus in the rat. *Brain Res.,* 82:178–182.
38. Lidbrink, P. and Jonsson, G. (1971): Semi-quantitative estimation of formaldehyde-induced fluorescence of noradrenaline in central noradrenaline nerve terminals. *J. Histochem. Cytochem.,* 19:747–757.
39. Lindvall, O. and Björklund, A. (1974): The organization of the ascending catecholamine neuron systems in the rat brain as revealed by the glyoxylic acid fluorescence method. *Acta Physiol. Scand.* (Suppl.), 412:1–48.
40. Maas, J. W., Dekirmenjian, H., Garver, D. L., Redmond, D. E., Jr., and Landis, D. H. (1972): Catecholamine metabolite excretion following intraventricular injection of 6-OH-Dopamine. *Brain Res.,* 41:507–511.
41. Mackay, E. M., Calloway, J. W., and Barnes, R. H. (1940): Hyperalimentation in normal animals produced by protamine insulin. *J. Nutr.,* 20:59–66.
42. Maeda, T., and Shimizu, N. (1972): Projections ascendantes du locus coeruleus et d'autres neurones aminergique pontiques au niveau du prosencephale du rat. *Brain Res.,* 36:19–35.
43. Margules, D. L. (1969): Noradrenergic synapses for the suppression of feeding behavior. *Life Sci.,* 8:693–704.
44. Margules, D. L. (1970): Alpha-adrenergic receptors in hypothalamus for the suppression of feeding behavior by satiety. *J. Comp. Physiol. Psychobiol.,* 73:1–12.
45. Marshall, J. F. and Teitelbaum, P. (1973): A comparison of the eating in response to hypothermic and glucoprivic challenges after nigral 6-hydroxydopamine and lateral hypothalamic lesions in rats. *Brain Res.,* 55:229–233.
46. McHugh, P. R., Morgan, T. H. and Bouton, G. N. (1975): Satiety: a graded behavioral phenomenon regulating caloric intake. *Science,* 190:167–169.
47. McHugh, P. R., Gibbs, J., Falasco, J. D., Moran, T., and Smith, G. P. (1975): Inhibitions

on feeding examined in rhesus monkeys with hypothalamic disconnexions. *Brain,* 98:441–454.

48. Miller, N. E., Gottesman, K. S. and Emery, N. (1964): Dose response to carbachol and norepinephrine in rat hypothalamus. *Am. J. Physiol.,* 206:1384–1388.
49. Montemurro, D. G. and Stevenson, J. A. F. (1955/56): The localization of hypothalamic structures in the rat influencing water consumption. *Yale J. Biol. Med.,* 28:396–403.
50. Morgane, P. J. and Jacobs, H. L. (1969): Hunger and Satiety, *World Review of Nutrition and Dietetics,* edited by G. H. Bourne, pp. 100–213. Karger, Basel.
51. Olsen, L. and Fuxe, K. (1972): Further mapping out of the central noradrenaline neuron systems: projections of the subcoeruleus area. *Brain Res.,* 43:289–295.
52. Osumi, Y., Oishi, R., Fujiwara, H. and Takori, S. (1975): Hyperdipsia induced by bilateral destruction of the locus coeruleus in rats. *Brain Res.,* 86:417–427.
53. Pfaff, D. W., (1969): Sex differences in food intake changes following pituitary growth hormone or prolactin injections. *Proc. Am. Psychol. Assoc.,* 4:211–212.
54. Pickel, V. M., Segal, M. and Bloom, F. E. (1974): A radioautographic study of the afferent pathways of the nucleus locus coeruleus. *J. Comp. Neurol.,* 155:15–42.
55. Redick, J. H., Nussbaum, A. L. and Mook, D. (1973): Estradiol induced suppression of feeding in the female rat: dependence on body weight. *Physiol. Behav.,* 10:543–557.
56. Redmond, D. E., Jr., Hinrich, R. H., Maas, J. W. and Kling, A. (1973): Behavior of free-ranging macaques after intraventricular 6-hydroxydopamine. *Science,* 181:1256–1258.
57. Redmond, D. E., Jr., Huang, Y. H., Snyder, D. R., Maas, J. W., and Baulu, J. (1976): Behavioral changes following lesions of the locus coeruleus in Macaca arctoides: *Neurosci. Abst.,* 2, 472.
58. Redmond, D. E., Jr., Swann, A., and Heninger, G. R. (1976): Phenoxybenzamine in anorexia nervosa. *Lancet,* 2:307.
59. Richter, C. P. and Hawkes, C. D. (1939): Increased spontaneous activity and food intake produced in rats by removal of the frontal poles of the brain. *J. Neurol. Psychiat.,* 2:231.
60. Schreiner, L., Rioch, McK. Pechtel, C. and Masserman, J. H. (1953): Behavioral changes following thalamic injury in cat. *J. Neurophysiol.,* 16:234–246.
61. Sclafani, A. (1971): Neural pathways involved in the ventromedial hypothalamic lesion syndrome in the rat. *J. Comp. Physiol. Psychol.,* 77:70–96.
62. Segal, M. and Landis, S. (1974): Afferents to the hippocampus of the rat studied with the method of retrograde transport of horseradish peroxidase. *Brain Res.,* 78:1–15.
63. Segal, M., Pickel, V. and Bloom, F. E. (1973): The projections of the nucleus locus coeruleus: an autoradiographic study. *Life. Sci.,* 13:817–821.
64. Smith, G. P. and Epstein, A. N. (1969): Increased feeding in response to decreased glucose utilization in the rat and monkey. *Am. J. Physiol.,* 217:1083–1087.
65. Smith, P. E. (1930): Hypophysectomy and a replacement therapy in the rat. *Am. J. Anat.,* 45:205–256.
66. Strominger, J. L. (1947): The relation between water intake and food intake in normal rats and rats with hypothalamic hyperphagia. *Yale J. Biol. Med.,* 19:279–288.
67. Ungerstedt, U. (1971): Adipsia and aphagia after 6-hydroxydopamine induced degeneration of the nigrostriatal dopamine system. *Acta Physiol. Scand.* (Suppl. 367), 81:95–122.
68. Ungerstedt, U. (1971): Stereotaxic mapping of the monoamine pathways in the rat brain. *Acta Physiol. Scand* (Suppl.), 367:1–48.
69. Worth, W. S., Collins, J., Kett, D., and Austin, J. H. (1976): Serial changes in norepinephrine and dopamine in rat brain after locus coeruleus lesions. *Brain Res.,* 106:198–203.

Anorexia Nervosa, edited by
R. A. Vigersky. Raven Press,
New York © 1977.

Brain Amines in Hypothalamic Obesity

Donald V. Coscina

Section of Neurochemistry, Clarke Institute of Psychiatry; and Department of Psychiatry, University of Toronto, Toronto, Ontario, Canada M5T 1R8

INTRODUCTION

Severe, persisting weight loss is at once a most apparent and distressing feature of anorexia nervosa. This self-imposed reduction of body mass by starvation has been associated with substantial mortality and morbidity (5,13). The physiological substrates of this feeding disorder are imperfectly understood. This fact is itself disturbing given the seeming increased prevalence of this syndrome (14). Accordingly, increasing our knowledge about those physiological mechanisms which mediate hunger and satiety should be valuable in understanding and, hopefully, treating certain aspects of this illness.

The present chapter summarizes experiments from this laboratory which examine the possible role of three brain monoamines (MAs) in eating disturbances: the two catecholamines (CAs), norepinephrine (NE) and dopamine (DA), and the indoleamine (IA) serotonin (5-hydroxytryptamine or 5-HT).

EXPERIMENTAL MODEL AND RATIONALE FOR USE

A frequently studied model of impaired satiety is the overeating (hyperphagia) and obesity which occur in rats with ventromedial hypothalamic (VMH) injury. The behavioral and physiological similarities between this induced pathology in animals and the obesity seen from overnutrition in humans (28) suggest common underlying mechanisms worthy of experimental attention. The work described here relates attempts to specify if brain CAs and/or IAs contribute to this VMH model of obesity.

ALTERED AMINES IN HYPOTHALAMIC OBESITY

My interest in brain MAs and hypothalamic obesity began in 1971. At that time it was already clear that the aphagia (29) which followed lateral hypothalamic (LH) damage was associated with transection of NE, DA, and 5-HT pathways ascending to forebrain structures via the medial forebrain bundle (30,31). If the integrity of either or both CA systems were essential to maintain normal feeding, prior disruption of both systems should substantially prevent the development of VMH hyperphagia and weight gain.

To test this possibility (10), we injected adult female rats in the cisterna magna with 300 μg (free base) of 6-hydroxydopamine (6-OH-DA), a neurotoxin known to chronically deplete brain NE and DA in this dose range (21). After an initial hypophagia and resultant weight loss (Fig. 1), rats began eating pellet chow and gaining weight normally. Fifty days after 6-OH-DA injection, bilateral radiofrequency heat lesions were made in the VMH area of rats pretreated with this drug or its vehicle (20 μl of 1% ascorbic acid in saline). Regardless of pretreatment, both groups overate food pellets and increased their weight 40% over the next 50 days (Fig. 1). However, additional tests of 24-hr acceptance of 0.02%, 0.01%, and 0.005% quinine sulfate solutions instead of tap water revealed that 6-OH-DA had reduced the heightened quinine rejection which occurs after VMH damage. Fluorometric assays of endogenous forebrain NE, DA, and 5-HT levels showed that although vehicle pretreatment had no effect on these MAs, 6-OH-DA produced 60% decrements in NE and 80% decrements in DA. 5-HT was minimally (−10%) affected.

To test further these results (10), we gave additional female rats VMH lesions, allowed them to become obese (Fig. 2), and then deprived them of

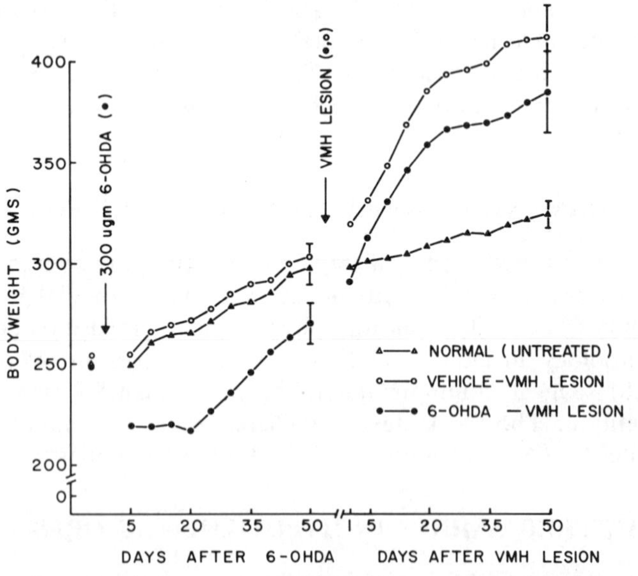

FIG. 1. Mean gram body weights plotted every 5 days for adult female rats receiving 6-OH-DA and VMH lesions ($N = 5$), vehicle and VMH lesions ($N = 5$), or no treatment ($N = 5$). Abbreviations explained in text. SEMs are shown 50 days after each treatment.

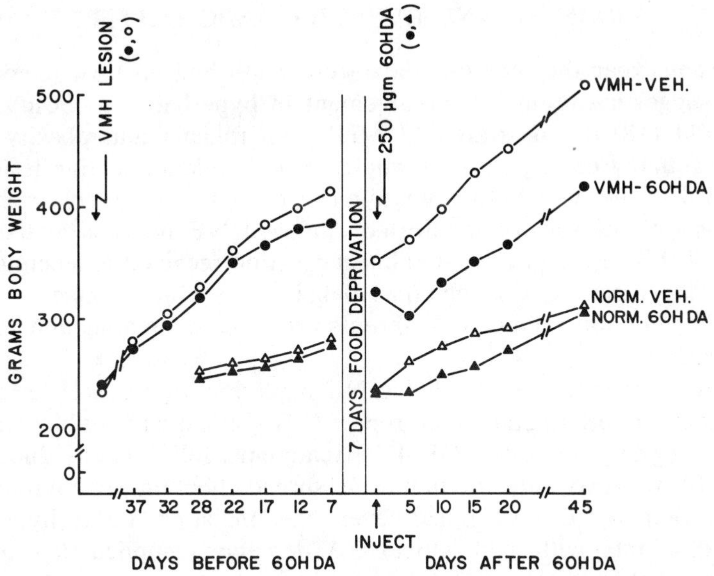

FIG. 2. Mean gram body weights plotted every 5 days for adult female rats receiving VMH lesions and 6-OH-DA ($N = 5$), VMH lesions and 6-OH-DA's vehicle ($N = 5$), no lesion and 6-OH-DA ($N = 12$), or no lesion and vehicle ($N = 8$). Abbreviations explained in text.

food for 7 days. At that time, a portion of lesioned rats and their normal controls received 250 µg 6-OH-DA intracisternally while the remaining rats received its vehicle. If intact NE and/or DA neurons were important in mediating the overeating required for VMH rats to reattain their elevated bodyweight "setpoint" (20), 6-OH-DA should block this eating and weight gain more in lesioned than in control rats. In fact, it did not (Fig. 2). Analyses of variance revealed that 6-OH-DA did suppress feeding and weight gain, but it did so equally for both drugged groups, i.e., there was no drug-lesion interaction. Tests of quinine acceptance in these same rats again revealed that 6-OH-DA attenuated the exaggerated rejection characteristic of VMH animals. Fluorometric assays of brain MAs confirmed that 6-OH-DA produced substantial (>60%) depletion of NE and DA with minimal (−9%) effects on 5-HT. Of particular interest were findings of small but reliable decrements in NE (−15%) and 5-HT (−8%) in brains from rats with VMH damage alone.

Although the above findings did not support the original hypothesis concerning brain CAs and hypothalamic obesity, they generated two interesting suggestions: (a) brain NE and 5-HT systems might be involved in VMH hyperphagia, and (b) brain CAs might mediate aspects of "finickiness" known to occur with such brain damage (26).

BRAIN NE AND HYPOTHALAMIC OBESITY

The same year the previous data were published (10), two reports appeared suggesting brain NE involvement in hypothalamic obesity. In the first, Gold (18) demonstrated "VMH" hyperphagia and obesity in rats without actually damaging these nuclei. Since Gold's effective lesion sites lay rostral to these traditional anatomical landmarks in an area rich in NE terminals (30), this work implicated damaged NE neurons in the pathogenesis of this feeding disorder. This suggestion received independent support from a paper by Ahlskog and Hoebel (1), in which damage seemingly restricted to hypothalamic NE afferents produced overeating and abnormal weight gain.

Our own observations of reliable NE depletion after VMH lesions (10) in conjunction with another such report (17) seemed compatible with these findings. The fact that our 6-OH-DA treatment itself did not induce hyperphagia (10) was probably due to its widespread effect on extrahypothalamic CAs, particularly DA (31). However, the unabated VMH hyperphagia observed in rats with such global CA depletions implied that sufficient satiety mechanisms survived 6-OH-DA treatment such that later VMH damage could disrupt them. Since hypothalamic NE neurons should have sustained severe injury from such drug treatment (21), it seemed unlikely that this degree of VMH hyperphagia was solely related to lesion-induced NE depletion. Indeed, careful examination of Ahlskog and Hoebel's data (1) revealed a magnitude of obesity considerably less than that associated with traditional hypothalamic obesity. Since we had observed reliable 5-HT depletion as well as NE depletion after VMH injury (10), the potential role of this IA system in classic hypothalamic obesity was explored.

[While these studies were in progress, additional experiments were reported which also questioned an exclusive role for NE in hypothalamic obesity. For example, Lorden et al. (24) provided convincing evidence that selective hypothalamic NE disruption seems neither necessary nor sufficient to induce overeating. In addition, hypophysectomy, which does not prevent VMH hyperphagia (12), abolishes the overeating due to hypothalamic NE deafferentation (2). Finally, VMH lesions plus hypothalamic NE deafferentation produce additive rather than subtractive effects on overeating and weight gain (3).]

RELIABLE 5-HT PLUS NE CHANGES AFTER VMH INJURY

As a first test of 5-HT's potential role in hypothalamic obesity, we replicated Gold's (18) observation of medial hypothalamic (MH) hyperphagia with lesions aimed rostral to the VMH nuclei and provided neurochemical scrutiny to the brains of these rats. This work (8) involved production of bilateral radiofrequency heat lesions of varying sizes according to Gold's coordinates in adult female rats. After 2 weeks of maintenance on Gold's

TABLE 1. *Body weight (BW) and brain amine or metabolite levels approximately 2 weeks after MH lesions or sham surgery*

Group		% Op BW	5-HT	NE	DA	5-HIAA
MH lesion	$\bar{X}$	+39.4	92.6	81.0	96.3	531
	SEM	1.910	1.13	1.79	1.46	14.7
	N	40	40	40	40	19
Sham lesion	$\bar{X}$	+5.04	100.0	100.0	100.0	541
	SEM	0.632	2.95	1.64	2.09	51.4
	N	20	20	20	20	9
	p	<0.001	<0.01	<0.001	ns	ns

Body weight expressed as percentage increase over weight at surgery. Levels of 5-HT, NE, and DA expressed as percentage of control levels. Levels of 5-HIAA expressed as nanograms per gram wet tissue weight.

high-fat diet (33% vegetable fat, 67% powdered chow), lesioned rats and sham-operated controls were sacrificed for fluorometric determinations of forebrain NE, DA, 5-HT, and 5-HT's major metabolite, 5-hydroxyindoleacetic acid (5-HIAA). Lesioned rats increased their weight by 40% after surgery, which was significantly greater than the 5% gain seen in controls (Table 1). Confirming our earlier work (10), MH lesions reliably decreased forebrain NE (−19%) and 5-HT (−8%) without reliably affecting DA and 5-HIAA (Table 1). Of added interest were findings of significant inverse correlations (Table 2) between degree of obesity in lesioned rats and levels of brain NE, 5-HT and 5-HIAA. In addition, levels of all three substances correlated positively with each other. These data supported and extended the suggestion of NE depletion in MH obese rats while simultaneously reinforcing our earlier suggestion of concomitantly changed 5-HT metabolism.

We have recently (7) obtained added support for hypotheses of NE and

TABLE 2. *Matrix of Pearson Product-Moment correlation coefficients for body weight and chemical variables shown in Table 1*

	BW	5-HT	NE	DA
5-HT	−0.2773[a]			
NE	−0.4005[b]	+0.6846[c]		
DA	+0.0170	+0.4173[d]	+0.3036	
5-HIAA	−0.5315[b]	+0.4843[a]	+0.4709[e]	+0.3735

All tests were performed on data obtained from lesioned rats alone (see Table 1 for number of observations per cell). All *p* values are two-tailed.

[a] $p < 0.10$.
[b] $p < 0.025$.
[c] $p < 0.01$.
[d] $p < 0.01$.
[e] $p < 0.005$.

TABLE 3. *Body weight and brain amine or metabolite levels approximately 1 month after GTG or control injection*

Group		BW (% increase/day over starting BW)	5-HT	5-HIAA	NE	DA
GTG	$\bar{X}$	2.36	969	315	385	1236
	SEM	0.304	18.3	9.56	14.0	16.3
	N	13	13	13	13	13
Control	$\bar{X}$	0.923	1029	339	445	1217
	SEM	0.088	22.4	10.4	11.1	22.2
	N	14	14	14	14	14
	p	<0.001	<0.06	ns	<0.01	ns

Body weight expressed as percentage increase per day over weight at time of injection. GTG mice received 8–14 mg of drug i.p.; controls received equal volumes of GTG's vehicle. Levels of 5-HT, 5-HIAA, NE, and DA expressed as nanograms per gram wet tissue weight.

5-HT involvement in hypothalamic obesity without the use of lesions. It is known that systemic injection of gold thioglucose (GTG) in mice can induce hyperphagia and obesity much as do MH lesions in rats (23). The presumed mechanism of this GTG action relates to its relatively high affinity for uptake into and subsequent neurotoxic action on neuronal elements in thc MH axis (15). If overeating and weight gain were mediated by altered NE and/or 5-HT neurons as indicated above, depletion of either or both MAs should be observed in brains from mice treated with GTG. This is what was found. Approximately 1 month after receiving 8 to 14 mg of GTG intraperitoneally, adult female mice surviving treatment showed substantial weight gain compared to controls maintained on the same pellet diet (Table 3). At the same time, fluorometric assays of endogenous forebrain MAs revealed decrements in NE and 5-HT but no changes in DA or 5-HIAA levels (Table 3). Unfortunately, the sample size remaining was not large enough (see ref. 8) to permit proper assessment of potential correlations between weight changes and these MA variables. Nevertheless, these findings provide independent evidence in a different experimental model of altered NE and 5-HT function in the genesis of overeating and obesity.

NECESSITY OF 5-HT IN MH OBESITY

If altered 5-HT metabolism were the sole factor producing hypothalamic obesity, prior disruption of those neurons involved in its synthesis, storage, uptake, release, and degradation should itself produce overeating and weight gain. A common method in attempts to impair forebrain 5-HT metabolism is to lesion the cell bodies giving rise to these neurons, namely, the midbrain raphe nuclei (16). Since the dorsal (B7) and median (B8) cell groupings seem the principal loci generating projections to or through the MH area destroyed by obesity-producing lesions (see refs. 6 and 16), such raphe destruction might be expected to produce overeating. However, it does not (9,11,25).

A priori, these negative findings do not invalidate the suggestion that 5-HT is important in central mechanisms mediating eating. The massive forebrain depletion following such raphe damage (e.g., 50 to 75%; 9,11, 19,25) is considerably greater than that observed after MH lesions producing hyperphagia (e.g., 6 to 10%; 8,10,11). Presumably, this added 5-HT depletion represents vast disruption of 5-HT networks outside those coursing through the MH axis. Such added damage could produce physiological and/or behavioral effects incompatible with the expression of overeating and/or fat deposition.

Although this possibility makes intuitive sense, it is difficult to reconcile with the recent finding that ventricular infusions of (a) the 5-HT metabolic inhibitor *p*-chlorophenylalanine (PCPA) produce short-term hyperphagia comparable to its transitory 5-HT depletory effects (4), or (b) the 5-HT neurotoxin 5,7-dihydroxytryptamine (5,7-DHT) can promote long-term overeating and exaggerated growth (but not fat deposition) in instances of substantial ($\geq$ 80%), seemingly specific 5-HT depletion (27). (Parenthetically, both findings support some primary role for 5-HT in overeating and weight gain.) However, a number of important differences likely exist between these two newer models of depleting brain 5-HT and the more traditional technique of raphe lesioning. These differences include: (a) level of action in central nervous system (e.g., depletion of forebrain alone with raphe lesions; depletion of whole brain plus spinal cord with ventricular PCPA or 5,7-DHT); (b) the magnitude of regional depletions in brain structures (e.g., possible decreased gradient of effect distal to ventricles for PCPA and 5,7-DHT versus raphe lesions); (c) different sites of neuronal action (e.g., entire neuronal axis plus innervations to cell bodies destroyed by raphe lesions; terminals primarily destroyed by 5,7-DHT with possibility for regenerative or collateral sprouting; no structural damage by PCPA); and (d) different modes of action on 5-HT metabolism (see ref. 22). Any or all of these factors could contribute to discrepancies obtained across these three methods used to study 5-HT roles in feeding.

RAPHE LESIONS BLOCK MH OBESITY

Although disruption of vast forebrain networks receiving midbrain 5-HT afferents may preclude demonstrations of behavioral changes restricted to feeding, combining such treatments with other manipulations known to alter feeding may provide clues about 5-HT's potential role in these latter models.

We have recently (11) employed this rationale to assess the importance of intact 5-HT systems to the development of the VMH syndrome. For this purpose, bilateral radiofrequency heat lesions were aimed rostral to the VMH nuclei (8,18) in adult female rats depleted of 5-HT by dorsal and median raphe lesions 50 days previously. Rats with both lesions showed no substantial weight gain compared to controls during the first postoperative week, plus they gained considerably less than sham + MH rats over 7 weeks. This was due to normal intake of food pellets during this time, which contrasted with the elevated intake of sham + MH rats (Fig. 3). Contrary to this capacity of raphe lesions to block MH hyperphagia, 24-hr acceptance tests of various sucrose and quinine solutions instead of water, as well as 24-day acceptance of high-fat diet instead of food pellets, showed raphe + MH rats to be overresponsive equivalent to obese sham + MH rats (11). Terminal fluorometric assays of forebrain NE, DA, 5-HT, and 5-HIAA revealed raphe lesions effective in chronically reducing both 5-HT and

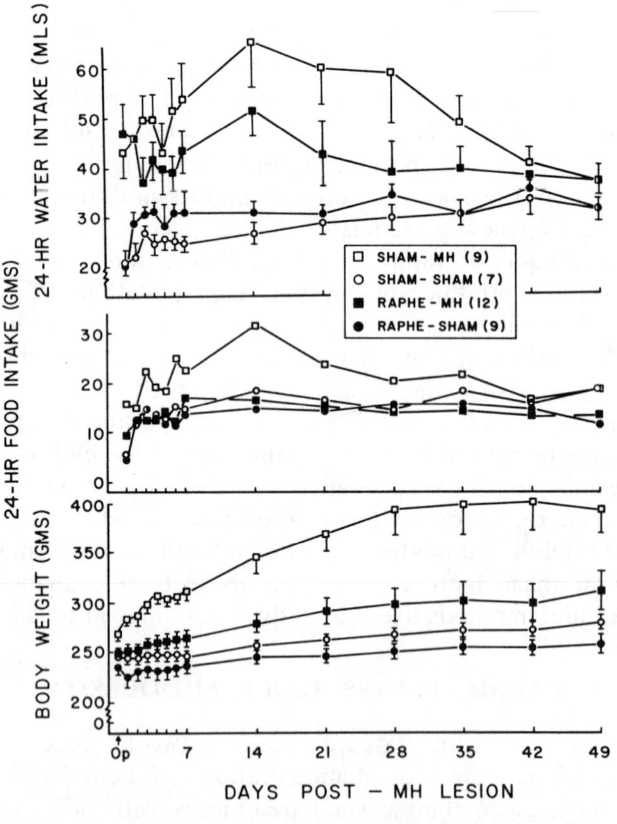

FIG. 3. Mean and SEM body weights (grams), 24-hr food intakes (grams), and 24-hr water intakes (milliliters) plotted daily (for the first week) or weekly (after the first week) following MH or sham surgery. Groups of adult female rats received lesions as shown in the figure. The first operation (raphe vs. sham lesions) occurred 50 days prior to the second operation (MH vs. sham lesions). Abbreviations explained in text.

5-HIAA by 75% with minimal effects on NE (−13%) and DA (+3%). As in our previous work (8,10), MH injury alone produced small but reliable depletion of NE (−14%) and 5-HT (−6%) without affecting DA or 5-HIAA.

The exact mechanisms by which raphe lesions can reduce MH hyperphagia are presently unknown. We cannot rule out possible nonspecific midbrain lesion effects in explaining some of these findings. However, the apparent histological and biochemical specificity of our midbrain lesions argues against this interpretation (11). In addition, correlations calculated between grams of weight gained 1 week after MH injury in raphe-lesioned rats with all their brain assay results revealed significant positive correlations with only 5-HT and 5-HIAA levels (r's = +0.6055 and +0.6078, respectively). This suggests that the initial suppression of MH obesity was specifically related to the magnitude of injury to 5-HT systems rather than to other neurons.

DISTINCT CA VERSUS IA ROLES IN THE MH SYNDROME

Altered 5-HT neurotransmission may have been instrumental in attenuating MH obesity (11). However, it clearly did not block the entire MH syndrome. Therefore, alterations to other neural systems must be involved in this classic eating disorder. From preceding data, brain NE subsystems seem clearly implicated. In support of this notion (11), correlations calculated between grams of weight gained 7 weeks after MH damage in raphe-lesioned rats with all their brain assay results revealed significant inverse correlations with only NE levels ($r = -0.6871$). This finding is compatible with earlier work suggesting inverse relationships between MH obesity and brain NE levels (1,2,3,8,10,11,17,18). Seemingly, the capacity for raphe lesions to limit the degree of initial MH obesity subsides with time. This could be due to compensatory increases in 5-HT turnover in undamaged neurons (see refs. 11 and 32; also note that MH lesions consistently lower 5-HT but not 5-HIAA; 8,10,11) and/or associated changes in postsynaptic receptor sensitivity compatible with reduced 5-HT release. Such changes could permit the eventual expression of moderate weight increments, which themselves seem related to altered NE metabolism.

When viewed collectively, our data imply concomitant but distinct roles for both CAs and IAs in aspects of the classic VMH syndrome. More specifically, the finding (10) that CA depletion via 6-OH-DA alters the quinine rejection but not the obesity associated with MH lesions points to some role for brain CAs in hypothalamic "finickiness." Conversely, raphe lesions, which attenuate MH-induced obesity but do not alter "finickiness" (11), imply some role for brain IAs in controlling long-term weight regulation (perhaps body weight "setpoint"). More precise delineations of how NE and 5-HT systems might mediate specific (e.g., autonomic nervous system balance, hormonal signals to the periphery modifying energy balance) or nonspecific (e.g., general arousal levels affecting broad categories of motivated behaviors) aspects of classic hypothalamic feeding disorders remain to be performed.

ACKNOWLEDGMENTS

All work reported from this laboratory was supported by funds from the Clarke Institute of Psychiatry. I warmly thank Drs. P. Garfinkel, D. Godse, H. Stancer, and J. Warsh for their various contributions to this work. R. Johnston, R. McArthur, P. Chan, M. Guttman, and C. Spegg provided excellent technical assistance throughout different phases of these studies.

REFERENCES

1. Ahlskog, J. E., and Hoebel, B. G. (1973): Overeating and obesity from damage to a noradrenergic system in brain. *Science,* 182:166–169.
2. Ahlskog, J. E., Hoebel, B. G., and Breisch, S. T. (1974): Hyperphagia following lesions of the noradrenergic pathway is prevented by hypophysectomy. *Fed. Proc.,* 33:463.
3. Ahlskog, J. E., Randall, P. K., and Hoebel, B. G. (1975): Hypothalamic hyperphagia: Dissociation from hyperphagia following destruction of noradrenergic neurons. *Science,* 190:399–401.
4. Breisch, S. T., Zemlan, F. P., and Hoebel, B. G. (1976): Hyperphagia and obesity following serotonin depletion by intraventricular p-chlorophenylalanine. *Science,* 192: 382–384.
5. Bruch, H. (1973): *Eating Disorders.* Basic Books, New York.
6. Conrad, L. C. A., Leonard, C. M., and Pfaff, D. W. (1974): Connections of the median and dorsal raphe nuclei in the rat: An autoradiographic and degeneration study. *J. Comp. Neurol.,* 156:179–206.
7. Coscina, D. V. (1976): Relationship of goldthioglucose-induced obesity in mice to levels of brain biogenic amines. Paper presented at Eastern Psychological Association Meeting, New York.
8. Coscina, D. V., Godse, D. D., and Stancer, H. C. (1976): Neurochemical correlates of hypothalamic obesity in rats. *Behav. Biol.,* 16:365–372.
9. Coscina, D. V., Grant, L. D., Balagura, S., and Grossman, S. P. (1972): Hyperdipsia after serotonin-depleting midbrain lesions. *Nature* [*New Biol.*], 235:63–64.
10. Coscina, D. V., Rosenblum-Blinick, C., Godse, D. D., and Stancer, H. C. (1973): Consummatory behaviors of hypothalamic hyperphagic rats after central injection of 6-hydroxydopamine. *Pharmacol. Biochem. Behav.,* 1:629–642.
11. Coscina, D. V., and Stancer, H. C. (1977): Selective blockade of hypothalamic hyperphagia and obesity in rats by serotonin-depleting midbrain lesions. *Science,* 195:416–419.
12. Cox, V. C., Kakolewski; J. W., and Valenstein, E. S. (1968): Effects of ventromedial hypothalamic damage in hypophysectomized rats. *J. Comp. Physiol. Psychol.,* 65:145–148.
13. Crisp, A. H. (1965): Some aspects of the evolution, presentation and follow-up of anorexia nervosa. *Proc. R. Soc. Med.,* 58:814–820.
14. Crisp, A. H., Palmer, R. L., and Kalucy, R. S. (1976): How common is anorexia nervosa? A prevalence study. *Br. J. Psychiatry,* 128:549–554.
15. Debons, A. F., Silver, L., Cronkite, E. P., Johnson, H. A., Brechner, G., Tenzer, D., and Schwartz, I. L. (1962): Localization of gold in mouse brain in relation to gold thioglucose obesity. *Am. J. Physiol.,* 202:743–750.
16. Fuxe, K., and Jonsson, G. (1974): Further mapping of central 5-hydroxytryptamine neurons: Studies with the neurotoxic dihydroxytryptamines. *Adv. Biochem. Psychopharmacol.,* 10:1–12.

17. Glick, S. D., Greenstein, S., and Waters, D. H. (1973): Ventromedial hypothalamic lesions and brain catecholamines. *Pharmacol. Biochem. Behav.,* 1:591–592.
18. Gold, R. M. (1973): Hypothalamic obesity: The myth of the ventromedial nucleus. *Science,* 182:488–490.
19. Grant, L. D., Coscina, D. V., Grossman, S. P., and Freedman, D. X. (1973): Muricide after serotonin depleting lesions of the midbrain raphe nuclei. *Pharmacol. Biochem. Behav.,* 1:77–80.
20. Hoebel, B. G., and Teitelbaum, P. (1966): Weight regulation in normal and hypothalamic hyperphagic rats. *J. Comp. Physiol. Psychol.,* 61:189–193.
21. Iversen, L. L., and Uretsky, N. J. (1971): Biochemical effects of 6-hydroxydopamine on catecholamine-containing neurones in the rat central nervous system. In: *6-Hydroxydopamine and Catecholamine Neurons,* edited by T. Malmfors and H. Thoenen, pp. 171–186. North-Holland, Amsterdam.
22. Knapp, S., and Mandell, A. J. (1976): Coincidence of blockade of synaptosomal 5-hydroxytryptamine uptake and decrease in tryptophan hydroxylase activity: Effects of fenfluramine. *J. Pharmacol. Exp. Ther.,* 198:123–132.
23. Liebelt, R. A., and Perry, J. H. (1967): Action of gold thioglucose on the central nervous system. In: *Handbook of Physiology, Section 6: Alimentary Canal,* edited by C. F. Code, pp. 271–286. American Physiological Society, Washington, D.C.
24. Lorden, J., Oltmans, G. A., and Margules, D. L. (1976): Central noradrenergic neurons: Differential effects on body weight of electrolytic and 6-hydroxydopamine lesions in rats. *J. Comp. Physiol. Psychol.,* 90:144–155.
25. Lorens, S. A., Sorenson, J. P., and Yunger, L. M. (1971): Behavioral and neurochemical effects of lesions in the raphe system of the rat. *J. Comp. Physiol. Psychol.,* 77:48–52.
26. Miller, N. E., Bailey, C. J., and Stevenson, J. A. F. (1950): Decreased "hunger" but increased food intake resulting from hypothalamic lesions. *Science,* 112:256–259.
27. Saller, C. F., and Stricker, E. M. (1976): Hyperphagia and increased growth in rats after intraventricular injection of 5,7-dihydroxytryptamine. *Science,* 192:385–387.
28. Schacter, S., and Rodin, J. (1974): *Obese Humans and Rats.* John Wiley & Sons, New York.
29. Teitelbaum, P., and Epstein, A. N. (1962): The lateral hypothalamic syndrome: Recovery of feeding and drinking after lateral hypothalamic lesions. *Psychol. Rev.,* 69:74–90.
30. Ungerstedt, U. (1971*a*): Stereotaxic mapping of the monoamine pathways in the rat brain. *Acta Physiol. Scand.* [*Suppl.*], 367:1–48.
31. Ungerstedt, U. (1971*b*): Adipsia and aphagia after 6-hydroxydopamine induced degeneration of the nigro-striatal dopamine system. *Acta Physiol. Scand.* [*Suppl.*], 367:95–122.
32. Warsh, J. J., Coscina, D. V., and Stancer, H. C. (1976): Effect of midbrain raphe lesions or intracisternal 6-hydroxydopamine administration on D,L-5-hydroxytryptophan-^{14}C metabolism after peripheral decarboxylase inhibition. *Brain Res. Bull.,* 1:273–278.

Anorexia Nervosa, edited by
R. A. Vigersky. Raven Press,
New York © 1977.

Anorexia Nervosa as a Model of Hypothalamic Dysfunction

Robert A. Vigersky and D. Lynn Loriaux

Reproduction Research Branch, National Institute of Child Health and Human Development, National Institutes of Health, Bethesda, Maryland 20014

INTRODUCTION

Although anorexia nervosa has been considered a psychiatric disease and the diagnosis is still made by psychologic criteria, patients with this disorder have numerous medical and endocrinologic abnormalities which have been the subject of intense investigation in recent years. Even though a specific cause of the disease has not yet been found, progress has been made in understanding the pathophysiology. Specifically, it has been suggested that anorexia nervosa represents a disease of altered hypothalamic function (9) because of the finding of specific hypothalamic regulatory abnormalities.

We have evaluated 29 patients with anorexia nervosa with both specific tests of hypothalamic function and endocrine studies of the hypothalamic-pituitary-end organ axis. This series expands and generally corroborates the finding in the five patients reported by Mecklenburg et al. (9) that patients with anorexia nervosa have hypothalamic dysfunction.

METHODS

All studies were begun at 8 a.m. with the subjects fasting. All polypeptide and steroid hormones were measured by radioimmunoassay. Triiodothyronine (T_3) and free thyroxine (fT_4) were determined as previously described (18). Mean ideal body weights (IBWs) were taken from the Metropolitan Life Insurance Company Statistical Bulletin.

Patients

The diagnosis of anorexia nervosa was made in 29 patients, ages 15 to 42 (mean $\pm$ SD was 24 $\pm$ 8 years), using the criteria of Feighner et al. (6). All medications were discontinued at least 30 days prior to patients' evaluation. Organic illness was ruled out by complete physical examination, hemogram, renal and liver function tests, urinalysis, X-rays of skull, sella turcica, and chest, electroencephalogram, electrocardiogram, and visual fields. These patients weighed 34.3 ± 6.6 kg (mean ± SD), which was 32 ± 10% below IBW.

Endocrine and Hypothalamic Tests

Seven regularly cycling young women (ages 20 to 29) free of endocrinologic disease were given 10 μg of synthetic LRF in the early follicular phase (days 2 to 5) of the menstrual cycle. Samples for gonadotropins were obtained via an indwelling scalp vein needle at −40, −30, −20, −10, 0, +5, +15, +30, +45, +60, +120, and +180 min from the time of injection. Basal luteinizing hormone (LH) and follicle-stimulating hormone (FSH) values represent the mean of five determinations obtained before injection of LRF. Thyroid-stimulating hormone (TSH) ($N = 9$) and prolactin (PRL) ($N = 14$) were obtained from normal subjects at 0, 10, 20, 30, 45, 60, 120, and 180 min after 500 μg of synthetic thyrotropin-releasing factor (TRF). Quantitative LH, FSH, TSH, and PRL responses were determined as previously described (18).

Ten normal subjects received the following provocative studies of growth hormone (GH) and cortisol: an insulin tolerance test (ITT) with 0.1 U/kg of regular insulin administered intravenously; an L-DOPA test with 500 mg given orally; and an arginine tolerance test (ATT) with arginine hydrochloride, 0.5 g/kg, given intravenously over 30 min. In addition, the rise of GH during slow-wave sleep was evaluated in eight normal subjects. A normal GH response in these studies was a rise to 7 ng/ml or greater with at least a doubling of the basal level. The normal cortisol response was the attainment of a plasma cortisol of 20 μg/100 ml or an increase of at least 5 μg/100 ml.

Free T_4 (fT_4), triiodothyronine (T_3), and TSH were obtained in euthyroid volunteers ($N = 47$). Plasma PRL was measured in the basal state in 21 normal women. In 10 of these women, PRL was suppressed with 500 mg of L-DOPA and stimulated with 500 μg of TRF. The normal response to L-DOPA is at least a 50% suppression of basal PRL levels, and the normal response to TRF is at least a doubling of the basal levels. A normal response to chlorpromazine (CPZ) is at least a doubling of PRL within 3 hr (16).

Studies of thermoregulation were performed in the NIH environmental chamber on 20 normal subjects within 15% of IBW. Subjects were clad in bathing suits and exposed to cold (10°C) and heat (49°C, 12% relative humidity) on different days. Core temperature was measured electronically at 1-min intervals using a rectal thermistor. The normal response to hyperthermia is an initial fall in core temperature due to peripheral vasodilatation (paradoxical change) followed by a rise in core temperature to within

0.40°C of the basal state. After 30 min of hyperthermia, the rate of change of core temperature per hour ($\Delta T°/\Delta t$) was +0.14 ± 0.16 (mean ± SD) (range −0.15 to +0.40). The normal response to hypothermia is an initial rise in core temperature due to peripheral vasoconstriction, shivering, and a fall to within 0.1°C of basal temperature. After 30 min of hypothermia, the $\Delta T°/\Delta t$ was −0.08 ± 0.28 (range +0.08 to −0.20).

Patients with anorexia nervosa were evaluated for the presence of partial diabetes insipidus by the method of Miller et al. (10).

RESULTS

Pituitary–End Organ Function

GH

As seen in Table 1, patients with anorexia nervosa had significantly higher basal plasma GH levels ($p < 0.001$) compared to normal subjects. The severity of weight loss was significantly correlated with the log basal plasma GH level ($r = 0.60$, $p < 0.05$). Of the 29 patients, 27 responded to at least one provocative test of GH release. Of the 2 who did not, 1 had basal plasma GH levels of 338 and 395 ng/ml, and those of the other patient rose from 12 to 17 ng/ml after insulin-induced hypoglycemia. There was no significant correlation between basal plasma GH and fasting blood sugar.

TABLE 1. *Pituitary–end organ function in anorexia nervosa*

	Normal	Anorexia nervosa
Growth hormone (ng/ml)	10.4 ± 12.2[a]	48.1 ± 80.7[b]
Prolactin (ng/ml)	16.2 ± 5.5	19.4 ± 14.4
TSH (μU/ml)	N.D. in 77% <7.6 in 23%	N.D. in 30% <6.0 in 70%
LH (mIU/ml)	7.9 ± 4.4	3.9 ± 2.5[b]
FSH (mIU/ml)	15.3 ± 2.7	5.6 ± 5.2[c]
Cortisol (μg/ml)	14.4 ± 3.9	14.8 ± 5.4
Free T_4 (ng/100 ml)	1.5 ± 0.2	1.5 ± 0.2
T_3 (ng/100 ml)	156 ± 30	76 ± 30[b]
Estradiol (pg/ml)	—	<10

[a] Values are mean ± SD.
[b] $p < 0.001$.
[c] $p < 0.01$.

PITUITARY-OVARIAN AXIS

Basal plasma LH and FSH were significantly lower in patients with anorexia nervosa compared to normals ($p < 0.001$ and $p < 0.01$, respectively). The quantitative responses, however, of plasma LH and FSH to

LRF (percent rise, incremental rise or area under the response curve) in the two groups are indistinguishable (*vide infra*). Plasma estradiol levels were less than 10 pg/ml in all patients.

PITUITARY-THYROID AXIS

Plasma T_3 levels were significantly lower than normal in patients with anorexia nervosa ($p < 0.001$) and were inversely correlated with severity of weight loss ($r = -0.73, p < 0.02$). Plasma free thyroxine (fT_4) and basal plasma TSH levels, however, were indistinguishable in the two groups.

PITUITARY-ADRENAL AXIS

The 8 a.m. plasma cortisol levels and the cortisol response to insulin-induced hypoglycemia in anorexia nervosa patients and normals were indistinguishable. There was no correlation between the 8 a.m. plasma cortisol level or magnitude of response to insulin-induced hypoglycemia and the severity of weight loss.

PROLACTIN

Basal plasma PRL was indistinguishable from normal. The maximum plasma PRL level following 500 μg TRF was 62 $\pm$ 37 ng/ml. This was indistinguishable from the level in normal women (82 $\pm$ 47 ng/ml).

Hypothalamic Function

WATER CONSERVATION

All patients had urinary osmolalities greater than plasma osmolalities after 15 hr of dehydration. After 2 hr of unchanged (< 5%) urinary osmolality, 12 patients responded with further increases (greater than 9%) in urinary osmolality to exogenous ADH (Table 2). There was no correlation between the magnitude of response to exogenous ADH or the maximum urinary osmolality attained just before ADH and the severity of weight loss.

THERMOREGULATION

A total of 85% of patients responded abnormally in a cold environment (Table 2). The mean $\pm$ SEM rate of temperature change ($\Delta T°/\Delta t$) after 30 min of exposure in the 10 abnormal responders was -1.44 ± 0.11 (Fig. 1). Shivering was not observed in any of the patients. In the heat, 86% of patients responded abnormally. The $\Delta T°/\Delta t$ at 30 min was $+3.04 \pm 0.38$ (Fig. 1). The heat intolerance was significantly more severe than the cold

TABLE 2. *Results of hypothalamic function tests in anorexia nervosa*

	No. tested	% Abnormal
Partial diabetes insipidus	27	44
Thermoregulation		
Heat	14	86
Cold	13	85
Time of peak pituitary hormone after LRF		
LH	29	93
FSH	29	76
after TRF		
TSH	20	80
PRL	24	29
Quantitative response to LRF		
LH	29	18
FSH	29	7
Diurnal variation of cortisol	11	54
Prolactin response to CPZ	14	0

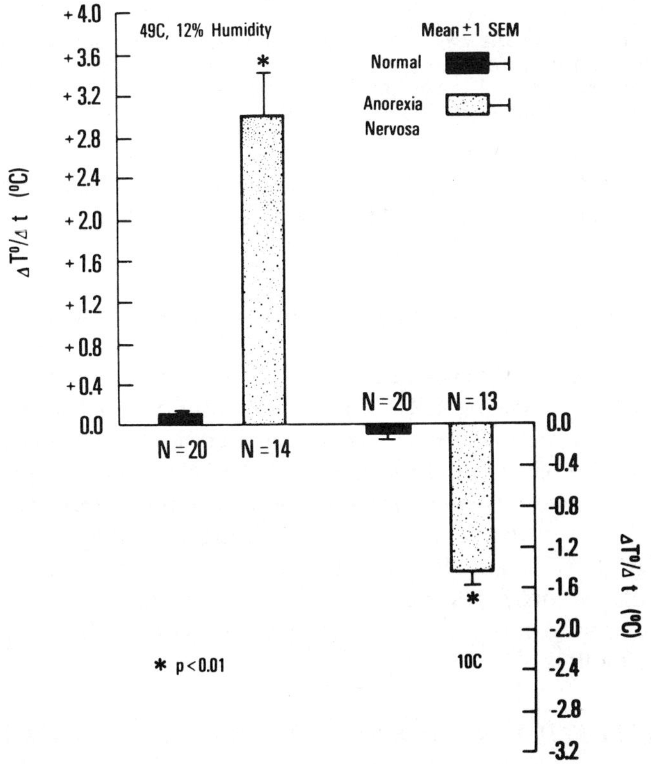

FIG. 1. Response (mean ± SEM) of normal subjects and patients with anorexia nervosa to hyperthermia and hypothermia. The $\Delta T°/\Delta t$ is the rate of change of core temperature (°C) per hour, which is a measure of thermoregulatory ability.

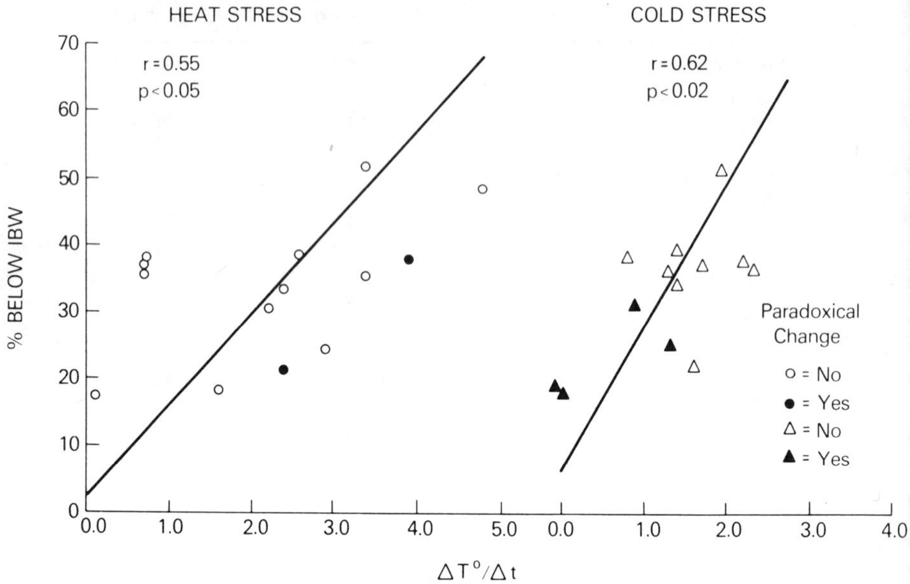

FIG. 2. Linear regression analysis of the severity of weight loss (% below IBW) in patients with anorexia nervosa vs the rate of change of core temperature per hour ($\Delta T°/\Delta t$). Paradoxical change refers to the initial rise in the cold or fall in the heat seen in the core temperature in normal subjects.

intolerance ($p < 0.01$). There was a significant correlation between the severity of weight loss and $\Delta T°/\Delta t$ in the cold ($r = 0.62$, $p < 0.02$) and in the heat ($r = 0.55$, $p < 0.05$) (Fig. 2).

KINETIC RESPONSES OF PITUITARY HORMONES

The time (mean ± SEM) of peak plasma LH (52 ± 5 min) and FSH (88 ± 7 min) response following LRF was significantly delayed in patients with anorexia nervosa compared to normal subjects ($p < 0.01$) (Fig. 3). The delayed response of peak plasma LH and FSH occurred in 93 and 76% of patients, respectively (Table 2). The time of the peak PRL response was significantly later in the group with anorexia nervosa compared to normal ($p < 0.05$) (Fig. 3). In all, 29% of patients had a delayed response (Table 2). The time of the peak plasma TSH value was significantly later in the anorexia nervosa group ($p < 0.001$) (Fig. 3). Response was delayed in 80% of patients (Table 2).

QUANTITATIVE RESPONSES OF PITUITARY HORMONE

There were no significant differences between anorexia and normal groups in their quantitative responses of plasma LH to LRF as measured in area

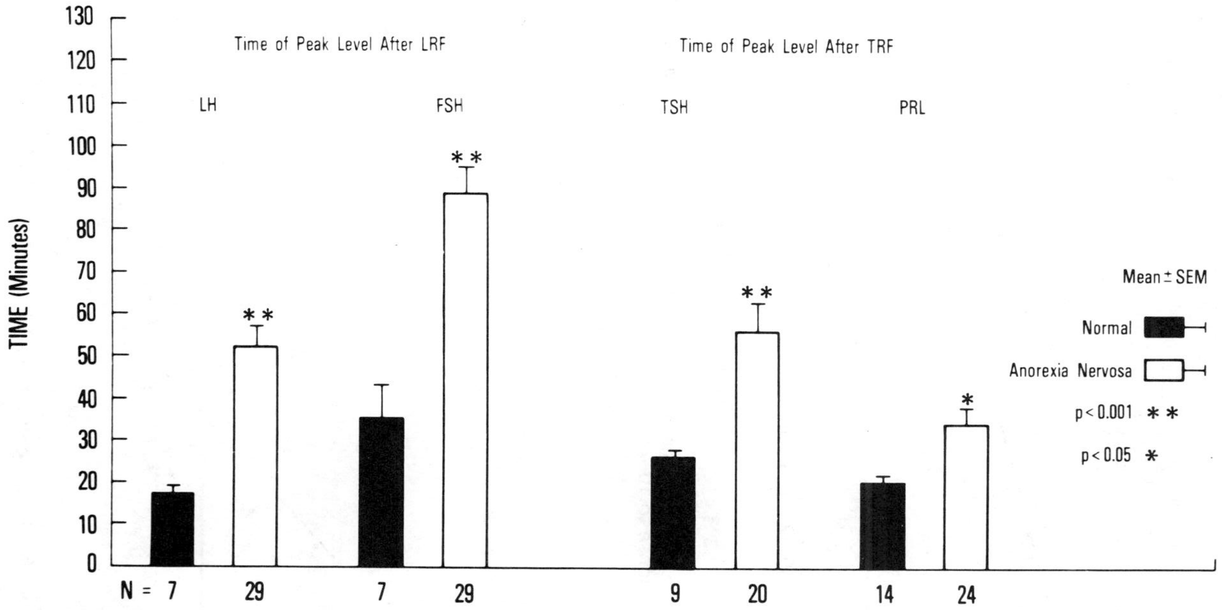

FIG. 3. Time (mean ± SEM) of peak pituitary hormone response after 10 μg of LRF or 500 μg of TRF in normal subjects and in patients with anorexia nervosa.

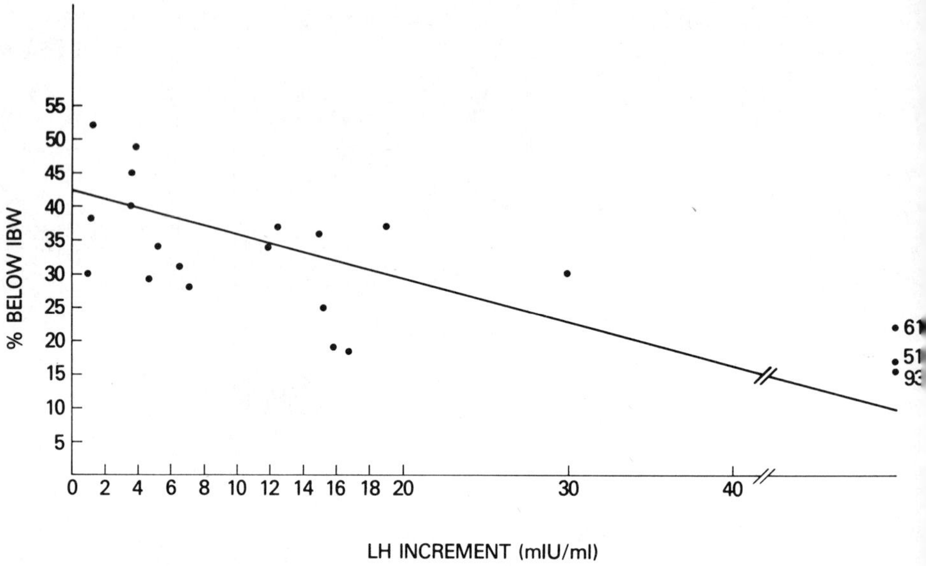

FIG. 4. Linear regression analysis of the severity of weight loss (% below IBW) vs the incremental LH response to 10 μg of LRF.

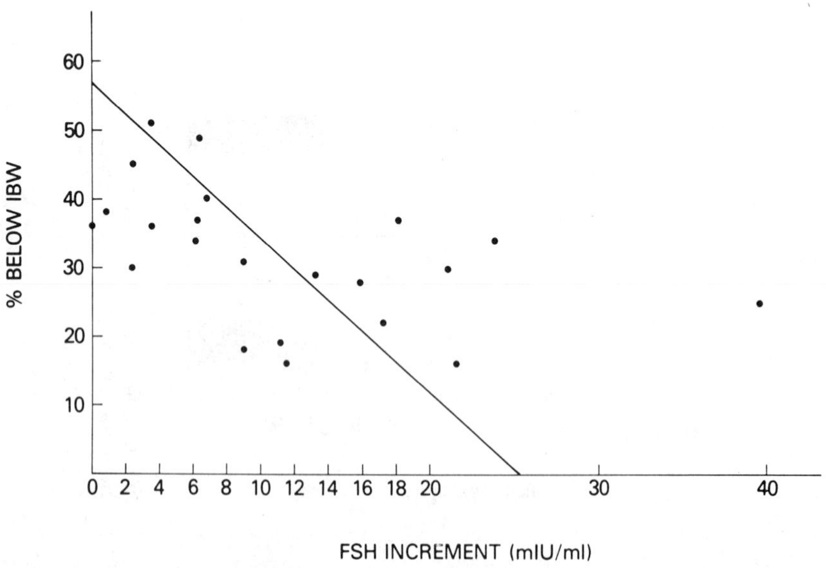

FIG. 5. Linear regression analysis of the severity of weight loss (% below IBW) vs the incremental FSH response to 10 μg of LRF.

units beneath the gonadotropin response curve, percent response, or incremental response. Integrated LH responses (mean ± SEM) were 2080 ± 318 mIU/ml/min and 1272 ± 559 mIU/ml/min in anorexia nervosa and normals, respectively. Six patients with anorexia nervosa (18%) did have subnormal (> 2 SD below mean) quantitative LH responses (Table 2). FSH responses were significantly greater in the anorexia nervosa group (1419 ± 395 mIU/ml/min) compared to normal (389 ± 115 mIU/ml/min) ($p < 0.05$). Two patients (7%) had subnormal quantitative FSH responses. There was a significant correlation between the severity of weight loss (percent below IBW) and the incremental LH ($r = 0.61$, $p < 0.01$) and FSH ($r = 0.46$, $p < 0.05$) response (Figs. 4 and 5) within the anorexia nervosa group.

The PRL responses to L-DOPA and CPZ were normal in all patients.

The TSH increment following 500 μg of TRF in anorexia nervosa patients (9.0 ± 4.0 μU/ml) was indistinguishable from that in nine normal subjects (8.6 ± 2.0 μU/ml).

OTHER HYPOTHALAMIC STUDIES

Despite normal basal 8 A.M. plasma cortisol levels, six patients (54%) did not have normal diurnal variation of cortisol.

All patients tested ($N = 11$) had at least a 7 ng/ml rise of plasma GH associated with stage 3 or 4 (delta-wave) sleep.

DISCUSSION

The hypothalamus controls numerous physiologic functions including regulation of the anterior pituitary hormones. In the diagnosis of hypothalamic disease or dysfunction, there should be: (a) no abnormality of end organ function not attributable to a pituitary cause; (b) no abnormality of pituitary function not attributable to a suprasellar cause; and/or (c) an abnormality of a specific hypothalamic function.

We have examined 29 patients with anorexia nervosa using these criteria to test for the presence of hypothalamic dysfunction.

End Organ Function

The status of thyroid function in anorexia nervosa is unclear. The constellation of normal fT_4, low T_3, normal basal TSH, and normal quantitative TSH response to TRF, which agrees with the findings of others (11,12), suggests that: (a) the thyroid gland itself is normal; (b) a peripheral abnormality of deiodination may be present; and (c) T_4 rather than T_3 may regulate the set-point of endogenous TRF. The question of whether or not these patients are hypothyroid is still unanswered. On the basis of abnormal androsterone/etiocholanolone, which is reversible with exogenous T_3,

Bradlow et al. (3) have recently suggested that these patients are biochemically hypothyroid.

The normal 8 A.M. plasma cortisol levels with no diurnal variation confirm the observation of others reporting elevated cortisol production rates in anorexia nervosa (2) and decreased metabolic clearance rates of cortisol in protein-calorie malnutrition (15). The adrenal hyperfunction may be related to the chronic hypoglycemia that is common in these patients, whereas the lack of diurnal variation may be due to hypothalamic causes as suggested by Krieger et al. (8).

The plasma estradiol level is less than 10 pg/ml in patients with anorexia nervosa. This is not unexpected in the face of chronically low gonadotropin secretions. Sherman et al. (14) have reported, however, that after patients returned to near-normal weight, plasma estradiol levels in anorexia nervosa were unchanged, despite higher basal LH levels and improved LH response to LRF. Recently, Beumont et al. (1) have reported that estradiol does increase as body weight increases. These observations suggest that either there is a primary ovarian abnormality, or, more likely, it is the time elapsed after return of normal body weight which determines the rate of ovarian recovery.

Pituitary Function

Basal plasma GH levels are significantly higher than normal but respond normally to one or more provocative stimuli. The reason for the elevated GH is not clear but may be related to chronic hypoglycemia. That this is not the case is suggested by the lack of correlation with basal blood sugar levels and the further GH rise during an ITT. Hypoaminoacidemia and/or deficiency in somatostatin may be a contributing factor, but this remains speculative.

Basal and TRF-stimulated plasma PRL and TSH are normal in anorexia nervosa. Basal plasma LH and FSH, however, are significantly lower than normal, as has been previously shown (14,18,19). The normal quantitative response to LRF in our patients does not agree with the observation of others (14,19). Our patients are older with a longer duration of disease than those previously reported, but other than these factors, we cannot explain the discrepancies.

Hypothalamic Function

Fully 44% of patients with anorexia nervosa have partial diabetes insipidus. This is a smaller percentage than originally reported by Mecklenburg et al. (9) but is nevertheless a specific hypothalamic function which is disordered in this illness.

Patients with anorexia nervosa have significant abnormalities of thermoregulation in both hot and cold environments. They do not shiver in the cold and have abnormal $\Delta T°/\Delta t$ in response to 30 min of hypo- or hyperthermia. The hypothalamus plays a central role in thermoregulation (9,17), and, therefore, abnormalities of this parameter constitute strong evidence for hypothalamic dysfunction. It is of some interest that the thermoregulatory abnormality is more severe at 49°C than at 10°C. This argues against the possibility that lack of adipose tissue is responsible for these changes. Furthermore, shivering is a hypothalamic function unrelated to the amount of adipose tissue.

Delayed TSH release after TRF has been reported to be suggestive of hypothalamic disease (5,7). We have previously reported (18) and confirm here that the delayed release is more generalized and includes the response of LH and FSH to LRF and of TSH and PRL to TRF. Low plasma T_3, high reverse T_3, and/or low plasma estradiol may contribute toward these abnormal kinetics (18). Alternatively, the clearance of the pituitary hormones in anorexia nervosa may be slow, a hypothesis as yet untested. That low plasma T_3 levels are not by themselves responsible for delayed TSH release is suggested by the data of Chopra et al. (4), who found a normal time of peak TSH after TRF in patients with low T_3 secondary to hepatic cirrhosis.

The constellation of low basal plasma LH and FSH with a normal quantitative response to exogenous LRF suggests that the pituitary is capable of synthesizing and releasing gonadotropins and that an abnormality of endogenous LRF exists. This may be due to low endogenous LRF levels or an abnormal form of LRF. The concept of hypothalamic hypogonadotropism in anorexia nervosa is supported by the data of Yoshimoto et al. (20), who produced acute LRF responsiveness with 3 to 5 days of 400 μg of LRF, and those of Nillius et al. (13), who produced follicular maturation with the administration of exogenous LRF.

In addition to the above, the lack of diurnal cortisol variation and the elevated basal GH levels suggest hypothalamic dysfunction.

Hypothalamic functions which appear to be normal are those regulating the PRL axis and the GH rise associated with delta-wave sleep.

CONCLUSIONS

That patients with anorexia nervosa have a primary hypothalamic *disease* is unclear. What is clear, however, is that these patients have disordered hypothalamic *function*. The hypothesis that this dysfunction is secondary to the weight change itself is supported by the correlations of the severity of weight loss and the severity of abnormalities of thermoregulation, time of peak TSH after TRF, quantitative gonadotropin response within the group, and basal plasma GH. Furthermore, a group of patients with secondary amenorrhea associated with weight loss (but who do not have anorexia nervosa), and whose percent below IBW is intermediate between normal and anorexia nervosa, are also intermediate in the severity of the specific hypothalamic tests (18). Patients with anorexia nervosa may also have pituitary dysfunction, but this, again, may be secondary to long-standing hypothalamic dysfunction. The hypothesis that anorexia nervosa may be a model of hypothalamic dysfunction, if valid, should then allow more rational approaches to therapy, which may include drugs that act at the hypothalamic level.

ACKNOWLEDGMENT

We would like to thank Ronald H. Thompson, Ph.D., for performing the thermoregulatory studies.

REFERENCES

1. Beumont, P. J. V., George, G. C. W., Pimstone, B. L., and Vinik, A. I. (1976): Body weight and the pituitary response to hypothalamic releasing hormones in patients with anorexia nervosa. *J. Clin. Endocrinol. Metab.,* 43:487–596.
2. Boyar, R. M., Kapen, S., Finkelstein, J. S., Fukishima, D. K., Weitzman, E. D., and Hellman, L. (1974): Delineation of the luteinizing hormone (LH) and cortisol (F) abnormalities in anorexia nervosa. *Abst. Am. Soc. Clin. Invest.,* 9a.
3. Bradlow, H. L., Boyar, R. M., O'Connor, J., Zumoff, B., and Hellman, L. (1976): Hypothyroid-like alterations in testosterone metabolism in anorexia nervosa. *J. Clin. Endocrinol. Metab.,* 43:571–574.
4. Chopra, I. J., Solomon, D., Chopra, U., Young, R. T., and Chua Teco, G. N. (1974): Alterations in circulating thyroid hormones and thyrotropin in hepatic cirrhosis: evidence for euthyroidism despite subnormal serum triiodothyronine. *J. Clin. Endocrinol. Metab.,* 39:501–511.
5. Faglia, G. P., Beck-Peccoz, P., Ferrari, C., Ambrosi, B., Spada, A., Travaglini, P., and Parocchi, S. (1975): Plasma thyrotropin-releasing hormone in patients with pituitary and hypothalamic disorders. *J. Clin. Endocrinol. Metab.,* 37:596–601.
6. Feighner, J. P., Robins, E., Guze, S. B., Woodruff, R. A., Jr., Winokur, G., and Munoz, R. (1972): Diagnostic criteria for use in psychiatric research. *Arch. Gen. Psychiatry,* 26:57–63.
7. Hall, R., Ornston, B. J., Besser, G. M., Cryer, R. J., and McKendrick, M. (1972): The thyrotropin-releasing hormone test in disease of the pituitary and hypothalamus. *Lancet,* 1:759–763.
8. Krieger, D. T., Allen, W., Rizzo, F., and Krieger, H. P. (1971): Characterization of the normal temporal pattern of plasma corticosteroid levels. *J. Clin. Endocrinol. Metab.,* 32:266–284.
9. Mecklenburg, R. S., Loriaux, D. L., Thompson, R. H., Andersen, A. E., and Lipsett, M. B. (1974): Hypothalamic dysfunction in patients with anorexia nervosa. *Medicine (Baltimore),* 53:147–159.
10. Miller, M., Dakas, T., Moses, A. M., Fellerman, H., and Streeten, D. (1970): Recognition of partial defects in antidiurectic hormone secretion. *Ann. Intern. Med.,* 73:721–729.
11. Miyai, K., Yamamoto, T., Azukizawa, M., Ishibashi, K., and Kumahara, Y. (1975): Serum thyroid hormones and thyrotropin in anorexia nervosa. *J. Clin. Endocrinol. Metab.,* 40:334–338.
12. Moshang, T., Jr., Parks, J. S., Baker, L., Vaidya, V., Utiger, R., Bongiovanni, A. M., and Snyder, P. J. (1975): Low serum triiodothyronine in patients with anorexia nervosa. *J. Clin. Endocrinol. Metab.,* 40:470–473.
13. Nillius, S. J., Fries, H., and Wide, L. (1975): Successful induction of follicular matura-

tion and ovulation by prolonged treatment with LH-releasing hormone in women with anorexia nervosa. *Am. J. Obstet. Gynecol.,* 122:921–928.
14. Sherman, B. M., Halmi, K. A., and Zamudio, R. (1975): LH and FSH response to gonadotropin releasing hormone in anorexia nervosa: effect of nutritional rehabilitation. *J. Clin. Endocrinol. Metab.,* 41:135–142.
15. Smith, S. R., Bledsoe, T., and Chhetri, M. K. (1975): Cortisol metabolism and the pituitary-adrenal axis in adults with protein calorie malnutrition. *J. Clin. Endocrinol. Metab.,* 40:43–52.
16. Tolis, G., Goldstein, M., and Friesen, H. G. (1973): Functional evaluation of prolactin secretion in patients with hypothalamic-pituitary disorders. *J. Clin. Invest.,* 52:783–788.
17. Vigersky, R. A., Loriaux, D. L., Andersen, A. E., and Lipsett, M. B. (1976): Anorexia nervosa: behavioural and hypothalamic aspects. *Clin. Endocrinol. Metab.,* 5:517–535.
18. Vigersky, R. A., Loriaux, D. L., Andersen, A. E., Mecklenburg, R. S., and Vaitukaitis, J. L. (1976): Delayed pituitary hormone response to LRF and TRF in patients with anorexia nervosa and with secondary amenorrhea associated with simple weight loss. *J. Clin. Endocrinol. Metab.,* 43:893–900.
19. Warren, M. P., and Vande Wiele, R. (1973): Clinical and metabolic features of anorexia nervosa. *Am. J. Obstet. Gynecol.,* 117:435–449.
20. Yoshimoto, Y., Moridera, K., and Imura, H. (1975): Restoration of normal pituitary gonadotropin reserve by administration of luteinizing-hormone-releasing hormone in patients with hypogonadotropic hypogonadism. *N. Engl. J. Med.,* 292:242–245.

Anorexia Nervosa, edited by
R. A. Vigersky. Raven Press,
New York © 1977.

Endocrine Profiles in Anorexia Nervosa

Gregory M. Brown, Paul E. Garfinkel, Nikolai Jeuniewic,
Harvey Moldofsky, and Harvey C. Stancer

Clarke Institute of Psychiatry, Toronto, Ontario, Canada M5T 1R8

INTRODUCTION

A variety of endocrine alterations have been reported in patients with anorexia nervosa. Because of these widespread effects, anorexia nervosa was confused with hypopituitarism until a number of differences were elaborated (27). Even today, there is disagreement as to the endocrine abnormalities present in anorexia nervosa. There is most agreement regarding the abnormality in gonadotropins in anorexia nervosa. Immaturity of circadian pattern of plasma luteinizing hormone (LH) (6) together with lowered daytime levels (3,12) and reduced responsiveness to clomiphene (3,20) and to luteinizing hormone–releasing hormone (LHRH) (23,28,30) have all been reported. Other reports are, however, less consistent: plasma cortisol (9,13,16,19) and plasma growth hormone (13,15,16,18,19) are reported as normal or elevated. Patients have also been reported as euthyroid (5,9, 13,25,26,31), although reduced levels of thyroxine and triiodothyronine have been described (22). Each of these alterations involves an abnormality in pituitary function, which is, in turn, dependent on hypothalamic function. Hormonal findings, therefore, have been postulated to be secondary to disturbed hypothalamic function.

It is now established that release of hormones from the anterior pituitary gland is controlled by hypothalamic-hypophyseal hormones (21). Three of these hormones have been identified to date: namely, thyrotropin-releasing hormone, luteinizing hormone–releasing hormone, and somatostatin (Fig. 1). Each of these hormones was initially characterized on the basis of action on a single pituitary hormone. However, each hypothalamic hormone has a dual action in normal individuals: thus, thyrotropin-releasing hormone in addition to releasing thyrotropin causes release of prolactin; luteinizing hormone–releasing hormone causes secretion of both LH and follicle-stimulating hormone, and somatostatin, which inhibits growth hormone release, also inhibits the secretion of thyrotropin (21). There is also considerable evidence that the hypothalamic factor inhibiting prolactin is dopamine, although the possibility of a separate peptide substance inhibiting dopamine has not been excluded (7).

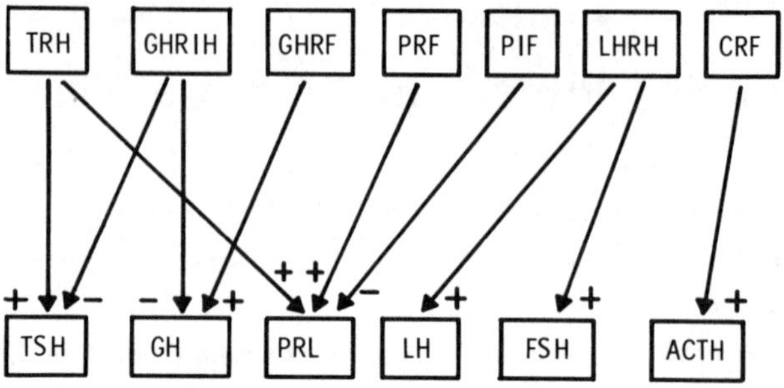

FIG. 1. Hypothalamic hormones (*upper boxes*) control release of anterior pituitary hormones (*lower boxes*) as indicated by the arrows. Identified hypothalamic hormones: TRH, thyrotropin-releasing hormone; GHRIH, somatostatin; LHRH, luteinizing hormone–releasing hormone; PIF, prolactin-inhibiting factor (dopamine).

Hypothalamic hormones whose structure is still unknown: GHRF, growth hormone–releasing factor; PRF, prolactin-releasing factor; CRF, corticotropin-releasing factor.

Anterior pituitary hormones: TSH, thyrotropin; GH, growth hormone; PRL, prolactin; LH, luteinizing hormone; FSH, follicle-stimulating hormone; ACTH, corticotropin.

From the foregoing, it is obvious that alteration in a single hypothalamic hormone would be an unlikely cause of the diversity of endocrine abnormalities that have been reported. The possibility must, therefore, be considered that the various endocrine features may be related to alterations in different hypothalamic mechanisms. In order to examine the hypothalamic-pituitary interrelationships with the clinical features of anorexia nervosa, we have examined 16 patients, paying particular attention to their nutritional status and to the course of the disorder.

EXPERIMENTAL METHOD

Of the 16 patients studied, only 1 was male (Table 1). All patients conformed with the criteria of Feighner et al. (10) for the diagnosis of anorexia nervosa. Female subjects all had secondary amenorrhea. Patients were studied on the clinical investigation unit of the Clarke Institute of Psychiatry. They were allowed free choice of diet until testing was complete. Caloric intake of each patient was observed and reported daily in all but patients 1 and 2. Patients were also weighed daily prior to breakfast while dressed in a hospital gown. At the time of testing, both the weight and caloric intake were noted. At the time of initial study, 13 of the 16 patients had a weight loss of 25% or greater, whereas 3 patients were studied during recovery from weight loss. In addition, 4 patients were retested after regaining weight. Duration of amenorrhea ranged from 4 months to 70 months (i.e., close to 6 years).

Patients were treated with an operant conditioning approach that rewarded weight gain (14). Only two patients received drugs: patient 6 re-

TABLE 1. *Clinical data*

Patient	Sex	Duration of amenorrhea prior to testing (months)	% Weight loss from standard	Caloric intake (cal/day)
1[a]	F	4	34	Poor
2	F	16	29	Poor
3	F	10	45	2,500
4	F	17	40	2,000
5	F	12	34	>4,000
6[a]	F	70	36	<1,500
7	F	25	37	1,800–2,000
8[a]	F	45	26	1,000–1,300
9[a]	M	–	48	800–1,200
10	F	16	13	2,000–2,500
11	F	18	0	1,000[b]
12	F	41	20	1,800–2,400
13	F	37	25	1,000–1,500
14	F	7	33	<1,200
15	F	13	28	1,800–2,200
16	F	22	35	<1,200

[a] Retested after regaining weight.
[b] This patient was unusual in maintaining a weight of 60 kg on an intake of 1,000 calories.

ceiving diazepam 10 mg/day as a bedtime hypnotic, and patient 9 receiving furosemide 40 mg/day for edema (13).

Testosterone, growth hormone, cortisol, and LH were measured as previously described (13). Prolactin and thyroid-stimulating hormone (TSH) were measured by radioimmunoassay with materials supplied by NIAMDD.

RESULTS

Growth Hormone

Growth hormone was found to be elevated in 8 out of 16 patients (Table 2), thus confirming observations made originally by Landon and co-workers in 1966 (16). In an earlier report (13) based on the first 9 patients in this study, we demonstrated a clear association of elevated plasma growth hormone levels with the nutritional status of the patients. We also noticed that in 4 of these patients studied after weight restoration, growth hormone levels decreased to normal. In confirmation of our previous study we find, in this expanded study, that resting morning levels of plasma growth hormone (GH) (Fig. 2) are significantly higher in those patients who have poor caloric intake (mean 16.4 ± SE 6.4; $N = 8$; versus 2.3 ± 0.6; $N = 8$; $t = 4.0$; $p = 0.001$ for log GH). No correlation was found between resting

TABLE 2. *Endocrine data*

Patient	T_3 resin uptake (%)	T_4 (μg/100 ml)	A.M. Plasma cortisol (μg/100 ml)	Blood glucose (mg/100 ml)	Plasma GH (ng/ml)	Plasma LH (μg/100 ml)	Plasma TSH (μU/ml)
1	36.7[a]	5.6	16.5	66	59.0	4.3	
2	27.0[a]	9.3	34.4	57	13.5	2.7	
3	29.0[a]	7.5	27.6	70	2.6	1.0	
4	27.2[a]	5.0	14.6	71	0.4	1.2	
5	47.7	7.1	14.3	76	1.0	2.1	
6	39.6	5.9	15.4	91	6.0	1.0	
7	55.5	8.5	30.0	97	0.6	1.8	
8	58	5.3	19.8	72	3.4	0.4	
9	35	8.5	19.0	70	19.3	0.8	
10			30.6	61	1.7	1.9	4.9
11	38	6.1	19.7	89	2.3	3.7	7.2
12	49	4.6	8.9	70	4.3	7.1	7.9
13	42	4.0	18.0	74	16.5	2.9	10.2
14	43	6.4	16.4	72	4.0	1.2	4.0
15	40	7.0	18.0	82	5.6	4.9	7.3
16			16.8	78	9.2	2.0	10.9

[a] Normal range differs from later subjects. For statistical analysis these data were transformed.

growth hormone levels and the percentage of weight loss or with the resting levels of any of the other hormones studied. GH levels also did not correlate with the duration of time since the onset of amenorrhea. The relationship of elevation of GH to poor nutrition in patients with anorexia nervosa was independently confirmed by Frankel and Jenkins in 1975 (11). They also confirmed that the elevation in resting GH levels was normalized by refeeding. In our earlier study, we reported that patients with elevated

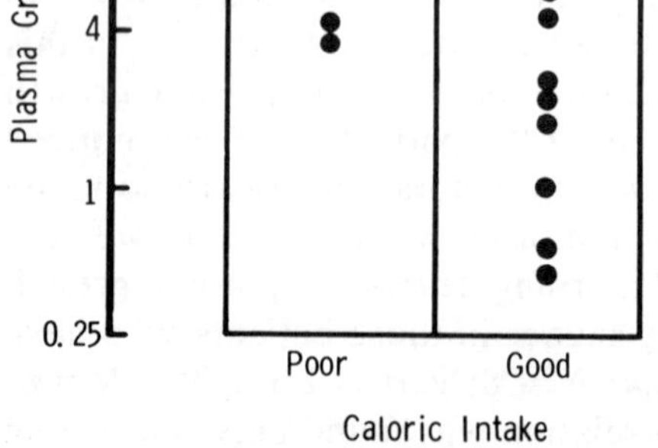

FIG. 2. Resting morning GH is higher in patients with poor caloric intake (Patients 1, 2, 6, 8, 9, 13, 14, 16) than in those with good caloric intake (Patients 3, 4, 5, 7, 10, 11, 12, 15).

resting GH levels uniformly showed a drop in growth hormone following glucose administration with a rebound to elevated levels thereafter. Frankel and Jenkins (11) also noted suppression of the elevated GH levels by a glucose load. However, in one of their patients they noted a paradoxical elevation in growth hormone following glucose. A paradoxical rise in GH following oral glucose in some patients with anorexia nervosa has been reported by Alvarez and co-workers (1) and Vanderlaan et al. (29). The reason for the discrepancy between these studies and the one reported here is not clear, although it may be related to the nature of the glucose stimulus and dose used.

Elevated levels of resting GH levels have been shown in a variety of states in which there is decreased caloric intake, including protein-calorie malnutrition, kwashiorkor, and marasmus (24). In kwashiorkor, normalization of GH occurs after protein refeeding but not after carbohydrate (24). The lack of relationship of GH levels to the degree of body weight loss and to duration of amenorrhea together with the finding that GH levels were elevated only in those with poor caloric intake strongly supports the contention that the elevation is secondary to starvation. Moreover, it is clear that weight alone is not related to the elevation in GH. Patients 3, 4, 5, and 7 who had weight loss ranging between 34 and 45% at the time of study all had good nutrition and had low growth hormone levels in the normal range. In contrast, patients 1, 6, 9, 14, and 16 who had similar weight loss—namely, between 33 and 48%—all had elevated growth hormone levels and had a poor caloric intake at the time of study.

Adrenal Function

Elevated morning plasma cortisol was found in 6 of our 16 patients as has been reported by others (1,16,19,29). In contrast to the findings with growth hormone, we found no significant relationship of plasma cortisol with caloric intake. In patients with poor caloric intake, mean (±SE) plasma cortisol was 19.5 ± 2.2 μg/100 ml ($N = 8$), compared to 20.5 ± 2.9 μg/100 ml ($N = 8$) in patients who were eating well. No correlation was found between cortisol levels and extent of weight loss or between cortisol and the duration of amenorrhea. Moreover, there was no correlation between resting cortisol levels and levels of glucose, luteinizing hormone, or TSH.

A significant correlation of 0.733 ($N = 14, p < 0.001$) was found between plasma cortisol and plasma thyroxine (Fig. 3). This relationship may occur because both substances are bound to globulins in plasma. It is known that levels of binding globulins may differ from individual to individual. Although the binding globulins for thyroxine and cortisol are not identical, it is likely that factors that affect one globulin could also affect another. Thus, with altered food intake the synthesis of both globulins might change resulting in similar changes in the two hormones. There is precedent for

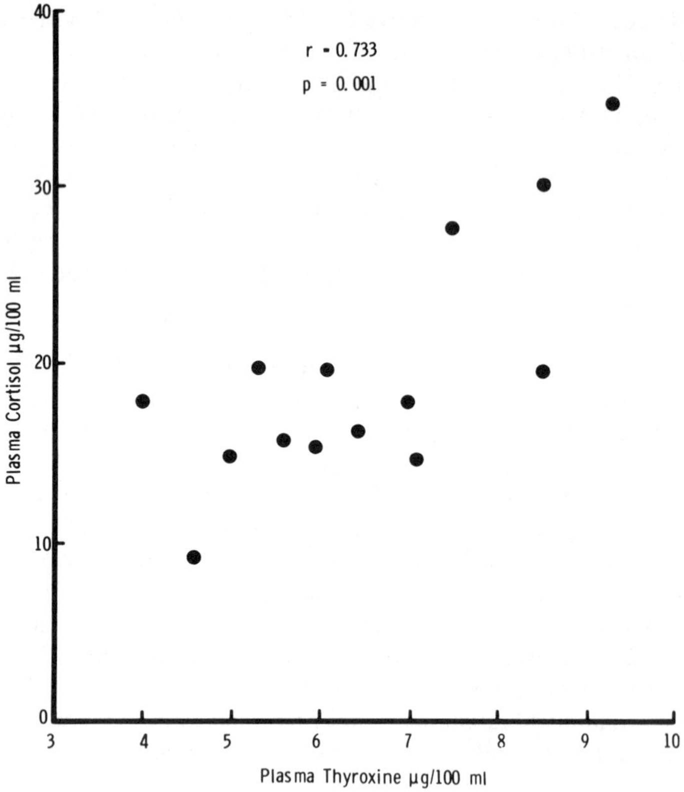

FIG. 3. Relationship of resting morning plasma cortisol and thyroxine levels.

such an effect as a decrease in cortisol binding in serum is found in kwashiorkor (17).

The nature of the factor which leads to elevation in cortisol in patients with anorexia nervosa is not clear as the elevation is not significantly correlated with calorie intake, weight loss, or duration of amenorrhea. However, the situation is complicated by the fact that cortisol is secreted episodically during the day so that resting morning samples taken at one time of the day do not give a full picture of adrenal function. Measures which give a better indication of the 24-hr pattern, such as urine free cortisol or frequent blood sampling through an indwelling cannula, may be required in order to better understand the altered adrenal function seen in these patients. Reduction in cortisol binding may also obscure elevation in plasma cortisol. In kwashiorkor, a decrease in cortisol binding in serum is found (2,17) so that the total cortisol is in the normal range even though the physiologically active free fraction is elevated (17).

Luteinizing Hormone

In the group of 16 patients that we have studied to date, there is a significant correlation (Fig. 4) between resting levels of LH and weight loss (−0.471; $N = 16$; $p = 0.033$). In contrast, there was no relationship of resting plasma LH levels to caloric intake, duration of amenorrhea, or resting levels of any of the other hormones studied. These findings agree with other reports (3) that plasma LH levels are reduced in some patients with anorexia nervosa but indicate that this lowering is related to the weight loss and not to the caloric intake. Boyar (6) has found that there is immaturity of the 24-hr LH secretory pattern in patients with anorexia nervosa. It is probable that the low morning LH levels seen in the present study reflect a prepubertal state of the patients. It has also been postulated that in normal pubertal girls menarche occurs at a critical weight (12).

In seven patients, the LH response to clomiphene was examined (Table 3). In these patients, this response was significantly correlated with weight loss (−0.834; $N = 7$; $p = 0.01$) (Fig. 5). Three patients with poor caloric intake had significantly smaller mean (±SE) LH responses to clomiphene (1.5 ± 0.76 μg/100 ml) than four patients with good caloric intake (9.3 ± 1.25 μg/100 ml). However, there was a major difference in weight loss between these two groups suggesting that this difference was actually due to the greater weight loss in the poorly nourished group. The LH response to clomiphene showed no relation to the duration of amenorrhea and was not significantly correlated with the resting level of any of the hormones studied.

Plasma LH response to LHRH infusion (Fig. 6) also showed a significant correlation with weight loss (−0.78; $N = 7$; $p = 0.02$). Plasma LH

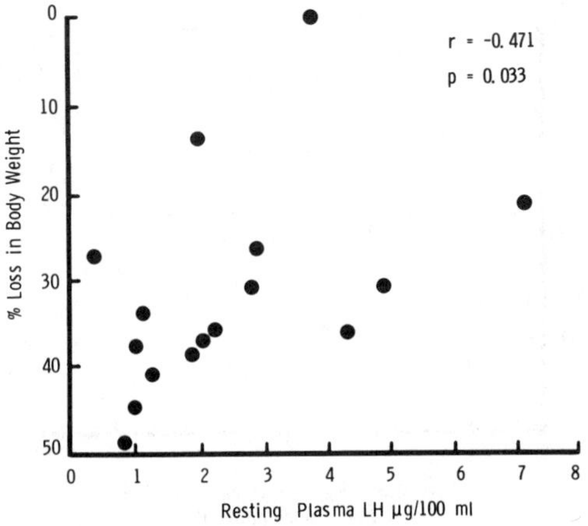

FIG. 4. Relationship of resting morning plasma luteinizing hormone to weight loss.

TABLE 3. *Peak hormone responses after clomiphene, TRH, and LHRH*

Patient	Increment in plasma LH after clomiphene (100 mg daily × 5)[a]	Increment in plasma TSH after TRH (500 μg)[b]	Increment in plasma LH after LHRH (100 μg)[a]
10	12	30.1	21.2
11	10	26.9	75.9
12	9	25.1	31.7
13	2.5	30.8	9.0
14	2.0	10.5	14.5
15	6.0	19.9	38.9
16	0.1	37.2	13.4

[a] μg/100 ml.
[b] μU/ml.

response (mean ±SE) to LHRH infusion was also significantly lower in the three patients with poor caloric intake (12.3 ± 1.7 μg/100 ml) than in the four patients with good caloric intake (41.9 ± 11.9 μg/100 ml). As is the case for LH responses to clomiphene, this apparent effect may be due to the greater weight loss rather than to reduced caloric intake.

In this study, a reduced LH response to clomiphene and a reduced LH response to LHRH showed a significant correlation with weight loss, in the same fashion as resting plasma LH showed a significant correlation with weight loss. These findings indicate that in patients with the lowest weight, not only was there a reduced resting level of plasma LH, there was also a reduced responsivity to the two agents which we used to stimulate LH secretion; namely, clomiphene and LHRH. These findings are in keep-

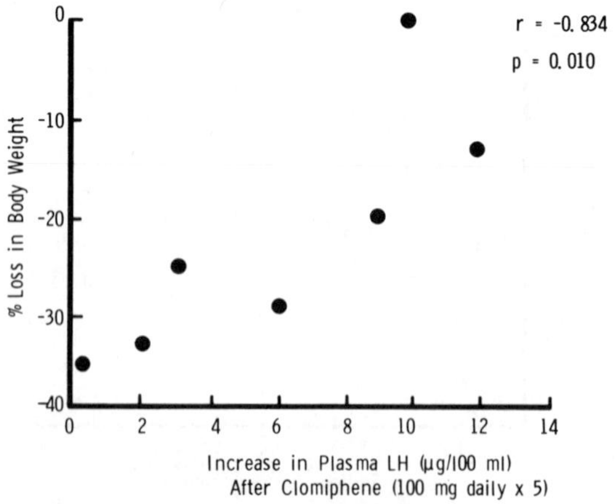

FIG. 5. Relationship of luteinizing hormone response to clomiphene (100 mg daily for 5 days) with weight loss.

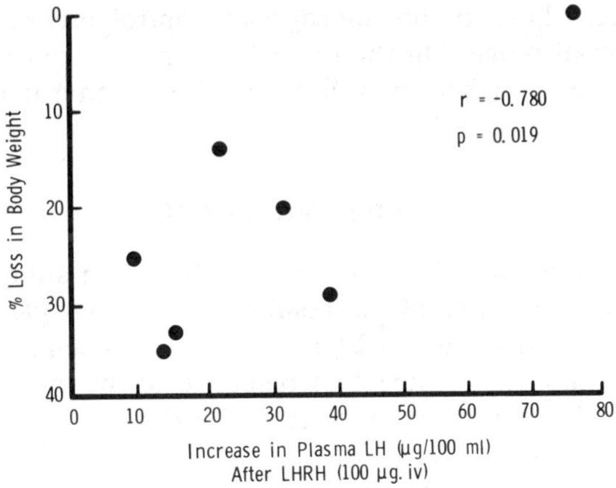

FIG. 6. Relationship of luteinizing hormone response to LHRH (100 μg i.v.) with weight loss.

ing with those of Beumont and co-workers (3) and of Marshall and Fraser (20), who showed that clomiphene is effective in increasing LH only in patients who had regained weight. A correlation of the LH response to LHRH with weight has been shown by other workers (23,28,30). Recently, Beumont and co-workers (4) have also shown a linear relationship of resting LH and of LH response to LHRH with body weight. In the present study, no correlation of resting plasma LH was found with caloric intake or the duration of amenorrhea even though there was a clear-cut correlation with weight loss.

Thyroid Function

Plasma thyroxine levels showed no significant correlation with percentage of weight loss or caloric intake. As mentioned previously, there was a significant correlation of plasma thyroxine and plasma cortisol. However, plasma thyroxine levels were not correlated with levels of any other hormone studied. T_3 resin uptake showed no significant relationship with weight loss, duration of amenorrhea, or caloric intake. Resting plasma TSH was measured in seven subjects. It showed no significant relationship with weight loss, duration of amenorrhea, or caloric intake. None of the patients investigated had abnormal TSH values. It thus appears that the patients we studied were all euthyroid. We confirm the finding of Beumont et al. (4) that plasma TSH is normal in anorexia nervosa. These findings are in contrast to those of Lundberg and co-workers (18), who found low TSH levels in three of eight patients, and with those of Miyai and co-workers (22), who found a significant lowering of serum thyroxine in patients with anorexia nervosa. However, in the latter study, although thyroxine levels were lower than those of an appropriate control group, they were not outside the normal range. On the other hand, patients with protein-calorie malnutrition have a higher dialyzable fraction of thyroxine than normal subjects (8).

TSH Response to TRH

The TSH response to TRH (500 μg i.v.) has been studied in seven patients. Preliminary analysis of the results shows that a clear-cut elevation of TSH occurred in response to TRH in all seven patients (Table 3). There was no relationship of the height of response to the loss in body weight, to the duration of amenorrhea, or to the caloric intake. The TSH response to TRH was significantly correlated with the resting TSH levels (0.73; $N = 7$; $p = 0.03$) but not with those of any other hormone studied. Miyai and co-workers (22) reported that the TSH response to TRH was delayed in patients with anorexia nervosa. This was not the case in the seven patients studied by us. Six of the seven showed a peak at 45 min. The responses observed ranged from 10.5 to 37.2 μU/ml and were well within normal limits. Our findings, therefore, agree well with those of Beumont and co-workers (4), who conclude that resting TSH and TSH responses to TRH are not abnormal in anorexia nervosa.

Hormone Profiles During Sleep

Repeated endocrine-sleep studies were performed in collaboration with a group at McMaster University[1] in a 20-year-old patient with anorexia nervosa. She was first studied soon after admission, 10 months after the onset of amenorrhea when her weight was down to 64% of her initial weight. She was studied again on two occasions while regaining weight when she was at 77 and 85% of the original weight. The final investigation was done after she again started to lose weight and her weight was 82% of her usual weight. Although the data are not completely analyzed, hormonal findings (on blood obtained every 20 min) during the first 2 hr of sleep (as monitored by EEG) are of considerable interest. On the first occasion when weight was 64% of initial weight, GH levels were high (>25 ng/ml) while LH was low (0.9 to 1.2 μg/100 ml), and prolactin was low normal (3.7 to 6.6 ng/ml). During recovery of weight, dramatic changes were found in these hormone measures on two separate occasions. GH levels became low (< 1.0 to 7.6) and on the first occasion showed no early-onset peak with all samples having undetectable levels. LH levels were higher (1.9 to 3.5), and prolactin was higher (4.2 to 15.4). On the final occasion, 2 weeks later, as she started to lose weight again, the findings

[1] Studied in collaboration with J. M. Cleghorn, V. Ward, L. H. Bernstein, and R. D. Kaplan.

reverted to the initial pattern with high GH (6.1 to 13.4), low LH (<1.0 to 1.0), and low-normal prolactin (1.0 to 6.8).

Although it is not possible to generalize from findings in this single subject, this case is nevertheless of considerable interest. In this patient, the endocrine findings changed rapidly, and yet another hormone, prolactin, showed an alteration in relation to nutritional status. It appears that endocrine-sleep studies with simultaneous monitoring of several pituitary hormones would be a valuable approach to the investigation of anorexia nervosa.

CONCLUSION

On the basis of the present findings, and a survey of the current literature, a number of conclusions appear to be warranted.

1. A variety of endocrine abnormalities may be seen in anorexia nervosa. These abnormalities are related to different clinical features of the disorder.
2. With poor nutritional status, as evidenced by low caloric intake, an elevation in growth hormone is seen. This elevation is readily reversed by refeeding, and the high growth hormone drops rapidly in response to a glucose load. The elevation is unrelated to body weight.
3. With loss in body weight, resting levels of plasma LH are reduced and inadequate LH responses to clomiphene and to LHRH are found. These findings are reversed as body weight is regained. In contrast to change in growth hormone, alterations in caloric intake produce no rapid changes in plasma LH.
4. Elevated plasma cortisol, seen in some but not all patients with anorexia nervosa, does not appear to be directly associated either with caloric intake or with body weight. To resolve this issue, detailed investigations of the hypothalamic-pituitary-adrenal axis will be necessary.
5. A correlation of resting plasma cortisol and plasma thyroxine has been found. Although the basis of this relationship is unknown, it may be speculated that with inadequate nutrition similar alterations in protein binding could occur for both hormones.

REFERENCES

1. Alvarez, L. C., Dimas, C. O., Castro, A., Rossman, L. G., Vanderlaan, E. F., and Vanderlaan, W. P. (1972): Growth hormone in malnutrition. *J. Clin. Endocrinol. Metab.*, 34:400–409.
2. Beas, F., Ferreira, E., and Rivarola, M. (1973): Adrenal cortical function in infants as seen in Chile. In: *Endocrine Aspects of Malnutrition, Marasmus, Kwashiorkor and*

Psychosocial Dwarfism, edited by L. I. Gardner and P. Amacher, pp. 343–353. Kroc Foundation, Saint Ynez, California.
3. Beumont, P. J. V., Carr, P. J., and Gelder, M. G. (1973): Plasma levels of luteinizing hormone and of immunoreactive oestrogens (oestradiol) in anorexia nervosa: response to clomiphene citrate. *Psychol. Med.,* 3:495–501.
4. Beumont, P. J. V., George, G. C. W., Pimstone, B. L., and Vinik, A. I. (1976): Body weight and the pituitary response to hypothalamic releasing hormones in patients with anorexia nervosa. *J. Clin. Endocrinol. Metab.,* 43:487–496.
5. Bliss, E. L., and Migeon, C. J. (1957): Endocrinology of anorexia nervosa. *J. Clin. Endocrinol. Metab.,* 17:766–776.
6. Boyar, R. M., Katz, J., Finkelstein, J. W., Kapen, S., Weiner, H., Weitzman, E. D., and Hellman, L. (1974): Anorexia nervosa: immaturity of the 24-hour luteinizing hormone secretory pattern. *N. Engl. J. Med.,* 291:861–865.
7. Brown, G. M., Seeman, P., and Lee, T. (1976): Dopamine/neuroleptic receptors in basal hypothalamus and pituitary. *Endocrinology,* 99:1407–1410.
8. Chopra, I. J., and Smith, S. R. (1975): Circulating thyroid hormones and thyrotropin in adult patients with protein-calorie malnutrition. *J. Clin. Endocrinol. Metab.,* 40:221–227.
9. Danowski, T. S., Livstone, E., Gonzales, A. R., Jung, Y., and Khurana, R. C. (1972): Fractional and partial hypopituitarism in anorexia nervosa. *Horm. Res.,* 3:105–118.
10. Feighner, J. P., Robins, E., Guze, S. B., Woodruff, R. A., Jr., Winokur, G., and Munoz, R. (1972): Diagnostic criteria for use in psychiatric research. *Arch. Gen. Psychiatry,* 26:57–63.
11. Frankel, R. J., and Jenkins, J. S. (1975): Hypothalamic pituitary function in anorexia nervosa. *Acta Endocrinol.* (*Kbh.*), 78:209–221.
12. Frisch, R. E., and Revelle, R. (1971): Height and weight at menarche and a hypothesis of menarche. *Arch. Dis. Child.,* 46:695–701.
13. Garfinkel, P. E., Brown, G. M., Stancer, H. C., and Moldofsky, H. (1975): Hypothalamic-pituitary function in anorexia nervosa. *Arch. Gen. Psychiatry,* 32:739–744.
14. Garfinkel, P. E., Kline, S. A., and Stancer, H. C. (1973): Treatment of anorexia nervosa using operant conditioning techniques. *J. Nerv. Ment. Dis.,* 157:428–433.
15. Giordano, G., Marugio, M., Minuto, F., and Barreca, T. (1971): Somatotropin increment in grave emaciation: Preliminary results. *Folia Endocrinol.* (*Roma*), 24:308–315.
16. Landon, J., Greenwood, F. C., Stamp, T. C. B., and Wynn, V. (1966): The plasma sugar, free fatty acid, cortisol, and growth hormone response to insulin, and the comparison of this procedure with other tests of pituitary and adrenal function: II. In patients with hypothalamic or pituitary dysfunction or anorexia nervosa. *J. Clin. Invest.,* 45:437–449.
17. Leonard, P. J. (1973): Cortisol-binding in serum in kwashiorkor: East African studies. In: *Endocrine Aspects of Malnutrition, Marasmus, Kwashiorkor and Psychosocial Dwarfism,* edited by L. I. Gardner and P. Amacher, pp. 355–362. Kroc Foundation, Saint Ynez, California.
18. Lundberg, P. O., Walinder, J., Werner, I., and Wide, L. (1972): Effects of thyrotrophin-releasing hormone on plasma levels of TSH, FSH, LH and GH in anorexia nervosa. *Eur. J. Clin. Invest.,* 2:150–153.
19. Marks, V., Howorth, N., and Greenwood, F. C. (1965): Plasma growth-hormone levels in chronic starvation in man. *Nature,* 208:686–687.
20. Marshall, J. C., and Fraser, T. R. (1971): Amenorrhoea in anorexia nervosa: assessment and treatment with clomiphene citrate. *Br. Med. J.,* 4:590–592.
21. Martin, J. B., Reichlin, S., and Brown, G. M. (1977): *Clinical Neuroendocrinology.* F. A. Davis, Philadelphia (*in press*).
22. Miyai, K., Yamamoto, T., Azukizawa, M., Ishibashi, K., and Kumahara, Y. (1975): Serum thyroid hormones and thyrotropin in anorexia nervosa. *J. Clin. Endocrinol. Metab.,* 40:334–338.
23. Palmer, R. L., Crisp, A. H., Mackinnon, P. C. B., Franklin, M., Bonnar, J., and Wheeler, M. (1975): Pituitary sensitivity to 50 μg LH/FSH-RH in subjects with anorexia nervosa in acute and recovery stages. *Br. Med. J.,* 1:179–182.
24. Pimstone, B. L., Becker, D. J., and Hansen, J. D. L. (1973): Human growth hormone and sulphation factor in protein-calorie malnutrition. In: *Endocrine Aspects of Malnutrition, Marasmus, Kwashiorkor and Psychosocial Dwarfism,* edited by L. I. Gardner and P. Amacher, pp. 73–90. Kroc Foundation, Saint Ynez, California.

25. Pops, M. A., and Schwabe, A. D. (1968): Hypercarotenemia in anorexia nervosa. *J.A.M.A.*, 205:533–534.
26. Seidensticker, J. F., and Tzagournis, M. (1968): Anorexia nervosa—clinical features and long-term follow-up. *J. Chronic Dis.*, 21:361–367.
27. Sheehan, H. L., and Summers, V. K. (1949): The syndrome of hypopituitarism, *Q. J. Med.*, 18:319–378.
28. Sherman, B. M., Halmi, K. A., and Zamudio, R. (1975): LH and FSH response to gonadotropin-releasing hormone in anorexia nervosa: effect of nutritional rehabilitation. *J. Clin. Endocrinol. Metab.*, 41:135–142.
29. Vanderlaan, W. P., Parker, D. C., Rossman, L. G., and Vanderlaan, E. F. (1970): Implications of growth hormone release in sleep. *Metabolism,* 19:891–897.
30. Warren, M. P., Jewelewicz, R., Dyrenfurth, I., Ans, R., Khalaf, S., and Vande Wiele, R. L. (1975): The significance of weight loss in the evaluation of pituitary response to LH-RH in women with secondary amenorrhea. *J. Clin. Endocrinol. Metab.*, 40:601–611.
31. Warren, M. P., and Vande Wiele, R. L. (1973): Clinical and metabolic features of anorexia nervosa. *Am. J. Obstet. Gynecol.*, 117:435–449.

Anorexia Nervosa, edited by
R. A. Vigersky. Raven Press,
New York © 1977.

The Effect of the Nutritional Status and Weight Changes on Hypothalamic Function Tests in Anorexia Nervosa

*Regina C. Casper, **John M. Davis, and
†Ghanshyam N. Pandey

**Department of Research, Illinois State Psychiatric Institute, Chicago, Illinois 60612, and Department of Psychiatry, Abraham Lincoln School of Medicine, University of Illinois, Chicago, Ill. 60680; **Illinois State Psychiatric Institute and University of Chicago, Pritzker School of Medicine, Chicago, Ill. 60601; and †Biological Research Laboratory, Illinois State Psychiatric Institute, Chicago, Ill. 60612*

INTRODUCTION

Although Simmonds' publication in 1914 (35) on hypophyseal cachexia did not include cases of anorexia nervosa, his observations nevertheless implied the possibility that endocrine factors contributed to the cachectic state associated with anorexia nervosa and gave the impetus for investigating the endocrine aspects of this disorder. There is substantial evidence (3,11,18,24,28) that pituitary function is intact in anorexia nervosa, and the interest has shifted to the hypothalamic level (21,24,33).

The hypothalamus is of interest in anorexia nervosa for another reason. Food intake and its associated subjective sensations hunger and satiety have been shown (20,27) to depend, so far only in animals, on arrays of cells in the ventromedial nucleus and in the lateral hypothalamus in close proximity to the median forebrain bundle.

Although there is general agreement that anorexia or loss of appetite rarely occurs in anorexia nervosa (17), other characteristic features such as a remarkable ability to suppress or deny hunger feelings and the experience of fullness and satiety after relatively small amounts of food are eaten, as well as occasional and sometimes regular bouts of overeating, suggest a disturbed balance between the so-called hunger and satiety centers.

There is no direct way to study the functioning of these hypothalamic regions in the human, but with the development of the neuroendocrine strategy (16) hypothalamic function can be indirectly evaluated through the measurement of circulating pituitary hormones—such as plasma growth hormone—known to be under hypothalamic control.

The study of growth hormone is appropriate in anorexia nervosa because the hypothalamic neurosecretory cells governing its release and inhibition form part of a neuronal relay system, located in the ventromedial nucleus and the median eminence, respectively (6,7,26), and have been shown to be sensitive to changes in concentrations of glucose, a metabolite which also influences feeding behavior (20,27).

The effects of starvation on both a psychological and biological level are intimately involved in the symptomatology and the endocrine changes of anorexia nervosa (10,33). One way to disentangle the effects of malnutrition would be through repeat testing of endocrine and metabolic measures after improved nutrition and weight gain. We took this approach, and in this study we are reporting on the growth hormone release pattern during a glucose tolerance test and after s.c. administration of subemetic doses of apomorphine, a dopaminergic substance, in patients with anorexia nervosa on admission and after weight gain.

METHODS

Female patients with anorexia nervosa, ages 12 to 32, conforming to Feighner's diagnostic criteria (13), were admitted to a psychiatric research unit. All medication was discontinued at least 10 days prior to testing. Most of the patients consumed, by their own choice, between 400 and 900 calories daily as recorded by a dietician. Patients were kept fasting after midnight, and all tests were started between 8 and 8:30 A.M. A 19-gauge scalp vein needle was placed in a forearm vein and kept patent with heparinized saline. Blood samples for growth hormone were withdrawn twice at 30-min intervals for base-line values and at various intervals after the injection of apomorphine (0.011 μg/kg) subcutaneously (e.g., 0.75 mg for a 70 kg woman). Initially we gave 0.75 mg apomorphine; however, two patients for whom this dose was used experienced strong nausea and retching, and subsequently the dose was adjusted based on weight. Nausea and drowsiness were experienced by all our patients after apomorphine injection. A normal response was defined as an increase in the GH level above 6 ng/ml, occurring 60 $\pm$ 20 min following the injection (12).

In the glucose tolerance (GT) test, a glucose load of 1.75 g/kg dextrose in the form of orangedex was administered orally, and blood was withdrawn at various intervals for the next 3 hr. The tests were repeated before discharge (after weight gain) when the daily caloric intake consisted of 2,000 to 3,000 calories. Part of the patient group received cyproheptadine. The plasma samples were stored at −20°C. Growth hormone was measured by a double-antibody radioimmunoassay (30). Human growth hormone antibody sera were kindly provided by the National Institute of Arthritis, Metabolism and Digestive Diseases. Serum proteins were measured as total solids and globulin determined with a colorimetric method. Serum glucose was determined by a colorimetric method using *o*-toluidine (15).

RESULTS

Growth hormone (GH) responses during a glucose tolerance test on admission and after weight gain were evaluated. All values were expressed as mean ± SD.

Table 1 shows the individual plasma GH and serum glucose levels during a GT test and their percentage of target weight adjusted for age and height. The mean weight loss for the patients was 35% of normal body weight, and the patients' food intake fluctuated between 400 and 900 cal/day. Fasting glucose levels were 71.8 ± 9.4 mg%. An impaired glucose tolerance curve with glucose concentrations exceeding 100 mg% after 180 min was observed in 11 out of 12 patients.

Basal plasma GH levels exceeded 5 ng/ml in 10 out of 12 patients. The mean ± SD GH level was 14.4 ± 5.6 ng/ml.

Most patients showed an unexpected rise in plasma GH levels after oral glucose, with only one patient showing the expected decline in plasma GH values. This was reflected in the plasma GH levels which rose from 14.4 ± 5.6 to 19.5 ± 17.3 ng/ml after 30 min with a peak of 21.0 ± 17.3 ng/ml at 1 hr and a slow but steady decline of GH levels thereafter with the lowest value of 9.8 ± 5.9 ng/ml after 3 hr.

After weight gain and with an increased nutritional intake (>2,000 cal/day), patients not only normalized their basal plasma GH levels, with a mean of 1.9 ± 1.4 ng/ml for the cyproheptadine (Periactin®) group and a mean of 4.04 ± 2.7 ng/ml for the placebo group, but GH levels remained low throughout the test (Table 2). The slightly elevated resting GH levels in two patients fell as anticipated in response to oral glucose, and one patient showed a secretory burst of GH after 120 min with the level rising to 19.9 ng/ml. The glucose tolerance curves essentially normalized after weight gain.

No significant differences were found in the GH or glucose response between the group of patients receiving placebo and the patients receiving cyproheptadine during treatment.

The observed changes between pretreatment plasma GH levels throughout the GT test and GH levels after weight gain were significant ($p < 0.03$; two-way analysis of variance); thus with increase in caloric intake and weight there was normalization of resting GH levels and the GH response to oral glucose.

The results of the apomorphine-stimulated GH response in patients with anorexia nervosa both on admission and after weight gain are shown in Tables 3 and 4.

Nine out of fourteen female patients with anorexia nervosa (Table 3) failed to show an increase in plasma GH levels of 6 ng/ml or more in response to apomorphine (12) before treatment. The absent or deficient GH rise cannot be due to an insufficient dose of apomorphine since Lal and co-workers (22) and Brown et al. (8) have shown a rise in GH after

TABLE 1. *Pretreatment plasma growth hormone and serum glucose levels after an oral glucose load (1.75 g/kg) in anorexia nervosa*

Patient	Growth hormone (ng/ml)						Glucose (mg%)						% Target weight
	0′	30′	60′	90′	120′	180′	0′	30′	60′	90′	120′	180′	
2	7.9	7.9	6.8	11.4	6.7	3.8	60	149	170	220	225	157	74
4	>20	>40	>40	>40	>20	>20	62	83	110	96	110	65	60
5	11.4	9.8	10.8	9.6	6.8	10.4	83	122	183	230	230	109	53
7	7.5	7.6	5.6	4.1	2.4	1.9	86	75	112	125	133	125	69
8	60.0	64.0	65.0	40.0	21.0	20.0	71	120	140	150	154	145	54
9	18.6	27.3	18.8	10.4	12.4	9.3	71	106	162	192	172	120	54
11	5.8	7.0	18.8	17.3	9.8	6.2	78	130	122	110	118	122	64
12	18.4	19.5	19.9	26.4	26.0	11.0	68	96	136	150	169	165	68
13	6.2	17.7	21.4	19.0	13.3	9.5	57	79	100	100	104	107	66
14	3.7	12.8	15.5	7.3	2.5	3.3	82	134	196	178	130	123	84
15	1.0	2.4	1.6	14.3	15.1	8.6	77	96	124	115	115	127	67
16	12.0	18.2	28.0	23.6	16.9	14.4	67	85	100	104	107	104	75
Mean	14.3	19.5	21.0	18.6	12.7	9.8	71.8	106.2	137.9	147.5	147.2	122.4	65.6
SD	15.6	17.3	17.3	11.9	7.4	5.9	9.4	24.3	32.7	47.4	44.0	26.2	9.4

Times are in minutes.

TABLE 2. *Plasma growth hormone and glucose levels after an oral glucose load (1.75 g/kg) in anorexia nervosa after weight gain*

	Growth hormone (ng/ml)						Glucose (mg%)						
Patient	0′	30′	60′	90′	120′	180′	0′	30′	60′	90′	120′	180′	% Target weight
Placebo group													
4	2.1	6.1	6.6	3.5	1.6	1.9	79	91	159	116	94	82	74
8	2.0	1.4	1.0	1.0	1.0	1.0	70	119	133	122	95	57	72
12	7.9	1.4	1.4	1.4	1.4	1.5	75	154	100	77	84	57	76
13	1.7	1.6	<1	<1	1.6	3.2	80	120	104	76	92	100	85
14	5.9	3.9	<1	<1	2	7.1	72	115	100	96	88	56	94
Mean	4.0	2.7	2.2	1.5	1.5	2.9	75.2	119.8	119.2	97.4	90.6	70.4	80.2
SD	2.7	2.1	2.4	1.0	0.3	2.4	4.32	22.4	26.1	21.3	4.5	19.8	±9.1
Cyproheptadine group													
2	5.0		2.6		1.6	3.1	71		61		77	79	90
5	2.4	3.4	<2	1.6	0.7	1.7	77	130	159	145	120	61	71
7	1.4	<1	<1	<1	1.2	1.2	80	118	115	111	86	94	81
9	2.1	4.4	2.0	2.3	1.7	2.3	70	103	157	153	92	89	71
11	0.8	1.6	1.6	2.3	2.9	6.1	57	73	96	84	57	77	78
15	<1	<1	1.6	2.6	19.9[a]	10.6[a]	75	107	93	61	68	75	82
16	<1	1.2	1.2	1.4	1.2	2.1	48	76	96	84	104	48	92
Mean	1.9	2.1	1.7	1.8	1.5	2.7	68.3	101.1	97.2	106.3	86.2	74.7	80.7
SD	1.4	1.4	0.5	0.6	0.7	1.7	11.6	22.7	51.1	36.7	21.4	15.8	±8.2

Times are in minutes.
[a] Not included in the calculation for the mean.

TABLE 3. *Pretreatment effect of apomorphine HCl on plasma growth hormone (ng/ml) in female anorexia nervosa patients*

Patient	Base line	Peak	Change	% Target weight	Disease duration (years)
2	4.4	22.0	+17.6	74	3
3	5.0	9.8	+ 4.8[a]	55	2
4	22.0	24.8	+ 2.8[a]	60	1
5	11.0	10.8	− 0.2[a]	53	6
6	1.7	1.9	+ 0.2[a]	70	4
7	1.0	2.7	+ 1.7[a]	69	4
8	2.9	13.2	+ 9.1	69	1
9	9.3	16.8	+ 7.5	54	5
10	1.1	1.96	+ 0.86[a]	67	5
12	13.5	44.0	+30.5	68	1.5
13	4.2	6.6	+ 2.2[a]	66	1.75
14	1.4	33.7	+32.3	84	2
15	2.8	6.4	+ 3.6[a]	67	0.58
16	12.5	11.2	− 1.3[a]	75	0.58
Mean	6.6	14.70	+ 7.97	69.8	2.67
SD	6.6	12.06	10.64		

[a] Growth hormone rise < 6 ng/ml.

half the amount (5.2 μg/kg) of apomorphine that was given to our patients. There was no significant correlation between lack of response and percent weight loss ($r = 0.41$) or disease duration ($r = 0.18$). Among the five responders to apomorphine, two had clearly elevated (9.3 ng/ml and 13.5 ng/ml) GH plasma levels.

After weight gain (Table 4) all fasting plasma GH levels, with one exception, were within normal range. The elevated GH concentration in patient 8 was probably due to activity since she was the only patient retested as an outpatient, after discharge.

After treatment five out of seven patients responded to apomorphine

TABLE 4. *Effect of apomorphine HCl on plasma growth hormone (ng/ml) after weight gain in female anorexia nervosa patients*

Patient	Base line	Peak	Change	% Target weight
4	1.6	10.1	+8.5	74
8	5.7	12.1	+6.4	100
12	2.3	2.3	0	76
13	1.4	15.2	+13.8	85
14	3.2	41.8	+38.6	94
15	1.3	18.8	+17.5[a]	82
16	1.0	1.0	0[a]	92
Mean	2.36	14.47	12.11	
SD	1.53	12.65	12.38	

[a] Patient received cyproheptadine.

normally, with a rise in GH beyond 6 ng/ml (Table 4). Three of the five responders had been nonresponders before weight gain. Of the two patients who did not respond, one had a positive response before treatment. Cyproheptadine, a serotonin antagonist, did not have a recognizable effect on growth hormone secretion in anorexia nervosa.

Serum proteins were within normal range with a total protein of 7.1 ± 0.3 g% before treatment and 7.1 ± 0.5 g% after weight gain. Pre- and post-treatment serum albumin (4.5 ± 0.1 and 4.6 ± 0.2 g%, respectively) and globulins (2.5 ± 0.1 and 2.5 ± 0.1, respectively) were unaffected by weight gain.

DISCUSSION

In our study improved nutrition and weight gain had a normalizing effect on the GH release pattern during the glucose tolerance test and after apomorphine as well as on resting growth hormone levels and the glucose tolerance curve.

These changes were noticeable because the majority of our anorexic patients had abnormal GH secretion curves during pretreatment.

In most of the severely malnourished patients, GH levels rose in response to oral glucose from already elevated resting levels. These findings are markedly different from observations in healthy adults, in whom hyperglycemia has an inhibiting effect on GH secretion (7,19). Such inhibition is difficult to prove in normals since resting GH levels are low and any further decrease is difficult to discern (38).

Vanderlaan et al. (36) have reported findings similar to ours. In eight out of ten patients with anorexia nervosa, plasma GH levels rose during a glucose tolerance test.

Garfinkel et al. (18) reported mixed results in anorexia nervosa: five patients showed a normal decline of elevated basal GH levels during the GT test; three of the patients had low resting GH levels with little change throughout the test, and in two patients GH levels rose after 90 min. One reason for these discrepancies might be that we used orangedex, a pure glucose solution which promptly raised blood glucose levels in most of our patients, whereas Garfinkel's group received glucola, containing 25% glucose and mostly di- and polysaccharides with only a few of the patients showing hyperglycemia. On retesting after weight gain, the data of Garfinkel et al. are in agreement with ours: continuous low GH levels throughout the GT test. Diabetic glucose tolerance curves have been described previously in anorexia nervosa (11,32,34,37) and in starvation (1,4). There is evidence that dietary intake, in particular the amount of carbohydrates consumed prior to the test, is associated with impaired glucose tolerance (9,32,34).

Even though the chemoreceptors of the emetic center in the medulla oblongata were sufficiently stimulated by apomorphine to produce nausea, the majority (64%) of patients with anorexia nervosa had no or deficient plasma growth hormone elevations, suggesting an impairment of hypothalamic receptor function. To our knowledge this is the first report on the use of apomorphine as a pharmacologic tool in anorexia nervosa. Ettigi et al. (12) found lower apomorphine-stimulated GH peaks in women without contraceptives than in women taking contraceptives. Both groups had lower levels than men. We have compared our group with the women in Ettigi's series who did not use contraceptives and found that women with anorexia nervosa had significantly more ($p < 0.02$, Fisher Exact Test) absent or deficient responses. Our finding that after weight gain 71% of the patients manifested an adequate response to apomorphine suggests that hypothalamic dopaminergic receptors have normalized in most patients and that such normalization is influenced by the nutritional status.

Hyperglycemia did not only act as a stimulus to GH release but also failed to suppress elevated GH levels; both findings suggest an impairment in the hypothalamic regulating system controlling pituitary GH release (2). There is evidence that the glucoreceptors and dopaminergic neurons interrelate in the hypothalamus. Mims and associates (29) and Ettigi et al. (12) have recently shown that glucose loading significantly attenuated GH response to L-DOPA and apomorphine. Therefore, the abnormalities in GH response to glucose and to apomorphine might be related in anorexia nervosa. Activation of serotonergic neurons does not seem crucial for the changes in GH levels since cyproheptadine, a serotonin antagonist, did not produce effects different from those of a placebo. These findings do support those of Parker and Rossman (31), who have shown that serotonergic mechanisms are involved in the sleep-associated GH release and that hyperglycemia did not affect the nocturnal GH rise.

Over half of our patients had high resting GH levels, a finding which helps differentiate anorexia nervosa from pituitary insufficiency. Others have reported elevated plasma GH levels in anorexia nervosa, usually in a smaller number of patients (11,18,23,25,37). The study by Garfinkel et al. (18) supports our findings, namely, that the caloric intake prior to the test influences plasma GH levels. Patients eating poorly showed elevated resting plasma GH levels, while plasma GH levels were low in well-nourished patients. It is unlikely that our high plasma GH values were due to the stress of the procedure since blood was drawn through an indwelling needle and patients remained resting. However, since GH values were consistently higher during the GT test, done 2 to 3 days after admission and 2 or 3 days prior to the apomorphine test, the stress of hospitalization might account for the differences in resting GH levels during the GT test and the apomorphine test.

Although most of our patients were adolescents or young adults, we do not think that the elevated base-line GH levels represent spontaneous secretory episodes as described by Finkelstein et al. (14). Such spontaneous rises in GH are usually followed by a decline consistent with the known half-life of GH, from 20 to 30 min, whereas in our sample the elevations persisted longer. It is also questionable whether these secretory pulses occur regularly in anorexic adolescent patients, who have minimal circulating levels of estradiol and whose LH-RH release has been shown to resemble more the prepubertal than the adolescent pattern (5).

Our results suggest that malnutrition and low caloric intake play a major role in producing changes in the GH release pattern in anorexic patients and that nutritional restoration and weight gain tend to normalize these changes.

Of course, the observed endocrine abnormalities may at the same time be part of the anorexic process. When retested, patients had improved, but most had not reached normal body weight and remained invested, although to a lesser degree, in the anorectic attitude. Continued longitudinal studies following patients through weight and psychologic fluctuations will serve to further tease out effects of malnutrition and define endocrine changes in anorexia nervosa.

ACKNOWLEDGMENTS

The authors wish to thank the staff of the 9 West Research Unit, in particular Mrs. Jan Schlemmer and Mrs. Mary Hagen, for their skillful assistance in the management and treatment of the patients.

REFERENCES

1. Baig, H. A., and Edozien, J. C. (1965): Carbohydrate metabolism in kwashiorkor. *Lancet,* 2:662–665.
2. Beck, P., Parker, M. L., and Daughaday, W. H. (1966): Paradoxical hypersecretion of growth hormone in response to glucose. *J. Clin. Endocrinol. Metab.,* 26:463–469.
3. Beumont, P. J. V., Friesen, H. C., Gelder, M. G., et al. (1974): Plasma prolactin and luteinizing hormone levels in anorexia nervosa. *Psychol. Med.,* 4:219–221.
4. Bowie, M. D. (1964) Intravenous glucose tolerance in kwashiorkor and marasmus, *S. Afr. Med. J.,* 38:328–329.
5. Boyar, R. M., Katz, J., Finkelstein, J. W., et al. (1974): Anorexia nervosa: immaturity of the 24-hour luteinizing hormone secretory pattern. *N. Engl. J. Med.,* 291:861–865.
6. Brazeau, P., Vale, W., Burgus, R., and Guillemin, R. (1974): Isolation of somatostatin (a somatotropin release inhibiting factor) of ovine hypothalamic origin. *Can. J. Biochem.,* 52:1067–1072.
7. Brown, G. M., and Reichlin, S. (1972): Psychologic and neural regulation of growth hormone secretion. *Psychosom. Med.,* 34:45–61.
8. Brown, W. A., Van Woert, M. H., and Ambani, L. M. (1973): Effect of apomorphine on growth hormone release in humans. *J. Clin. Endocrinol. Metab.,* 37:463–465.
9. Conn, J. W. (1940): Interpretation of the glucose tolerance test. The necessity of a standard preparatory diet. *Am. J. Med. Sci.,* 199:555–564.
10. Dally, P. (1969): *Anorexia Nervosa.* Heineman Medical Books Ltd., London.
11. Danowski, T. S., Livstone, E., Gonzales, A. R., et al. (1972): Fractional and partial hypopituitarism in anorexia nervosa. *Horm. Res.,* 3:105–118.

12. Ettigi, P., Lal, S., Martin, J., and Friesen, H. G. (1975): Effects of sex, oral contraceptives and glucose loading on apomorphine-induced growth hormone secretion. *J. Clin. Endocrinol. Metab.*, 40:1094–1098.
13. Feighner, J. P., Robins, E., Guze, S. B., Woodruff, R. A., Winokur, G., and Munoz, R. (1972): Diagnostic criteria for use in psychiatric research. *Arch. Gen. Psychiatry,* 26:57–62.
14. Finkelstein, J. W., Roffwarg, H. P., Boyar, R. M., Kream, J., and Hellman, L. (1972): Age-related changes in the twenty-four hour spontaneous secretion of growth hormone. *J. Clin. Endocrinol. Metab.*, 35:665–670.
15. Frings, C. S., Ratcliff, C. R., and Dunn, R. T. (1970): Automated determination of glucose in serum and plasma by a direct toluidine procedure. *Clin. Chem.,* 16:282–284.
16. Frohman, L. A. (1975): Neurotransmitters as regulators of endocrine function. *Hosp. Pract.,* 10:54–67.
17. Garfinkel, P. E. (1974): Perception of hunger and satiety in anorexia nervosa. *Psychol. Med.,* 4:309–315.
18. Garfinkel, P. E., Brown, G. M., Stancer, H. C., and Moldofsky, H. (1975): Hypothalamic-pituitary function in anorexia nervosa. *Arch. Gen. Psychiatry,* 32:739–744.
19. Glick, S. M., Roth, J., Yalow, R., and Berson, S. A. (1969): *Frontiers in Neuroendocrinology,* edited by W. F. Ganong and L. Martini, pp. 141–182. Oxford University Press, New York.
20. Grossman, S. P. (1975): Role of the hypothalamus in the regulation of food and water intake. *Psychol. Rev.,* 82:200–224.
21. Katz, J. L. (1975): Psychoendocrine considerations in anorexia nervosa. In: *Topics in Psychoendocrinology,* edited by E. J. Sachar, pp. 121–133 & Grune & Stratton, New York.
22. Lal, S., de la Vega, C. E., Sourkes, T. L., and Friesen, H. G. (1973): Effect of apomorphine on growth hormone, prolactin, luteinizing hormone and follicle-stimulating hormone levels in human serum. *J. Clin. Endocrinol. Metab.*, 37:719–724.
23. Landon, J., Greenwood, F. C., Stamp, T. C. B., and Wynn, V. (1966): The plasma sugar, free fatty acid, cortisol and growth hormone response to insulin and the comparison of this procedure with other tests of pituitary and adrenal function. II. In patients with hypothalamic or pituitary dysfunction or anorexia nervosa. *J. Clin. Invest.,* 45:437–449.
24. Lundberg, P. O., Walinder, J., Werner, I., et al. (1972): Effects of thyrotrophin-releasing hormone on plasma levels of TSH, FSH, LH and GH in anorexia nervosa. *Eur. J. Clin. Invest.,* 2:150–153.
25. Marks, V., Howorth, N., and Greenwood, F. C.: Plasma growth hormone levels in chronic starvation in man. *Nature,* 208:686–687.
26. Martin, J. B. (1976): Brain regulation of growth hormone secretion. In: *Frontiers in Neuroendocrinology, Vol. 4,* edited by L. Martini and W. F. Ganong, pp. 129–168. Raven Press, New York.
27. Mawson, A. R. (1974): Anorexia nervosa and the regulation of food intake: A review. *Psychol. Med.,* 4:289–308.
28. Mecklenburg, R. S., Loriaux, D. L., Thompson, R. H., Anderson, A. E., and Lipsett, M. B. (1974): Hypothalamic dysfunction in patients with anorexia nervosa. *Am. J. Obstet. Gynecol.,* 117:435–449.
29. Mims, R. B., Scott, C. L., Modebe, O. M., and Bethune, J. E. (1973): Prevention of L-dopa-induced growth hormone stimulation by hyperglycemia. *J. Clin. Endocrinol. Metab.,* 37:660–663.
30. Odell, W. D., Rayford, P. L., and Ross, G. T. (1967): Simplified, partially automated method for radioimmunoassay of human thyroid-stimulating, growth, luteinizing and follicle stimulating hormones. *J. Lab. Clin. Med.,* 70:973–979.
31. Parker, D. C., and Rossman, L. G. (1971): Human growth hormone release in sleep: Nonsuppression by acute hyperglycemia. *J. Clin. Endocrinol. Metab.,* 32:65–69.
32. Ross, C. W. (1938): Anorexia nervosa with special reference to the carbohydrate metabolism. *Lancet,* 1:1041–1045.
33. Russell, G. F. M. (1965): Anorexia nervosa. *Proc. R. Soc. Med.,* 58:811–814.
34. Sheldon, J. H., and Young F. (1938): On the carbohydrate metabolism in anorexia nervosa. *Lancet,* 1:257–259.
35. Simmonds, M. (1914): Uber hypophysis-schwund mit tödlichem ausgang. *Dtsch. Med. Wochenschr.,* 40:322.

36. Vanderlaan, W. P., Parker, D. C., Rossman, L. G., and Vanderlaan, E. F. (1970): Implications of growth hormone release in sleep. *Metabolism,* 19:891–897.
37. Warren, M. P., and Vande Wiele, R. L. (1973): Clinical and metabolic features of anorexia nervosa. *Am. J. Obstet. Gynecol.,* 117:435–449.
38. Whichelow, M. J., Sturge, R. A., Keen, H., Jarrett, R. J., Stimmler, L., and Grainger, S. (1974): Diurnal variation in response to intravenous glucose. *Br. Med. J.,* 1:488–491.

Anorexia Nervosa, edited by
R. A. Vigersky. Raven Press,
New York © 1977.

Food Intake, Fatness, and Reproductive Ability

Rose E. Frisch

Department of Population Sciences, and Harvard Center for Population Studies, Cambridge, Massachusetts 02138

TOO LITTLE OR TOO MUCH FAT

It is commonly observed that human beings, like other mammals, must "grow up" before becoming capable of reproduction. But on what scale is the "growing up" best measured: age, height, weight, skeletal age, or some other measure of the body? And how is the synchronization of the "grown-upness" and reproductive ability brought about (27)?

Undernutrition delays sexual development in both human beings (9,15) and animals (24,27). Some factor other than chronological age is therefore controlling. Undernutrition, chronic or acute, also causes the cessation of established reproductive ability in the human female (15) and male (30), as well as in other mammals (24).

Recent findings that the onset and maintenance of regular menstrual function in the human female are each dependent on the maintenance of a minimum weight for height, apparently representing a critical fat storage (15), imply that a particular body composition of fat/lean or fat/body weight may be an important determinant for reproductive ability in the human female (12,15).

Data from both nonanorectic (15,44) and anorectic female patients (5,44) show that a loss of body weight in the range of 10 to 15% of normal weight for height, which represents a loss of about one-third of body fat (15), results in amenorrhea. Data from obese women show that excessive fatness also causes amenorrhea (25,37). Too little fat or too much fat therefore turns off sexual function in the human female (12).

WEIGHT AT PUBERTY

The idea that relative fatness is important for female reproductive ability follows from our first findings that the events of the adolescent growth spurt in boys and girls, and particularly menarche in girls, are each closely related to a critical body weight (18,19). This finding was unexpected for human beings, although it was well known for other mammals (6,24,28), including primates (42), that sexual maturity (defined by vaginal opening, or more precisely by first estrus) is more closely related to body weight than to chronological age (6,24,28). Each event of the adolescent growth spurt was analyzed using longitudinal United States growth data. A velocity curve of height and weight growth from birth to age 18 years was plotted for each of the 201 girls and 209 boys of the three studies. The height and weight of each child at each adolescent event were determined and studied as a function of the age of the event.

We found that the mean weight of girls at the time of initiation of the adolescent growth spurt (30 kg) (20), at the time of maximum rate of weight gain (39 kg) (16), and at menarche (47 kg) (19) did not differ for early and late maturing girls, whereas their mean height at each of these events increased significantly with age of the event.

These results accounted for the many observations in the literature (41) that early maturers have more weight for height than late maturers at spurt initiation and throughout the adolescent spurt, including menarche.

Based on these early findings of an invariant mean weight in girls, we first proposed that there is a direct relation between a critical body weight and menarche. The mechanism was adapted from Kennedy's food intake–lipostat-metabolic signal (27,28). We proposed that the attainment of the *average* critical weight, which we now know represents a critical body composition of fatness attained at varying heights and weights by individual girls (10,12,15), causes a change in metabolic rate per unit mass, which in turn affects the hypothalamus-ovarian feedback by decreasing the sensitivity of the hypothalamus to estrogen. There is evidence for such a change of sensitivity of the hypothalamic "gonadostat" in girls and boys (31).

COMPONENTS OF WEIGHT AT MENARCHE

In order to make the notion of a critical weight meaningful for an individual girl, we studied the components of the body weight at menarche of each girl (21).

Although weight is considered a reasonably good measure of metabolism in the normal child, total body water (TW) and lean body weight (LBW, TW/0.72)(38) are more closely correlated with metabolic rate than is body weight, since they represent the metabolic mass, as a first approximation (29). These components and fat (body weight minus LBW) were calculated for each girl at menarche and at the initiation of the spurt, using the equations of Mellits and Cheek (33) from deuterium oxide measurements, and also those of Moore et al. (35) for comparison (21). The total body water values at menarche for all subjects calculated by both methods were comparable, 26.2 $\pm$ 0.18 (SD 2.4) liters and 26.8 $\pm$ 0.16 (SD 2.2) liters, respectively (21). Total water calculated by either equation did not change significantly with increasing age of menarche. Since lean body weight is calculated by TBW/0.72, lean body weight also is invariant with increasing age of menarche (21). All further results were calculated by the Mellits-

Cheek equation (33). The mean lean body weight at menarche, 36.3 ± 0.3 kg, and mean fat at menarche, 11.5 ± 0.3 kg, are similar to those obtained at ages 12.5 to 13 years from ^{40}K counting (7).

The greatest change in body composition of both early and late maturing girls during the adolescent growth spurt is a large increase in body fat, from about 5 to 11 kg, a 120% increase, compared to a 44% increase in lean body weight. There is thus a change in ratio of LBW to fat from 5:1 at initiation of the spurt to 3:1 at menarche (21).

A FATNESS INDEX: TOTAL WATER AS PERCENT OF BODY WEIGHT

Total body water as percent of body weight (TW/BWt%) is a more important index than the absolute amount of total water because it is an

TABLE 1. *Total water/body weight percent as an index of fatness*

	Female	Male
Weight (kg)	65	65
Total water (liters)	33	40
LBW (kg) (TW/0.72)	46	56
Fat (kg)	19	9
Fat/BWt%	29	14
TW/BWt%	51	62

$$\text{Fat/BWt\%} = 100 - \frac{\text{TW/BWt\%}}{0.72}$$

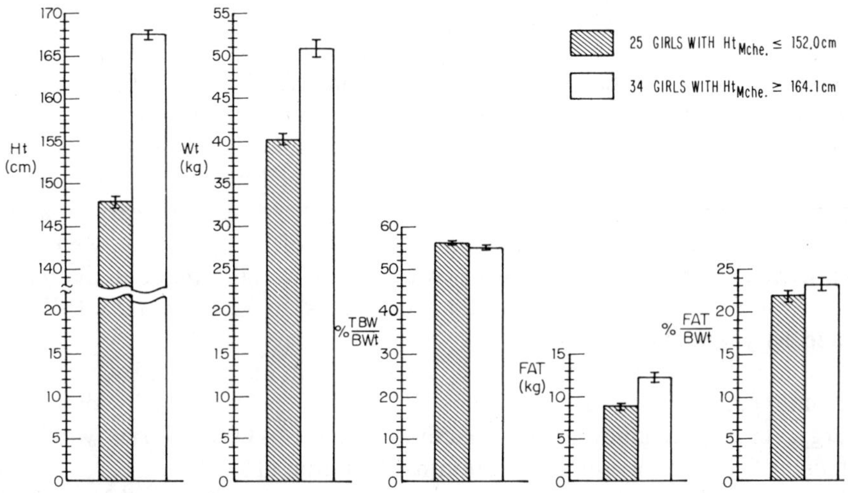

FIG. 1. Height, weight, total water/body weight percent (TBW/BWt%), fat, fat/body weight percent (fat/BWt%) of girls at the extremes of the height range at menarche. (From ref. 13 with permission.)

index of fatness (8) (Table 1). When girls are grouped by height at menarche rather than by age at menarche, the shortest, lightest girls and the tallest, heaviest girls differ in height by 20 cm and in weight by 12 kg. But these two extreme groups have the same relative fatness, as shown by their similar percentages of total water/body weight, 56.3 ± 0.5% and 55.3 ± 0.5%, respectively. Both these values are similar to the mean for all subjects, 55.1 ± 0.3% (Fig. 1).

FATNESS AS A DETERMINANT OF MINIMAL WEIGHTS FOR MENSTRUAL CYCLES

The total water/body weight percent data of 181 girls followed from menarche to the completion of growth at ages 16 to 18 years provided a simple method of estimating a minimal weight for height necessary for the onset of menstrual cycles (menarche) (Fig. 2) in primary amenorrhea and for the restoration of menstrual cycles in cases of secondary amenorrhea (Fig. 3) when the amenorrhea is due to weight loss (15).

Percentiles of total water/body weight percent, which are percentiles of fatness, were made at menarche and at age 18 years, the age at which body composition was stabilized (12) (Fig. 4).

For patients with secondary amenorrhea, we found that 56.1% of total water/body weight, the 10th percentile at age 18 years, which is equivalent to about 22% fat of body weight, indicates a minimal weight for height necessary for the restoration and maintenance of menstrual cycles. For example, a 20-year-old woman whose height is 160 cm (63 in.) should weigh at least 46.3 kg (102 lb) before menstrual cycles would be expected to resume (Fig. 3) (Table 2).

The weights at which menstrual cycles ceased or resumed in postmenarcheal patients ages 16 and older are about 10% heavier than the minimal weights for the same height observed at menarche (Table 2) (Fig. 2).

In accord with this finding, the body composition data show that both early and late maturing girls gain an average of 4.5 kg of fat from menarche to age 18 years. Almost all of this gain is achieved by age 16 years, when mean fat is 15.7 ± 0.3 kg, 27% of body weight. At age 18 years mean fat is 16.0 ± 0.3 kg, 28% of the mean body weight of 57.1 ± 0.6 kg. Reflecting this increase in fatness, the total water/body weight percent decreases from 55.1 ± 0.2% at menarche (12.9 ± 0.1 years) to 52.1% ± 0.2% (SD 3.0) at age 18 years (12) (Fig. 4).

The main function of the 16 kg of fat stored on an average by both early and late maturers by age 18 years may be to provide easily mobilized energy for a pregnancy and for lactation; the 144,000 calories would be sufficient for a pregnancy and 3 months' lactation (15).

Because girls are less fat at menarche than when they achieve stable reproductive ability, the minimal weight for height for the onset of men-

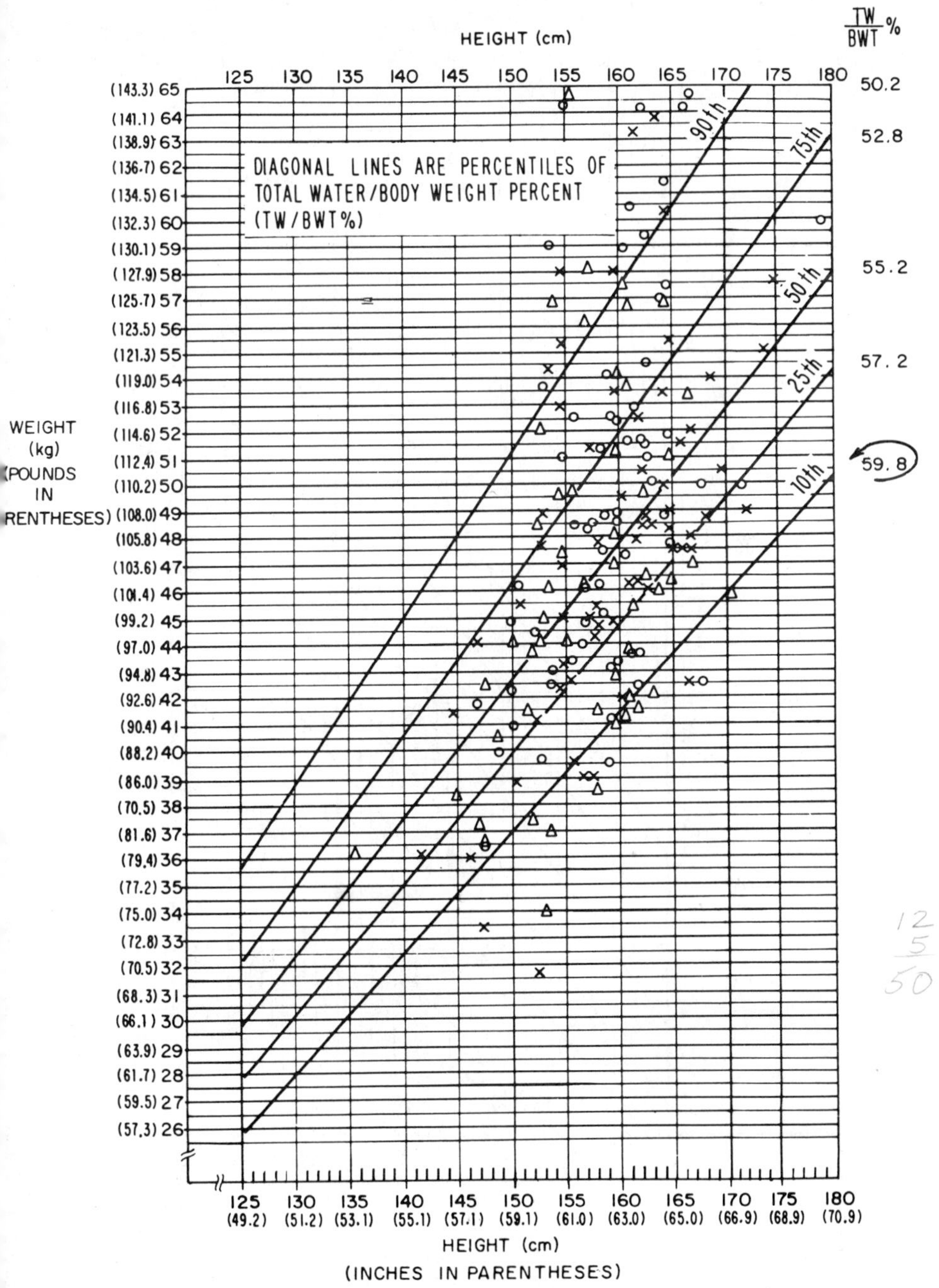

FIG. 2. Minimal weight necessary for a particular height for onset of menstrual cycles is indicated on the weight scale by the 10th percentile diagonal line of TW/BWt%, 59.8%, as it crosses the vertical height lines. Height growth of girls must be completed, or approaching completion. For example, a 15-year-old girl whose completed height is 160 cm (63 in.) should weigh at least 41.4 kg (91 lb) before menstrual cycles can be expected to start. Symbols are the height and weight at menarche of each of the 181 girls of the Berkeley Guidance Study, O; Child Research Council Study, X; and Harvard School of Public Health Study, △. (From ref. 15 with permission.)

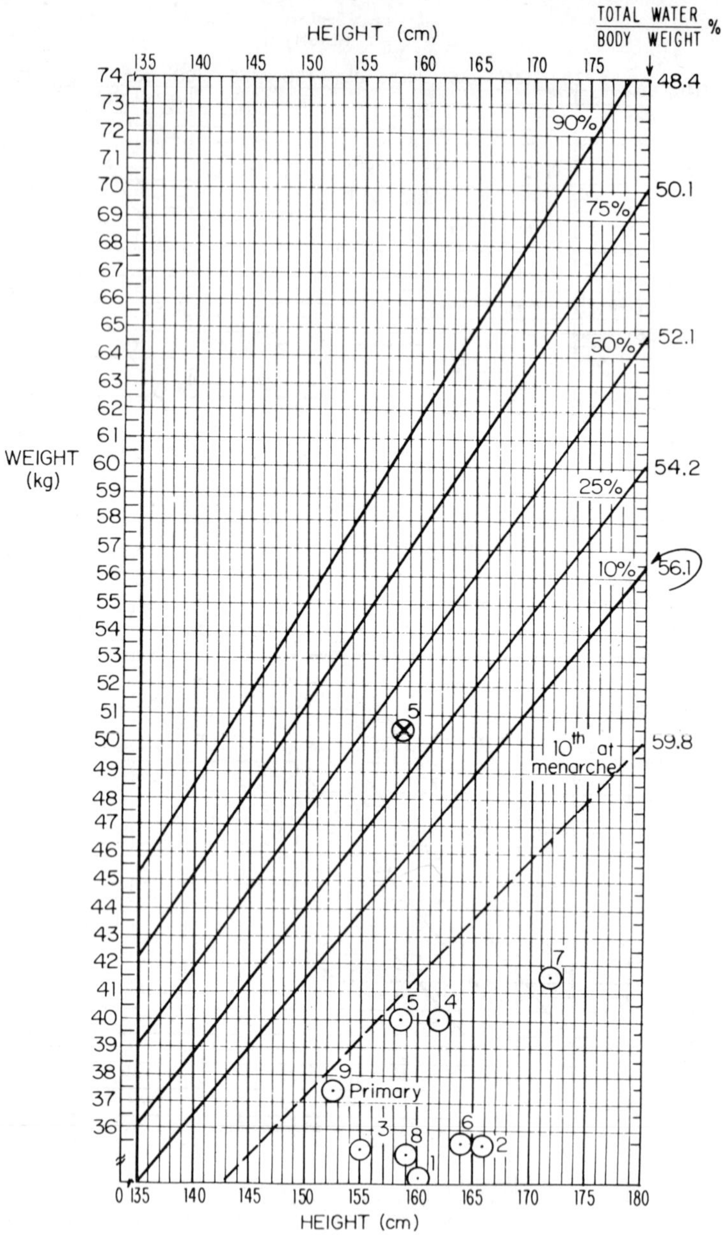

FIG. 3. Minimal weight necessary for a particular height for restoration of menstrual cycles is indicated on the weight scale by the 10th percentile diagonal line of TW/BWt%, 56.1%, as it crosses the vertical height line. For example, a 20-year-old woman whose height is 160 cm should weigh at least 46.3 kg (102 lb) before menstrual cycles would be expected to resume. (Modified from ref. 15.)

The 10th percentile at menarche (taken from Fig. 2) is shown by the dashed line.

⊙1–9: Amenorrheic, anorectic patients described in Boyar et al. (2) in comparison with normal, minimal weights. ⊗: Patient #5 at the time of resumption of normal cycles.

TABLE 2. *Minimal weight for particular height necessary for the onset or restoration of menstrual cycles*

		Menarche or primary amenorrhea			Secondary amenorrhea		
	Height	Minimal[a] weight (10th percentile)		Average weight (50th percentile)	Minimal[b] weight (10th percentile)		Average weight (50th percentile)
(inches)	(cm)	(lb)	(kg)	(kg)	(lb)	(kg)	(kg)
53.1	135	66.7	30.3	34.9	74.6	33.9	38.9
53.9	137	68.6	31.2	36.0	76.8	34.9	40.1
54.7	139	70.6	32.1	37.0	79.0	35.9	41.2
55.5	141	72.6	33.0	38.0	81.2	36.9	42.4
56.3	143	74.4	33.8	39.0	83.4	37.9	43.5
57.1	145	76.3	34.7	40.1	85.6	38.9	44.7
57.9	147	78.3	35.6	41.1	87.8	39.9	45.8
58.7	149	80.3	36.5	42.1	90.0	40.9	47.0
59.4	151	82.3	37.4	43.1	92.2	41.9	48.1
60.2	153	84.3	38.3	44.2	94.4	42.9	49.3
61.0	155	86.2	39.2	45.2	96.6	43.9	50.4
61.8	157	88.2	40.1	46.2	98.8	44.9	51.5
62.6	159	90.2	41.0	47.2	101.0	45.9	52.7
63.4	161	92.2	41.9	48.3	103.2	46.9	53.8
64.2	163	93.9	42.7	49.3	105.4	47.9	55.0
65.0	165	95.9	43.6	50.3	107.6	48.9	56.1
65.7	167	97.9	44.5	51.4	109.8	49.9	57.3
66.5	169	99.9	45.4	52.4	112.0	50.9	58.4
67.3	171	101.9	46.3	53.4	114.0	51.8	59.6
68.1	173	103.8	47.2	54.4	116.2	52.8	60.7
68.9	175	105.8	48.1	55.5	118.4	53.8	61.8
69.7	177	107.8	49.0	56.5	120.6	54.8	63.0
70.5	179	109.6	49.8	57.5	122.8	55.8	64.1
71.3	181	111.8	50.8	58.5	125.2	56.9	65.3

From ref. 15, Figs. 1 and 2.
[a] Equivalent to 17% fat/body weight.
[b] Equivalent to 22% fat/body weight.

strual cycles in cases of primary amenorrhea due to undernutrition is indicated by the 10th percentile of fractional body water at menarche, 59.8%, which is equivalent to about 17% fat of body weight (Fig. 2).

The standards of Fig. 2 would be used also for girls who become amenorrheic as a result of weight loss shortly after menarche, as is often found in cases of anorexia nervosa in adolescent girls (5,15). Of course, other factors, such as emotional stress, affect the maintenance or onset of menstrual cycles. Therefore, menstrual cycles may cease without weight loss and may not resume in some subjects even though the minimum weight for height has been achieved (15).

Our standards apply as yet only to Caucasian U.S. females (15) and European females since different races have different critical weights at

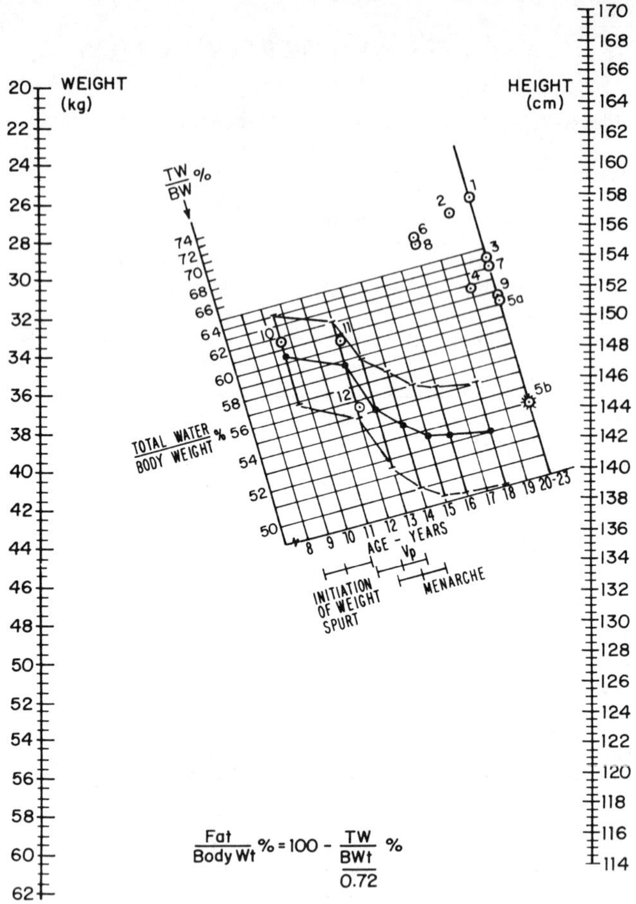

FIG. 4. Nomogram to estimate an index of fatness, total water as percentage of body weight, from the height and weight of a girl, to compare with the normal values (mean ± 1SD) at each adolescent event and at reproductive maturity (age 16 to 18 years). V_p is age of peak weight velocity. (Modified from ref. 12.)

Procedure. 1. Connect the points representing the subject's height and weight with a transparent rule. 2. Mark the point at which the connecting line crosses the numbered scale of TW/BWt%. 3. To compare with the normal values, read horizontally from the point on the TW/BWt% scale until reaching the vertical line indicating the age of the subject; mark the percent on her age line.

For example, a 15-year-old girl with secondary amenorrhea after severe dieting weighs 39 kg at height of 158 cm. Her estimated TW/BWt% is 61.0%, abnormally high for her age. This percentage, equivalent to 15% fat/body weight, is normally found at ages 9 to 10 years, at the time of the initiation of the adolescent growth spurt. After weight gain to 47 kg, the subject's percentage of total water/weight falls to 55.0%, equivalent to 24% fat/weight, a value in the normal range for her age.

Total body water as percent of body weight is calculated directly by the following equation from Mellits and Cheek (33): $TW = -10.313 + 0.252\ (\text{wt.})_{(\text{kg})} + 0.154\ (\text{ht.})_{(\text{cm})}$ when height $\geqq 110.8$ cm. Then divide TW by BWt (kg).

⊙1–9: Amenorrheic, anorectic patients described in Boyar et al. (2) compared to normal TW/BWt% values (mean ± 1 SD) at each adolescent event and at reproductive maturity (age 16 to 18 years.) ☼ 5b: Patient #5 after resumption of cycles; #10: a normal 9.6-year-old girl, height 134.0 cm, weight 28.2 kg; #11 and #12: normal identical twins. Twin #11 (correctly predicted from the body composition as the lighter of the two at birth) is 140.0 cm, 31.9 kg; #12 is 145.5 cm and 40.3 kg. Twin #11 had an earlier premenarcheal pubertal LH secretory pattern than did twin #12. The TW/BWt% of subjects off the normal scale (e.g., cases 1,2,6,8) are considered approximations only. Data made available by Dr. R. Boyar.

menarche (17), and it is not yet known whether the different critical weights represent the same critical body composition of fatness.

AMENORRHEA IN ANOREXIA NERVOSA

The controversy in the literature about the relation of amenorrhea to weight loss in anorexia nervosa may be clarified by the use of the minimum weight for height standards, keeping in mind that the weight is necessary but not sufficient, i.e., other factors may be overriding.

In a detailed study of anorexia nervosa in identical twins, Gifford et al. (23) note that although the twin with anorexia "gradually returned to 100 pounds (45.5 kg), only 4 pounds (1.8 kg) below her customary weight, her menstrual periods were still absent." This patient's height was 63 in. (160.0 cm) at age 19 years; her minimum weight for the resumption of cycles was therefore 46.5 kg (102.3 lb), and she still had to gain 1 kg before attaining the minimum weight for her height for the resumption of cycles (Fig. 3; Table 2). We have observed other cases of secondary amenorrhea with a similar, surprisingly sharp threshold in both anorectic and nonanorectic females.

BODY WEIGHT CHANGES AND THE LH SECRETORY PATTERN

The findings that (a) urinary and plasma gonadotropins are low in underweight patients with or without anorexia nervosa; (b) the response to luteinizing hormone releasing hormone (LH-RH) is diminished when body weight is low and is restored when body weight returns to normal (2,39,44); and (c) a normal response to clomiphene citrate occurs only after body weight returns to the normal range (32) suggest that a central nervous system signal affects hypothalamic function, and thus the secretion of gonadotropins by the anterior pituitary (2,40). Stephens (40), in an excellent review of the effects of inanition on hypophyseal function, presents detailed data on the deleterious effect of undernutrition on both female and male reproductive organs and function.

Further evidence comes from findings of Boyar et al. (2) that the type of LH secretory pattern, prepubertal or pubertal, is closely correlated with the extent of loss or gain of body weight. Comparison of TW/BWt% with the normal pattern of adolescent changes and the normal menarcheal and postmenarcheal standards shows that a prepubertal body composition is correlated with a prepubertal LH secretory pattern, and a pubertal body composition is correlated with a pubertal LH secretion. Figures 3 and 4 show that the nine amenorrheic patients with prepubertal LH secretory patterns reported by Boyar et al. (2) are far below the minimum weight for height corresponding to about 22% fat/body weight, or even the minimal menarcheal level of 17% fat/body weight. Note that when patient #5 resumed normal menstrual cycles her body composition and her LH secretory pattern (2) were both normal for such function.

A HYPOTHETICAL SCHEME OF SYNCHRONIZATION OF "THE BODY" AND REPRODUCTIVE ABILITY: SEX FAT

No causal relationship is proven by the close association of the LH secretory pattern and changes in the fat/lean and fat/body weight body composition. However, it is economical and teleologically and evolutionarily reasonable to hypothesize that the physical ability to reproduce successfully and the hypothalamic control of reproduction are synchronized by the central nervous system. The most likely signals are metabolic, relating food intake to core temperature (3) and fat depots (26). The fat gained during the adolescent growth spurt, particularly after peak velocity, which I call sex fat, could be a special part of this mechanism. Sex fat is differentiated from vital fat, the fat necessary for the minimum maintenance of basal metabolic rate and the vital functions. Both the absolute and relative amounts of fat are important, since the lean body mass and the fat obviously must be in a particular absolute range, as well as a relative range, i.e., the individual must be big enough to reproduce. For example, babies are approximately 14 to 16% fat/body weight at birth, and they obviously do not reproduce.

Sex fat could affect the control of gonadal hormone secretion in four ways: (a) aromatization of androgens to estrogen takes place in human abdominal and breast fat tissue (36); adipose tissue therefore may provide a significant extragonadal source of estrogen; (b) the excretion of estrogen varies with body weight and fatness, and estrogen metabolism is influenced by "factors involved in fat metabolism, including the thyroid hormones" (4); (c) vital fat and sex fat in relation to the lean body mass would be a determinant of metabolic rate; and (d) adipose tissue can affect the rate of blood flow (22). Since steroids, prostaglandins, and catecholamines are all present in adipose tissue, it may be a modulator of the concentrations of these substances available to the ovary and other reproductive organs.

Conversely, the increase of sex fat may be affected by increases in estrogen secretion, and a rise in estrogen may also contribute to the fall in caloric intake observed after peak velocity in both rats (14) and adolescent girls and boys (34).

BODY TEMPERATURE, FOOD INTAKE, OVULATION, AND "FLUSHING"

Wakeling and Russell (43) observed that the central body temperature of anorectic patients rises in response to a standard meal, whereas in normal subjects central body temperature remains constant.

The importance to the human female of a normal lack of such a response to a meal is suggested by the phenomenon of "flushing" in animals (13). Flushing is the increase in the rate of twinning in sheep resulting from short-term (e.g., a week) high caloric feeding before mating to the ram. The well-nourished human female fortunately does not normally superovulate in response to a high caloric intake, such as a large steak dinner (13).

The large amount of fat deposited during the human adolescent growth spurt may be the intervening factor which makes the sexually mature female less responsive sexually to caloric stimulation, as well as protecting her from the harmful effects of low caloric intake (13).

CONCLUSIONS

Figure 5 summarizes the interaction of food intake, fatness, and reproductive ability over the whole female reproductive span. At each milestone, a reduction in food intake can affect reproductive function (11). The physio-

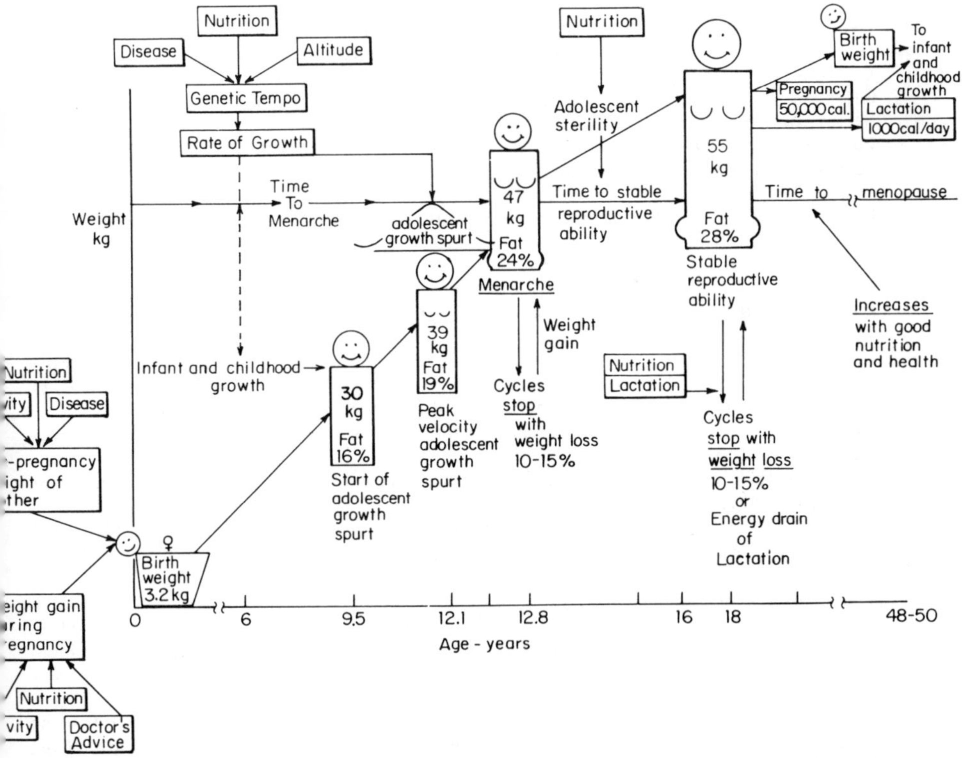

FIG. 5. Biological determinants of female reproductive ability (fecundity). Each reproductive milestone can be affected by environmental factors, as shown. The maintenance of regular ovulatory cycles is related to a minimum level of fat storage and is thus directly affected by undernutrition and energy-draining activities, such as lactation. (From ref. 11 with permission.)

logical and endocrinological mechanisms for most of these interactions are still unknown. Their clarification may identify pathways helpful in the understanding and treatment of anorexia nervosa.

ACKNOWLEDGMENTS

The preparation of this paper was supported by NIH Biomedical Research Grant 5-S07-2RR-05446-15. The hypothetical section is based on research done while a Fellow of the John Simon Guggenheim Memorial Foundation (1975 to 1976).

REFERENCES

1. Bishop, M. W. H. (1970): Ageing and reproduction in the male. *J. Reprod. Fertil.* [*Suppl.*], 12:65–87.
2. Boyar, R. M., Katz, J., Finkelstein, J. W., Kapen, S., Weiner, H., Weitzman, E. D., and Hellman, L. (1974): Anorexia nervosa: Immaturity of the 24-hour luteinizing hormone secretory pattern. *N. Engl. J. Med.*, 291:861–865.
3. Brobeck, J. R. (1960): Food and temperature. *Recent Prog. Horm. Res.*, 16:439–466.
4. Brown, J. B., and Strong, J. A. (1965): Effect of nutritional status and thyroid function on the metabolism of estradiol. *J. Endocrinol.*, 32:107–115.
5. Crisp, A. H. (1970): Anorexia nervosa: 'Feeding disorder', 'nervous malnutrition' or 'weight phobia'? *World Rev. Nutr. Diet.*, 12:452–504.
6. Dickerson, J. W. T., Gresham, G. A., and McCance, R. A. (1964): The effect of undernutrition and rehabilitation on the development of the reproductive organs: pigs. *J. Endocrinol.*, 29:111–118.
7. Forbes, G. B. (1972): Growth of the lean body mass in man. *Growth*, 36:325–337.
8. Friis-Hansen, B. J. (1956): Changes in body water compartments during growth. *Acta Paediatr. Scand.* [*Suppl.*], 110:1–67.
9. Frisch, R. E. (1972): Weight at menarche: similarity for well-nourished and undernourished girls at differing ages, and evidence for historical constancy. *Pediatrics*, 50(3): 445–450.
10. Frisch, R. E. (1974): Critical weight at menarche, initiation of the adolescent growth spurt, and control of puberty. In: *Control of Onset of Puberty*, edited by M. M. Grumbach, G. D. Grave, and F. E. Mayer, pp. 403–423. John Wiley & Sons, New York.
11. Frisch, R. E. (1975): Demographic implications of the biological determinants of female fecundity. *Soc. Biol.*, 22:17–22.
12. Frisch, R. E. (1976a): Fatness of girls from menarche to age 18 years, with a nomogram. *Hum. Biol.*, 48:353–359.
13. Frisch, R. E. (1976*b*): The physiological basis of reproductive efficiency. In: *Meat Animals*, edited by D. Lister, D. N. Rhodes, V. R. Fowler, and M. F. Fuller, pp. 327–354. Plenum Publishing Corp., New York.
14. Frisch, R. E., Hegsted, D. M., and Yoshinaga, K. (1975): Body weight and food intake at early estrus of rats on a high-fat diet. *Proc. Natl. Acad. Sci. U.S.A.*, 72:4172–4176.
15. Frisch, R. E., and McArthur, J. W. (1974): Menstrual cycles: Fatness as a determinant of minimum weight for height necessary for their maintenance or onset. *Science*, 185:949–951.
16. Frisch, R. E., and Revelle, R. (1969*a*): The height and weight of adolescent boys and girls at the time of peak velocity of growth in height and weight: longitudinal data. *Hum. Biol.*, 41:536–559.
17. Frisch, R. E., and Revelle, R. (1969*b*): Variation in body weights and the age of the adolescent growth spurt among Latin American and Asian populations in relation to calorie supplies. *Hum. Biol.*, 41:185–212.
18. Frisch, R. E., and Revelle, R. (1970): Height and weight at menarche and a hypothesis of critical body weights and adolescent events. *Science*, 169:397–399.

19. Frisch, R. E., and Revelle, R. (1971*a*): Height and weight at menarche and a hypothesis of menarche. *Arch. Dis. Child.,* 46:695–701.
20. Frisch, R. E., and Revelle, R. (1971*b*): Height and weight of girls and boys at the time of initiation of the adolescent growth spurt in height and weight and the relationship to menarche. *Hum. Biol.,* 43:140–159.
21. Frisch, R. E., Revelle, R., and Cook, S. (1973): Components of the critical weight at menarche and at initiation of the adolescent spurt: estimated total water, lean body mass and fat. *Hum. Biol.,* 45:469–483.
22. Gersh, I., and Still, M. A. (1945): Blood vessels in fat tissue. Relation to problems of gas exchange. *J. Exp. Med.,* 81:219.
23. Gifford, S., Murawski, B. J., and Pilot, M. L. (1970): Anorexia nervosa in one of identical twins. *Int. Psychiatry Clin.,* 7:139–228.
24. Hammond, J. (Ed.) (1955): *Progress in the Physiology of Farm Animals, Vol. 2.* Butterworths, London.
25. Iizuka, R., and Kawakami, S. (1968): Body weight change and sexual function in women. *Sanfujinka No Jissai* (*Tokyo*), 17:388–394.
26. Kennedy, G. C. (1957): Development with age of hypothalamic restraint upon the appetite of the rat. *J. Endocrinol.,* 16:9–17.
27. Kennedy, G. C., and Mitra, J. (1963): Body weight and food intake as initiating factors for puberty in the rat. *J. Physiol.,* 166:408–418.
28. Kennedy, G. C. (1969): Interactions between feeding behavior and hormones during growth. *Ann. N. Y. Acad. Sci.,* 157:1049–1061.
29. Keys, A., and Brozek, J. (1953): Body fat in adult man. *Physiol. Rev.,* 33:245–325.
30. Keys, A., Brozek, J., Henschel, A., and Mickelsen, O. (1950): *The Biology of Human Starvation, Vol. 1,* p. 753. University of Minnesota Press, Minneapolis.
31. Kulin, H. E., Grumbach, M. M., and Kaplan, S. L. (1972): Gonadal-hypothalamic interaction in prepubertal and pubertal man: effect of clomiphene citrate on urinary follicle-stimulating hormone and luteinizing hormone and plasma testosterone. *Pediatr. Res.,* 6:162–171.
32. Marshall, J. C., and Fraser, T. R. (1971): Amenorrhoea in anorexia nervosa: Assessment and treatment with clomiphene citrate. *Br. Med. J.,* 4:590–592.
33. Mellits, E. D., and Cheek, D. B. (1970): The assessment of body water and fatness from infancy to childhood. *Monogr. Soc. Res. Child. Devel.,* 35:12–26.
34. Mitchell, H. S., Reed, R. B., Valadian, I., and Hoff, M. (1966): The adolescent growth spurt and nutrient intake. *Proc. Int. Congr. Nutr.,* 4:1–8.
35. Moore, F. K., Olesen, H., McMurrey, J. D., Parker, V., Ball, M. R., and Boyden, C. M. (1963): *The Body Cell Mass and Its Supporting Environment.* W. B. Saunders Co., Philadelphia.
36. Nimrod, A., and Ryan, K. J. (1975): Aromatization of androgens by human abdominal and breast fat tissue. *J. Clin. Endocrinol. Metab.,* 40:367–372.
37. Nodate, Y. (1969): Estrogen metabolism. *Sanfujinka No Jissai* (*Tokyo*), 18:219–229.
38. Pace, N., and Rathbun, E. N. (1945): Studies on body composition. III: The body water and chemically combined nitrogen content in relation to fat content. *J. Biol. Chem.,* 158:685–691.
39. Palmer, R. L., Crisp, A. H., MacKinnon, P. C. B., Franklin, M., Bonnar, J., and Wheeler, M. (1975): Pituitary sensitivity to 50 μg LH/FSH-RH in subjects with anorexia nervosa in acute and recovery stages. *Br. Med. J.,* 1:179–182.
40. Stephens, D. J. (1941): Endocrine factors in undernutrition. *J. Clin. Endocrinol. Metab.,* 1:257–268.
41. Tanner, J. M. (1962): *Growth at Adolescence, Ed. 2.* Blackwell, Oxford.
42. van Wagenen, G. (1949): Accelerated growth with sexual precocity in female monkeys receiving testosterone propionate. *Endocrinology,* 45:544–546.
43. Wakeling, A., and Russell, G. F. M. (1970): Disturbances in the regulation of body temperature in anorexia nervosa. *Psychol. Med.,* 1:30–39.
44. Warren, M. P., Jewelewicz, R., Dyrenfurth, I., Ans, R., Khalaf, S., and Vande Wiele, R. L. (1975): The significance of weight loss in the evaluation of pituitary response to LH-RH in women with secondary amenorrhea. *J. Clin. Endocrinol. Metab.,* 40:601–611.

Anorexia Nervosa, edited by
R. A. Vigersky. Raven Press,
New York © 1977.

Studies on Secondary Amenorrhea, Anorectic Behavior, and Body-Image Perception: Importance for the Early Recognition of Anorexia Nervosa

Hans Fries

Department of Psychiatry, University Hospital, S-750 14 Uppsala, Sweden

INTRODUCTION

The provocative syndrome of anorexia nervosa has attracted much attention from different medical aspects, but with regard to phenomenology the most detailed definitions of the syndrome have emerged from a psychiatric viewpoint. Thus, the "typical case" of anorexia nervosa has been that referred to and investigated by a psychiatrist. Considerable effort and acumen led to definition of a specific syndrome of "primary" or "true" anorexia nervosa and its distinction from other unspecific feeding disorders, as those for example seen in primary depressions, schizophrenia, or obsessive-compulsive or hysterical neurosis (2,23). One of the specific features of anorexia nervosa is the anorectic behavior with a disruption of normal eating patterns and a stubborn resistance to food intake in order to reach extreme thinness. The delusional disturbances of bodily perception or body image first postulated by Bruch (1) have also been regarded as a fundamental disorder of anorexia nervosa, possibly explaining the self-perpetuating course of the illness (21). In recent years, some psychological studies have shown that it is possible to quantify the degree of behavioral abnormality (20) and, still more interesting, that the degree of bodily misperception in anorexia nervosa can be objectively measured (21). Thus, methods which seem fairly reliable can be used to distinguish anorexia nervosa patients from normals or nonanorectic patients.

Another characteristic feature of the anorexia nervosa syndrome is the endocrine disorder signaled by the loss of menstruation. The occurrence of secondary amenorrhea is an early symptom of the illness, as shown in Table 1. From this, it appears clearly that early amenorrhea occurs in approximately 70% of the cases. However, most authors have difficulties differentiating retrospectively between the onset of the feeding disorder (i.e., the anorectic behavior) and the onset of weight loss, which causes uncertainty regarding the amount of weight really lost before the onset of amenorrhea. It has been concluded that menstruation ceases early in anorexia nervosa but usually after some real weight loss (6), which would be in agreement with the hypothesis of a "critical body weight" necessary for the maintenance of regular menstruations (14).

TABLE 1. *Relation between eating disorder/weight loss and onset of secondary amenorrhea in anorexia nervosa*

		Secondary amenorrhea (%)		
References	*N*	Preceding other symptoms	Coinciding with debut of eating disorder or early weight loss	After manifest eating disorder or significant weight loss
Dally (7)	134	11	63	26
Fey and Hauser (9)	263	24	38	38
Theander (24)	94	7	88	5
Halmi (15)	94	21	52	18
Morgan and Russell (17)	41	18	34	45
	total 628	mean 16.2	mean 55.0	mean 26.4
		71.2		

Since secondary amenorrhea is an essential criterion for the diagnosis of anorexia nervosa in females, it might be rewarding to exchange the psychiatric viewpoint for that of the gynecologist or endocrinologist. Thus, the following question would arise: how frequently is the symptom of secondary amenorrhea associated with weight loss or anorectic symptomatology? The answer to this question is important because it could imply an early recognition of the syndrome and thereby better results of treatment.

EARLY STUDIES ON SECONDARY AMENORRHEA IN GYNECOLOGICAL PATIENTS AND IN A RANDOM SAMPLE OF A FEMALE POPULATION

During the late 1960s, several authors paid attention to a new iatrogenic syndrome, the so-called post-pill amenorrhea. In a study of 75 young women with prolonged amenorrhea after discontinuance of oral contraceptive treatment, we found a surprisingly high occurrence of early dieting behavior (12). More than half of these women had been dieting or losing weight for other reasons during the oral contraceptive treatment, especially in connection with its discontinuance, the average weight loss being 9 kg. Approximately 75% were judged to be underweight at the time of onset of amenorrhea. Primary anorexia nervosa was diagnosed in four cases, and another six women showed anorectic traits. It was concluded that weight loss rather than the oral contraceptive agents was the cause of the amenorrhea.

These findings initiated a study of a population sample of 2,000 women aged 18 to 45 years within Uppsala County, Sweden (19). To our knowledge, this is the only study so far on the epidemiology of secondary amenorrhea in a random population sample. In a postal inquiry all women were interviewed with regard to the occurrence of secondary amenorrhea and the use of oral contraceptives. Answers were obtained from 93% of the population. From these the incidence and prevalence rates of secondary amenorrhea were calculated (Table 2). The 1-year prevalence rate of secondary amenorrhea of more than 3 months' duration for women under 25 years of age was 6.3%.

TABLE 2. *Incidence and prevalence rates of secondary amenorrhea*

	Secondary amenorrhea (%)		
	>3 months	>6 months	>12 months
1-year incidence rate	3.3	0.7	—
1-year period prevalence rate	4.4	1.8	1.1
Point prevalence rate	1.8	1.5	1.2

From Pettersson et al. (19)

In a follow-up investigation, the amenorrheic women in the same study were compared to age-matched, nonamenorrheic control subjects with respect to background variables of etiologic interest, e.g., psychogenic factors and weight loss (13). A significantly higher proportion of underweight women was found in the amenorrheic group. Two women were diagnosed as having anorexia nervosa, yielding an estimated minimum prevalence of 1 per 1,000, but there was also evidence of other women with anorectic symptomatology and marked underweight.

In another study, 30 women with secondary amenorrhea associated with self-induced weight reduction were investigated (10). They were selected from a total of 40 consecutive cases with secondary amenorrhea. The median age of these 30 women was 22.3 years (range 18 to 34), and the duration of their present amenorrhea varied between 8 and 80 months (median 20.5). The amenorrhea was not related to previous use of oral contraceptive agents. Their average weight loss was 14 kg, and almost all women were judged to be underweight at onset of amenorrhea (Fig. 1). Twenty-six women admitted a conscious dieting behavior, mostly initiated

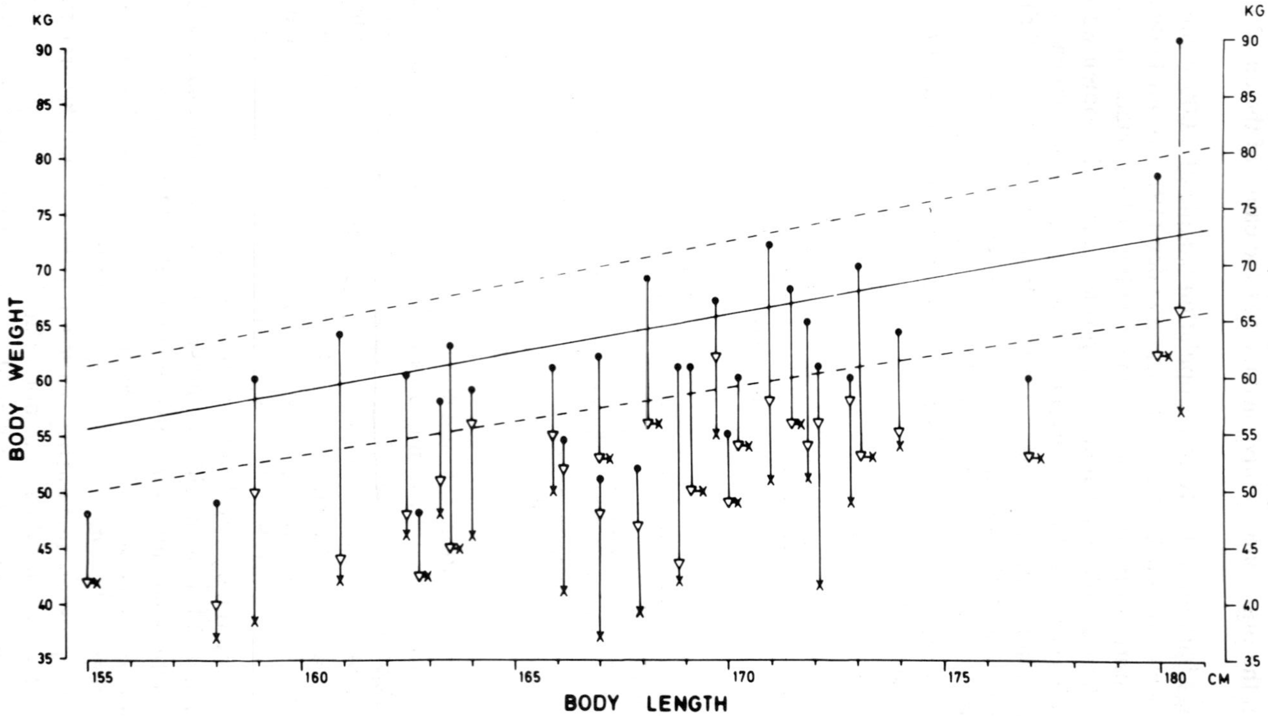

FIG. 1. Weights in relation to height before, during, and after onset of amenorrhea. The period of onset = L.M.P. + 2 months. Each woman is represented by a vertical line. ● = maximum weight immediately before weight loss. ▽ = minimum weight at onset of amenorrhea. x = minimum weight during the period of amenorrhea. Solid line, mean weight distribution of Norwegian women 25 to 30 years old; broken lines, ±10% deviation from the mean weight distribution, considered as a range of normal variation. (From ref. 10.)

for "cosmetic" reasons. At investigation, four different patterns or stages of dieting behavior were distinguished:

1. Dieting for obvious cosmetic reasons.
2. Dieting due to a neurotic fixation on weight/food intake. This dieting behavior had become a goal in itself and appeared as quite unjustified with regard to initial or current weight. Anxious attention to caloric intake, "appropriate" foodstuffs, and frequent weight control were constant features. Rules and restrictions regarding food intake had to be followed in an almost compulsory manner, deviations causing anxiety and increased fixation, etc. However, the weight loss was not extreme.
3. Anorectic behavior. In addition to the behavioral pattern just described, these women showed a pronounced change of attitude or ambivalence toward eating with disruption of normal eating patterns, stubborn resistance to food intake, and, according to reports of several of the women, periods of bulimia, vomiting, purging, and physical overactivity. Most of them showed nervous symptoms, usually of a rather unspecific, asthenic, depressive, or anancastic kind, and a few suffered from primary psychiatric disorders. They appeared to maintain some degree of insight and did not deny their eating disorder in any obvious way. Most of these women showed a pronounced weight loss.
4. "True" anorexia nervosa according to the diagnostic criteria given by Bruch (1,2). These women exhibited loss of insight, strong denial of symptoms, however conspicuous, and disturbed body perception in connection with extreme weight reduction.

Among the 30 women, 13 displayed anorectic behavior, and another 4 women were judged to suffer from "true" anorexia nervosa. Profound emotional disturbances and sexual maladjustment were more common at the anorectic stages. A "continuum hypothesis" was proposed since it was evident that the same woman could develop anorectic behavior or a full-blown picture of anorexia nervosa even from a point of seemingly understandable dieting for cosmetic reasons. Thus, anorexia nervosa may be considered as the final stage after a continuous change from conscious, voluntary slimming for more or less legitimate reasons toward an uncontrollable dieting behavior with loss of insight and an obviously defective body image perception. This process may stop at any stage, either spontaneously or by therapeutic intervention, and the factors determining a serious turn of the development are considered to be multivariate.

PRESENT STUDY

During the last 18 months a rather heterogenous group of female patients with a picture of "true" anorexia nervosa or secondary amenorrhea with anorectic behavior/weight loss has been investigated and treated at the Departments of Gynecology and Psychiatry, University Hospital, Uppsala. By using rigorous diagnostic criteria for anorexia nervosa (8), we could divide these women into two groups: those who satisfied the criteria and those who did not. Both groups and an additional group of healthy female control subjects were investigated with regard to their degrees of anorectic behavior and bodily misperception. The main purposes of the study were to see (a) whether or not the tests used were specific for the diagnosis of "true" anorexia nervosa, and (b) if so, whether the patients with anorexia nervosa could be clearly differentiated from other patients with secondary amenorrhea and self-induced weight reduction, who do not satisfy strict criteria of anorexia nervosa.

Patients and Methods

Thirty-eight women with a history of anorexia nervosa or secondary amenorrhea and self-imposed weight loss were classified by strict research criteria for anorexia nervosa (8) (see Chap. 2).

In all, 21 women satisfied the criteria for anorexia nervosa and formed group A. However, they represented very different stages of the illness, with approximately one-half of the women in acute or subacute stages and the other half in a probable stage of healing after previous treatment and weight gain. Their body weights were expressed as percent of the "average body weight" (% ABW) according to actuarial tables (3,4). At investigation, only 11 of the women in group A had a body weight below 75% ABW, and of the remaining 10 women who had increased their weights after treatment, 5 had recently regained spontaneous menstruations at more or less regular intervals (all 5 women at body weights more than 80% ABW).

The 17 women who did not satisfy the diagnostic criteria for anorexia nervosa formed group B. They all had a history of long-standing secondary amenorrhea in association with self-imposed weight loss. At the time of investigation, 6 of these 17 women had recently regained some spontaneous menstrual activity after weight gain (5 women at body weights more than 85% ABW), but 5 of these 6 women were still judged to be oligoamenorrheic. The women in group B did not satisfy the following criteria for anorexia nervosa: 6 women did not satisfy criterion A (i.e., their age at onset was 25 or more, the oldest being 28); 8 women did not satisfy criterion B (i.e., their weight loss was less than 25% of original body weight); 1 woman did not satisfy criterion D (the possibility of Bartter's syndrome could not be ruled out); 3 women did not satisfy criterion E (2 with signs of primary depression and 1 with severe conversion symptoms); 5 women did not satisfy criterion F [i.e., except for amenorrhea, none of the manifestations specified in criterion F (2)–(6) was found]. The diagnostic demarcation from other primary psychiatric syndromes needs further comments: there was no case with productive schizophrenic symptoms, but the personality of a few women in both groups could well be characterized as schizoid. There was no case with manifest manic-depressive psychosis, but depressive symptoms were very frequent in both group A and group B. However, it is extremely difficult to determine whether these depressions were of primary or secondary nature. To sum up, schizoid, depressive, hysterical, and anancastic features were common in different blendings in both groups and mainly were interpreted to reflect early personality disorder.

Twenty-two young, healthy, and regularly menstruating women volunteered as control subjects and formed group C. This control group was chiefly made up of hospital staff, but none was professionally involved in the care of anorectic patients.

All women in groups A through C were investigated with respect to their anorectic behavior and body image perception by the following two methods. First, the magnitude of the behavioral disorder was measured by means of an anorectic behavior rating scale[1] (11). This scale was designed to fit outpatients as well as inpatients and is similar to the rating scale previously introduced by Slade (20). In contrast to the format of Slade's "anorexic behaviour scale," however, the questions are put directly to the patient by a doctor or a clinical psychologist, who rates the answers from 0 to 2 in anorectic direction. There are 25 items, and the maximum score is 50. If necessary, the rater has freedom to give a more detailed explanation of each item. Thus, the rating scale is simply a standardized and focused psychiatric interview. To minimize the effect of denial, rationalizations, etc. from the patient, the rating is performed in a psychotherapeutic atmosphere after the patient's biography has been taken in a free interview. It was considered desirable that the patient had been previously acquainted with the rater and had some confidence in him.

The second method of investigation was a "visual body size estimation apparatus," by which the degree of body image misperception was quantified. This method was introduced by Slade and Russell (21), and the apparatus and techniques used in the present investigation are exactly the same as those described in their study. In short, each woman was asked to estimate her own widths across four defined body regions (the zygomas, axillae, waist at the narrowest part, and hips at the widest part) by means of two movable lights on a horizontal bar. She could move the lights symmetrically outward or inward at desirable speed by a turnable potentiometer. She was then asked to stop the lights when she felt that the distance between them corresponded to the width asked for. Each body region was estimated four times, and the mean of these four measures constituted the "perceived size" of the region. This "perceived size" was compared with the "real size," which was obtained by use of an anthropometer. Thus a body image perception index could be calculated as follows:

$$\text{body perception index} = \frac{\text{perceived size}}{\text{real size}}$$

To minimize the amount of data given in the present chapter, we use only a total body perception index, which is defined as the mean of the body indices of all four body regions investigated.

Results

GROUPS A THROUGH C

These results are given in Tables 3 and 4, in which data regarding age, weight, anorectic behavior scores, and total body perception indices are compared.

---

[1] Available upon request from the author.

TABLE 3. *Clinical data—groups A through C*

	Group A ($N = 21$)	Group B ($N = 17$)	Group C ($N = 22$)
Age (years) at investigation	20.8 ± 4.8^a	25.0 ± 6.0	24.3 ± 3.0
Weight (% ABW) at investigation	78.5 ± 9.4^b	82.8 ± 18.7^c	93.7 ± 7.6
Anorectic behavior scores	23.1 ± 10.4^b	21.4 ± 9.1^b	3.2 ± 2.2
Body perception indices	1.36 ± 0.31^b	1.26 ± 0.27^c	1.09 ± 0.12

Clinical data of patients with anorexia nervosa (group A) and secondary amenorrhea with self-imposed weight loss but not anorexia nervosa (group B) compared to healthy women with normal menses (group C).

[a] $p < 0.01$ group A vs group C.

[b] $p < 0.001$ group A or group B vs group C.

[c] $p < 0.02$ group B vs Group C.

TABLE 4. *Comparisons of groups A and B*

	Group A		Group B		
	Mean	SD	Mean	SD	*t*-test values
Age (years)					
At onset of weight loss	16.6	3.2	21.5	4.7	3.85: $p < 0.001$
At investigation	20.8	4.8	25.0	6.0	2.43; $p < 0.025$
Weight					
Total weight loss during illness (kg)	21.6	7.7	14.3	6.0	3.22; $p < 0.005$
Weight at investigation (% ABW)	78.5	9.4	82.8	18.7	0.92; ns
Anorectic behavior scores	23.1	10.4	21.4	9.1	0.54; ns
Body perception indices	1.36	0.31	1.26	0.27	1.04; ns

Data about age, weight, anorectic behavior, and body perception from a group (A) of 21 female patients satisfying the diagnostic criteria of anorexia nervosa (8) as compared to a group (B) of 17 patients with self-imposed weight loss and secondary amenorrhea who do not satisfy these criteria.

WEIGHT AT INVESTIGATION

No significant differences regarding anorectic behavior scores and body perception indices were obtained between groups A and B (Table 4). This could possibly be explained by the inclusion of several cases of anorexia nervosa in recovery in group A. Thus, these patients were excluded in a further comparison, in which only group A patients weighing less than

75% ABW were compared to group B patients. However, the results were still very similar with no significant differences between the groups.

When comparing the anorectic behavior scores between group A patients weighing more than 75% ABW (N = 10) and those weighing less than 75% ABW (N = 11), we found no significant difference (t = 1.24), and the same was true of an analogous comparison of the body perception indices (t = 0.49). The same comparisons were also made within group B, in which the patients weighing more than 75% ABW (N = 10) scored higher on the anorectic behavior scale than those weighing less than 75% ABW (N = 7), the mean scores being 26.2 and 14.4, respectively ($t = 3.35$; $p < 0.005$). An analogous intragroup comparison of the body perception indices within group B yielded no significant difference (t= 1.77).

ALL PATIENTS

Although the age at investigation was significantly lower in the group A patients than in the control subjects of group C, there was no significant difference as to age distribution when all 38 women in groups A and B (mean age 22.7 years) were compared to the control subjects (t = 1.23).

When data from all 38 women in groups A and B were added together, the following correlations were made:

1. between total weight loss and anorectic behavior scores ($r = +0.16$; ns);
2. between total weight loss and body perception indices ($r = +0.21$; ns);
3. between % ABW and anorectic behavior scores ($r = +0.36$; $p < 0.05$);
4. between % ABW and body perception indices ($r = -0.04$; ns); and
5. between body perception indices and anorectic behavior scores ($r = +0.41$; $p < 0.01$).

DISCUSSION

Validity and Interpretation of the Testing

The anorectic behavior scale seemed to be very useful in distinguishing healthy females from those with anorectic behavior. None of the controls scored higher than 8, and a score above 10 could be considered diagnostic. It is obvious that the results of the rating scale also depend on the patient's degree of insight or denial or the cooperation and emotional rapport obtained. Thus, the positive correlation found between % ABW and anorectic behavior scores might be explained by increased faking or denial on the part of the anorexia nervosa patients in acute or subacute stages, who had low weights at investigation. This is, however, contradicted by the finding that the anorexia nervosa patients of group A, who weighed less than 75% ABW, still had diagnostic scores which did not differ significantly from those of the anorexia nervosa patients weighing more than 75% ABW. It was therefore concluded that the possible occurrence of denial or rationalizations had a negligible effect on the result.

It seems that the patients in group B were those chiefly responsible for the positive correlation between % ABW and anorectic behavior scores. It may be that some of the group B patients who displayed low anorectic behavior scores had low body weights due to other reasons, e.g., a primary depression with loss of appetite. However, few patients were found to have primary psychiatric illness. Then the positive correlation found between weight and anorectic behavior might be explained by an increasing anxiety and a consequent decision to starve oneself with increasing weight, and that the desire to continue intense dieting or anorectic behavior decreases with the amount of weight lost. This latter conclusion is in contrast to the clinical experience of an accelerating behavioral disorder with progressive weight loss and to the hypothesis of "a vicious circle" proposed by Slade and Russell (21) on the basis of their finding of a direct association between the degree of perceptual disorder and that of malnutrition. However, such an association was not found in the present study. Although it is evident that some severe cases, especially those seen by psychiatrists, run a very malignant course, it is questionable if this tempting theory of anorexia nervosa as a self-perpetuating illness holds true for the majority of cases. It may instead be argued that the disease often is self-delimiting, especially if the less severe or mitigated forms are included. Anorexia nervosa is a much more frequent disorder than previously realized (5), and it is a common observation that many anorectic patients reach some point of compromise or *modus vivendi,* where they maintain social functions (such as studies or work) at a relatively stable level of malnutrition and without seeking further medical help. By this reasoning, it would in fact be logical to expect a positive rather than a negative correlation between weight gain and increase of anorectic behavior.

The body perception indices differentiated anorectic patients from normals also very convincingly. As in the previous study of Slade and Russell (21), most normal females were found to be remarkably exact in the estimations of their body widths, in contrast to the marked overestimation of the anorectic subjects. Also, the magnitude of the perceptional disorder was positively correlated to the anorectic behavior scores, which confirms earlier findings (20) and supports the assumption that the techniques used are specific for anorexia nervosa.

There are, however, arguments which indicate that this assumption is too simple. Firstly, 5 of the 22 control subjects of group C overestimated their body widths by 21 to 33%, and none showed an underestimation of a similar degree. This may indicate that a substantial number of normals do overestimate themselves in about the same degree as that found in anorexia nervosa patients. This observation, together with the fact that the origin and the fundamental roles of the perceptual disorder measured by this technique are unknown, underlines the great need of further studies in different populations with regard to age, sex, presence of any illness affecting body size, other perceptional disorders, etc. Such studies have presently been initiated, and the preliminary results from a study of 20 hyperobese patients showed that many of them overestimated themselves between 8 and 60% (mean body perception index 1.24; SD 0.14), which agrees with a short note on this subject made earlier (22). In another pilot study of 7 young schizophrenic patients with productive symptoms, such as delusions and hallucinations, but who were not too ill to cooperate in the investigation, all were shown to overestimate themselves between 15 and 48% (mean 31%). It was expected that the general perceptual disorder so characteristic of schizophrenia would manifest itself in both under- and overestimation, and it is difficult to explain this finding, provided that the method of investigation in itself is not biased toward overestimation. This is, however, contradicted by the exact estimations made by the majority of the healthy control subjects.

In spite of these questions and a call for future studies, it is concluded that the body perception index represents a bodily experience, which is essential and of great importance for patients with anorexia nervosa—but it cannot be maintained that a defect in body perception, as measured by this technique, is specific only for this diagnosis.

Diagnostic and Therapeutic Implications

The main finding in the present study is the striking similarity between groups A and B with regard to their degrees of anorectic behavior and body misperception. In spite of the strict diagnostic criteria and the seemingly important diagnostic parameters investigated, it was not possible to distinguish the groups from one another.

The significant differences in age at onset and at investigation are, of course, due to selection by the use of the age criterion of Feighner et al. (8) for the diagnosis of anorexia nervosa. If the few women with an age of onset of 25 or more, who were primarily regarded as suffering "true" anorexia nervosa, had been included in group A (instead of group B), this would not have changed the results of the group comparisons in any significant way. From clinical experience, the age limit of Feighner et al. (8) is too low since it is obvious that there exists a group of women with a slightly later onset who satisfy all other criteria of anorexia nervosa. There are also reports of cases who start much later in life (16). Therefore, it is recommended that the age limit of onset should be increased at least to the age of 30.

As to the degree of total weight loss, there was also a striking difference due to selection by the weight criterion of Feighner et al. This underlines the opinion that many of the patients in group B had less severe illness and could be regarded as mitigated cases of anorexia nervosa, in accordance with earlier descriptions of patients with secondary amenorrhea and self-induced weight reduction (10). The finding that the weight at investigation did not differ between the groups might be explained by the fact that half of the group A patients were in a stage of healing and had gained considerable weight. As this was thought to affect the results of the testings, comparisons were also made with consideration of the present weight (more or less than 75% ABW) within groups A and B. However, the results of the testings were still very similar, both in the intergroup comparison and within the groups (with the exception of the anorectic behavior scores in group B earlier commented on).

Thus, it is concluded that women who have a long-standing history of secondary amenorrhea and self-imposed weight loss, but who do not satisfy strict diagnostic criteria of anorexia nervosa, show diagnostic anorectic behavior scores and marked overestimation of body widths, not quantitatively different from those of patients with "true" anorexia nervosa in acute or subacute stages. What is then the difference between these two groups? Probably this is more a matter of degree of illness (e.g., as measured by the total weight loss or secondary effects of severe malnutrition) than a matter of diagnosis.

The early recognition of anorexia nervosa cannot be overemphasized. We know that secondary amenorrhea is an early symptom in the majority of cases with anorexia nervosa, and that secondary amenorrhea in itself is frequently associated with weight loss or anorectic behavior. We know that many of these patients do consult gynecologists early and of their own free will, in sharp contrast to the later and often reluctant confrontation with a psychiatrist. We know that every woman with anorexia nervosa has had a starting point. Thus, it is important that physicians, and especially gynecologists, pay great attention to a history of dieting behavior and weight loss in women who consult them for secondary amenorrhea. In this context, simple diagnostic techniques, such as those used in the present investigation, might facilitate classification of doubtful cases.

The prospects of a successful (psycho)therapy are more favorable at an early stage when the patient, before taking refuge in various forms of denial or rationalizations, still preserves some degree of insight. A Finnish follow-up study (18) of 48 patients with anorexia nervosa, who had been followed during a mean period of 5 years, confirmed the results of others (7,24), namely, that anorexia nervosa is a serious condition, which is difficult to treat effectively and has considerable mortality. However, it was shown that the prognosis with regard to a later freedom of symptoms was four times as good in those patients who were treated within the first 3 years after onset (58% symptom-free) as in those who received treatment later (13% symptom-free). In another recent study (17), a more doubtful outcome was associated with a longer illness before admission, and it was concluded that "the long-term outcome will depend more on factors influencing patient referral according to the severity of their illness, rather than on the method of treatment itself." Thus, in order to improve the prognosis, every woman with secondary amenorrhea and self-induced weight reduction who does not suffer other obvious primary psychiatric illness should be regarded as a potential patient with anorexia nervosa.

The importance of early recognition and psychotherapy for mitigated cases with anorexia nervosa has been commented on elsewhere (10). The major reason for a progressive refinement of diagnostic descriptions is, of course, the inherent possibility to obtain meaningful therapeutic programs. Regrettably, the impressive work invested in elucidating the cause and psychopathology of anorexia nervosa has so far yielded few specific or new therapeutic methods. This rather gloomy prognostic outlook might be exchanged for a more optimistic one if we included "anorectics in-the-making" in our diagnostic and therapeutic efforts.

ACKNOWLEDGMENTS

The author is indebted to Ass. Psychologist Sven Holmgren for valuable advice and competent performance of the testings, and to Mrs. Birgitta Söderblom for skillful secretarial assistance. Ass. Professor Sven Johan Nillius has kindly contributed by referring amenorrheic patients to the present investigation. The study was supported by the Swedish Medical Research Council (Grant No. 21X-5001).

REFERENCES

1. Bruch, H. (1962): Perceptual and conceptual disturbances in anorexia nervosa. *Psychosom. Med.*, 24:188–194.
2. Bruch, H. (1973): *Eating Disorders: Obesity, Anorexia Nervosa and the Person Within.* Basic Books, New York.
3. Ciba-Geigy (1970*a*): Average weights of adults [from: *Build and Blood Pressure Study, Vol. 1.* Society of Actuaries, Chicago, 1959]. *Scientific Tables,* p. 711. Ciba-Geigy, Basle
4. Ciba-Geigy (1970*b*): Normal measurements during growth [from: Heimendinger, J. (1964): Measurements made in the period 1956–1957 on 2150 boys and 2150 girls in Basle, Switzerland. *Helv. Paediatr. Acta,* 19: Suppl. 13]. *Scientific Tables,* pp. 701–705. Ciba-Geigy, Basle.
5. Crisp, A. H., Palmer, R. L., and Kalucy, R. S. (1976): How common is anorexia nervosa? A prevalence study. *Br. J. Psychiatry,* 128:549–554.
6. Crisp, A. H., and Stonehill, E. (1971): Relation between aspects of nutritional disturbance and menstrual activity in primary anorexia nervosa. *Br. Med. J.,* 3:149–151.
7. Dally, P. (1969): *Anorexia Nervosa.* Heinemann, London.

8. Feighner, J. P., Robins, E., Guze, S. B., Woodruff, R. A., Winokur, G., and Munoz, R. (1972): Diagnostic criteria for psychiatric research. *Arch. Gen. Psychiatry,* 26:57–63.
9. Fey, M., and Hauser, G. A. (1970): *Die Postpubertäts-Magersucht.* Huber, Bern.
10. Fries, H. (1974): Secondary amenorrhoea, self-induced weight reduction and anorexia nervosa. *Acta Psychiatr. Scand.* [*Suppl.*], 248.
11. Fries, H. (1975): Anorectic behaviour: nosological aspects and introduction of a behaviour scale (abstract in English). *Scand. J. Behav. Ther.,* 4:137–148.
12. Fries, H., and Nillius, S. J. (1973): Dieting, anorexia nervosa and amenorrhoea after oral contraceptive treatment. *Acta Psychiatr. Scand.,* 49:669–679.
13. Fries, H., Nillius, S. J., and Pettersson, F. (1974): Epidemiology of secondary amenorrhea. II. A retrospective evaluation of etiology with special regard to psychogenic factors and weight loss. *Am. J. Obstet. Gynecol.,* 118:473–479.
14. Frisch, R. E., and McArthur, J. W. (1974): Menstrual cycles: fatness as a determinant of minimum weight for height necessary for their maintenance or onset. *Science,* 185:949–951.
15. Halmi, K. A. (1974): Anorexia nervosa: demographic and clinical features in 94 cases. *Psychosom. Med.,* 36:18–26.
16. Kellett, J., Trimble, M., and Thorley, A. (1976): Anorexia nervosa after the menopause. *Br. J. Psychiatry,* 128:555–558.
17. Morgan, H. G., and Russell, G. F. M. (1975): Value of family background and clinical features as predictors of long-term outcome in anorexia nervosa: four-year follow-up study of 41 patients. *Psychol. Med.,* 5:355–371.
18. Niskanen, P., Jääskeläinen, J., and Achté, K. (1974): Prognosen vid anorexia nervosa (no abstract in English). *Nord. Psykiatr. Tidskrift,* 28:160–165.
19. Pettersson, F., Fries, H., and Nillius, S. J. (1973): Epidemiology of secondary amenorrhea. I. Incidence and prevalence rates. *Am. J. Obstet. Gynecol.,* 117:80–86.
20. Slade, P. D. (1973): A short anorexic behaviour scale. *Br. J. Psychiatry,* 122:83–85.
21. Slade, P. D., and Russell, G. F. M. (1973*a*): Awareness of body dimensions in anorexia nervosa: cross-sectional and longitudinal studies. *Psychol. Med.,* 3:188–199.
22. Slade, P. D., and Russell, G. F. M. (1973*b*): Experimental investigations of bodily perception in anorexia nervosa and obesity. *Psychother. Psychosom.,* 22:359–363.
23. Sours, J. A. (1969): Anorexia nervosa: nosology, diagnosis, developmental patterns and power-control dynamics. In: *Adolescence: Psychosocial Perspectives,* edited by G. Caplan, and S. Lebovici, pp. 185–212. Basic Books, New York.
24. Theander, S. (1970): Anorexia nervosa. *Acta Psychiatr. Scand.* [*Suppl.*], 214.

Anorexia Nervosa, edited by
R. A. Vigersky. Raven Press,
New York © 1977.

Twenty-four Hour Gonadotropin Secretory Patterns in Anorexia Nervosa

†Robert M. Boyar and Jack Katz

Departments of Oncology and Psychiatry, Montefiore Hospital and Medical Center, Bronx, New York 10467

INTRODUCTION

Anorexia nervosa is a disorder primarily of young women that is characterized by marked weight loss in the obsessive pursuit of thinness and hyperactivity in the presence of emaciation and amenorrhea. Previous studies in markedly underweight patients with anorexia nervosa have shown low plasma gonadotropins (1,14) and a failure to respond to clomiphene citrate (2,11). With the return of body weight to normal, basal gonadotropin levels rise and the LH response to clomiphene returns toward normal (15).

In an attempt to delineate more precisely the mechanism responsible for the gonadotropin abnormality in anorexia nervosa, we measured plasma LH at 20-min intervals for 24 hr in nine young women with this disorder who had lost 23.8 to 40.5% of their ideal body weight (5). The results of these studies showed that the 24-hr LH secretory patterns resembled those found in normal prepubertal or pubertal girls. In a single patient who was restudied after clinical remission and weight gain, the LH secretory pattern showed a "maturation" to one characteristic of normal adult young women.

These studies suggested that weight loss could affect the 24-hr secretory pattern of LH; however, it is possible that the psychiatric disturbance and its neurochemical correlate could also be responsible. This latter possibility could explain the known occurrence of amenorrhea prior to the onset of weight loss in one-quarter to one-half of patients with this disorder (7,9,10).

The present chapter concerns studies of the 24-hr LH and FSH secretory patterns in four patients with the psychiatric abnormalities of anorexia nervosa but who maintained near-normal ideal body weight. These patients were in the bulimic phase of their disease that was characterized by periods of gorging, food hoarding, forced vomiting, and maintenance of normal body weight. All four patients had had anorexia nervosa for at least 6 years and

† Present address: Department of Internal Medicine, University of Texas Health Science Center, Dallas, Texas 75235.

had been at least 20% below ideal body weight at some time in the past. Three of the four were menstruating irregularly, and the fourth had secondary amenorrhea.

MATERIALS AND METHODS

Patients

The four patients (Tables 1 and 2) ranged in age from 23 to 26 and were sexually mature. They all had normal menarche but developed amenorrhea associated with the onset of their disease. Three of the four had irregular

TABLE 1. *Clinical data in 4 patients with anorexia nervosa*

Case no.	1	2	3	4
Age at illness onset (years):	19	17	14	17
Weight at illness onset (kg):	61.4	56.8	63.6	59.1
Age at study (years):	26	23	26	23.5
Weight at study (kg):	47.7	50.0	50.0	48.2
Height at study (cm):	152.4	160.0	163.8	165.1
% below ideal weight at study:	0	2	7	12
Lowest weight (kg) (age):	38.6 (22)	44.5 (17.5)	45.5 (21)	36.4 (22)

menstrual cycles at the time of the present study period, whereas the fourth had persistent amenorrhea associated with recurrent episodes of fluid retention. The patients gave histories consistent with primary anorexia nervosa for at least 6 years. They were all preoccupied with thoughts about food and body weight, and engaged in episodes of gorging, food hoarding, and self-induced vomiting. The patients were white and from middle-class families in which diet, weight, and physical appearance were important concerns. All four patients were able to relate some precipitating event that was associated with the onset of their illness.

Methods

All four patients were admitted to the Clinical Research Center at Montefiore Hospital and Medical Center. They were on no medication during the study, nor had they been on any medication for the 6 months prior to the study. The patients were studied in a lightproof, soundproof sleep study

TABLE 2. *Clinical history in 4 patients with anorexia nervosa*

Case no.	1	2	3	4
Menstrual status:	Menarche: 12; periods regular; amenorrhea at age $22\frac{1}{2}$ through present	Menarche: $13\frac{1}{2}$; periods regular; amenorrhea at age $15\frac{1}{2} \times 4\frac{1}{2}$ years; currently irregular	Menarche: 12; periods irregular; amenorrhea at age 20×3 years after 1 year use of oral contraceptive; currently irregular	Menarche: $15\frac{1}{2}$; periods regular; amenorrhea at age 20×3 years; currently irregular
Clinical history:	Began dieting in context of new job and urging by friend; currently: obsessive dieting alternating with binging (no vomiting), distorted body image, insomnia, rapid weight changes	Began dieting to lose weight for ballet lessons; currently: obsessive dieting with binging and vomiting, food stealing and hoarding, distorted body image, insomnia, hyperactivity	Began dieting in context of first sexual relationship; could not diet successfully so forced self to vomit regularly; currently: vomiting compulsively after meals, binging, distorted body image, hyperactivity, insomnia, cold intolerance, rapid weight changes (fluid retention and diuresis)	Began dieting in context of tensions at home; currently: obsessive dieting alternating with binging and vomiting, distorted body image, hyperactivity, insomnia, rapid weight changes
Comments:	Compulsive features	Hysterical, depressive, impulsive (borderline) features; father and paternal grandfather have manic-depressive illness	Depressive, impulsive, dependent (borderline) features	Depressive, anxious, hysterical, impulsive (borderline) features

room for a 24-hr period. A catheter was inserted into an antecubital vein and connected to a longer tube extending into an adjoining room. The details of obtaining and handling blood specimens have been reported previously (8). During the study, one blood sample was obtained every 20 min for 24 hr. During nocturnal sleep, polygraphic monitoring of sleep was performed and sleep stages were scored according to standardized criteria (13). Plasma LH (6) and FSH (4) were measured by double antibody radioimmunoassay. In our laboratory, 5 ng of LER 907 is equivalent to 1 mIU/ml of 2nd IRP-HMG. For FSH, 20 ng of LER 907 is equivalent to 1 mIU/ml of 2nd IRP-HMG. The coefficient of variation for duplicate samples is approximately 10%. All samples from each 24-hr study were assayed simultaneously. The 24-hr LH and FSH mean hormone concentrations as well as the mean LH and FSH values during sleep and waking are listed in Table 3. Student's t-test was used to evaluate the statistical significance between the mean LH and FSH levels asleep compared with waking.

TABLE 3. *The 24-hr mean and sleep-wake LH and FSH levels (mIU/ml)*

	LH			FSH		
Cases	Sleep	Wake	24-hr LH	Sleep	Wake	24-hr FSH
1	7.8 ± 4.8^a	3.0 ± 0.25	5.1 ± 3.3	7.5 ± 1.9^a	5.2 ± 0.3	6.2 ± 1.5
2	11.4 ± 10.1^b	6.9 ± 0.69	10.4 ± 6.8	11.8 ± 3.7^c	10.3 ± 1.4	11.4 ± 2.0
3	11.2 ± 7.5^a	4.8 ± 1.6	6.7 ± 5.3	11.3 ± 1.7^a	8.1 ± 1.3	9.2 ± 2.4
4	18.9 ± 8.3^a	10.0 ± 3.4	14.2 ± 6.5	4.6 ± 2.0^c	3.3 ± 0.9	4.2 ± 1.7

[a] Mean LH and FSH during sleep significantly greater than mean LH awake ($p < 0.001$).
[b] Mean LH and FSH during sleep significantly greater than mean LH awake ($p < 0.01$).
[c] There was no significant difference between the mean FSH asleep compared with waking.

RESULTS

Anorexia Nervosa and Low Body Weight

Figure 1 shows the LH and FSH secretory patterns in a 17-year-old girl with typical anorexia nervosa when she was 35% below her ideal body weight. The mean LH concentration was 6.1 mIU/ml during sleep and 3.8 mIU/ml during waking ($p < 0.001$). The mean FSH concentration was 13.0 mIU/ml during sleep and 10.6 mIU/ml during waking ($p < 0.001$).

Figure 2 shows the LH and FSH secretory patterns in a 20-year-old patient who was 24% below her ideal body weight. The mean LH concentration during sleep was 26 mIU/ml compared with 13.2 mIU/ml during waking ($p < 0.001$). The mean FSH concentration was 10.3 during sleep and 7.8 during waking ($p < 0.001$).

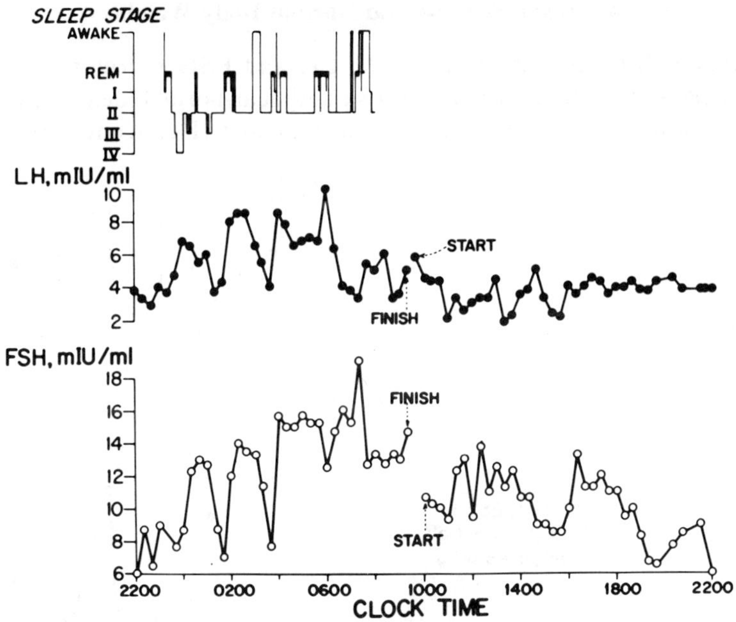

FIG. 1. The 24-hr LH and FSH secretory patterns in a 17-year-old girl with anorexia nervosa who was 35% below her ideal body weight.

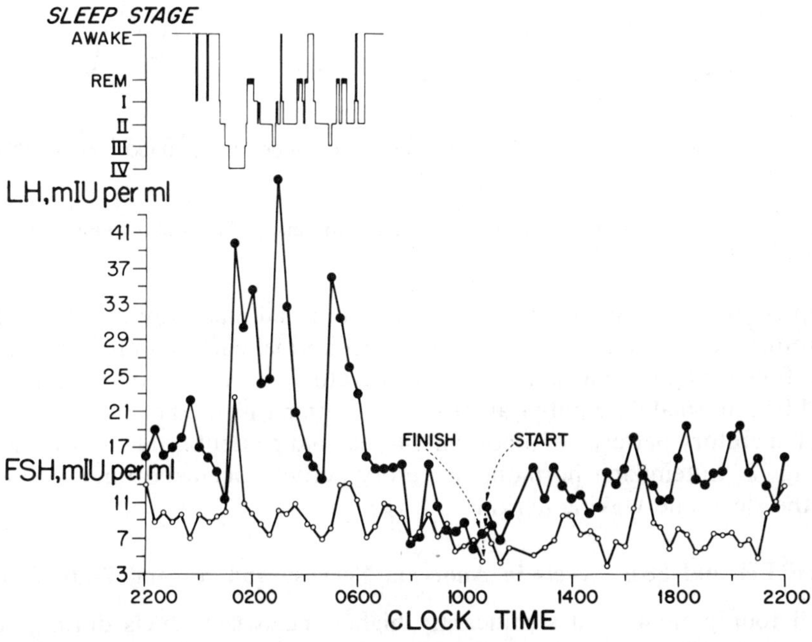

FIG. 2. The 24-hr LH and FSH secretory patterns in a 20-year-old girl with anorexia nervosa who was 24% below her ideal body weight.

Anorexia Nervosa and Normal Body Weight

Figures 3 through 6 show the 24-hr LH and FSH secretory patterns in the four patients with anorexia nervosa and near-normal ideal body weight. All four patients had significantly higher mean LH concentrations during

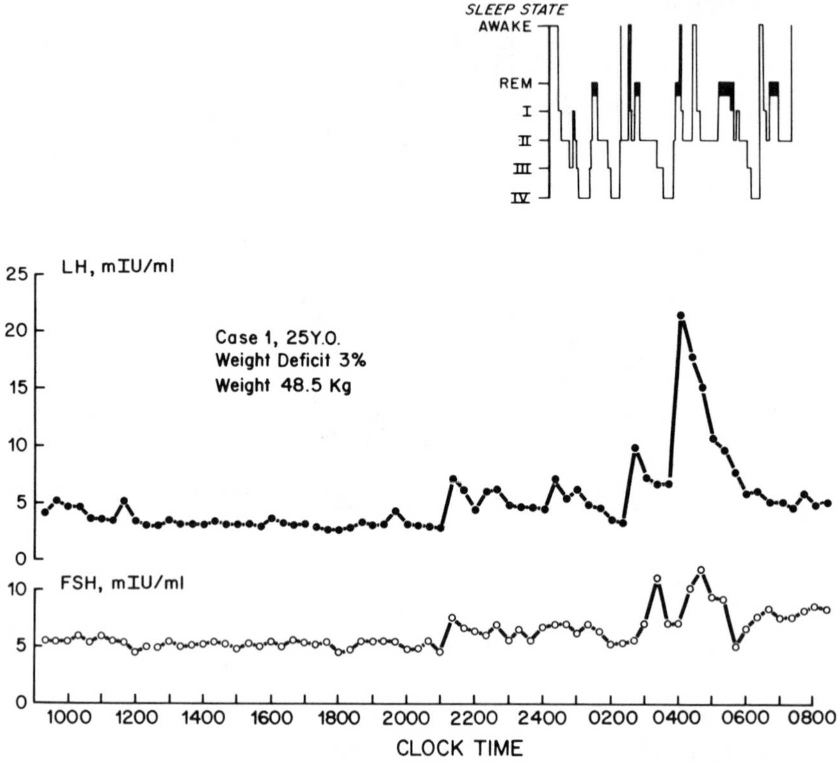

FIG. 3. The 24-hr LH and FSH secretory patterns in case 1. The sleep histogram is displayed for the hours of nocturnal sleep.

sleep compared with waking. Two of the four had markedly decreased LH secretory activity during waking similar to normal early-mid pubertal girls. The fourth patient had episodic LH secretory activity during waking resembling normal late-pubertal girls. For comparison, the 24-hr LH and FSH secretory patterns of a normal 14-year-old postpubertal girl are shown in Fig. 7. Luteinizing hormone secretory activity occurred randomly during the sleep and waking periods.

Mean LH and FSH Levels in Anorexia Nervosa and Normal Body Weight

All four patients had significantly higher mean LH levels during sleep compared with waking (Table 3). The 24-hr mean LH levels ranged from

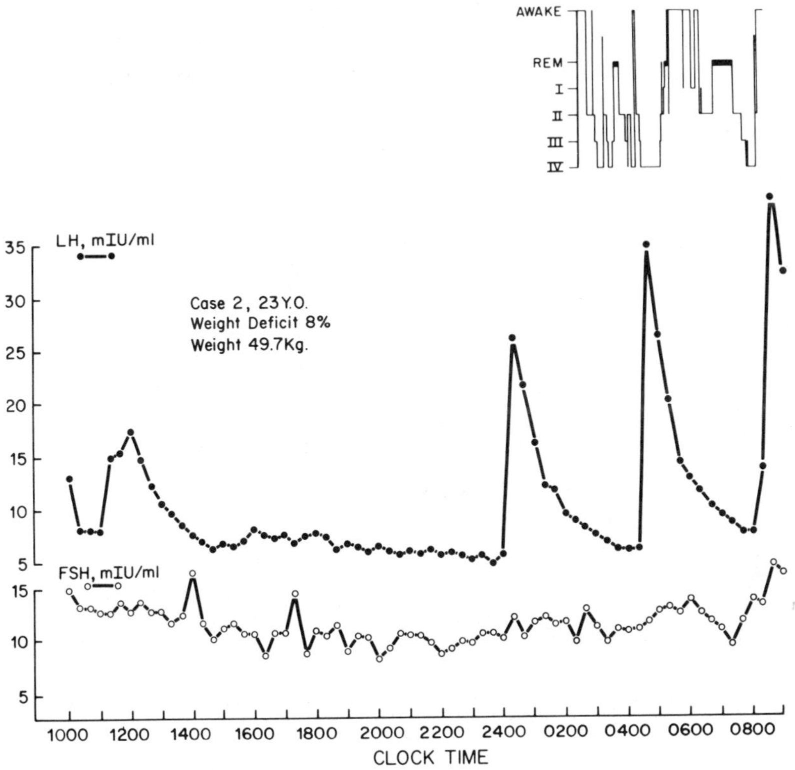

FIG. 4. The 24-hr LH and FSH secretory patterns in case 2. The sleep histogram is displayed for the hours of nocturnal sleep.

5.1 to 14.2 mIU/ml with a mean of 9.1 mIU/ml. The 24-hr mean FSH levels ranged from 4.2 to 11.4 mIU/ml with a mean of 7.8 mIU/ml. Two of the four also had significantly higher mean FSH levels asleep compared with waking.

DISCUSSION

The results of the present study indicate that a regression or arrest of the 24-hr LH secretory "program" is not solely dependent on weight loss in patients with anorexia nervosa. The finding that "immature" LH secretory patterns can occur in patients who fulfill the psychiatric criteria for anorexia nervosa but who are of near-normal ideal body weight suggests that the psychiatric abnormality and its neurochemical correlate can also be associated with abnormalities of gonadotropin secretion.

This does not exclude weight loss in the emaciated patient with anorexia nervosa as an additional factor that can also result in the changes reported

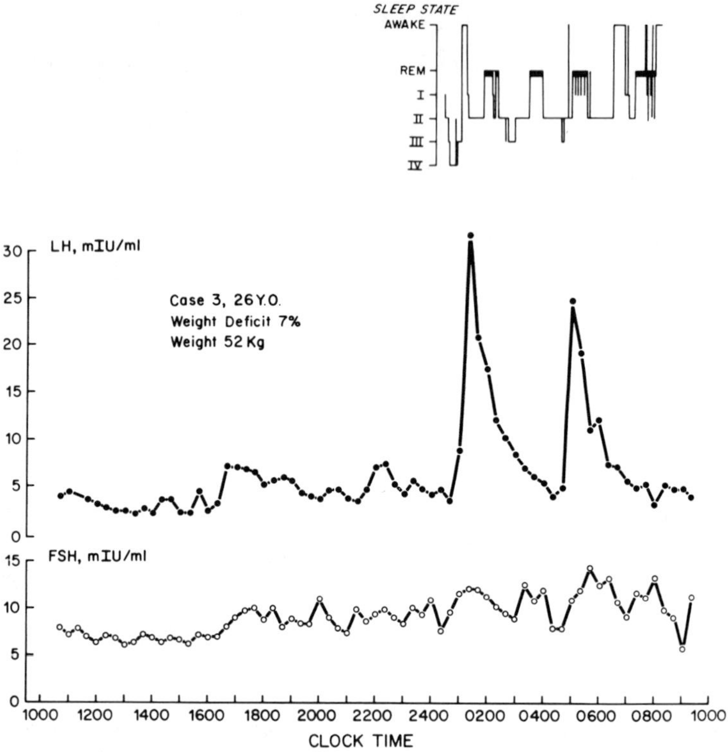

FIG. 5. The 24-hr LH and FSH secretory patterns in case 3. The sleep histogram is displayed for the hours of nocturnal sleep.

previously (5). These results suggest that abnormal LH secretory patterns may be present in the one-quarter to one-half of patients with anorexia nervosa who develop amenorrhea prior to the onset of weight loss; however, additional studies in these patients will be required to resolve this point definitively.

Recently, Beumont et al. (3) showed that the basal LH and FSH levels and response to gonadotropin-releasing hormone (GnRH) correlated with body weight when the latter was expressed as the percent deficit from standard body weight. These observations agree with studies reported by Warren and Vande Wiele (16), but not with those of other groups (12,17,19). These differences may be the result of differences in the degree of weight loss as well as the duration of the illness. It is clear that the response to GnRH is a response to a pharmacologic test and may not provide a true depiction of the endogenous hormonal milieu.

Furthermore, since the immature gonadotropin secretory patterns can occur in the absence of significant weight loss, it seems reasonable to suggest that this abnormality may be a manifestation of a reversible hypo-

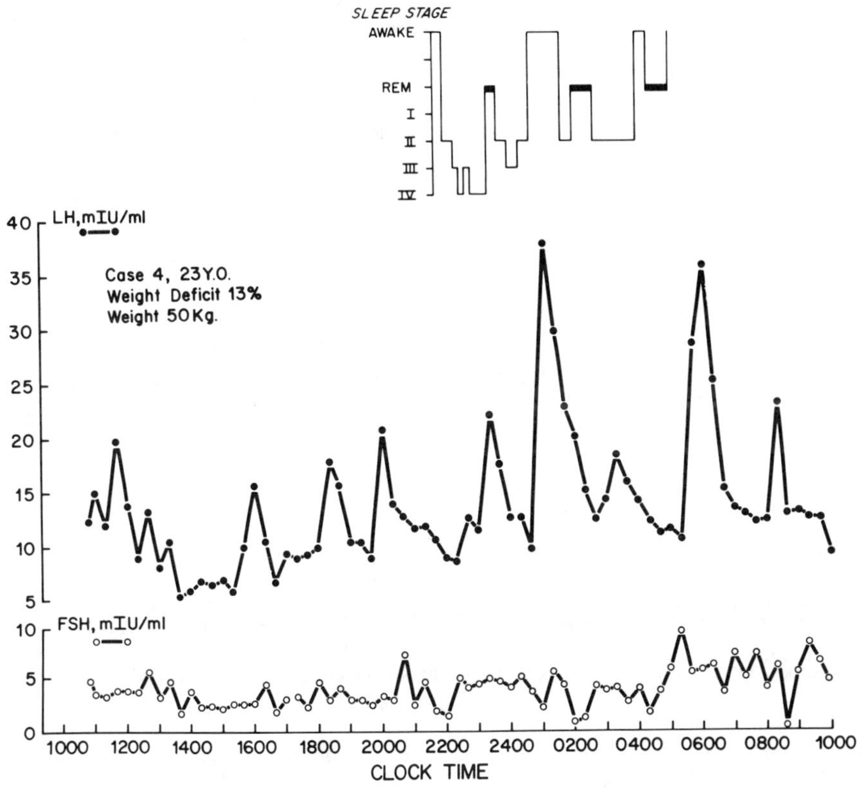

FIG. 6. The 24-hr LH and FSH secretory patterns in case 4. The sleep histogram is displayed for the hours of nocturnal sleep.

thalamic abnormality. Since the secretion of GnRH may be controlled by biogenic amines, it is possible that the changes in monoamines that occur in response to the psychiatric aberrations associated with this disorder may also affect GnRH activity.

Finally, it is of interest that these patients maintained normal body weight by gorging themselves with large quantities of carbohydrate. This raises the possibility that abnormal dietary constituents may affect gonadotropin-releasing hormone synthesis and/or release. Recently, Wurtman and Fernstrom (18) have summarized the available data concerning the control of brain neurotransmitter synthesis by precursor availability and nutritional state. Since neurotransmitter function plays an important role in release of the gonadotropin-releasing hormone regulating pituitary LH and FSH secretion, it is not unreasonable to suggest that a relationship may exist between the aberrant eating patterns exhibited by these patients and their gonadotropin abnormalities. This is obviously an important area that warrants future study.

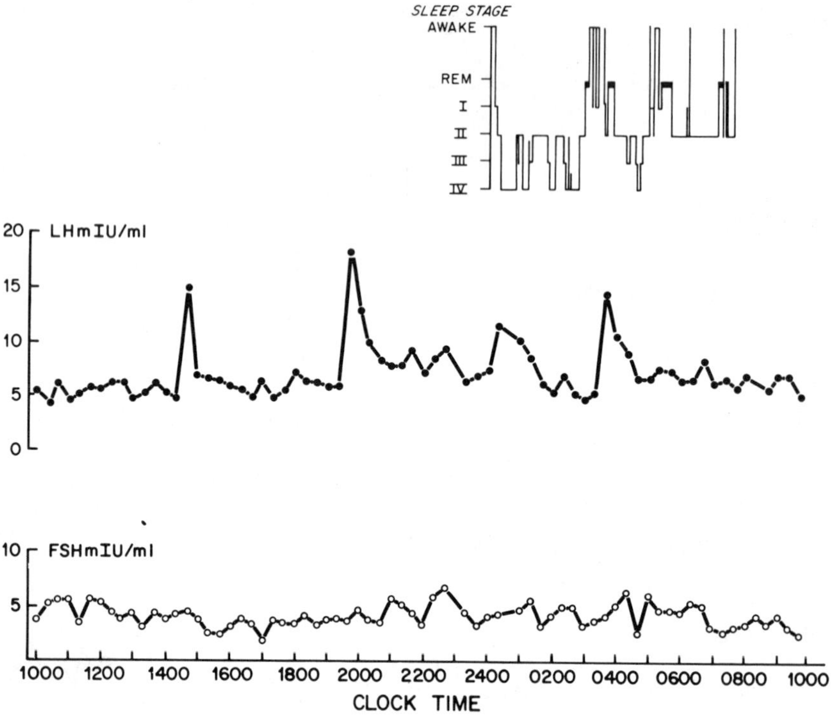

FIG. 7. The 24-hr LH and FSH secretory patterns in a normal 14-year-old post-menarchal girl. Note the random LH secretory activity of equal magnitude during sleep and waking periods.

ACKNOWLEDGMENTS

These studies were supported by NIH Grants CA07304, HL-14734, and RR-53. The technical assistance of Mira Fein, Nate Katz, and Ed Rosario is appreciated. The LH and FSH reagents were supplied by the NIAMDD.

REFERENCES

1. Bell, E. T., Harkness, R. A., Loraine, J. A., and Russell, G. F. M. (1966): Hormone assay studies in patients with anorexia nervosa. *Acta Endocrinol.* (*Kbh.*), 51:140–148.
2. Beumont, P. J. V., Carr, P. J., and Gelder, M. G. (1973): Plasma levels of luteinizing hormone and of immunoactive oestrogens (oestradiol) in anorexia nervosa: Response to clomiphene citrate. *Psychol. Med.,* 3:495–501.
3. Beumont, P. J. V., George, G. C. W., Pimstone, B. L., and Vinik, A. I. (1976): Body weight and the pituitary response to hypothalamic releasing hormones in patients with anorexia nervosa. *J. Clin. Endocrinol. Metab.,* 43:487–496.
4. Boyar, R. M., Finkelstein, J. W., Roffwarg, H., Kapen, S., Weitzman, E. D., and Hellman, L. (1973): Twenty-four hour luteinizing hormone and follicle-stimulating hormone secretory patterns in gonadal dysgenesis. *J. Clin. Endocrinol. Metab.,* 37:521–525.
5. Boyar, R. M., Katz, J., Finkelstein, J. W., Kapen, S., Weiner, H., Weitzman, E. D., and

Hellman, L. (1974): Anorexia nervosa: Immaturity of the 24-hour luteinizing hormone secretory pattern. *N. Engl. J. Med.*, 291:861–865.
6. Boyar, R. M., Perlow, M., Hellman, L., Kapen, S., and Weitzman, E. (1972): Twenty-four hour patterns of luteinizing hormone secretion in normal men with sleep stage monitoring. *J. Clin. Endocrinol. Metab.*, 35:73–81.
7. Halmi, K. A. (1974): Anorexia nervosa: Demographic and clinical features in 94 cases. *Psychosom. Med.*, 36:18–26.
8. Hellman, L., Nakada, F., Curti, J., Weitzman, E. D., Kream, J., Roffwarg, H. R., Ellman, S., Fukushima, D. K., and Gallagher, T. F. (1970): Cortisol is secreted episodically by normal man. *J. Clin. Endocrinol. Metab.*, 30:411–422.
9. Kay, D. W. K., and Leigh, D. (1954): Natural history, treatment, and prognosis of anorexia nervosa, based on a study of 38 patients. *J. Ment. Sci.*, 100:411–431.
10. King, A. (1963): Primary and secondary anorexia nervosa syndromes. *Br. J. Psychiatry*, 109:470–479.
11. Marshall, J. C., and Fraser, T. R. (1971): Amenorrhea in anorexia nervosa: Assessment and treatment with clomiphene citrate. *Br. Med. J.*, 4:590–592.
12. Mecklenburg, R. S., Loriaux, D. L., Thompson, R. H., and Lipsett, M. (1974): Hypothalamic dysfunction in patients with anorexia nervosa. *Medicine* (*Baltimore*), 53:147–159.
13. Rechtschaffen, A., and Kales, A. (Eds.) (1968): *A Manual of Standardized Terminology, Techniques and Scoring System for Sleep Stages of Human Subjects.* NIH Publication 204, Government Printing Office, Washington, D.C.
14. Russell, G. F. M., Loraine, J. A., Bell, E. T., and Harkness, R. A. (1965): Gonadotrophin and oestrogen excretion in patients with anorexia nervosa. *J. Psychosom. Res.*, 9:79–85.
15. Russell, G. F. M., and Wakeling, A. (1974): The endocrine and menstrual response to clomiphene citrate in patients with anorexia nervosa. Presented at the Tenth European Conference on Psychosomatic Research, Edinburgh, Scotland, September 1974.
16. Warren, M. P., and Vande Wiele, R. L. (1973): Clinical and metabolic features of anorexia nervosa. *Am. J. Obstet. Gynecol.*, 117:435–449.
17. Wiegelmann, W., and Solbach, H. G. (1972): Effects of LH-RH on plasma levels of LH and FSH in anorexia nervosa. *Horm. Metab. Res.*, 4:404.
18. Wurtman, R. J., and Fernstrom, J. D. (1976): Control of brain neurotransmitter synthesis by precursor availability and nutritional state. *Biochem. Pharmacol.*, 25:1691–1696.
19. Yoshimoto, Y., Moridera, K., and Imura, H. (1975): Restoration of normal pituitary gonadotropin reserve by administration of luteinizing-hormone-releasing hormone in patients with hypogonadotropic hypogonadism. *N. Engl. J. Med.*, 292:242–245.

Anorexia Nervosa, edited by
R. A. Vigersky. Raven Press,
New York © 1977.

Weight Loss and Responsiveness to LH-RH

Michelle P. Warren

Departments of Medicine and Obstetrics and Gynecology, The Roosevelt Hospital, Columbia College of Physicians and Surgeons, New York, New York 10019

Selected acquired gonadotropin deficiency has been reported in women who have developed amenorrhea in the setting of severe self-imposed weight loss, in particular patients with anorexia nervosa. This deficiency is manifested by low LH, and to a lesser extent, decreased FSH levels in plasma (4,10,19) and appears to be a selective acquired deficiency which reverses with recovery (weight gain) (16,18). Preliminary investigations indicate that the defect is hypothalmic in origin since synthetic LH-RH has been reported effective in releasing both LH and FSH in such patients (11,14,21). However, our studies done in women with weight loss indicate that the degree of pituitary responsiveness to LH-RH is related to body weight with the most severely underweight having blunted or absent responses. Since resumption of menses and presumably pituitary responsiveness return in the majority of patients regaining their original weight, our study was initiated to observe the effect of weight loss on pituitary response to LH-RH in women with weight loss related secondary amenorrhea.

METHODS

Sixteen women, ages 15 to 30, with amenorrhea occurring in the setting of severe self-imposed weight loss were given synthetic LH-RH, 50 μg, i.v. Plasma samples were drawn at base line and 30 min intervals for 2 hr. Seven normal menstruating women, ages 23 to 33 years with cycle lengths ranging from 27 to 32 days, were also studied for a total of 14 injections during different phases of the cycle: early follicular (days 1 and 2), late follicular (day 11), midcycle (day 14 of a 28-day cycle and day 18 of a 32-day cycle), luteal (days 18–25), and late luteal (day 28).

Seventeen patients with secondary amenorrhea of idiopathic origin were also studied. Their ages ranged from 15 to 33 years. The duration of the amenorrhea was from 8 months to 12 years. Excluded from this group were patients with a pituitary tumor or primary ovarian failure. None of these patients had a history of self-imposed dieting or recent weight loss, or was receiving exogenous estrogens.

The synthetic decapeptide (LH-RH, Abbott Laboratories) was dissolved in physiological saline and stored at 4°C. In both the patients and normal controls LH-RH at doses of 50 μg was injected intravenously. Blood samples were taken at base-line and half-hourly intervals for 2 hr. In addition, one patient received a dose of 200 μg LH-RH i.v. In eleven patients, LH-RH was continuously infused through a separate indwelling catheter at a dose of 25 μg/hr for a period of 30 hr using a Harvard infusion pump. Bloods were sampled every 15 min for the first 2 hr and hourly thereafter.

Three patients improved during the study and were followed serially with repeated LH-RH tests, vaginal smears, menstrual histories, and weekly weights. No exogenous therapy was given. LH, FSH (12,13), and total plasma estrogens (7) were measured by radioimmunoassay. The antibody used in the estrogen assay was generated against estradiol 17-BSA and cross-reacted with estrone. The values reported, therefore, represent a combined value of estradiol and estrone. Ideal body weights were adopted from the Metropolitan Life Insurance Company tables (20).

RESULTS

Initial results in these patients indicated that women with weight loss could be separated into several groups (Fig. 1).

First, an extremely unresponsive group with body weights less than 25%

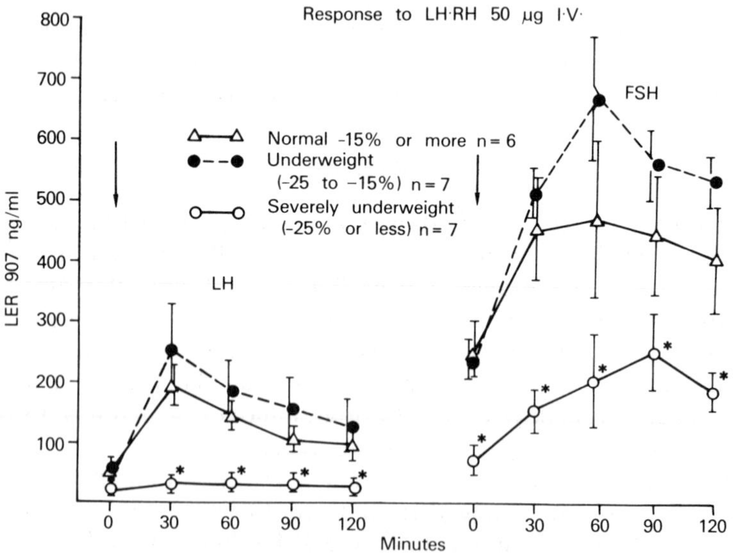

FIG. 1. Effect of 50 μg LH-RH in 20 women with amenorrhea and weight loss. Vertical bars represent SEM. *Values significantly different from the two other groups $p < 0.05-p < 0.001$. (From ref. 18.)

of ideal showed little or no response. When the relatively unresponsive early follicular phase of the cycle is taken for comparison, an absent or blunted response occurred in all women who were more than 25% below ideal weight for LH and more than 34% for FSH ($p < 0.05$ to $p < 0.005$).

Second, an intermediate group who were between −25% and −15% of their ideal body weight occasionally demonstrated a greatly increased response to LH-RH (Fig. 1), indicating that the pituitary may hyper-respond to LH-RH during certain phases of recovery. For this reason, the mean values appear higher than the group who was near normal in weight (−15% below ideal or greater) (Fig. 1), but they did not differ significantly.

Although it has been reported that plasma FSH values rise to a lesser degree following LH-RH than do plasma LH values, these patients were conspicuous in that the plasma FSH response was always considerably

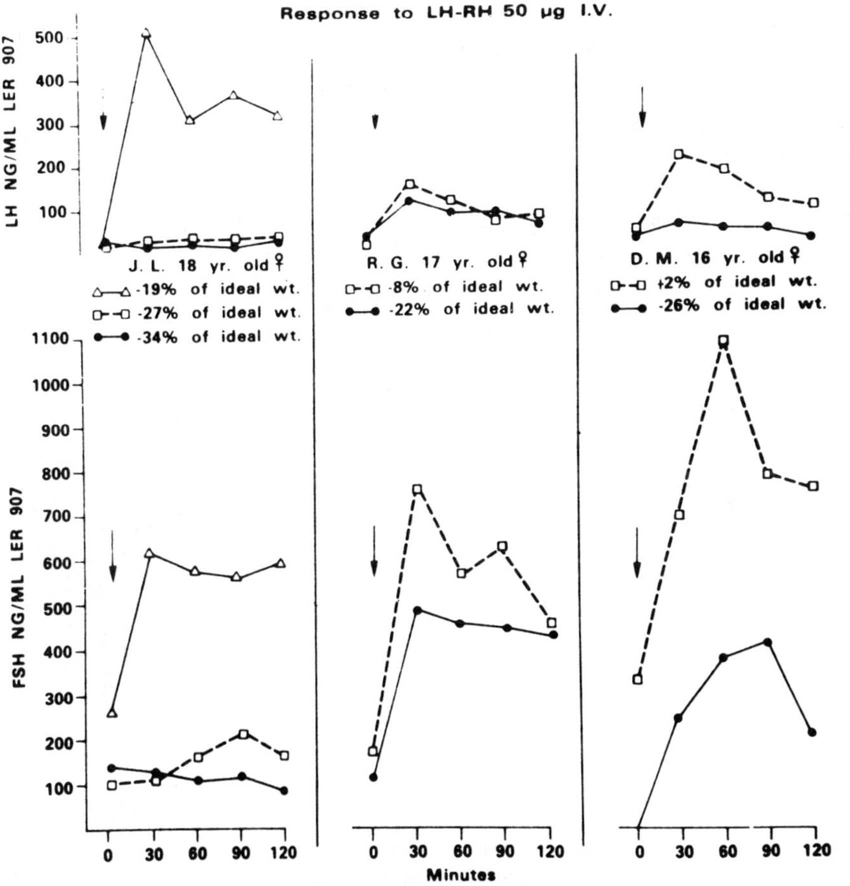

FIG. 2. Repeated LH-RH injections (50 μg i.v.) in 3 patients with weight loss and secondary amenorrhea during recovery (weight gain). (From ref. 18.)

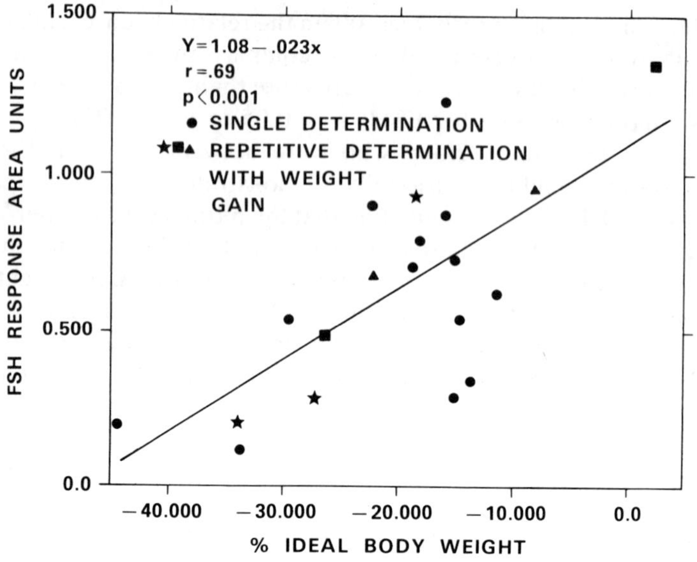

FIG. 3. Correlation of FSH response to LH-RH (50 μg i.v.) and weight expressed as percent of ideal body weight. (From ref. 18.)

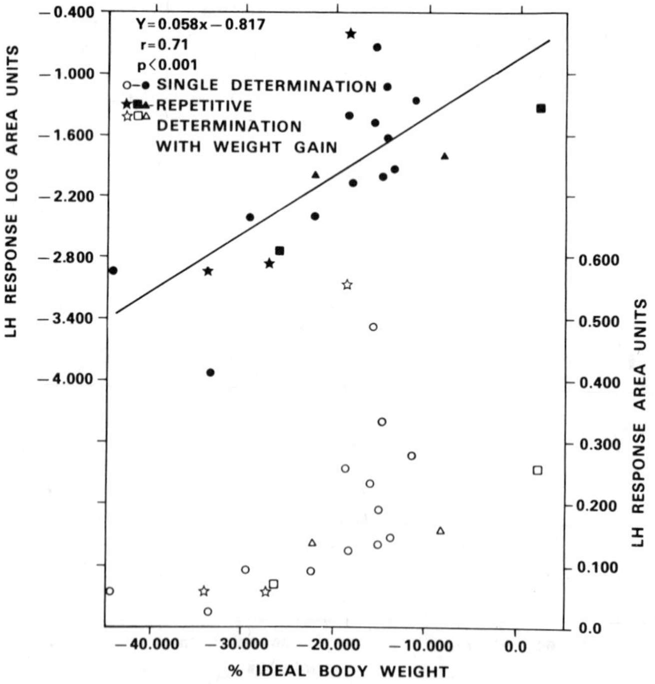

FIG. 4. Correlation of LH response to LH-RH (50 μg i.v.) and weight expressed as percent of ideal body weight. Upper part of graph represents logarithmic scale, lower part represents uniform scale. (From ref. 18.)

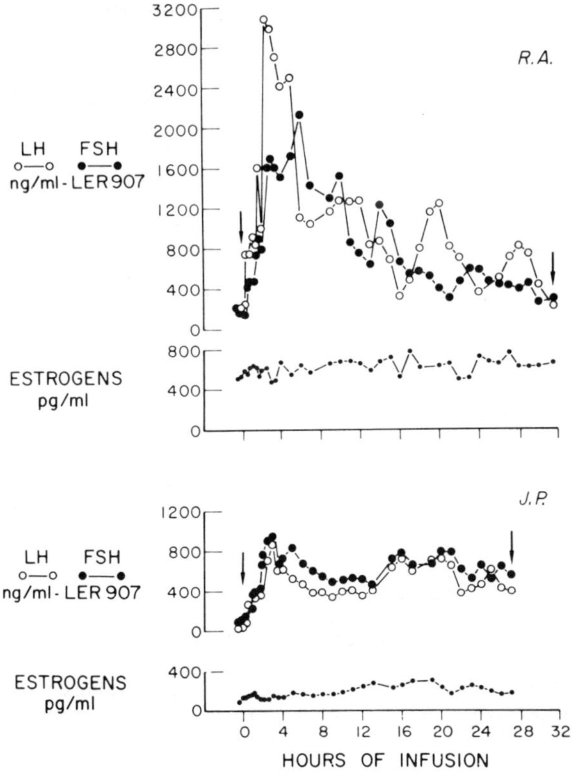

FIG. 5. Levels of LH, FSH, and estrogens in plasma during continuous infusion of LH-RH in two normal subjects in the late proliferative phase of the cycle. (Arrows mark beginning and end of the infusion—25 μg/hr). (From ref. 8.)

greater than the LH response. Although obviously blunted, the plasma FSH response to LH-RH was always present, even in the severely underweight group.

Several patients followed serially as weight gain occurred demonstrated the same pattern (Fig. 2). One patient (J.L.) was first seen when her weight was 34% below ideal. Her response to LH-RH was absent at this level. With an 8 pound weight gain, some increase in response was evident, especially for FSH, and with a 17 pound weight gain, a remarkable increase in responsiveness to LH-RH was evident even though the patient had not resumed menstrual bleeding. Two other patients followed during weight gain demonstrated the same pattern.

Due to variability in base-line levels, the measurement of absolute increase in response, or percent increase, was not felt to be an accurate quantitation of the patient's total response to LH-RH. Therefore, the areas circumscribed by the LH and FSH levels over a 2-hr period were measured using a compensating polar planimeter and expressed in planimeter units. The result obtained could then be compared to body weight and the regression

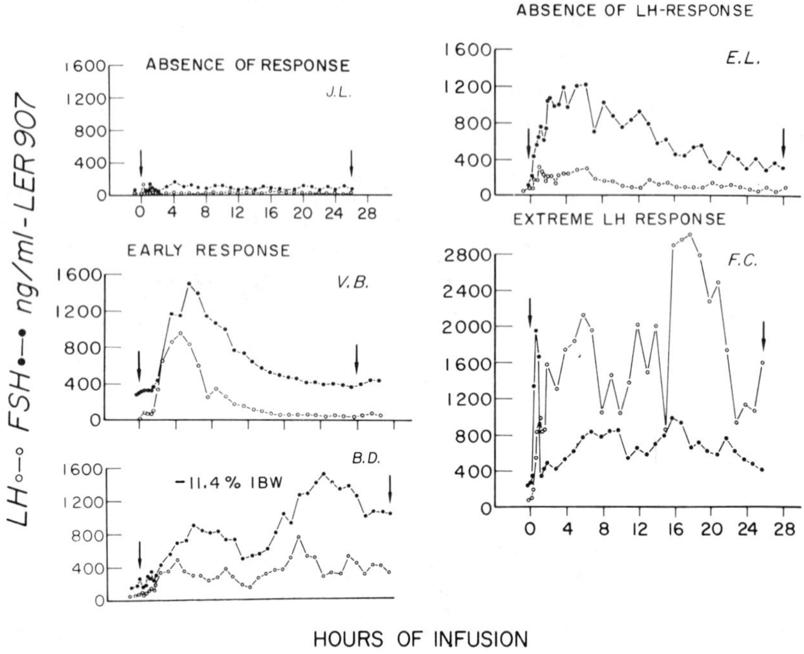

FIG. 6. Levels of LH and FSH in plasma during continuous infusion of LH-RH in 5 subjects with amenorrhea. (Arrows mark beginning and end of the infusion—25 μg/hr). (From ref. 8.)

analysis applied to the data. Twenty LH-RH injections of 16 patients at different weight levels were analyzed in this manner.

The results indicated that the return of FSH responsiveness was linear and correlated directly with an increase in body weight (Fig. 3). A high correlation was therefore demonstrated between FSH responsiveness and increasing body weight. Patients followed serially adhered to this linear correlation with increasing responsiveness as their weight approached ideal.

On the other hand, the LH response (Fig. 4) differed in that regression analysis indicated the best fit for the data was linear on a logarithmic scale ($r = .71$). Therefore, an exponential relation for this response was observed with LH responsiveness increasing exponentially with body weight. Around −15% below ideal, LH responsiveness in terms of the original area units increased dramatically. Stepwise regression up to the fourth power did not improve the fit.

An attempt was made to determine whether increasing responsiveness could be demonstrated in severely underweight patients by increasing doses of releasing factor. One patient was given 200 μg LH-RH i.v. with no increase in response. Another patient, also severely underweight, was given LH-RH 25 μg/hr for 30 hr with essentially no response.

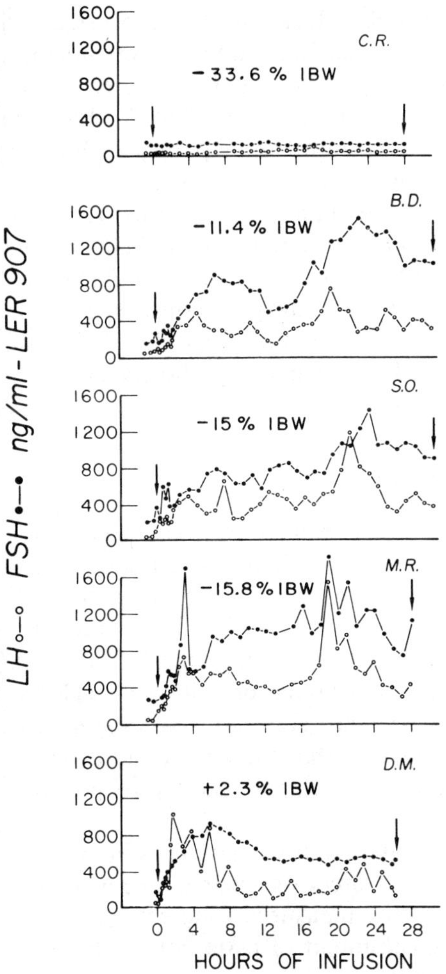

FIG. 7. Levels of LH and FSH in plasma during continuous infusion of LH-RH in 5 subjects with amenorrhea due to weight loss. (Arrows mark beginning and end of the infusion —25 μg/hr.)

Increasing responsiveness to LH-RH is not related to estrogen levels or the duration of amenorrhea. For both the variables correlation was insignificant. Increasing responsiveness to LH-RH both for LH and FSH was demonstrated well before detectable total plasma estrogens or before evidence of estrogen effect on vaginal smear. Several patients had responsive pituitaries with barely detectable plasma estrogens, while on the other hand, several unresponsive patients had levels of plasma estrogens comparable to that found in the mid-follicular phase of the menstrual cycle or higher. The 3 patients tested serially, however, did have some increase in plasma estrogens associated with increase in pituitary responsiveness.

With prolonged (24 to 32 hr) LH-RH infusions (25 μg/hr) in 2 normal women in mid-follicular phase of the cycle, an initial increase in gonadotropins lasting 6 to 8 hr occurred after which levels declined although remained above base-line (Fig. 5). When various amenorrheic states were studied, a variety of patterns were observed, including early response, late response, or absence of response of either or both gonadotropins (Fig. 6). Patients with anorexia nervosa showed particularly interesting patterns (Fig. 7). When severely underweight, a patient with anorexia nervosa since prepubertal age showed no response. On the other hand, four patients who were all within 15% of their ideal body weight but remained amenorrheic showed a peak of gonadotropins which occurred toward the end of the infusion. Of interest also is a shift from late response to the early response in patients who were more nearly approximate their ideal weight. Patient D. M., whose weight was closest to ideal, menstruated spontaneously shortly after the infusion.

DISCUSSION

Patients with anorexia nervosa are known to have disturbances in dynamic patterns affecting temperature control, cyclicity of adrenocorticotropic hormone, water conservation, TSH and gonadotropin release, all attributed to hypothalamic abnormalities (10,11,14,19,21). Our study reveals that basal pituitary gonadotropic function is undoubtedly affected. In our study the gonadotrophic response to stimulation with LH-RH was impaired in women who had undergone severe self-imposed weight loss. The disparate FSH and LH recovery suggests that the LH gonadotroph is more severely affected than the FSH gonadotroph and that the responsible regulatory mechanisms are different.

A puzzling fact was the presence of fairly high total estrogens in many of these patients without evidence of estrogen effect on vaginal smear. It was felt that estrone might be contributing to the measured total estrogens in a higher than anticipated amount and measurement of estradiol levels might have better reflected physiologic changes.

Fishman et al. (5) have demonstrated that women with anorexia nervosa have an increase in the catechol estrogen 2-hydroxyestrone over normal, an estrogen with much less biologic activity than estradiol. This may account for the wide variation in estrogen levels obtained in our patients. They also postulated that body weight may influence the direction of estradiol metabolism, with low body weight such as seen in anorexia associated with an increase in 2-hydroxyestrone formation and less estrogenic activity of the endogenous hormone.

Several authors have shown that with increasing body weight, basal gonadotropin responses to LH-RH return to normal or are even exaggerated (1,2,11,17). It is interesting in this regard that women who have developed amenorrhea in a setting other than weight loss did not appear to have LH-RH responsiveness which could be correlated to body weight.

Even when underweight, these patients' responses as quantitated by planimetry did not demonstrate any significant correlation with body mass. In contrast to the group with weight loss, 5 of the 17 patients showed an LH response which was considerably greater than the FSH response. It is significant to note that in this study the patients with a normal body weight remained amenorrheic despite a presumably normal pituitary response to LH-RH. In these individuals, prolonged infusions of LH-RH to test pituitary reserve were more likely to uncover abnormalities not reflected in single pulse studies.

Studies by a number of authors have demonstrated that the dynamics of LH-RH-stimulated gonadotropin release from the pituitary have a multiphasic pattern (3,8,9). With continuous LH-RH infusion there appear to be in men two pools of LH secretion characterized by early (30 to 60 min) and late (90 to 120 min) peaks. The first pool represents a readily accessible pool of prestored gonadotropins stimulated by LH-RH and controlled by feedback inhibition. The second pool is probably closely associated with gonadotropin biosynthesis as inhibitors of protein synthesis appear to interfere with sustained release of LH. This second pool is also secreted in response to continuous stimulation, but in the normal person is secreted at a greatly reduced rate despite a continued infusion. Our patients with anorexia nervosa appeared to be deficient in the early phase response although continued stimulation elicited significant rises in both gonadotropins late in the infusion. Restoration of normal responsiveness by repeated administration of LH-RH has been reported in anorexia nervosa (22). This suggests that the blunted or delayed responses seen may be due to loss of stimulation by endogenous LH-RH.

This and other evidence indicate that weight may be critical to pituitary responsiveness and basal pituitary function. The onset of puberty in girls is associated with a critical body weight (6). The heightened LH response to LH-RH seen in children as they enter puberty (15) may be triggered as the adolescent child approaches this critical weight.

While we have shown that pituitary gonadotropic function is affected in anorexia nervosa, the primary defect may still lie in the hypothalamus. The change in sensitivity of the pituitary with weight loss may be secondary to atrophy of the gonadotrophs as a result of lack of stimulation from endogenous LH-RH. Further investigation is necessary however, to determine if weight loss may also have a direct effect on basal pituitary function.

REFERENCES

1. Akande, E. O., Carr, P. J., Dutton, A., Bonnar, J., Corker, C. S., and MacKinnon, P. C. B. (1972): Effect of synthetic gonadotropin-releasing hormone in secondary amenorrhea. *Lancet,* 2:112–116.
2. Aono, T., Minagawa, J., Kinugasa, T., Miyake, A., and Kurachi, K. (1974): The diagnostic significance of LH-releasing hormone test in patients with amenorrhea. *Am. J. Obstet. Gynecol.,* 119:740–748.

3. Bremner, W. J. and Paulsen, C. A. (1974): Two pools of luteinizing hormone in the human pituitary: Evidence from constant administration of luteinizing hormone-releasing hormone. *J. Clin. Endocrinol. Metab.*, 39:811–814.
4. Danowski, T. S., Livstone, E., Gonzales, A. R., Jung, T., and Kharana, R. C. (1972): Fractional and partial hypopituitarism in anorexia nervosa. *Horm. Res.*, 3:105–118.
5. Fishman, J., Boyar, R., and Hellman, L. (1975): The influence of body weight on estradiol metabolism in young women. *J. Clin. Endocrinol. Metab.*, 41:989–991.
6. Frisch, R. E. and Revelle, R. (1971): Height and weight at menarche and a hypothesis of menarche. *Arch. Dis. Child,* 46:695–701.
7. Hotchkiss, E., Atkinson, L. E., and Knobil, E. (1971): The time course of serum estrogen and luteinizing hormone (LH) concentrations during menstrual cycle of rhesus monkey. *Endocrinology,* 89:177–183.
8. Jewelewicz, R., Dyrenfurth, I., Warren, M., and Vande Wiele, R. L. (1974): Clinical studies with gonadotropin-releasing hormone. *Bull. N.Y. Acad. Med.,* 50:1097–1119.
9. Jewelewicz, R., Dyrenfurth, I., Ferin, M., Bogumil, J., and Vande Wiele, R. L. (1977): Gonadotropin and steroid response to long term gonadotropin-releasing hormone (Gn-RH) infusions at various stages of the menstrual cycle in women. *J. Clin. Endocrin. Metab.* (*In press.*)
10. Lundberg, P. O., Walinder, J., Werner, I., and Wide, L (1972): Effects of thyrotropin releasing hormone on plasma levels of TSH, FSH, LH, and GH in anorexia nervosa. *Eur. J. Clin. Invest.,* 2:150–153.
11. Mecklenberg, R. S., Loriaux, D. L., Thompson, R. H., Anderson, A. E., and Lipsett, M. B. (1974): Hypothalamic dysfunction in patients with anorexia nervosa. *Medicine,* 53:147–159.
12. Midgley, A. R. (1966): Radioimmunoassay: A method for human chorionic gonadotropin and human luteinizing hormone. *Endocrinology,* 79:10–18.
13. Midgley, A. R. (1967): Radioimmunoassay for human follicle stimulating hormone. *J. Clin. Endocrinol. Metab.,* 27:295–299.
14. Nillius, S. J. and Wide, L. (1972): The LH-releasing hormone test in 31 women with secondary amenorrhea. *J. Obstet. Gynecol. Br. Comm.,* 79:874–882.
15. Roth, J. C., Kelch, R. P., Kaplan, S. L., and Grumbach, M. M. (1972): FSH and LH response to luteinizing hormone-releasing factor in prepubertal and pubertal children, adult males and patients with hypogonadotropic and hypergonadotropic hypogonadism. *J. Clin. Endocrinol. Metab.* 35:926–930.
16. Sherman, B. M., Halmi, K. A., and Zamudio, R., (1975): LH and FSH response to gonadotropin-releasing hormone in anorexia nervosa: Effect of nutritional rehabilitation. *J. Clin. Endocrinol. Metab.,* 41:135–142.
17. Taymor, M. L., Thompson, I. E., Berger, M. J., and Patton, W. (1974): Luteinizing hormone–releasing hormone (LH-RH) as a diagnostic and research tool in gynecologic endocrinology. *Am. J. Obstet. Gynecol.,* 120:721–732.
18. Warren, M. P., Jewelewicz, R., Dyrenfurth, I., Ans, R., Khalaf, S., and Vande Wiele, R. L. (1975): The significance of weight loss in the evaluation of pituitary response to LH-RH in women with secondary amenorrhea. *J. Clin. Endocrinol. Metab.,* 40:601–611.
19. Warren, M. P. and Vande Wiele, R. L. (1973): Clinical and metabolic features of anorexia nervosa. *Am. J. Obstet. Gynecol.,* 117: 435–449.
20. Weights of insured persons in the United States associated with lowest mortality, from Metropolitan Life Insurance Company statistical bulletin 40 (Nov–Dec., 1959), p. 3.
21. Wiegelmann, W. and Solbach, H. G. (1972): Effects of LH-RH on plasma levels of LH and FSH in anorexia nervosa. *Horm. Metab. Res.,* 4:404.
22. Yoshimoto, Y., Moridera, K., and Imura, H. (1975): Restoration of normal pituitary gonadotropin reserve by administration of luteinizing hormone releasing hormone in patients with hypogonadotropic hypogonadism. *N. Engl. J. Med.,* 292:242–245.

Anorexia Nervosa, edited by
R. A. Vigersky. Raven Press,
New York © 1977.

Effects of Administered Estrogen on Luteinizing Hormone Release in Subjects with Anorexia Nervosa in Acute and Recovery Stages

A. Wakeling, V. De Souza, and C. J. Beardwood

Academic Department of Psychiatry, Royal Free Hospital, London NW3, England

INTRODUCTION

Secondary amenorrhea is an essential feature of anorexia nervosa when the illness occurs in postpubertal girls. It usually arises early in the course of the illness following some initial weight loss but may antedate weight loss in a number of cases (10). During the acute stage of the illness associated with marked weight loss, pituitary gonadotropin and gonadal steroid levels are low. As weight gain ensues during recovery these levels tend to rise, but this is not an invariable finding (2,13,23). Amenorrhea persists until normal weight is restored, but even then many patients fail to menstruate and continue for long periods to show an absence of the cyclical changes in gonadotropins and estrogens which characterize the normal menstrual cycle (2,20). Many recent studies (15,17,21,25) have demonstrated an effective gonadotropin response to synthetic hypothalamic gonadotropin releasing hormone (LH-RH) in patients with anorexia nervosa after weight gain. The failure to resume menstruation does not therefore appear to be consequent on primary pituitary gonadotropin failure. These data suggest that the amenorrhea in anorexia nervosa is not determined solely by malnutrition and, furthermore, point to the possibility of an abnormality in the regulation of gonadotropic output at the level of the hypothalamus.

The regulation of normal menstruation depends on an intact hypothalamic-pituitary gonadal axis. The cyclical pattern of pituitary gonadotropin release is determined in large part by the complex negative and positive feedback effects of the gonadal steroids, particularly estrogen, on the hypothalamic-pituitary unit. Recent work (8,11,24,28) has suggested that gonadal steroids may exert part of their regulatory effect on gonadotropin release by a direct action on the pituitary gonadotrophs by altering the sensitivity of these cells to the action of the hypothalamic releasing hormone. However, it is well established that estrogen, particularly estradiol, exerts an important role in the feedback regulation of pituitary gonadotropin secretion through a direct action on the hypothalamus, controlling the release of LH-RH (9). During the follicular phase of the menstrual cycle, the tonic secretion of luteinizing hormone (LH) and follicle-stimulating hormone (FSH) is regulated by a negative feedback action of estrogen which allows normal ovarian follicular development. At mid-cycle, in primates, the rising production of estrogen from the developing follicle initiates, by a positive feedback action, the ovulatory surge of LH and FSH (12).

Knobil and his collaborators (4,12,26) have shown in the adult rhesus monkey that the negative and positive feedback effects of estrogen on gonadotropin release can be demonstrated experimentally by the administration of estrogen during the follicular phase of the menstrual cycle. The resulting increments in circulating estrogen under these conditions consistently invoke gonadotropin surges which are indistinguishable from those occurring spontaneously at mid-cycle. Tsai and Yen (22,27) have reported similar findings in regularly menstruating adult women. These workers administered ethinyl estradiol 200 μg daily for a period of 3 days during the follicular phase of the cycle and noted a fall in LH and FSH levels during the treatment period (negative feedback effects of estrogen) followed by an acute rise in serum LH approximating the normal mid-cycle surge of LH (positive feedback effects of estrogen). The administration of exogenous estrogen to simulate mid-cycle conditions can therefore be used as an experimental tool for assessing the gonadotropin-releasing function of the hypothalamic-pituitary unit in its entirety.

The present study was undertaken to test directly the capacity of the hypothalamic-pituitary unit to respond with changes in LH release to the negative and positive feedback of exogenously administered estrogen at different stages of treatment in subjects with anorexia nervosa. It was anticipated that such a study might allow a more precise definition of the mechanisms underlying the amenorrhea in this disorder.

PATIENTS AND METHODS

Patients

Nineteen postpubertal female patients in whom the diagnosis of anorexia nervosa was made according to previously outlined criteria (19) were studied. All were inpatients when the investigations were carried out. The patients had been admitted to the hospital in a malnourished state and were treated by intensive nursing care and associated supportive psychotherapy with the aim of persuading them to achieve a high calorie intake. This treatment regime was invariably successful such that weight gain was achieved in each case without recourse to medication of any kind. In 11 patients (cases 1 through 11), a course of exogenous estrogen was given shortly after admission. Nevertheless, by this time they were already eating full meals and had shown some initial weight gain.

Twelve patients were given an estrogen test after they had achieved a normal weight and had remained at that weight for at least 2 weeks. Four of these patients had previously been tested during the earlier phase of treatment.

Normal Subjects

Five regularly menstruating females (ages 19 to 35) were given the estrogen test during the follicular phase of a menstrual cycle, starting on day 7 of the cycle.

Estrogen Test Procedure

The estrogen test consisted of giving 100 μg ethinyl estradiol orally twice daily for a period of 3 days. The capacity of the hypothalamic-pituitary axis to respond with changes in gonadotropin release to the negative and positive feedback effects of the administered estrogen was assessed by measuring serum LH values. Samples for LH estimations were taken on the day prior to estrogen administration then daily throughout the 3-day period of drug administration and for the next 4 to 5 consecutive days. Serum 17β-estradiol levels were measured on the day prior to the test. Blood samples were all taken between 9 and 10 A.M., and the serum samples were frozen until the time of assay. All the samples obtained from one patient were assayed for LH in a single assay.

Radioimmunoassay Measurements

Serum LH and 17β-estradiol levels were measured in duplicate by double-antibody radioimmunoassay techniques. The LH assay used was a modification of the method described by Midgley (14). MRC pituitary standard ICSH 68/40 was used as the standard preparation. The sensitivity of the assay allowed measurement down to 1 mIU/ml in terms of the standard preparation MRC ICSH 68/40. With this assay the normal range for the follicular phase of the cycle is 3.5 to 16.0 mIU/ml. Values for the mid-cycle peak in normal subjects exceed 18 mIU/ml. The 17β-estradiol assay used was a modification of the method of Emment et al. (6), with chromatographic separation of the estrogens using Sephadex LH-20. The steroid was labeled with ^{125}I as described by Nars and Hunter (16). The lowest level of 17β-estradiol detectable was 10 pg/ml. The normal range for the follicular phase of the menstrual cycle in our laboratory is 50 to 150 pg/ml.

RESULTS

Normal Subjects

The LH response to 200 μg ethinyl estradiol administered daily for 3 days during the mid-follicular phase of the cycle is shown in Table 1. Estrogen produced an initial lowering of LH values in each subject demonstrating the negative feedback effects of estrogen. All the subjects showed subsequent positive feedback effects with elevation of LH significantly above base-line levels. These peak increases occurred either on the last day of estrogen administration or on the subsequent day. The peak LH values reached were variable ranging between 18.0 and 75.0 mIU/ml, but all fell within the range of levels seen in normal women at the time of the mid-cycle peak of LH. The highest peak values were seen in the two women with the highest levels of basal 17β-estradiol. By the second day after cessation of estrogen, LH levels had returned to base-line concentrations.

TABLE 1. *LH response to 200 μg ethinyl estradiol*

Subject Patient	17β-estradiol (pg/ml) Day 6	LH mIU/ml Days 6	7	8	9	10	11
1	140	11.0	14.0	8.5	75.0[a]	19.0[a]	7.5
2	150	6.1	4.1	3.5	30.0[a]	55.0[a]	6.2
3	53	8.2	3.9	3.1	18.0[a]	13.0[a]	6.1
4	50	9.0	3.5	3.5	8.5	21.0[a]	7.6
5	72	7.5	<1.0	<1.0	20.0[a]	8.0	8.5

The effect of ethinyl estradiol (200 μg daily) administered during the mid-follicular phase of the cycle (days 7–9), on LH levels in 5 regularly menstruating females.
[a] Donates values significantly above basal values ($p < 0.001$).

Patients Tested During the Early Stage of Treatment

Table 2 summarizes the relevant clinical data prior to the administration of estrogen in eleven patients before substantial weight gain had been achieved. Basal LH and 17β-estradiol levels were generally low with only two patients (cases 2 and 4) having LH concentrations and two patients (2 and 10) 17β-estradiol concentrations within the normal follicular range.

The LH values in the 11 patients during and after estrogen administration are shown in Table 3. Estrogen produced a lowering of LH levels in those patients with detectable basal levels of LH, demonstrating the negative feedback effect of estrogen. This effect was more obvious in the patients with higher basal LH levels.

TABLE 2. *Clinical data prior to estrogen administration and before weight gain*

Patient	Age (years)	Duration of amenorrhea (months)	Wt. on admission (kg)	Wt. at test (kg)	% of standard weight	Basal 17β-estradiol levels (pg/ml)	Basal LH levels (mIU/ml)
1	21	60	36.6	46	87	25	2.4
2	30	120	36.0	39.9	69	75	4.3
3	27	84	35.0	36	64	36	2.8
4	28	24	32.2	41.6	78	18	5.5
5	18	24	35.0	36.8	69	15	1.3
6	24	18	42.0	44	80	31	<1.0
7	25	18	37.7	44.6	75	35	<1.0
8	19	24	36.2	38	78	17	2.0
9	38	6	41.0	43	79	28	<1.0
10	16	9	33.5	40	78	60	1.7
11	31	84	40.0	46	79	15	<1.0
Mean			36.8	41.4		32.3	

Relevant clinical details and weight, LH, and 17β-estradiol levels in 11 patients with anorexia nervosa before marked weight gain, on the day preceding estrogen administration.

None of the patients showed any clear-cut positive feedback effect with elevation of LH above base line during the period of estrogen administration or on the day following cessation of estrogen. Four patients, however (cases 1, 6, 8, and 11), showed increased values of LH above base-line levels at some time during the subsequent 4 days. Because of this time sequence, these increased levels of LH may have reflected the spontaneous increase in gonadotropin associated with weight gain since each patient was gaining weight throughout the test. Moreover, these increased levels tended to remain elevated over the next 2 weeks.

TABLE 3. *LH values before, during, and after estrogen administration*

Patient	Days 0	LH mIU/ml 1	2	3	4	5	6	7	8
1	2.4	1.0	<1.0	<1.0	<1.0	<1.0	<1.0	5.2	4.7
2	4.3	<1.0	<1.0	1.0	1.0	1.0	<1.0	1.7	4.5
3	2.8	3.0	2.3	<1.0	1.0	1.8	1.3	1.3	1.8
4	5.5	5.0	1.0	1.5	4.0	1.0	<1.0	<1.0	<1.0
5	1.3	<1.0	<1.0	<1.0	<1.0	1.0	<1.0	<1.0	<1.0
6	<1.0	<1.0	<1.0	<1.0	<1.0	<1.0	4.0	3.8	4.3
7	<1.0	1.0	<1.0	<1.0	<1.0	<1.0	<1.0	<1.0	–
8	2.0	2.5	<1.0	<1.0	1.2	<1.0	2.8	9.5	5.0
9	<1.0	<1.0	<1.0	1.0	<1.0	<1.0	<1.0	<1.0	<1.0
10	1.7	1.8	1.0	1.8	1.4	<1.0	<1.0	<1.0	<1.0
11	<1.0	1.0	<1.0	<1.0	1.0	<1.0	<1.0	<1.0	3.7

Serum LH levels before, during, and after administration of ethinyl estradiol (200 μg daily for 3 days) in 11 patients with anorexia nervosa prior to marked weight gain.

Patients Tested after Restoration of a Normal Weight

Table 4 summarizes the relevant clinical data prior to the estrogen test, in twelve patients after restoration of a normal weight in ten of them and approximation of a normal weight in two. Basal LH levels were higher than those in patients tested earlier in treatment and fell within the normal follicular range in nine of them. With the restoration of a more normal weight there was a tendency for basal 17β-estradiol levels to rise, but these levels remained low in eight of the patients. There was no statistically significant correlation between 17β-estradiol levels and basal LH levels ($r = 0.25$).

The effects of the administration of estrogen on LH levels are shown in Table 5. Ethinyl estradiol induced an initial lowering of LH levels in eleven of the patients. Only one patient (case 2) failed to demonstrate these negative feedback effects of estrogen, but basal LH levels were very low in this subject. Three patients (1, 12, and 13) showed clear-cut positive feedback effects of estrogen with elevation of LH levels above base-line on the last day of estrogen administration or on the following day with subsequent return to base-line values. Basal LH levels were normal in each of these patients and in two of them (1 and 12) the peak LH values fell within the range of levels occurring in normal women during the mid-cycle LH peaks.

The eight patients who showed no positive feedback effects of estrogen on LH release all demonstrated negative feedback effects with diminution of LH levels during estrogen administration. Basal LH levels were normal in six of these subjects.

TABLE 4. *Clinical data prior to estrogen test after restoration or approximation of normal weight*

Patient	Age (years)	Duration of amenorrhea (months)	Wt. on admission (kg)	Wt. at test (kg)	% of standard weight	Basal 17β-estradiol levels (pg/ml)	Basal LH levels (mIU/ml)
1	21	60	36.6	52	99	37	9.3
2	30	120	36.0	50.5	90	17	1.0
3	27	84	35.0	49	88	31	6.8
5	18	24	35.0	47	90	18	8.5
12	14	18	38.6	53.1	105	130	8.6
13	21	30	38.0	52.6	91	30	6.4
14	26	36	38.5	58.1	102	56	1.8
15	15	28	40.0	52.8	90	35	7.5
16	23	12	40.2	50	93	53	6.0
17	25	24	33.2	51.6	89	99	6.7
18	16	9	42.0	50	93	50	8.3
19	17	12	33.1	51.5	105	29	3.2
Mean			37.2	51.5		48.8	

Clinical details and weight, LH, and 17β-estradiol levels in 12 patients with anorexia nervosa after restoration or approximation of normal weight, on the day prior to estrogen administration.

TABLE 5. *Effects of estrogen administration*

	LH mIU/ml								
Patient	Days 0	1	2	3	4	5	6	7	8
1	9.3	7.8	3.9	7.5	24.0	18.0	6.8	2.8	2.2
2	1.0	1.0	1.2	3.8	1.0	1.0	1.0	1.4	9.0
3	6.8	3.7	1.3	1.0	<1.0	1.0	<1.0	<1.0	<1.0
5	8.5	4.6	4.1	3.4	2.4	2.3	3.5	3.7	—
12	8.6	5.0	5.3	27.0	31.0	1.0	7.0	4.6	7.2
13	6.4	3.4	3.9	10.0	9.0	5.0	3.4	6.0	—
14	1.8	<1.0	1.0	<1.0	<1.0	1.0	1.2	<1.0	1.2
15	7.5	2.7	1.8	3.2	3.3	5.3	2.3	2.2	—
16	6.0	<1.0	<1.0	<1.0	<1.0	<1.0	2.5	5.3	—
17	6.7	6.7	4.5	3.4	4.5	4.5	5.3	5.2	—
18	8.3	8.2	2.5	2.6	3.8	5.2	3.7	6.8	6.4
19	3.2	1.3	1.0	1.0	1.7	3.0	1.8	2.1	—

Serum LH level before, during, and after administration of ethinyl estradiol (200 μg daily for 3 days) in 12 patients with anorexia nervosa after restoration of normal weight.

There were no consistent features—age, duration of illness, weight on admission, weight at the time of the test, or period of time the patient had remained at a normal weight prior to the test—which differentiated patients who showed unequivocal positive feedback effects of estrogen from the others. One of the patients showing the complete estrogen response had normal basal 17β-estradiol levels, whereas these levels were low in the other two.

Course During Subsequent 6 Months of Patients Tested after Restoration of Normal Weight

Of the three patients who showed a positive feedback response to estrogen, two (cases 12 and 13) had subsequent menstrual bleeding. Menstruation started 3 weeks after the course of estrogen in one patient (12) and 4 weeks after in the other (13). Thereafter, both patients experienced regular menstrual cycles. Normal weight was maintained, and both were considered to have made a full psychological and nutritional recovery. The third patient (case 1) failed to menstruate. Following the estrogen test her weight remained normal for approximately 3 weeks, and she then gradually began to lose weight again.

Of the nine patients who failed to demonstrate any positive feedback release of LH after estrogen administration, three (cases 14, 16, and 18) maintained a normal weight during the subsequent 6 months. Only one of these patients (18), however, resumed menstruation, with the onset some 3 months after the estrogen test.

The remaining six patients all started to lose weight within a few weeks of the estrogen test and none of them menstruated.

DISCUSSION

The results in healthy women were similar to those reported by Yen and Tsai (27), who used the same regime of exogenous estrogen administration.

In contrast to healthy women, patients with anorexia nervosa prior to marked weight gain failed to show any positive feedback release of LH after estrogen administration. In these patients basal LH levels were generally low, but when LH levels were measurable, negative feedback action of estrogen was demonstrated by a lowering of LH levels.

In patients following weight gain, the negative feedback effects of estrogen were more apparent. With weight gain there had been a coincident increase in LH levels, such that nine out of twelve patients had achieved normal LH concentrations. Negative feedback effects of estrogen with lowering of LH levels were achieved in each of these patients, but only three of them showed a complete response to estrogen with a subsequent positive feedback release of LH. In two patients with persisting low basal levels of LH only negative feedback effects of estrogen were observed.

These findings suggest that in anorexia nervosa the ability of the hypothalamus to respond to the positive feedback effects of estrogen is more impaired than its ability to respond to the negative feedback effects. Furthermore, the ability to respond to these positive feedback effects is clearly influenced by the patient's weight. They were not demonstrated prior to the resumption of a normal weight and until basal LH levels had risen to normal. However, the capacity of the hypothalamus to respond to the positive feedback effects of estrogen was still impaired in the majority of patients even after these criteria had been fulfilled.

It is of course possible that more patients would have been induced to produce positive feedback LH surges with larger doses of ethinyl estradiol or a longer period of administration. It is known that in normal women the sensitivity of the hypothalamus to respond to the positive feedback effects of administered estrogen increases toward mid-cycle when circulating levels of endogenous estrogen are rising (27). Circulating 17β-estradiol levels tended to be low in the patients in the present investigation even after weight gain. Nevertheless, there was no obvious difference between the basal 17β-estradiol levels of those subjects who demonstrated positive feedback effects and those who failed to do so. Furthermore, the ability of the patient to respond to the positive feedback effects of estrogen seemed to be related to her subsequent menstrual history. A positive feedback release of LH to ethinyl estradiol 200 μg daily for 3 days was predictive of an early return of menstruation provided the patient maintained a normal weight.

The present results support those studies in which clomiphene citrate has been used to study the integrity of the hypothalamic-pituitary-gonadal axis in anorexia nervosa (1,13,23). Thus, in patients in the malnourished state, clomiphene fails to invoke a gonadotropin response. With the resumption of normal weight, clomiphene invariably induces an initial rise in LH, indicating that the negative feedback effects of estrogen on gonadotropin release are operating. Many patients, however, fail to menstruate, suggesting an impaired hypothalamic response to the positive feedback effects of estrogen. The complete clomiphene response tends to occur only in patients with normal follicular basal levels of LH, although such levels do not guarantee a response. The results of the present investigation also suggest that there must be a return to normal basal levels of LH prior to the resumption of a positive feedback capacity between estrogen and LH.

These findings taken together suggest that in recovery from anorexia nervosa there is a return to normal hypothalamic-pituitary-gonadal activity in a definite sequence which recapitulates puberty (5). With marked weight loss there are low circulating levels of gonadotropins and estrogens. With weight gain these levels rise, and this is associated with a return of the capacity of the hypothalamus to respond normally to the negative feedback effects of estrogen. The capacity of the hypothalamus to respond to the positive feedback effects of estrogen returns at a later stage. The development of a positive feedback capacity between estrogen and LH, necessary for ovulation to take place, occurs late in puberty (3,18).

It has been postulated that the sequence of maturational events occurring during normal puberty is closely dependent on critical weight changes (7). It is of course possible that in anorexia nervosa the return of the capacity of the hypothalamus to respond normally to the feedback effects of estrogen is also dependent on weight or nutritional thresholds specific for each patient. However, the fact that in some patients the return of menstruation is delayed for long periods following the resumption of normal weight and eating patterns suggests that other non-weight-dependent factors are operating. The psychological disturbance itself is usually the last abnormality to be resolved, and it is possible that this bears some relationship to the hypothalamic disturbance underlying the amenorrhea. Nevertheless, the maturational changes in the hypothalamic-pituitary-gonadal axis associated with puberty occur over a long time span, and it is possible that the recapitulation of these events during recovery from anorexia nervosa might in some patients require a long time sequence. Longitudinal studies in which nutritional, psychological, and endocrine parameters are assessed concurrently in individual patients may provide insight into these issues.

ACKNOWLEDGMENT

This study was aided by a grant from the Medical Research Council (S.972/499/C).

REFERENCES

1. Beumont, P. J. V., Carr, P. J., and Gelder, M. G. (1973): Plasma levels of luteinizing hormone and of immunoreactive oestrogens (oestradiol) in anorexia nervosa: response to clomiphene citrate. *Psychol. Med.,* 3:495–501.
2. Crisp, A. H., Chen, C., Mackinnon, P. C. B., and Corker, C. (1973): Observations of gonadotrophic and ovarian hormone activity during recovery from anorexia nervosa. *Postgrad. Med. J.,* 49:584–590.
3. Dierschke, D. J., Weiss, G., and Knobil, E. (1974): Sexual maturation in the female rhesus monkey and the development of estrogen-induced gonadotropin hormone release. *Endocrinology,* 94:198–206.
4. Dierschke, D. J., Yamaji, T., Karsch, F. J., Weick, R. F., Weiss, G., and Knobil, E. (1973): Blockade by progesterone of estrogen induced LH and FSH release in the rhesus monkey. *Endocrinology,* 92:1496–1501.
5. Donovan, B. T., and Van Der Werff Ten Bosch, J. J. (1965): *Physiology of Puberty.* Monographs of the Physiological Society. Edward Arnold, London.
6. Emment, Y., Collins, W. P., and Somerville, I. F. (1972): Radioimmunoassay of oestrone and oestradiol in human plasma. *Acta Endocrinol. (Kbh.),* 69:567–582.
7. Frisch, R. E., and Revelle, R. (1970): Height and weight at menarche and a hypothesis of critical body weight and adolescent events. *Science,* 169:397–398.
8. Jaffe, R. B., and Keye, W. R. (1974): Estradiol augmentation of pituitary responsiveness to gonadotropin-releasing hormone in women. *J. Clin. Endocrinol. Metab.,* 39:850–855.
9. Kastin, A. J., Gual, C., and Schally, A. V. (1972): Clinical experience with hypothalamic releasing hormones. Part 2. Luteinizing and other hypophysiotropic releasing hormones. *Recent Prog. Horm. Res.,* 28:201–117.
10. Kay, D. W. K., and Leigh, D. (1954): The natural history, treatment and prognosis of anorexia nervosa, based on a study of 38 patients. *J. Ment. Sci.,* 100:411–431.
11. Keye, W. R., and Jaffe, R. B. (1974): Modulation of pituitary gonadotropin response to gonadotropin-releasing hormone by estradiol. *J. Clin. Endocrinol. Metab.,* 38:805–810.
12. Knobil, E., Dierschke, R. J., Yamaji, T., Hotchkiss, J., and Weick, R. F. (1972): Role of oestrogen in the positive and negative feedback control of LH secretion during the menstrual cycles of the rhesus monkey. In: *Gonadotrophins,* edited by R. B. Saxena. John Wiley & Sons, New York.
13. Marshall, J. C., and Fraser, Russell T. (1971): Amenorrhoea in anorexia nervosa: assessment and treatment with clomiphene citrate. *Br. Med. J.,* 4:590–592.
14. Midgley, A. R. (1966): Radioimmunoassay: a method for human chorionic gonadotrophin and human luteinizing hormone. *Endocrinology,* 79:10–18.
15. Mortimer, C. H., Besser, G. M., McNeilly, A. S., Marshall, J. C., Harsoulis, P., Tunbridge, W. M. G., Gomez-Pan, A., and Hall, R. (1973): Luteinizing hormone and follicle stimulating hormone-releasing test in patients with hypothalamic-pituitary-gonadal dysfunction. *Br. Med. J.,* 4:73–77.
16. Nars, P. W., and Hunter, W. H. (1973): A method for labelling oestradiol 17β with radioiodine for radioimmunoassays. *J. Endocrinol.,* 57:xlviii.
17. Palmer, R. L., Crisp, A. H., Mackinnon, P. C. B., Franklin, M., Bonnar, J., and Wheeler, M. (1975): Pituitary sensitivity to 50 μg LH/FSH-RH in subjects with anorexia nervosa in acute and recovery stages. *Br. Med. J.,* 1:197–182.
18. Reiter, E. O., Kulin, H. E., and Hamwood, S. M. (1974): The absence of positive feedback between oestrogen and luteinizing hormone in sexually immature girls. *Pediatr. Res.,* 8:740–745.
19. Russell, G. F. M. (1970): Anorexia nervosa: its identity as an illness and its treatment. In: *Modern Trends in Psychological Medicine, 2,* edited by J. H. Price. Butterworths, London.
20. Russell, G. F. M., and Beardwood, C. J. (1968): The feeding disorders, with particular reference to anorexia nervosa and its associated gonadotrophic changes. In: *Endocrinology and Human Behaviour,* edited by R. P. Michael. Oxford University Press, London.
21. Sherman, B. M., Halmi, K. A., and Zamudio, R. (1975): LH and FSH response to gonadotropin-releasing hormone in anorexia nervosa: effect of nutritional rehabilitation. *J. Clin. Endocrinol. Metab.,* 41:135–142.
22. Tsai, C. C., and Yen, S. S. C. (1971): The effect of ethinyl estradiol administration during

early follicular phase of the cycle on the gonadotropin levels and ovarian function. *J. Clin. Endocrinol. Metab.,* 33:917–923.

23. Wakeling, A., Marshall, J. C., Beardwood, C. J., De Souza, V. F. A., and Russell, G. F. M. (1977): The effects of clomiphene citrate on the hypothalamic-pituitary-gonadal axis in anorexia nervosa. *Psychol. Med. Psychol. Med.,* 6:371–380.
24. Wang, C. F., and Yen, S. S. C. (1975): Direct evidence of estrogen modulation of pituitary sensitivity of luteinizing hormone-releasing factor during the menstrual cycle. *J. Clin. Invest.,* 55:201–204.
25. Warren, M. P., Jewelewicz, R., Dyrenfurth, I., Ans, R., Khalaf, S., and Vande Wiele, R. L. (1975): The significance of weight loss in the evaluation of pituitary response to LH-RH in women with secondary amenorrhoea. *J. Clin. Endocrinol. Metab.,* 40:601–611.
26. Yamaji, T., Dierschke, D. J., Hotchkiss, J., Battacharya, A. H., Surve, A. H., and Knobil, E. (1971): Estrogen induction of LH release in the rhesus monkey. *Endocrinology,* 89:1034–1041.
27. Yen, S. S. C., and Tsai, C. C. (1972): Acute gonadotropin release induced by exogenous estradiol during the mid-follicular phase of the menstrual cycle. *J. Clin. Endocrinol. Metab.,* 34:298–305.
28. Yen, S. S. C., Vandenberg, G., and Siler, T. M. (1974): Modulation of pituitary responsiveness to LRF by estrogen. *J. Clin. Endocrinol. Metab.,* 39:170–177.

Anorexia Nervosa, edited by
R. A. Vigersky. Raven Press,
New York © 1977.

Effect of Nutritional Rehabilitation on Hypothalamic-Pituitary Function in Anorexia Nervosa

Barry M. Sherman and Katherine A. Halmi

Division of Endocrinology and Metabolism, Departments of Internal Medicine and Psychiatry, University of Iowa College of Medicine, Iowa City, Iowa 52242

INTRODUCTION

Study of alterations in endocrine function in patients with anorexia nervosa has provided seemingly endless fascination for clinical investigators. The development of hypothalamic releasing factors and pharmacologic agents that alter pituitary hormone secretion has increased our ability to detect changes in hypothalamic-pituitary function in this syndrome. In an attempt to better understand the role of nutrition and body weight on alterations in neuroendocrine function, we have evaluated pituitary function before, during, and after a program of nutritional rehabilitation using operant conditioning techniques. We report here the results of studies using gonadotropin releasing hormone (GnRH) to assess the adequacy of pituitary LH and FSH secretion and L-DOPA as a stimulus of growth hormone secretion.

MATERIALS AND METHODS

To date, 45 patients have been studied as a part of a comprehensive program of evaluation and treatment of anorexia nervosa in the Clinical Research Center at the University of Iowa. All patients met rigid criteria for the diagnosis (11). The initial 15 patients were treated with an operant conditioning program that used positive reinforcement of social activities, increased physical activity, and visiting privileges contingent on weight gain. The remaining 30 patients have been part of a double-blind study designed to assess the efficacy of cyproheptadine, with and without operant conditioning, on weight gain. In all cases, patients had an initial observation period during which base-line studies were done. These studies were repeated after completion of the inpatient treatment program. Details of body weight before and after treatment are summarized in Table 1.

TABLE 1. *Changes in body weight during inpatient nutritional rehabilitation in 30 patients with anorexia nervosa*

	Admission		Discharge	
	Body wt (kg)	% Normal wt	Wt gain (kg)	% Normal wt
Range	27–45	48–84	2–14.3	51–98
Mean ± SD	36.5 ± 5.2	70.1 ± 8.9	7.7 ± 3.2	84.6 ± 9.6

Fourteen patients with anorexia nervosa had assessment of gonadotropin response to GnRH. In eight patients (group I) the response to the releasing hormone was tested during the pretreatment evaluation period when the patients were 53 to 64% of ideal body weight, and this test was repeated prior to hospital discharge when they were 79 to 88% of ideal body weight. Six patients were readmitted to assess the response to GnRH 4 to 11 months following initial hospitalization and treatment (group II). This group did not have pretreatment GnRH studies. When readmitted they were more than 90% of ideal body weight, but none had resumed menstruation.

Seven women with histories of regular menses served as paid volunteers and received a single dose of the releasing hormone on the seventh day following the onset of menstrual bleeding.

Synthetic GnRH was supplied by Ayerst Laboratories. All subjects received 100 μg of the releasing hormone intramuscularly. Blood samples were obtained 10 min before and immediately prior to administration of the drug, and at 15, 30, 60, 90, 120, 180, 240, and 360 min thereafter. The serum was frozen and stored at −20°C prior to hormone assay. The LH and FSH responses following intramuscular administration of GnRH tend to be more prolonged than after an equal dose given intravenously (24). Serum LH and FSH were measured by radioimmunoassay with reagents provided by the National Pituitary Agency (4,19). Results are expressed in nanograms per milliliter of the reference preparation LER-907. All samples from an individual pateint were measured in a single assay.

The net increase in gonadotropin concentration above basal levels was computed by calculating the area under the response curve by the method of summation of trapezoids. Because of the considerable variance in response within groups, a log transformation of the data was performed and analyzed by analysis of variance and Tukey's multiple comparison procedure. Serum estradiol was measured by a radioimmunoassay recently described (13).

Twenty-two patients and twelve healthy young women had determination of fasting serum growth hormone concentration and the growth hormone response to a single oral 0.5-g dose of L-DOPA. Growth hormone was measured by radioimmunoassay with reagents supplied by the National Pituitary Agency (27).

Response to GnRH

At the time of hospital admission, mean basal levels of LH (21 ± 13 ng/ml), FSH (52 ± 32 ng/ml), and estradiol (16.5 ± 6.5 pg/ml) in the 14 anorexia nervosa patients were significantly ($p < 0.001$) lower than mid-follicular phase values in normal women: 117 ± 47 ng/ml, 171 ± 47 ng/ml, and 110 ± 30 pg/ml, respectively (Table 2). Hospital treatment and return to near 80% of ideal body weight resulted in the return of the mean FSH concentration to the normal range, 159 ± 51 ng/ml. However, LH remained low, 30 ± 24 ng/ml. In the six patients who were readmitted after they had returned to more than 90% of ideal body weight, the basal serum LH was further increased to 63 ± 7 ng/ml, but this was still significantly lower ($p < 0.05$) than the normal follicular phase concentrations. The mean serum FSH concentration in this group was normal. The initial serum estradiol concentration was less than 33 pg/ml in all of these patients and did not increase after weight gain, even in that group who had returned to more than 90% of ideal body weight (Table 2).

The LH response to GnRH was markedly impaired in the anorexia nervosa patients who were studied prior to treatment when they were at 53 to 64% of ideal body weight (Fig. 1A, Table 2). Three of the eight patients had no measurable response. After the patients were treated and returned to 79 to 88% of ideal body weight, the LH response increased but remained substantially less than in normal women. By contrast, in the patients studied on readmission after they had returned to more than 90% of ideal body weight, the LH response was normal. When measured as the area under the curve, this LH response was greater but not significantly different from that observed in the normal women and resembled the type of response seen in women with amenorrhea secondary to causes other than anorexia nervosa (Fig. 2).

Whereas the LH response to GnRH was markedly diminished at very low body weights, the FSH response was equal to or greater than that observed in the normal reference population even in those patients studied before treatment at 53 to 64% of ideal body weight (Fig. 1B, Table 2). Although the mean integrated FSH response in each of the anorexia nervosa groups was greater than in the normal women, the differences were not significant.

If the impaired LH response in untreated patients was due to a deficiency of the hypothalamic releasing hormone, then repeated administration of GnRH might restore the response toward normal. Based on this presumption, we gave four patients with untreated anorexia nervosa 100 μg of GnRH on 5 consecutive days while they were taking a diet designed to maintain their admission body weight. The initial LH response was impaired in four patients, and in one subject the LH response was restored toward normal after repeated administration of GnRH (Fig. 3).

In an attempt to assess the relationship between low serum levels of

TABLE 2. *Changes in serum LH and FSH and response to GnRH during nutritional rehabilitation in patients with anorexia nervosa*

	Age	Wt (kg)	% IBW	E_2 (pg/ml)	Basal LH (ng/ml)	FSH (ng/ml)	Response to GnRH LH (μg/ml/-360 min)	Response to GnRH FSH (μg/ml/-360 min)
Group I admission	19 ± 5	31 ± 4	60 ± 5	16 ± 8	16 ± 8	46 ± 36	7 ± 9	41 ± 17
Group I discharge		43 ± 3	82 ± 3	23 ± 8	30 ± 24	159 ± 51	17 ± 22	49 ± 36
Group II admission	17 ± 4	33 ± 4	63 ± 7	17 ± 5	23 ± 16	67 ± 29	—	—
Group II readmission		47 ± 3	92 ± 2	20 ± 7	66 ± 29	167 ± 55	65 ± 41	41 ± 26
Normal follicular phase				110 ± 30	117 ± 47	171 ± 47	46 ± 19	20 ± 13

IBW, ideal body weight; E_2, estradiol.

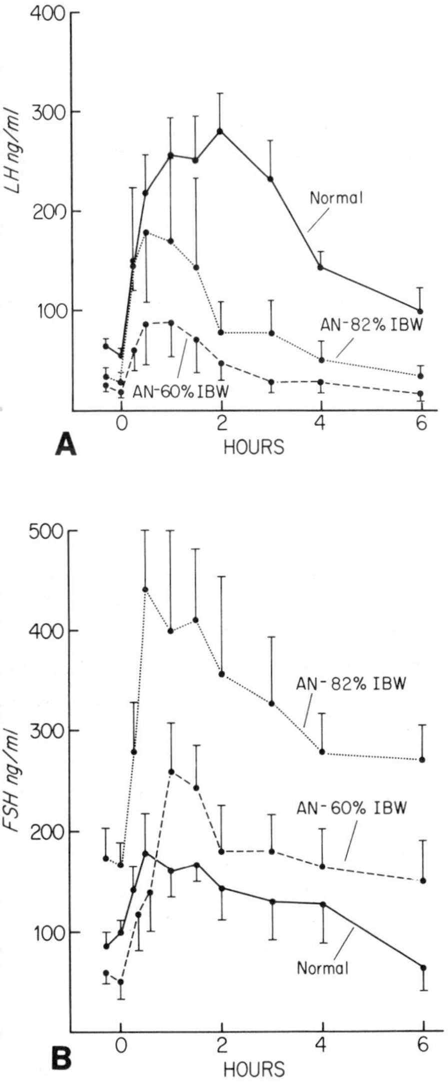

FIG. 1. LH **(A)** and FSH **(B)** responses to the administration of 100 μg of GnRH in patients with anorexia nervosa at 53 to 64% (60%) and 79 to 88% (82%) of ideal body weight, and in 8 normally cycling women during the midfollicular phase. Vertical bars represent ± 2 SEM.

estradiol and the diminished LH response to GnRH, we performed a second test after 3 days of treatment with ethinyl estradiol, 25 μg/day. In all cases the basal levels of LH and FSH were lower after estradiol treatment. Substantial absolute increases in the LH and FSH responses to GnRH over the pre-estradiol test were noted in several patients; however, when these figures were analyzed for net increase in gonadotropin concentration above basal values for the entire group, there was no statistically significant increase after estrogen treatment (Fig. 4).

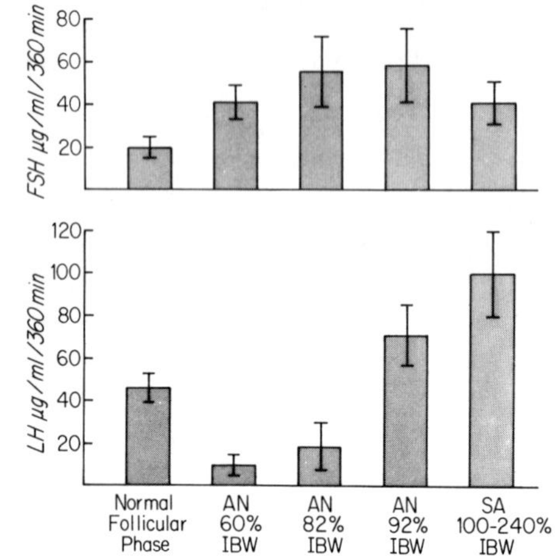

FIG. 2. LH and FSH responses to GnRH expressed as the integrated response above basal levels in normal women during the follicular phase, patients with anorexia nervosa at 53 to 64% (60%), 79 to 88% (82%), and 90 to 94% (92%) of ideal body weight, and patients with secondary amenorrhea (SA) owing to causes other than anorexia nervosa.

Growth Hormone Response to L-DOPA

Twenty-two patients had determination of fasting serum growth hormone concentration on at least two occasions during the pretreatment evaluation. The mean growth hormone concentration before treatment was 13.4 ± 29.4 (SD) ng/ml. One patient had extreme elevation of the fasting growth hormone concentration, 120 to 150 ng/ml. When that value was deleted, the mean fasting level for the remaining 21 patients was 7.0 ± 8.3 ng/ml. In 13 patients growth hormone was measured following oral administration of 100 g of glucose. In all but two patients there was prompt suppression of the growth hormone concentration to less than 5 ng/ml.

Of these 22 patients, 11 received cyproheptadine and 11 a placebo. After treatment and weight gain, the mean fasting growth hormone was 7.9 ± 13.7 ng/ml in the control group and 2.9 ± 2.8 in the cyproheptadine-treated patients, $p < 0.05$. All 12 patients who had an oral glucose load after

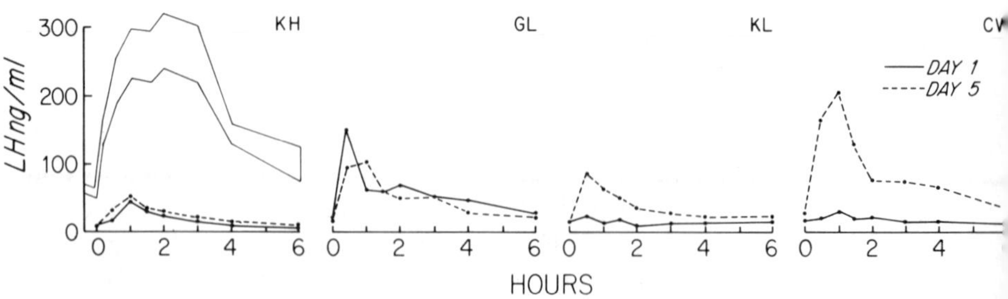

FIG. 3. LH response on the first and final days of 5 daily doses of 100 μg of GnRH in patients with untreated anorexia nervosa. The enclosed area represents the LH response of normal subjects to 100 μg of GnRH during the midfollicular phase of the menstrual cycle.

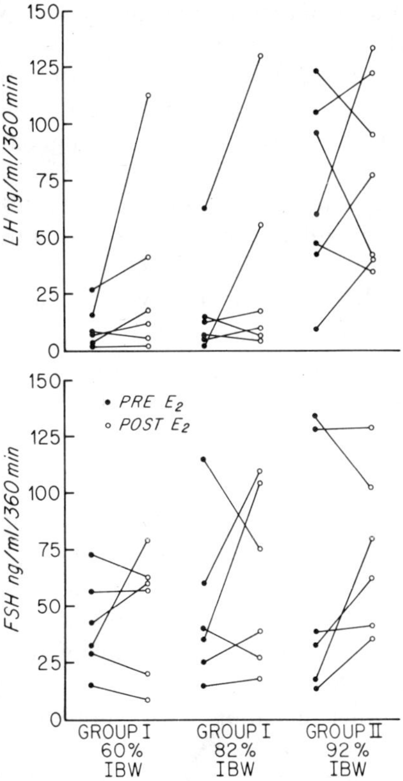

FIG. 4. LH and FSH responses to GnRH expressed as the integrated response above basal levels, before and after 3 days of ethinyl estradiol, 12.5 μg every 12 hr in patients with anorexia nervosa during nutritional rehabilitation. The second test was performed 8 hr after the last dose of estradiol.

treatment (5 drug, 7 placebo) had normal suppression of serum growth hormone to less than 5 ng/ml.

Twenty-two patients had pretreatment assessment of growth hormone response to 0.5 g of L-DOPA given orally (Table 3). Only eight patients had an increment in serum growth hormone concentration greater than 6 ng/ml. In a control group of 12 young, healthy women, 10 responded with

TABLE 3. *Serum growth hormone response to oral administration of L-DOPA before and after nutritional rehabilitation*

	Healthy subjects	Anorexia nervosa		
		Admission	Discharge	
			Control	Cyproheptadine
N	12	22	11	10
Responses > 6 ng/ml	10	8	2	4
Increment hGH ng/ml	31.5 ± 30.5	7.0 ± 12	11.8 ± 23.8	8.2 ± 12.5

increments of greater than 6 ng/ml, and the mean increment for the group was 31.5 ± 30.5 ng/ml. When the L-DOPA test was repeated after nutritional rehabilitation, increments of 6 ng/ml or more were found in only 6 of the 22 patients, 2 in the control and 4 in the cyproheptadine group. There was no difference in the mean increment in growth hormone concentration in the two groups either before or after treatment.

Seven patients had the L-DOPA test repeated after 2 days of diethylstilbestrol (5.0 mg/day), with no significant enhancement of the growth hormone response to L-DOPA.

Twelve patients had assessment of growth hormone response to apomorphine, a dopamine receptor agonist, given in a dose of 0.75 mg subcutaneously. Only four patients responded with an increase in growth hormone concentration of more than 6 ng/ml.

DISCUSSION

The development of agents that assist in the detection of disorders of neuroendocrine regulation has provided new means to investigate the endocrinologic features of anorexia nervosa. When the hypothalamic releasing hormone for LH and FSH was synthesized and became available for clinical investigation, it was quickly applied to the study of this syndrome by us and several other groups (1,18,20,32,36).

Unstimulated LH and FSH concentrations in patients with untreated anorexia nervosa were low, consistent with many other studies. After weight gain there was an increase in the unstimulated gonadotropin concentration that occurred more readily for FSH than for LH. That is, in patients who returned to about 82% of body weight FSH levels were normal, whereas LH concentrations remained significantly less than normal follicular phase values even after return to more than 90% of ideal body weight.

In normal women administration of 100 μg of GnRH caused a four- to sixfold increase in serum LH concentration and an elevation in serum FSH up to double the prestimulated value (7,17,34). Near the time of the midcycle LH peak and during the luteal phase, the LH response to GnRH is greater than during the follicular phase, an effect attributed to the increased concentrations of estradiol (7,34). In women with secondary amenorrhea without evidence of pituitary destruction, LH and FSH responses to GnRH are usually preserved and may be greater than in normal menstruating women (33). This suggests that in a majority of patients with secondary amenorrhea the regulatory abnormality lies at or above the level of the hypothalamus.

In those anorexia nervosa patients tested after treatment and return to more than 90% of ideal body weight, the LH and FSH responses were often greater than those observed in normal women during the follicular phase, and they were not unlike the exaggerated responses observed in women with secondary amenorrhea owing to causes other than anorexia nervosa. This observation suggests that the impaired LH response to GnRH at initial hospitalization and the progressive improvement in response with nutritional rehabilitation reflected the result of severe malnutrition on hypothalamic secretion of GnRH rather than an abnormality peculiar to patients with anorexia nervosa. These findings are in agreement with those of Palmer et al. (20), who showed a significant relationship between the response to GnRH and increase in body weight during treatment in individual patients.

Inadequate hypothalamic secretion of GnRH in untreated anorexia nervosa could explain these findings. If true, then prolonged administration of GnRH might result in the restoration of normal LH responsiveness in patients at low body weights. We observed an improved LH response to GnRH in one of four subjects treated with 100 μg of the releasing hormone daily for 5 days. Using 400 μg of GnRH daily for 3 to 5 days, Yoshimoto et al. (36) reported that the impaired response to GnRH was restored to normal in each of four patients with anorexia nervosa. These results suggest that the impaired LH response to GnRH in patients with severe untreated anorexia nervosa was a result of diminished endogenous secretion of the releasing hormone during the period of malnutrition and that the restoration of a normal response by administration of exogenous GnRH may be dose and time related.

It has been shown that estradiol can enhance as well as suppress the LH response to GnRH (12,30,35). When estradiol was given to anorexia nervosa patients and the GnRH test repeated, we observed an enhanced response in several patients but no statistically significant increase in the LH or FSH response compared to the test done without estradiol pretreatment. We cannot exclude the possibility that the same or different dose of estrogen given for a different period of time might enhance the response more generally. Because the serum estradiol concentrations remained very low, even in patients who returned to normal body weight and regained the capacity to secrete LH, the low circulating estradiol levels may not be causally related to the impaired LH response observed at very low body weights.

The striking disparity in LH and FSH responses to GnRH and in basal LH and FSH concentrations during nutritional rehabilitation raised several questions regarding control of pituitary gonadotropin secretion. Quantitative reduction in LH response suggests that there was a severe decrease in synthesis and/or storage of LH but not FSH during the period of severe malnutrition. If the current evidence that LH and FSH are synthesized in the same pituitary cell (21) is correct, then these data imply that independently regulated systems for the synthesis and secretion of each hormone must exist. It is unclear whether the factors which independently modulate LH and FSH are hypothalamic, pituitary, or peripheral in origin. These data can be interpreted as a reflection of differential sensitivity of the mechanisms that control synthesis and/or release of LH and FSH to what may be reduced concentrations of a single releasing hormone. Although they do not favor either conclusion, they are also consistent with the existence of separate hypothalamic releasing factors for each hormone.

The observation of an FSH response to GnRH that was greater than the LH response in women at very low body weight is not unlike the pattern reported in prepubertal girls (7,21). Evaluating nocturnal gonadotropin secretion, Boyar et al. (2) recently demonstrated that in patients with anorexia nervosa there was a "regression" to a prepubertal pattern of hormone secretion with restoration of a more mature pattern after weight gain. This observation and the reversion to a mature pattern of response to GnRH after weight gain further support the hypothesis that sexual maturation may be related to attainment of a critical body mass (8,9).

Studies of serum growth hormone in patients with anorexia nervosa have emphasized the observation of increased basal growth hormone concentrations (10). In our study, the mean pretreatment fasting growth hormone level was mildly elevated, and in most instances there was a normal response to the administration of oral glucose. Only one patient exhibited an extreme elevation of fasting growth hormone concentration. The increase in serum growth hormone has been attributed to various aspects of caloric deprivation as observed during short-term experimental starvation or protein calorie malnutrition (22,26). The mechanisms of growth hormone elevation in anorexia nervosa and protein calorie malnutrition may differ. It has been suggested that in protein calorie malnutrition the increase in serum growth hormone is related to deficiencies of alanine and albumin, both of which are normal in anorexia nervosa. Moreover, the elevated growth hormone concentrations seen in protein calorie malnutrition were not suppressed normally following a glucose load and often exhibited a paradoxical increase after glucose and an exaggerated response to the intravenous infusion of arginine (29).

The administration of 0.5 g of L-DOPA orally is a widely accepted means of assessing pituitary growth hormone responsiveness with results comparable to those obtained after the infusion of arginine or the induction of hypoglycemia with insulin administration (23,25,31). Failure to respond to L-DOPA has been reported in up to 15% of normal subjects. A surprisingly small proportion of our anorexia nervosa patients had normal increases in serum growth hormone after L-DOPA, and there was no change in response to L-DOPA after estrogen treatment or after weight gain in either the control or cyproheptadine-treated patients. The small number of patients that responded to apomorphine administration strengthens the suggestion that there may be a specific abnormality in dopaminergic regulation of growth hormone secretion in anorexia nervosa (6,14).

These findings are consistent with two recent reports of marked attenuation of the growth hormone response to insulin-induced hypoglycemia as compared with normal weight or weight-matched control subjects (3,5). By contrast, others have reported normal growth hormone responses to arginine infusion in patients with anorexia nervosa (16,28). Studies of pituitary growth hormone secretion after administration of thyrotropin releasing hormone (TRH) provide additional evidence of abnormal growth hormone secretion in anorexia nervosa. In normal subjects, the administration of TRH has no effect on growth hormone secretion. However, in patients with depression, anorexia nervosa, and acromegaly, there was prompt release of growth hormone in addition to thyrotropin (TSH) and prolactin (15). Adequate growth hormone response after TRH and intravenous arginine infusion indicates that in patients with anorexia nervosa the pituitary gland maintained its ability to secrete growth hormone; moreover, it suggests that failure to respond to the dopaminergic agonists L-DOPA and apomorphine reflects a disorder of regulation above the level of the pituitary gland.

The results of these studies using available agents to probe hypothalamic-pituitary function suggest that the disturbances of gonadotropin and growth hormone secretion seen in anorexia nervosa are manifestations of abnormalities at or above the hypothalamus. Normal regulation of gonadotropin and growth hormone secretion is exceedingly complex, and the precise role of biogenic amines in the regulation of these hormones and perhaps in feeding behavior as well remains unclear. It is therefore impossible to synthesize a hypothesis that will explain our observations on the basis of a single abnormality of neuroendocrine regulation. Hopefully, the identification of these and other specific defects of pituitary hormone secretion will help provide the basis for a better understanding of the biologic disturbances that result in the behavioral and hormonal features of anorexia nervosa.

ACKNOWLEDGMENT

Supported by NIH Grant RR59 from the General Clinical Research Centers Branch.

REFERENCES

1. Aono, T., Kinugasa, T., Yamamoto, T., Miyake, A., and Kurachi, K. (1975): Assessment of gonadotropin secretion in women with anorexia nervosa. *Acta Endocrinol.* (*Kbh.*), 80:630–641.
2. Boyar, R. M., Katz, J., Finkelstein, J. W., Kapen, S., Weiner, H., Weitzman, E. D., and Hellman, L. (1974): Anorexia nervosa: Immaturity of the 24-hour luteinizing hormone secretory pattern. *N. Engl. J. Med.*, 291:861–865.
3. Brauman, H., and Gregoire, F. (1975): The growth hormone response to insulin induced

hypoglycaemia in anorexia nervosa and control underweight or normal subjects. *Eur. J. Clin. Invest.*, 5:289–295.
4. Cargille, C. M., and Rayford, P. L. (1970): Characterization of antisera for human follicle-stimulating hormone radioimmunoassay. *J. Lab. Clin. Med.*, 75:1030–1040.
5. Devlin, J. G. (1975): Obesity and anorexia nervosa, a study of growth hormone release. *Ir. Med. J.*, 68:227–231.
6. Ettigi, P., Lal, S., Martin, J. B., and Friesen, H. G. (1975): Effect of sex, oral contraceptives, and glucose loading on apomorphine-induced growth hormone secretion. *J. Clin. Endocrinol. Metab.*, 40:1094–1098.
7. Franchimont, P., Becker, H., Ernould, Ch., Thys, Ch., Demoulin, A., Bourguignon, J. P., Legros, J. J., and Valcke, J. C. (1974): The effect of hypothalamic luteinizing hormone releasing hormone (LH-RH) on plasma gonadotropin levels in normal subjects. *Clin. Endocrinol.*, 3:27–39.
8. Frisch, R. E., and McArthur, J. W. (1974): Menstrual cycles: Fatness as a determinant of minimum weight for weight necessary for their maintenance or onset. *Science*, 185:949–951.
9. Frisch, R. E., and Revelle, R. (1970): Height and weight at menarche and a hypothesis of critical body weights and adolescent events. *Science*, 169:397–399.
10. Garfinkel, P. E., Brown, G. M., Stancer, H. C., and Moldofsky, H. (1975): Hypothalamic-pituitary function in anorexia nervosa. *Arch. Gen. Psychiatry*, 32:739–744.
11. Halmi, K. A. (1974): Anorexia nervosa: Demographic and clinical findings. *Psychosom. Med.*, 36:18–26.
12. Keye, W. R., and Jaffe, R. B. (1974): Modulation of pituitary gonadotropin response to gonadotropin-releasing hormone by estradiol. *J. Clin. Endocrinol. Metab.*, 38:805–810.
13. Korenman, S. G., Stevens, R. H., Carpenter, L. R., Robb, M., Niswender, G., and Sherman, B. M. (1974): Estradiol radioimmunoassay without chromatography: Procedure, validation and normal values. *J. Clin. Endocrinol. Metab.*, 38:718–720.
14. Maany, I., Frazer, A., and Mendels, J. (1975): Apomorphine: Effect on growth hormone. *J. Clin. Endocrinol. Metab.*, 40:162–163.
15. Maeda, K., Kato, Yamaguchi, N., Chihara, K., Ohga, S., Iwasaki, Y., Yoshimoto, Y., Moridera, K., Kuromaru, S., and Imura, H. (1976): Growth hormone release following thyrotrophin-releasing hormone injection into patients with anorexia nervosa. *Acta Endocrinol.* (*Kbh.*), 81:1–8.
16. Neri, V., Ambrosi, B., Beck-Peccoz, P., Travaglini, P., and Faglia, G. (1972): Growth hormone regulation and hypothalamic-pituitary-adrenal function in anorexia nervosa. *Folia Endocrinol.* (*Roma*), 25:143–151.
17. Nillius, S. J., and Wide, L. (1972): Variation in LH and FSH response to LH-releasing hormone during the menstrual cycle. *J. Obstet. Gynaecol. Br. Commonw.*, 79:865–873.
18. Nillius, S. J., and Wide, L. (1975): Gonadotropin-releasing hormone treatment for induction of follicular maturation and ovulation in amenorrhoeic women with anorexia nervosa. *Br. Med. J.*, 3:405–408.
19. Odell, W. D., Parlow, A. F., Cargille, C. M., and Ross, G. T. (1968): Radioimmunoassay for human follicle-stimulating hormone: Physiological studies. *J. Clin. Invest.*, 47:2551.
20. Palmer, R. L., Crisp, A. H., MacKinnon, P. C. B., Franklin, M., Bonnar, J., and Wheeler, M. (1975): Pituitary sensitivity to 50 μg LH/FSH-RH in subjects with anorexia nervosa in acute and recovery stages. *Br. Med. J.*, 1:179–182.
21. Phifer, R. F., Midgley, A. R., and Spicer, S. S. (1973): Immunohistologic and histologic evidence that follicle-stimulating hormone and luteinizing hormone are present in the same cell type in the human pars distalis. *J. Clin. Endocrinol. Metab.*, 36:125–141.
22. Pimstone, B. L., Barbezat, G., and Hansen, J. P. L. (1968): Studies on growth hormone secretion in protein calorie malnutrition. *Am. J. Clin. Nutr.*, 21:482–485.
23. Porter, B. A., Rosenfield, R. L., and Lawrence, A. M. (1973): The levodopa test of growth hormone reserve in children. *Am. J. Dis. Child.*, 126:589–592.
24. Rannevik, G., and Thorell, J. (1974): Effects of synthetic LH/FSH-releasing hormone (LRH) on plasma LH and FSH in amenorrhoeic women. *Acta Endocrinol.* (*Kbh.*), 75:647.
25. Root, A. W., and Russ, R. D. (1972): Effect of L-dihydroxyphenylalanine upon serum growth hormone concentrations in children and adolescents. *J. Pediatr.*, 81:808–813.
26. Samuel, A. M., and Deshpande, U. R. (1972): Growth hormone levels in protein calorie malnutrition. *J. Clin. Endocrinol. Metab.*, 35:863–867.

27. Schalch, D. S., and Parker, M. L. (1964): A sensitive double antibody assay for human growth hormone. *Nature,* 203:1141–1142.
28. Sizonenko, P. C., Rabinovitch, A., Schneider, P., Paunier, L., Wollheim, C. B., and Zahnd, G. (1975): Plasma growth hormone, insulin, and arginine infusion in children and adolescents with idiopathic short stature, isolated growth hormone deficiency, panhypopituitarism, and anorexia nervosa. *Pediatr. Res.,* 9:733–738.
29. Smith, S. R., Edgar, P. J., Pozefsky, T., Chhetri, M. K., and Prout, T. E. (1974): Growth hormone in adults with protein-calorie malnutrition. *J. Clin. Endocrinol. Metab.,* 39:53–62.
30. Wang, S. F., and Yen, S. S. C. (1975): Direct evidence of estrogen modulation of pituitary sensitivity to luteinizing hormone-releasing factor during menstrual cycle. *J. Clin. Invest.,* 55:201–204.
31. Weldon, V. V., Gupta, S. K., Haymond, M. W., Paglara, A. S., Jacobs, L. S., and Daughaday, W. H. (1973): The use of L-DOPA in the diagnosis of hyposomatotropism in children. *J. Clin. Endocrinol. Metab.,* 36:42–46.
32. Wiegelmann, W., and Solbach, H. G. (1972): Effects of LH-RH on plasma levels of LH and FSH in anorexia nervosa. *Horm. Metab. Res.,* 4:404.
33. Yen, S. S. C., Rebar, R., VandenBerg, G., and Judd, H. (1973): Hypothalamic amenorrhea and hypogonadotropinism. *J. Clin. Endocrinol. Metab.,* 36:811–816.
34. Yen, S. S. C., VandenBerg, G., Rebar, R., and Ehara, Y. (1972): Variation of pituitary responsiveness to synthetic LRF during different phases of the menstrual cycle. *J. Clin. Endocrinol. Metab.,* 35:931–937.
35. Yen, S. S. C., VandenBerg, G., and Siler, T. M. (1974): Modulation of pituitary responsiveness to LRF by estrogen. *J. Clin. Endocrinol. Metab.,* 39:170–177.
36. Yoshimoto, Y., Moridera, K., and Imura, H. (1975): Restoration of normal pituitary gonadotropin reserve by administration of luteinizing-releasing hormone in patients with hypogonadotropic hypogonadism. *N. Engl. J. Med.,* 292(5):242–245.

Anorexia Nervosa, edited by
R. A. Vigersky. Raven Press,
New York © 1977.

The Pituitary Responsiveness to Acute and Chronic Administration of Gonadotropin-Releasing Hormone in Acute and Recovery Stages of Anorexia Nervosa

Sven Johan Nillius and Leif Wide

Departments of Obstetrics and Gynecology and Clinical Chemistry, University Hospital, S-750 14 Uppsala Sweden

INTRODUCTION

Anorexia nervosa (AN) is characteristically accompanied by disturbances in gonadotropin secretion from the anterior pituitary gland, and amenorrhea is an obligatory symptom in women.

Studies on gonadotropin secretion in AN by radioimmunological assay methods revealed that the pituitary secretion of LH was impaired in the acute stages although FSH secretion was usually preserved (1,4,10,11,26). After weight gain, the LH values increased (1,11). Age-inappropriate LH secretory patterns, which resembled those found in prepubertal and pubertal children, were found in women with AN (2). The LH secretion was very low during wakefulness with an augmentation of the secretion synchronous with sleep, and this immature LH secretory pattern seemed to be reversible on restoration of weight (2). In the acute stage of AN, patients did not respond to clomiphene citrate with an increase of LH, indicating hypothalamic dysfunction (1,11). The hypothalamic responsiveness to clomiphene reappeared following regain of weight (1,11).

The isolation, structural determination, and synthesis of a hypothalamic gonadotropin-releasing hormone by Schally et al. (21) in 1971 opened a new field of reproductive endocrinology and created possibilities for direct studies of the pituitary gonadotropic function in health and disease. This hormone, LH-releasing hormone (LRH), was found to be capable of evoking a release of both LH and FSH in the human and could be used for diagnostic tests to evaluate the pituitary reserve capacity for gonadotropin secretion. In early studies with LRH in AN, the patients were found to respond to LRH with a small but significant release of both LH and FSH, which indicated that their impaired gonadotropin secretion was due to hypothalamic rather than pituitary dysfunction (3,5,12,13,16,28). Patients with AN, anorectic behavior, or severe dieting in connection with the onset of amenorrhea had a significantly lower LH response than other patients with functional amenorrhea (16). In normal adult women and in patients with amenorrhea not related to weight loss, the LH response to LRH is four to six times larger than the FSH response (15). An inverted response pattern with a marked FSH response in combination with a low or absent LH response to LRH was later described in advanced stages of AN (7,14,17,19,22–24,25,29). Such an inverted response to LRH is characteristic of normal prepubertal children (6,9,20). Recent studies have shown that the LH responsiveness to LRH improved as weight gain occurred, and the inverted prepubertal-like response pattern returned to that normally found in adult women (17,19,22,25).

This chapter is a review of studies on the pituitary gonadotropin secretion in women undergoing evaluation and treatment for AN at the University Hospital in Uppsala. The gonadotropic function was investigated in acute and recovery stages of AN under basal conditions and after acute and chronic administration of synthetic gonadotropin-releasing hormone, LRH.

A radioimmunosorbent technique (27) was used for the assay of immunoreactive FSH and LH in serum. The results are expressed in nanograms per milliliter of highly purified FSH and LH preparations. The LH preparation had a biological activity of 14,000 IU (2nd IRP-HMG) per mg, and the FSH preparation had a biological and immunological activity of 12,000 IU (2nd IRP-HMG) per mg. Estradiol and progesterone concentrations in serum were also determined by radioimmunological assay methods.

The LRH test was performed with an intravenous dose of 100 μg of LRH as previously described (15). The FSH and LH response to LRH was defined as the difference between the mean of the two values at 30 and 45 min after the injection and the mean of the two control values at -10 and 0 min before the injection. For calculation of differences between mean values, formulas based on the Student's t-distribution were used.

PITUITARY RESPONSIVENESS TO GONADOTROPIN-RELEASING HORMONE IN THE ACUTE STAGE OF ANOREXIA NERVOSA

Twenty-six amenorrheic women, aged 13 to 24 years (mean 18.4 years), with AN were studied with the LRH test while they were hospitalized for treatment in the acute stage of the disease. Their mean body weight at the time of the investigation was 36.3 kg (range 27 to 44 kg), which corresponds to 66% (range 52 to 77%) of mean ideal body weight (IBW) (8).

Their basal gonadotropin secretion was very low. The mean FSH and LH levels in serum were approximately 30% of those observed in 10 healthy women in the early follicular phase of the menstrual cycle (Table 1). All but eight of the AN patients had basal FSH values below 2 SDs from the mean

TABLE 1. *Basal gonadotropin levels and gonadotropin responses to LRH in acute and recovery stages of anorexia nervosa*

	FSH				LH				FSH/LH ratio	
	Basal ng/ml	$p <$	Response to LRH ng/ml	$p <$	Basal ng/ml	$p <$	Response to LRH ng/ml	$p <$	Basal	Response to LRH
I. AN, acute stage, $N = 26$ Mean weight 66% of IBW	0.36		0.60		0.29		0.46		1.24	1.30
		0.02		0.001		ns		0.001		
II. AN, recovery stage 1, $N = 28$ Mean weight 75% of IBW	0.66		0.92		0.28		1.43		2.36	0.64
		ns		ns		0.01		0.001		
III. AN, recovery stage 2, $N = 10$ Mean weight 100% of IBW	0.80		0.68		0.54		3.68		1.48	0.18
		ns		0.05		0.05		0.05		
IV. Control, healthy women, $N = 10$ Early follicular phase	1.1		0.31		0.94		1.41		1.17	0.22
		0.001		ns		0.001		0.001		

of the control group, and all but four had pathologically low basal LH levels.

The mean FSH and LH responses to LRH in the acute stage of AN in comparison with those obtained in the healthy women are shown in Table 1, which also indicates the FSH/LH ratio of the responses to LRH in the two groups. The mean FSH response in the AN group was twice as high as that of the control group, but the difference was not statistically significant. The LH response, however, was only one-third of the normal response. Eight of the nineteen women who responded with an LH release after LRH had subnormal LH responses.

The FSH/LH ratio of the responses to LRH was above unity in the AN group and six times larger than that of the control group of normal women.

PITUITARY RESPONSIVENESS TO GONADOTROPIN-RELEASING HORMONE DURING RECOVERY STAGES OF ANOREXIA NERVOSA

The pituitary gonadotropic function was reassessed during clinical improvement in 19 of the 26 women with AN. The basal gonadotropin secretion and the pituitary reserve capacity for FSH and LH secretion were investigated by 38 intravenous LRH tests during different recovery stages of AN.

In all, 28 LRH tests were performed in 14 women while they were at less than 85% of IBW (mean 75%). The mean basal FSH level at those tests was significantly higher than in the acute stage of AN, whereas the mean LH level remained low. In 10 LRH tests performed in 9 women at 85% of IBW or higher (mean 100%), the mean basal LH level was significantly

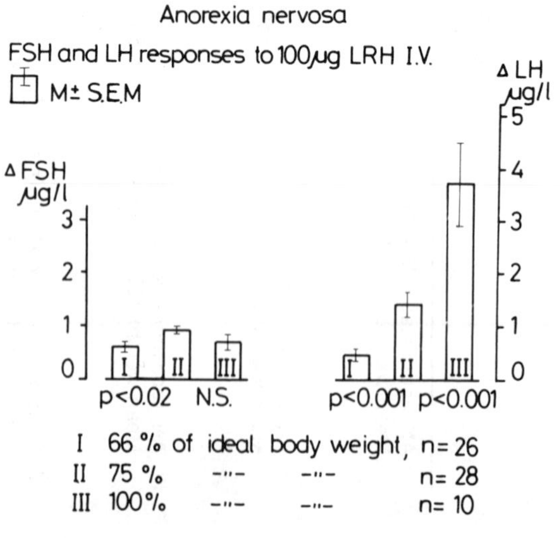

FIG. 1. Mean FSH and LH responses to LRH in acute and recovery stages of AN.

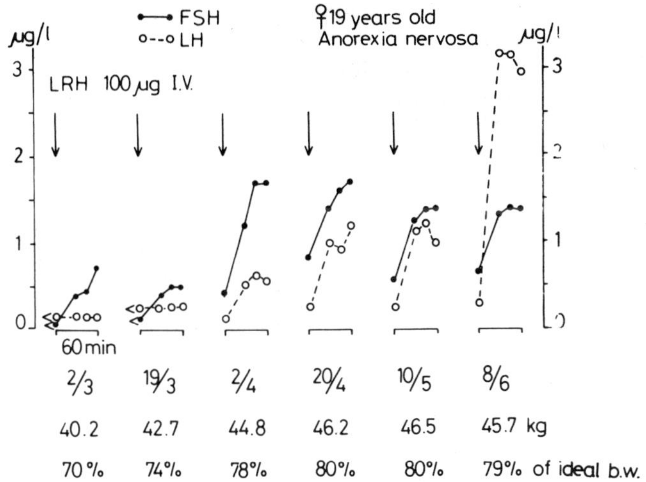

FIG. 2. FSH and LH results from serial LRH tests during clinical improvement in a 19-year-old woman with AN.

higher than at weights below 85% of IBW. The mean FSH level was also slightly higher, but this difference was not statistically significant (Table 1).

Mean gonadotropin responses to intravenous LRH in the acute and recovery stages of AN are shown in Table 1 and Fig. 1. The increase of the LH responsiveness was greater than that of FSH so that the FSH/LH ratio of the responses became less than unity. The mean LH response to LRH at this recovery stage (75% of IBW) was exactly the same as in the normal women, but the FSH response was higher than in the control group. When LRH tests were performed at body weights of 85% of IBW or higher, the mean LH response to LRH had further increased and was 2.6 times higher than in the control group, while the FSH response was unchanged and similar to that of the normal women.

The changes in the pituitary gonadotropic function during clinical improvement in AN are illustrated by Fig. 2, which shows FSH and LH results from serial LRH tests performed in a 19-year-old woman during hospitalization for treatment of AN. The impaired pituitary reserve capacity for gonadotropin secretion seen in the acute stage of AN improved and was restored to normal during clinical remission with weight gain, and the prepubertal-like response pattern after acute LRH administration reversed to normal.

LONG-TERM TREATMENT WITH GONADOTROPIN-RELEASING HORMONE IN ANOREXIA NERVOSA

Nine women with AN were given prolonged treatments with 500 μg of synthetic LRH every 8 hr during 13 treatment courses (14,17,18). Their

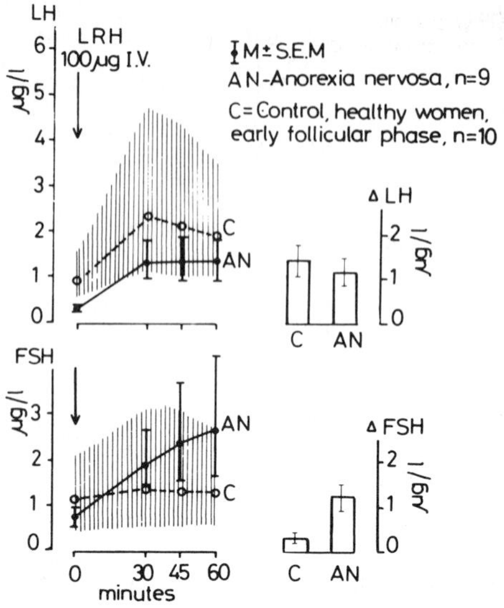

FIG. 3. Mean LH and FSH levels before and after intravenous LRH, and mean LH and FSH responses to LRH before prolonged LRH treatment of 9 women with AN. (From ref. 18.)

gonadotropin levels before and after an acute intravenous injection of 100 μg of LRH before the treatment are shown in Fig. 3, together with the corresponding results in ten healthy women in the early follicular phase of the menstrual cycle. Before the treatment, the basal LH levels were below the normal range in all the patients while only three of the nine women had pathologically low FSH levels. All but one of the AN patients responded to the pretreatment LRH test with an evident LH and FSH release into the blood. The mean LH response was similar to that in the healthy women, whereas the FSH response was four times larger (Fig. 3). Thus, the pretreatment LRH test showed an inverse prepubertal-like response pattern.

Treatment with LRH alone

Prolonged therapy with LRH alone was given to seven women with AN during 8 treatment cycles (14,17,18). The treatment was monitored by basal body temperature recordings and frequent determinations of FSH, LH, estradiol, and progesterone in blood or urine. A total of 500 μg of LRH was administered parenterally every 8 hr until menstruation occurred after 24 to 36 days of treatment. Follicular maturation and ovulation, as judged by increased blood levels of estradiol and progesterone, were induced during all the treatment cycles.

Ovarian hormone levels during an ovulatory menstrual cycle induced by LRH alone are shown in Fig. 4. Before the treatment, this AN patient had a very low endogenous estrogen production. After 11 days of treatment with 1,500 μg of LRH daily, the plasma estradiol levels had risen to levels consistent with follicular maturation. At that time, the basal body temperature

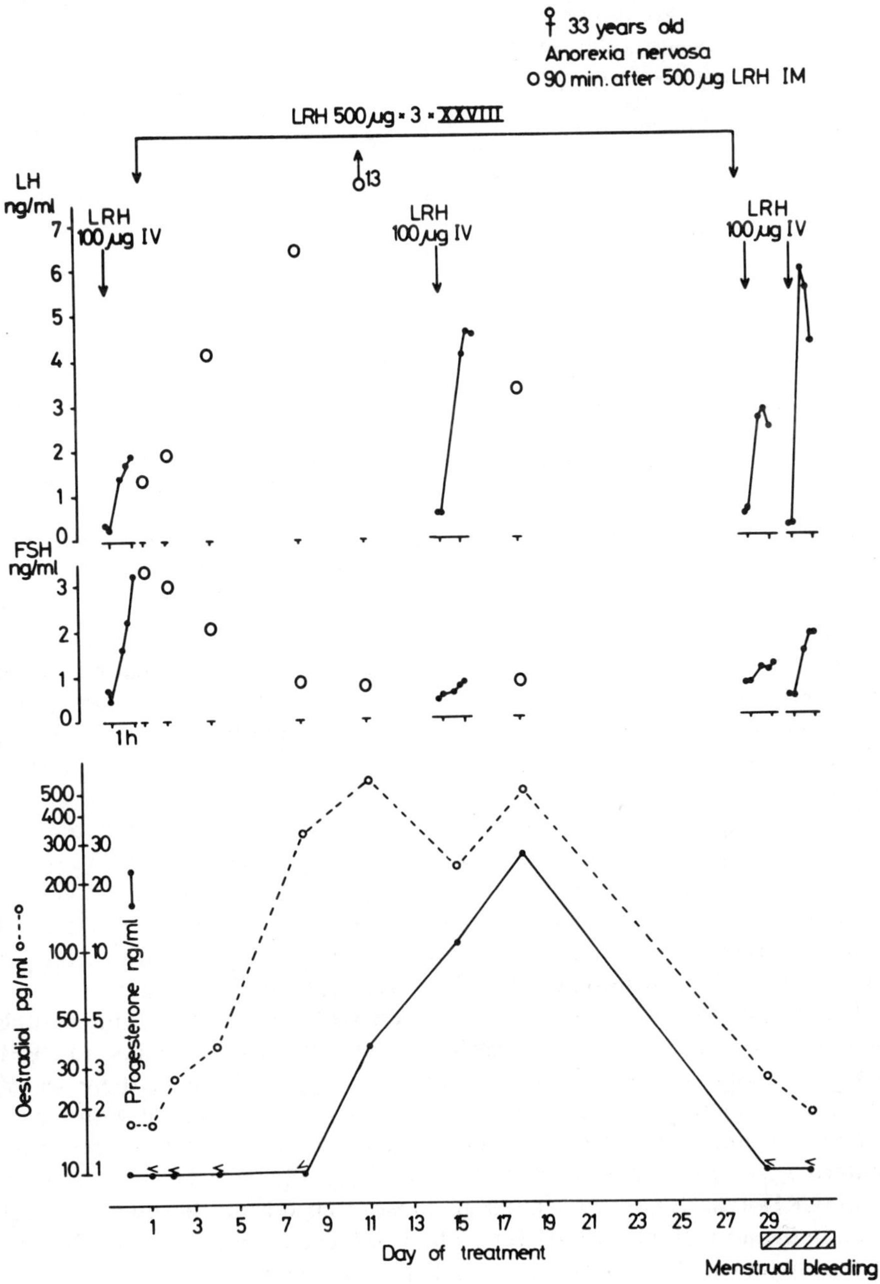

FIG. 4. Serum levels of LH, FSH, estradiol, and progesterone before, during, and after the LRH treatment cycle of an AN patient.

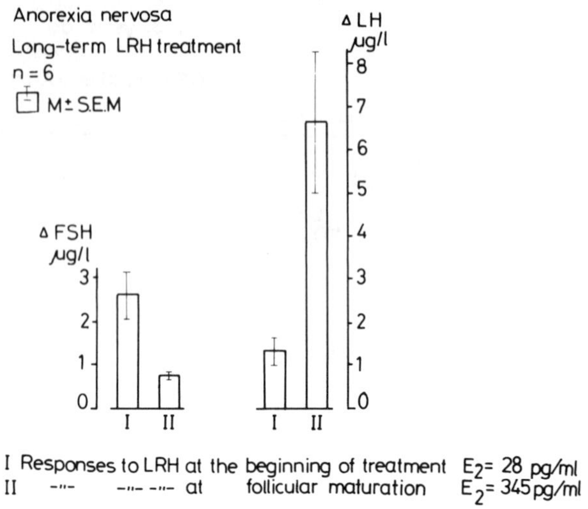

FIG. 5. Mean FSH and LH responses to 500 μg of LRH in 6 women with AN at the beginning of prolonged LRH treatment and at follicular maturation during the treatment. (From ref. 18.)

increased as did the blood level of progesterone, confirming that ovulation occurred. One week later, a high-normal progesterone value was observed, indicating normal corpus luteum function. The estrogen and progesterone patterns during the treatment cycle are similar to those seen during normal ovulatory menstrual cycles.

Thus, by prolonged treatment with LRH it was possible not only to restore normal basal ovarian steroid secretion but also to induce a normal ovarian cycle with follicular growth and maturation, ovulation, and corpus luteum formation in this amenorrheic woman who was practically devoid of any ovarian activity before the treatment. Surprisingly, this was achieved by constant administration of a single gonadotropin-releasing hormone.

During the prolonged treatment with constant doses of LRH, interesting qualitative and quantitative changes in the pituitary responsiveness to LRH were observed (Fig. 4). During the first 11 days of therapy, there was a progressive increase of the LH response to LRH concomitant with a progressive decrease of the FSH response, and the prepubertal-like response pattern reversed to normal. On treatment day 12, the LH concentration after LRH reached levels similar to those seen during the midcycle LH peak in the normal menstrual cycle. The FSH level, however, was only 20% of that obtained after LRH on day 2 of the treatment.

After the prolonged LRH treatment, the patient had a normal adult response pattern with a marked LH response in combination with a small FSH response. One month later, however, the patient had reversed to a prepubertal-like response pattern again with a very large FSH response, nearly twice as high as the LH response. The ovarian steroid production remained low after the treatment, and amenorrhea persisted.

Thus, a cyclical gonadotropin secretory pattern with differential changes of the LH and FSH responses to LRH could also be induced by constant administration of the single gonadotropin-releasing hormone in AN. At the time of the maximum LH response, the blood level of estradiol had increased from 20 to more than 500 pg/ml, and there was also a small increase of the progesterone level. Influence of the ovarian hormones, estradiol, and possibly also progesterone, may be one possible explanation for these differential changes of the LH and FSH responses during the treatment.

Changes in the Pituitary Responsiveness to LRH During Prolonged LRH Treatments

The changes in the pituitary gonadotropin responses to LRH during chronic administration of LRH in AN are summarized in Fig. 5, which is a composite illustration of FSH and LH levels after LRH administration at the beginning and after 10 to 19 days of treatment with 500 μg of LRH every 8 hr in six women with AN. During the first days of treatment at a mean serum estradiol level of 28 pg/ml, the FSH level after LRH was twice as high as the LH level, an inverted prepubertal-like response pattern. After 14 days of treatment, on the average, at a mean estradiol level of 345 pg/ml consistent with follicular maturation, the situation had changed dramatically. The mean LH concentration in blood after LRH had risen to a level similar to that observed during the midcycle peak in the normal menstrual cycle. The LH level after LRH was nine times higher than the FSH level, which had decreased considerably at that time.

The change from a pronounced inverted prepubertal-like response pattern after LRH to a normal preovulatory response pattern after approximately 2 weeks of LRH treatment in women with AN may be due to self-priming effects of LRH on the pituitary responsiveness to LRH acting together with modulatory feedback effects of estradiol at the pituitary level.

Corpus Luteum Function During Treatments with LRH Alone

Ovulation, as judged by increased progesterone levels in serum, was induced during all the treatment cycles with LRH alone. However, the maximum progesterone values observed during the luteal phase in six of the eight induced cycles were rather low, suggesting inadequate luteal function. Possible explanations of the insufficient corpus luteum function might be inadequate FSH stimulation early in the cycle or inadequate LH stimulation at follicular maturation and during the luteal phase for normal ovulation and corpus luteum function to occur. In an attempt to improve luteal function, we gave LRH in combination with human chorionic gonadotropin (HCG) to some women with AN.

Treatment with LRH in Combination with Human Chorionic Gonadotropin

Five women with AN were treated with LRH in combination with HCG during six treatment courses (17,18). This combined treatment was monitored by daily determinations of estradiol in blood and total estrogens in urine. When the estrogens reached levels consistent with follicular maturation, the 8-hourly injections of 500 μg of LRH were interrupted, and a single intramuscular injection of HCG (6,000 to 9,000 IU) was given. The HCG administration was repeated at least once during the luteal phase of the induced cycle. Follicular maturation and ovulation were induced in all the

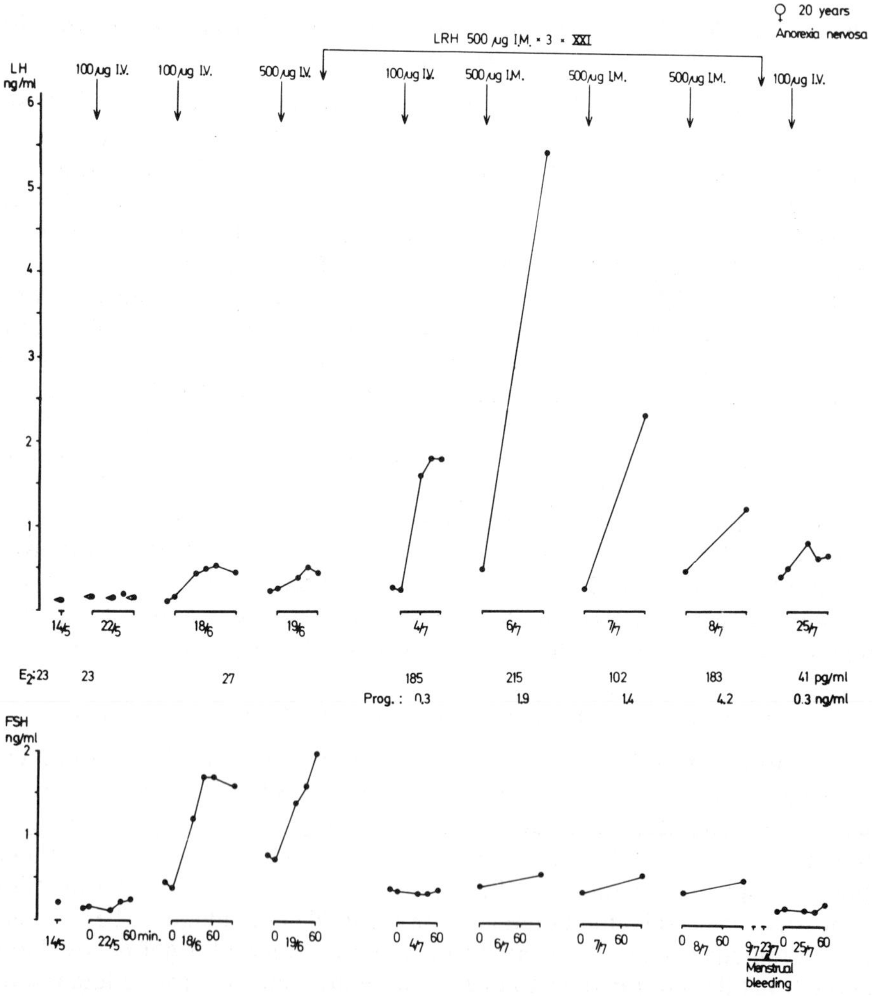

FIG. 6. Basal LH and FSH levels as well as LH and FSH responses to LRH before, during, and after prolonged LRH treatment in a 20-year-old woman with AN.

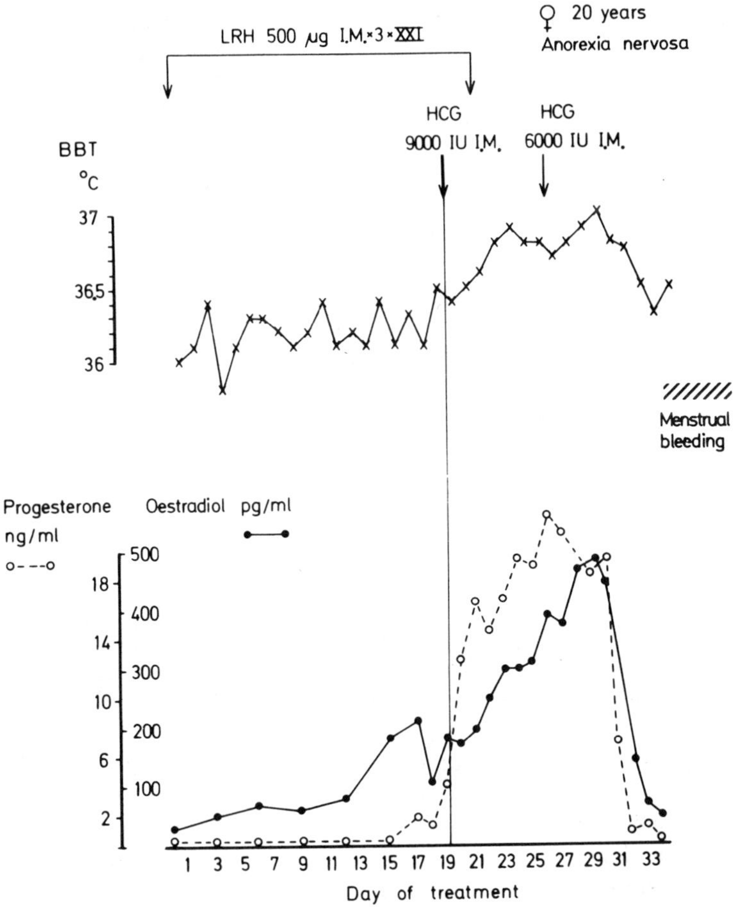

FIG. 7. Basal body temperature (BBT) and blood levels of estradiol and progesterone during the treatment with LRH and HCG in the AN patient from Fig. 6.

treatment cycles, and the corpus luteum function was adequate, as judged by high-normal progesterone levels in blood.

Results from the combined LRH-HCG treatments in two of the amenorrheic patients with AN are shown in Figs. 6 through 9. The pituitary responsiveness to LRH in one of these patients before, during, and after the LRH treatment is shown in Fig. 6. After 16 days of treatment with LRH, 500 μg every 8 hr, the response pattern to LRH had changed markedly. The LH response was pronounced, and there was no longer any significant FSH response. As can be seen in Fig. 7, which shows estradiol and progesterone levels in blood during the treatment cycle, the induced LH peak during the constant administration of LRH presumably induced ovulation. The blood level of estradiol reached a peak 2 days before HCG was ad-

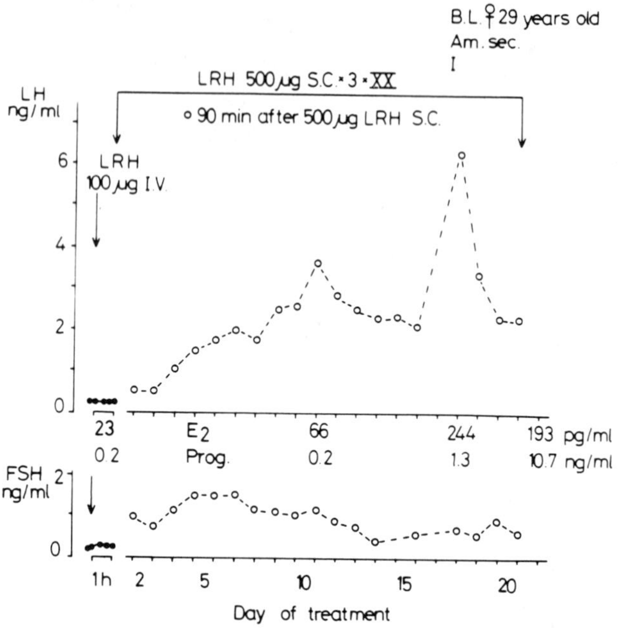

FIG. 8. Basal LH and FSH levels as well as LH and FSH responses to LRH before, during, and after prolonged LRH treatment of a 29-year-old woman with AN. (From ref. 18.)

ministered. This peak was followed by a fall, and at the same time there was an increase of the progesterone concentration in serum to 4.2 ng/ml when HCG was given. Thus, ovulation had presumably already occurred at that time. It is evident from Fig. 7 that the combined treatment with LRH and HCG resulted in a normal ovulatory cycle with good corpus luteum function, as evidenced by the perfectly normal luteal phase progesterone curve.

A complete lack of pituitary responsiveness to LRH was observed in the pretreatment LRH test of another of the AN patients (Fig. 8). During the prolonged LRH treatment, both LH and FSH responses to LRH appeared. The FSH response was more marked than the LH response during the first 3 days, and a prepubertal-like FSH/LH ratio of the gonadotropin responses was seen during the first week of treatment. On treatment day 18, the LH level reached a midcycle-like peak, which was followed by increased progesterone levels in blood (Fig. 9). Thus, ovulation was induced during the constant administration of LRH, before HCG was administered. The characteristic fall of the estradiol peak level, concomitant with the increase of the progesterone level found at ovulation in the normal menstrual cycle, is also seen during the LRH-induced cycle of this patient (Fig. 9). The progesterone concentration was 10.7 ng/ml when HCG was administered, in-

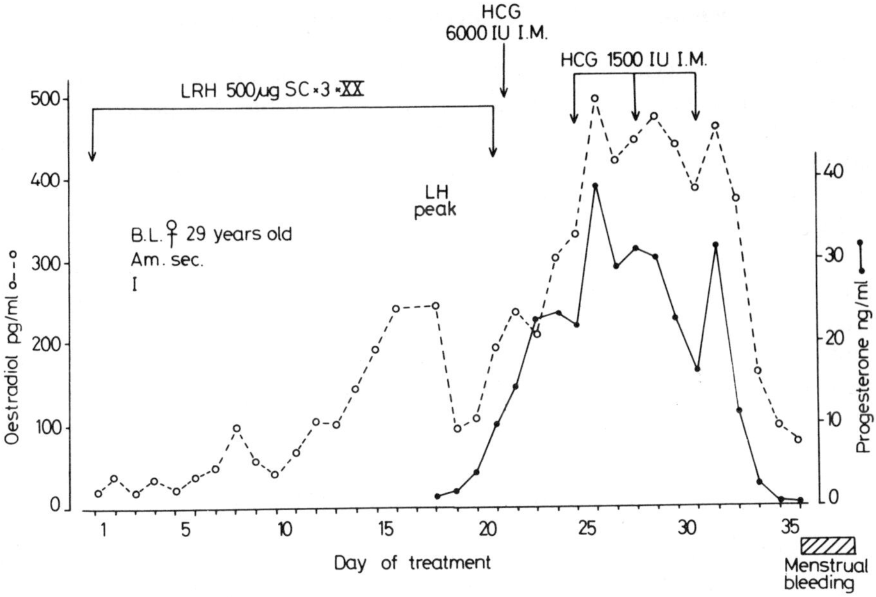

FIG. 9. Blood levels of estradiol and progesterone during the prolonged treatment with LRH in combination with HCG of the AN patient from Fig. 8. (From ref. 18.)

dicating that ovulation had already occurred. Repeated injections of HCG were given during the luteal phase, which was slightly prolonged with high estradiol and high-normal progesterone levels.

Induction of Follicular Maturation and Ovulation, Confirmed by Pregnancy

One involuntarily sterile 28-year-old AN patient with a 13-year duration of illness conceived during the combined LRH-HCG treatment, thus proving that adequate follicular growth and maturation occurred during the prolonged treatment with LRH. Previously, she had been given 10 treatment courses with human menopausal gonadotropins (HMG). The last treatment had resulted in a multiple pregnancy which ended in abortion of quadruplets. During the next treatment cycle, HMG was replaced by LRH for induction of follicular growth and maturation (17).

Treatment with 500 μg of LRH every 8 hr was given until follicular maturation, and then HCG was administered to induce ovulation. The first treatment course resulted in ovulation, but no pregnancy occurred. The second treatment course was successful, and resulted in a single pregnancy which continued uneventful to term. After delivery, she breast-fed the child for 3 months, and then she had to stop because of sore nipples.

Extraendocrine Effects of Prolonged LRH Treatment in AN

Regular global assessments of the psychiatric condition were continuously made by a psychiatrist or psychologist in some of the AN patients before, during, and after the prolonged LRH treatment to evaluate if the therapy had any extraendocrine effects on eating behavior, weight gain, mood, or libido (14).

No obvious changes were reported or observed during the treatment. All the women became markedly relieved when they regained menstruations, although none of them was cured of the anorectic disorder at that time. Thus, prolonged LRH therapy did not seem to be successful overall treatment of AN. This is not surprising since LRH deficiency is probably only one manifestation of the hypothalamic dysfunction in the complex disorder AN.

SUMMARY AND CONCLUSIONS

The pituitary gonadotropic function was investigated in women with AN under basal conditions and after acute and chronic administration of the hypothalamic gonadotropin-releasing hormone LRH. In the acute stages of AN, there was a markedly reduced pituitary secretion of both FSH and LH. The impairment was usually more pronounced for LH than for FSH secretion. The endogenous estrogen production was low or absent as in women after the menopause. Postmenopausal women, however, have a greatly increased gonadotropin secretion due to the loss of negative feedback effects of the ovarian hormones on the hypothalamic-pituitary system. The combination of reduced estrogen levels and impaired gonadotropin secretion in the women with AN indicated that they had a defect in the hypothalamus or the pituitary.

The pituitary reserve capacity for gonadotropin secretion was studied by measurements of the gonadotropin levels in serum after an acute intravenous injection of synthetic LRH. Most patients with AN responded to LRH with an evident increase of both FSH and LH in serum, which indicated that their pituitary can synthesize the gonadotropins and, in response to exogenous LRH, release them into the blood; it also suggested that they had hypothalamic rather than pituitary dysfunction.

In the acute stage of AN, however, the pituitary reserve capacity for LH secretion was greatly impaired while the pituitary capacity to release FSH in response to LRH was preserved or sometimes even increased. However, some women showed neither any FSH nor LH response to an acute intravenous injection of LRH. These results suggested pituitary dysfunction in the acute stage of AN, either primary due to defects at the pituitary level or secondary to dysfunction at the hypothalamic level with insufficient hypothalamic stimulation of the pituitary gonadotrophs by endogenous gonadotropin-releasing hormone.

During clinical remission with weight gain, the pituitary gonadotropic function improved. At first, the basal FSH secretion increased while the LH secretion remained low. On restoration of weight, the basal LH secretion also increased, but the LH levels were still lower than in regularly menstruating women. The FSH levels, however, did not differ from normal. The pituitary reserve capacity for LH secretion increased progressively during recovery stages of AN. Thus, the changes in the pituitary gonadotropic function in the acute stage of AN were reversible and possibly related to body weight.

The gonadotropin response pattern after LRH in the acute stage of AN resembled that of normal prepubertal children, who have minimal LH responses and normal FSH responses to LRH. It has been suggested that the decreased LH response to exogenous LRH in prepubertal subjects is secondary to deficient endogenous secretion of LRH (20). This might be true also for patients with AN. Long-term treatment with exogenous LRH was therefore given to women with AN. The therapy was found to induce gonadotropin responses in patients who had neither FSH nor LH responses to LRH before the treatment. The reduced pituitary reserve capacity for LH secretion was augmented, and the prepubertal-like response pattern after LRH reversed to normal. The results suggested that there was a deficient production and/or secretion of endogenous LRH from the hypothalamus in the acute stages of AN.

Prolonged treatment with LRH in AN not only restored the pituitary reserve capacity for gonadotropin secretion but also induced cyclic changes in the gonadotropin secretion from the pituitary. Normal ovulatory menstrual cycles could be induced by LRH therapy in amenorrheic AN patients, who were practically devoid of any gonadotropic and ovarian activity before the treatment. The results from the prolonged LRH therapy in AN supported the suggestion that there was a deficiency of the endogenous LRH secretion in AN.

Induction of follicular maturation and ovulation could be achieved by LRH treatment in amenorrheic women with AN. However, during menstrual cycles induced by LRH alone, inadequate luteal phases were sometimes observed. Treatment with LRH in combination with HCG improved the corpus luteum function. Prolonged LRH therapy can be used to induce ovulation in infertile anovulatory women with partially recovered AN but does not represent a successful overall treatment of AN since no obvious extraendocrine effects on mood and behavior were observed during the treatments.

In conclusion, studies on the gonadotropin secretion in anorexia nervosa suggest that there is a reversible suprapituitary disturbance in the acute stages with a deficient secretion of endogenous gonadotropin-releasing hormone from the hypothalamus.

ACKNOWLEDGMENTS

This work was supported by the Swedish Medical Research Council (Grant No. 13X-3145).

REFERENCES

1. Beumont, P. J. V., Carr, P. J., and Gelder, M. G. (1973): Plasma levels of luteinizing hormone and of immunoreactive oestrogens (oestradiol) in anorexia nervosa: response to clomiphene citrate. *Psychol. Med.,* 4:495–501.
2. Boyar, R. M., Katz, J., Finkelstein, J. W., Kapen, S., Weiner, H., Weitzman, E. D., and Hellman, L. (1974): Anorexia nervosa. Immaturity of the 24-hour luteinizing hormone secretory pattern. *N. Engl. J. Med.,* 291:861–865.
3. Crosignani, P. G., Reschini, E., D'Alberton, A., Trojsi, L., Cantalamessa, L., and Giustina, G. (1974): Variability of gonadotropin response to luteinizing hormone-releasing hormone in amenorrheic women. *Am. J. Obstet. Gynecol.,* 120:376–384.
4. Danowski, T. S., Livstone, E., Gonzales, A. R., Jung, Y., and Khurana, R. C. (1972): Fractional and partial hypopituitarism in anorexia nervosa. *Horm. Res.,* 3:105–118.
5. Espinosa-Campos, J., Robles, C., Gual, C., and Perez-Palacios, G. (1974): Hypothalamic, pituitary, and ovarian function assessment in a patient with anorexia nervosa. *Fertil. Steril.,* 25:453–458.
6. Franchimont, P., Becker, H., Ernould, Ch., Thys, Ch., Demoulin, A., Bourguignon, J. P., Legros, J. J., and Valcke, J. C. (1974): The effect of hypothalamic luteinizing hormone releasing hormone (LH-RH) on plasma gonadotrophin levels in normal subjects. *Clin. Endocrinol.,* 3:27–39.
7. Franchimont, P., Demoulin, A., and Bourguignon, J. P. (1975): Clinical use of LH-RH test as a diagnostic tool. *Horm. Res.,* 6:177–191.
8. Geigy Scientific Tables (1970): Average weights of adults (from insured person in the United States, Society of Actuaries, *Build and Blood Pressure Study, Vol.* 1, 1959, p. 16). Ciba-Geigy, Basel.
9. Job, J. C., Garnier, P. E., Chaussain, J. L., and Milhaud, G. (1972): Elevation of serum gonadotropins (LH and FSH) after releasing hormone (LH-RH) injection in normal children and in patients with disorders of puberty. *J. Clin. Endocrinol. Metab.,* 35:473–476.
10. Lundberg, P. O., Wålinder, J., Werner, I., and Wide, L. (1971): Effects of thyrotrophin-releasing hormone on plasma levels of TSH, FSH, LH and GH in anorexia nervosa. *Eur. J. Clin. Invest.,* 2:150–153.
11. Marshall, J. C., and Fraser, T. R. (1971): Amenorrhoea in anorexia nervosa: Assessment and treatment with clomiphene citrate. *Br. Med. J.,* 4:590–592.
12. Mecklenburg, R. S., Loriaux, D. L., Thompson, R. H., Andersen, A., and Lipsett, M. B. (1974): Hypothalamic dysfunction in patients with anorexia nervosa. *Medicine (Baltimore),* 53:147–159.
13. Mortimer, C. H., Besser, G. M., McNeilly, A. S., Marshall, J. C., Harsoulis, P., Tunbridge, W. M. G., Gomez-Pan, A., and Hall, R. (1973): Luteinizing hormone and follicle stimulating hormone-releasing hormone test in patients with hypothalamic-pituitary-gonadal dysfunction. *Br. Med. J.,* 4:73–77.
14. Nillius, S. J., Fries, H., and Wide, L. (1975): Successful induction of follicular maturation and ovulation by prolonged treatment with LH-releasing hormone in women with anorexia nervosa. *Am. J. Obstet. Gynecol.,* 122:921–928.
15. Nillius, S. J., and Wide, L. (1972*a*): Variation in LH and FSH response to LH-releasing hormone during the menstrual cycle. *J. Obstet. Gynaecol. Br. Commonw.,* 79:865–873.
16. Nillius, S. J., and Wide, L. (1972*b*): The LH-releasing hormone test in 31 women with secondary amenorrhoea. *J. Obstet. Gynaecol. Br. Commonw.,* 79:874–882.

17. Nillius, S. J., and Wide, L. (1975): Gonadotrophin-releasing hormone treatment for induction of follicular maturation and ovulation in amenorrhoeic women with anorexia nervosa. *Br. Med. J.,* 3:405–408.
18. Nillius, S. J., and Wide, L. (1977): Changes in the pituitary responsiveness to luteinizing hormone-releasing hormone (LRH) during prolonged LRH treatment for induction of follicular maturation and ovulation in amenorrheic women with anorexia nervosa. (submitted for publication.)
19. Palmer, R. L., Crisp, A. H., Mackinnon, P. C. B., Franklin, M., Bonnar, J., and Wheeler, M. (1975): Pituitary sensitivity to 50 μg LH/FSH-RH in subjects with anorexia nervosa in acute and recovery stages. *Br. Med. J.,* 1:179–182.
20. Roth, J. C., Kelch, R. P., Kaplan, S. L., and Grumbach, M. M. (1972): FSH and LH response to luteinizing hormone-releasing factor in prepubertal and pubertal children, adult males and patients with hypogonadotropic and hypergonadotropic hypogonadism. *J. Clin. Endocrinol. Metab.,* 35:926–930.
21. Schally, A. V., Arimura, A., Kastin, A. J., Matsuo, H., Baba, Y., Redding, T. W., Nair, R. M. G., and Debeljuk, L. (1971): Gonadotropin-releasing hormone: One polypeptide regulates secretion of luteinizing and follicle-stimulating hormones. *Science,* 173:1036–1037.
22. Sherman, B. M., Halmi, K. A., and Zamudio, R. (1975): LH and FSH response to gonadotropin-releasing hormone in anorexia nervosa: Effect of nutritional rehabilitation. *J. Clin. Endocrinol. Metab.,* 41:135–142.
23. Travaglini, P., Beck-Peccoz, P., Ferrari, C., Ambrosi, B., Paracchi, A., Severgnini, A., Spada, A., and Faglia, G. (1976): Some aspects of hypothalamic-pituitary function in patients with anorexia nervosa. *Acta Endocrinol.* (*Kbh.*), 81:252–262.
24. Vandekerckhove, D., Dhont, M., and Van Eyck, J. (1975): Diagnostic value of the LH-releasing hormone stimulation test in functional amenorrhea. *Acta Endocrinol.* (*Kbh.*), 78:625–633.
25. Warren, M. P., Jewelewicz, R., Dyrenfurth, I., Ans, R., Khalaf, S., and Vande Wiele, R. L. (1975): The significance of weight loss in the evaluation of pituitary response to LH-RH in women with secondary amenorrhea. *J. Clin. Endocrinol. Metab.,* 40:601–611.
26. Warren, M. P., and Vande Wiele, R. L. (1973): Clinical and metabolic features of anorexia nervosa. *Am. J. Obstet. Gynecol.,* 117:435–449.
27. Wide, L., Nillius, S. J., Gemzell, C., and Roos, P. (1973): Radioimmunosorbent assay of follicle-stimulating hormone and luteinizing hormone in serum and urine from men and women. *Acta Endocrinol.* (*Kbh.*) [*Suppl.*], 174:1–58.
28. Wiegelmann, W., and Solbach, H. G. (1972): Effects of LH-RH on plasma levels of LH and FSH in anorexia nervosa. *Horm. Metab. Res.,* 4:404.
29. Yoshimoto, Y., Moridera, K., and Imura, H. (1975): Restoration of normal pituitary gonadotropin reserve by administration of luteinizing-hormone-releasing hormone in patients with hypogonadotropic hypogonadism. *N. Engl. J. Med.,* 292:242–245.

Anorexia Nervosa, edited by
R. A. Vigersky. Raven Press,
New York © 1977.

Thyroid Hormone Metabolism in Prolonged Experimental Starvation in Man

Apostolos G. Vagenakis

Department of Medicine, Endocrinology Division, University of Massachusetts Medical School, Worcester, Massachusetts 01605

INTRODUCTION

Prolonged starvation, experimental or occurring from natural causes, has been for many years the subject of basic and clinical research. This research has been addressed primarily to nitrogen-amino acids and carbohydrate metabolism where dramatic changes and adaptations occur (10). The striking drop of basal metabolic rate (BMR) from 62 to 160 kcal/hr to 45 to 95 kcal/hr after 21 days of fasting has been noted (2,6,15), but adequate explanation of this phenomenon is lacking. Studies of thyroid hormone economy in experimental starvation are few and the findings inconsistent. Thus, the serum thyroxine (T_4) in prolonged starvation remains unchanged or slightly decreased (1,21,27), and the free thyroxine (FT_4) has been found to increase slightly (21,27). Measurements of serum concentration of triiodothyronine (T_3) have not been reported in starvation. Recent studies have revealed that patients with severe illness often display a normal or slightly decreased serum T_4 concentration with an increase in the concentration of free T_4 (13,19,20), findings similar to those reported during starvation. Of particular interest was the observation that serum T_3 concentration in these patients was depressed.

During the past several years, rapid progress has been made in elucidating the pathways of peripheral thyroxine metabolism in man and their physiological significance. The generation of T_3 from monodeiodination of T_4 has been clearly demonstrated (3), and quantitative studies revealed that half of T_4 that undergoes monodeiodination is converted to T_3 in the peripheral tissues (4,24). Furthermore, these findings together with the observation that oxygen consumption decreases during starvation led us to conduct a prospective study of the effects of prolonged starvation on the concentration, binding, and production rates of T_4 and T_3. Since the pathway of monodeiodination of T_4 has been demonstrated to be operative in man forming the inactive reverse T_3 (rT_3), the serum concentration of rT_3 was assessed in prolonged starvation and refeeding in an attempt to explore whether T_3 and rT_3 in man are products of alternate pathways of peripheral T_4 metabolism.

MATERIALS AND METHODS

Studies were performed in seven female and two male (subjects 2 and 8) obese euthyroid volunteers aged 21 to 48 years. During an initial control period of 1 to 3 weeks, patients received a liquid diet containing 1,500 cal and 850 $\pm$ 50 μg (mean $\pm$ SD) iodide daily in a volume of 1,500 ml. At the end of the third week, while the subjects were on an experimental diet, a thyrotropin-releasing hormone (TRH) test was performed: 400 μg was injected i.v. and blood was withdrawn at −15, 0, 10, 20, 30, 45, 60, and 90 min thereafter. The following day, subjects were injected i.v. with sterile $^{131}T_4$ and $^{125}T_3$ (80 and 100, μci, respectively), and blood was withdrawn at 2, 4, 6, 8, 10, 16, and 24 hr and every 12 hr thereafter for 7 days. The serum was quickly removed and a small amount of propylthiouracil (PTU) and 1 drop of saturated solution of potassium iodide (SSKI) were added to the serum. The serum was frozen in aliquots and analyzed when all the serum for the 7-day period was collected. Serum T_4, T_3, and rT_3 were assayed in the same samples allowing sufficient time for the decay of radioactive $^{131}T_4$ and $^{125}T_3$. After the completion of the control observations, the food was totally withdrawn for 4 weeks and patients were maintained on 1,500 ml of tap water supplemented with 850 μg iodine as KI daily together with multivitamins. On the 20th day of the fasting period, a TRH test was again performed and the protocol of control period was repeated.

In addition, four euthyroid obese volunteers, three women and one man (patient 13, Table 2) received 0.25 mg sodium L-T_4 p.o. daily in order to suppress endogenous thyroid function. Approximately 3 weeks later they were started on a 7- to 10-day period of 1,500-cal mixed diet. Serum samples were obtained daily on the last 3 days of this period. Food was then totally withdrawn for 6 to 11 days, but sodium L-T_4 was continued. Serum samples were obtained daily for the last 3 days of the fasting period. Patients were then refed with the control 1,500-cal diet for the next 5 days, serum samples being obtained on the final 3 days.

Methods of Hormone Assay

Serum T_4 concentrations were measured by the Tetralute® method (5) and serum T_3 and thyrotropin-stimulating hormone (TSH) by radioimmunoassay. Percent free T_4 (%FT_4) and T_3 (%FT_3) were measured by equilibrium dialysis, and free T_4 (FT_4) and T_3 (FT_3) concentrations were calculated as the product of the total hormone concentrations and the percentage that was free. Serum reverse T_3 (rT_3) was measured by a very sensitive and specific radioimmunoassay (16,26). All tests were run in duplicate, and serum samples obtained during the control and starvation periods were assayed concurrently. Aliquots of serum and standards containing the $^{131}T_4$ and $^{125}T_3$ from the turnover studies were passed via small ion-exchange columns for removal of iodoproteins as previously described (18). The recovery was 65 ± 3% (mean ± SD) for $^{131}T_4$ and 75 ± 2% for $^{125}T_3$. The purified fractions of $^{131}T_4$ and $^{125}T_3$ were then counted in a γ-counter spectrometer, and the slope and Y intercept were assessed by the method of least squares. The integral approach first suggested by Tait (25) and adapted for thyroid hormone kinetics by Surks et al. (24) was then applied for calculation of daily production rate of T_4 and T_3. Statistical analyses were carried out by the paired *t*-test.

RESULTS

Serum T_4 Concentrations

Serum T_4 concentration (Table 1) averaged 7.0 ± 1.6 μg/dl during the control period and was essentially unchanged during the last 8 days of the fast (6.8 ± 1.9 μg/dl) in the nine patients who were not receiving suppressive doses of L-T_4. During starvation there occurred a small but significant increase of %FT_4. Thus the %FT_4 was 0.016 ± 0.0009% during the control period and increased to 0.020 ± 0.0005% during starvation ($p < 0.02$), and this resulted in a small but significant increase in FT_4 (1.1 ± 0.2 versus 1.3 ± 0.4 ng/dl; $p < 0.05$).

In the four patients receiving 0.25 mg sodium L-T_4 daily (Table 2), serum T_4 averaged 12.4 ± 1.5 μg/dl during the control period and increased slightly in all subjects during the 6- to 11-day period of fast (mean 15.1 ± 2.9 μg/dl). The latter value returned almost exactly to control values during the 5 days of refeeding (12.0 ± 2.3 μg/dl).

Metabolic Clearance Rate and Production Rate of T_4

In the nine euthyroid obese volunteers not receiving L-T_4 replacement therapy, the metabolic clearance rate (Fig. 1) averaged 1.2 ± 0.3 liters/day during the control period and remained essentially unchanged during starvation. Since the serum concentration of T_4 remained unchanged, the daily degradation or production rate of T_4 also remained unchanged (80 ± 28 versus 75 ± 26 μg/day).

Serum T_3 Concentration

During the last 8 days of starvation, serum T_3 concentration (Table 1) was strikingly decreased from control values in all nine subjects not receiving sodium L-T_4 (145 ± 22 versus 66 ± 28 ng/dl; $p < 0.001$). Values

TABLE 1. *Effect of starvation on the concentration and binding of T_4 and T_3 in serum and on the response to TRH*

Subject	T_3(RIA)[a] (ng/100 ml) C	F	%FT_3 ($\times 10^3$) C	F	FT_3 (pg/100 ml) C	F	T_4(D)[a] (μg/100 ml) C	F	%FT_4 ($\times 10^3$) C	F	FT_4 (ng/100 ml) C	F	TSH[a] (μU/ml) C	F	TRH test[b]: Max ΔTSH (μU/ml) C	F	TRH test[b]: ΔT_3[c] (ng/100 ml) C	F
1	120	68	154	179	185	121	7.1	6.3	16	19	1.2	1.2	3.0	2.7	26	21	55	35
2	162	117	142	164	230	192	7.0	6.4	15	16	1.0	1.0	2.7	3.7	13	14	40	30
3	126	44	181	223	228	97	5.3	4.4	16	20	0.8	1.0	1.3	1.7	10	7	35	35
4	178	101	157	187	279	188	9.9	10	15	21	1.4	2.1	1.8	3.1	5.6	10	40	20
5	113	43	196	188	221	81	5.9	5.0	17	23	1.0	1.1	1.0	1.1	8	11	35	50
6	155	54	157	159	243	86	6.7	8.2	17	19	1.1	1.2	1.4	0.9				
7	158	80	132	159	209	127	9.2	9.3	14	20	1.3	1.9	0.6	1.4	14	9	23	53
8	133	43	166	173	221	73	6.8	5.4	17	19	1.1	1.0	0.6	0.8				
9	158	58	146	167	231	96	5.3	6.1	15	22	0.8	1.3	0.7	1.6	18	13	10	15
Mean	145	68	166	188	227	118	7.0	6.8	16	20	1.1	1.3	1.5	1.9	14	12	34	34
SD	22	28	22	22	25	44	1.6	1.9	0.9	2.5	0.2	0.4	0.8	1.0	6.9	4.5	14	14
p-value	<0.001		<0.05		<0.001		ns		<0.02		<0.05		ns		ns		ns	
Normal range	80–180		140–230		120–440		4.0–11.6		14–28		0.8–2.5		0–5					

[a] Values for each test are the mean of those in serum samples obtained daily during the last 8 days of the control period (C) and of the 4-week fast (F).
[b] 400 μg TRH administered i.v.
[c] Difference between basal T_3 concentration and values obtained 90 min after TRH.

TABLE 2. *Effect of fasting and refeeding on the serum concentrations of T_4, T_3, and rT_3 in obese, euthyroid volunteers*

		Serum T_4 (μg/dl)			Serum T_3 (ng/dl)			Serum rT_3 (ng/dl)		
Patient	Rx[a]	Control	Fast	Refeed	Control	Fast	Refeed	Control	Fast	Refeed
1	0	7.0	6.2	—	116	65	—	38	57	—
2	0	5.6	4.4	—	121	48	—	30	33	—
3	0	5.6	4.8	—	131	48	—	42	45	—
4	0	10.4	9.9	—	183	106	—	69	106	—
5	0	7.7	6.3	—	185	123	—	48	63	—
6	0	5.7	6.8	—	157	62	—	19	38	—
7	0	7.3	4.3	—	133	45	—	22	31	—
8	0	6.1	9.6	—	165	55	—	25	42	—
9	0	10.1	8.8	—	155	81	—	31	68	—
Mean ± SD		7.3 ± 1.8	6.8 ± 2.0	—	149 ± 26[b]	70 ± 27	—	36.0 ± 15[b]	54 ± 23	—
10	+	12.1	12.7	10.1	158	93	141	75	122	76
11	+	13.7	18.9	13.9	214	140	225	69	162	71
12	+	10.5	13.1	9.9	131	99	136	70	146	92
13	+	13.5	16.0	14.1	171	97	156	77	188	63
Mean ± SD		12.4 ± 1.5	15.1 ± 2.9	12.0 ± 2.3[c]	168 ± 35[d]	107 ± 22	164 ± 41[c]	73 ± 4[d]	154 ± 28	76 ± 12[c]

[a] 0, not receiving sodium L-T_4; +, suppressed with 0.25 mg sodium L-T_4 daily.
[b] $p < 0.001$ as compared to value obtained during fasting.
[c] $p < 0.02$ as compared to value obtained during fasting.
[d] $p < 0.01$ as compared to value obtained during fasting.

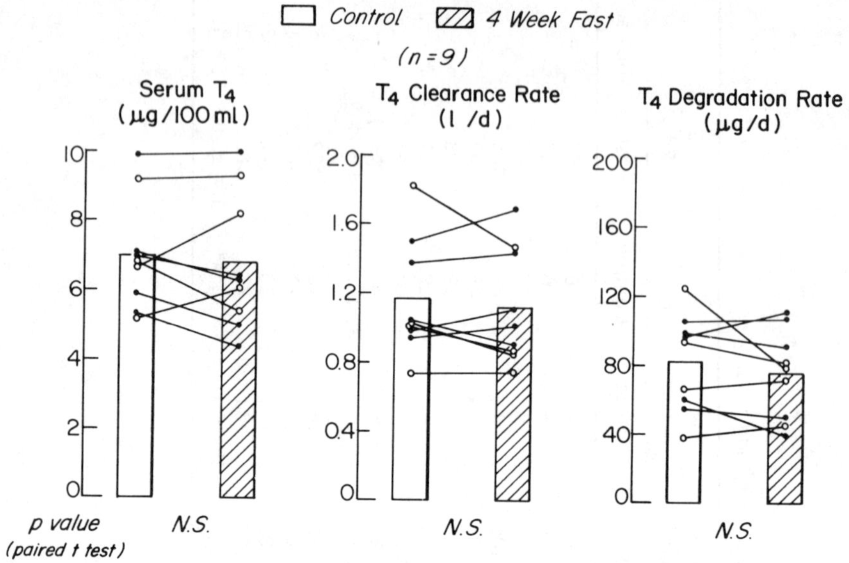

FIG. 1. T_4 kinetics in 9 obese subjects before and during starvation.

were in the hypothyroid range in six (< 80 ng/dl). As with the $\%FT_4$, a small but statistically significant increase was noticed during starvation (0.166 ± 0.022 versus $0.188 \pm 0.0022\%$; $p < 0.01$). However, in contrast to FT_4, FT_3 was markedly decreased (227 ± 25 versus 118 ± 44 pg/dl; $p < 0.001$).

Similar results were obtained during fasting in the four patients receiving 0.25 mg sodium L-T_4 (Table 2). During the control period, serum T_3 averaged 168 ± 35 ng/dl and decreased to 107 ± 22 ng/dl during the period of starvation. The latter values returned to control values in all subjects during the 5 days of refeeding (164 ± 41 ng/dl).

Metabolic Clearance Rate and Production Rates of T_3

In the nine euthyroid obese volunteers not receiving L-T_4 replacement in whom the T_3 kinetics studies were performed and analyzed by the single-compartment method, T_3 clearance rate did not change during starvation. As expected, the production rate was markedly decreased during starvation, and it was the result of the decreased serum values. Since the single-compartment method overestimates the clearance rate by 30% (24), in four of the above patients in whom early serum samples were drawn after the injection of $^{125}T_3$, the integral analysis was applied (Fig. 2). As expected, the results were qualitatively similar to but quantitatively different from those

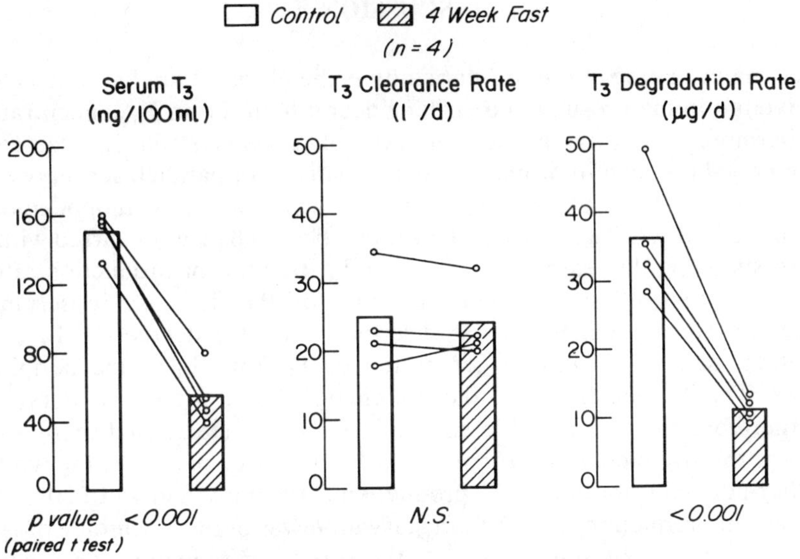

FIG. 2. T_3 kinetics in 4 obese subjects before and during starvation. The disappearance curve of $^{125}T_3$ in the serum was analyzed by the integral method (24).

of the single-compartment analysis. The metabolic clearance rate was unchanged during starvation, but the production rate was decreased by 70% during the last 8 days of fasting (36 ± 9 versus 11 ± 4 μg/day; $p < 0.001$).

Serum Reverse T_3 Concentration

In the nine patients not receiving sodium L-T_4, serum rT_3 concentration averaged 36.0 ± 15 ng/dl during the control period (Table 2). By the end of the prolonged fast, serum rT_3 increased in all nine patients, averaging 54 ± 23 ng/dl ($p < 0.001$). Concomitantly, serum T_3 concentration in the same sample of serum decreased strikingly. Control serum rT_3 concentration in the four patients receiving sodium L-T_4 averaged 73 ± 4 ng/dl, increased strikingly in all during the 6- to 11-day fast (154 ± 28 ng/dl; $p < 0.01$), and decreased to control values in each patient during the 5 days of refeeding (76 ± 12 ng/dl).

Basal Serum TSH and Response to TRH

No significant change in the serum TSH concentration occurred during starvation. The maximum serum TSH concentration achieved in response to TRH was also unchanged by starvation, as was the increment in T_3 (RIA) that TRH induced at 90 min (Table 1).

DISCUSSION

The major finding of the present study is the observation that total caloric deprivation in man results in a striking decrease in serum T_3 concentration. Furthermore, the total production rate of T_3 was strikingly decreased reaching values seen in primary hypothyroidism. In parallel, serum reverse T_3 concentration, the other alternate metabolic product of T_4 monodeiodination, increased strikingly during starvation. These changes occurred without a corresponding decrease in total serum T_4, free T_4, or production rate of T_4. Three possible sources may account for the decrease in serum T_3 concentration: (a) enhanced T_3 clearance rate, (b) decreased T_3 or T_4 secretion, and (c) decreased generation of T_3 from T_4 in the peripheral tissues. The T_3 clearance rate did not change during prolonged starvation, and therefore the first possible source is excluded. Decreased secretion of T_3 from the thyroid does not appear to be the case, since it is known that the thyroidal contribution to T_3 production is no more than 15 to 20%. The decrease in production rate of T_3 in starvation was of the magnitude of 70%, thus making thyroid suppression as the source of reduction of serum T_3 in starvation unlikely. Moreover, low T_3 concentration was observed in patients receiving fully suppressive doses of T_4, strongly indicating that suppression of endogenous thyroidal activity does not contribute to a significant extent to the low serum T_3 concentration observed in the nonreplaced patients. It appears, therefore, that the decrease of conversion of T_4 to T_3 in the peripheral tissues accounts for the observed decrease in T_3 production during starvation in man.

A second important observation from the present studies was the increase in reverse T_3 during starvation. Most importantly, the studies have revealed a close reciprocal relation between changes in the serum T_3 concentration and rT_3. Thus, the prompt decrease in serum T_3 in nonreplaced and T_4-replaced patients that accompanied starvation was followed by a concomitant increase in rT_3, and these changes were promptly returned to control values following refeeding.

Since the clearance rate of rT_3 during starvation was not assessed, these changes in reverse T_3 may reflect changes in clearance rate of rT_3. Decreased clearance rates have been recently reported in other conditions where reciprocal changes of T_3 and rT_3 occur (12). Preliminary studies in our laboratory appear to indicate that a 20 to 35% decrease in rT_3 clearance rate is found during starvation. However, the overall production rate appears to be increased in some patients.

In view of the recent studies which report relatively high concentrations of rT_3 in association with low concentrations of T_3 in the serum of patients with chronic and acute illness (8,9,12,13,16), in human umbilical cord, and in anorexia nervosa, it is likely that such alterations in peripheral T_4 metabolism are not confined to total starvation only. However, further studies have revealed that the decrease of T_3 seen in various illnesses and in patients receiving a hypocaloric diet is not always accompanied by an increase in serum reverse T_3 concentration since high, normal, or low serum reverse T_3 has been found (11,12,16,23). It appears, therefore, that the primary event in all these conditions is the decrease in T_3 production. An increase in rT_3 production may or may not be present.

Since the T_3 is more potent metabolically than T_4, conversion of T_4 to T_3 must enhance the metabolic activity of the parent hormone. It has been found that overfeeding, particularly with carbohydrates, results in an increased generation of T_3 as a result of an apparent increase in conversion of T_4 to T_3 (7,14). Furthermore, the rT_3 concentration is decreased during overfeeding, suggesting an enhancement of the peripheral action of T_4 through its conversion to T_3. This may have metabolic significance since it may be related to the enhanced thermic effects observed in individuals following acute weight gain (22). The decrease in T_3 production in starvation, therefore, may explain the decreased oxygen consumption often seen in prolonged starvation, which cannot be explained by the reduction of body mass only. It may represent a defense of the starving individual to conserve energy and nitrogen resources as long as possible.

Another possible implication of these findings stems from the normality of basal serum TSH concentration and the normal response to TRH found during starvation. One would expect an increased response to TRH secondary to decreased serum T_3 concentration during starvation. The possibility that the increase in serum rT_3 may account for the observed normal TRH responses in starvation by exerting a negative feedback control in the pituitary has been excluded by the fact that rT_3 administration in normal euthyroid individuals in quantities sufficient to raise serum rT_3 to values commonly seen in starvation had no effect on TRH-induced TSH release (17). If starvation *per se* does not offset the enhanced TRH response which follows the decrease in serum thyroid hormone concentration, then the normal TSH response to TRH seen in starvation suggests that T_4 and not only T_3 plays a significant role in the homeostatic control of TSH secretion.

Finally, as indicated by these studies, deiodination of T_4 to form T_3 or rT_3 is not a random process. It appears that diversion of peripheral T_4 metabolism from T_3 toward rT_3 generation can be considered to reflect diversion from activating to inactivating pathways of hormone metabolism and is enzymatic in nature. Starvation and overfeeding would appear to provide a fine model for further studies of the potentially important metabolic control point.

ACKNOWLEDGMENTS

I would like to thank my colleagues in collaboration with whom these studies have been carried out: L. E. Braverman, S. H. Ingbar, A. Burger,

G. Portnay, F. Azizi, R. Arky, and J. O'Brian. The secretarial assistance of Mrs. S. O'Neil is greatly appreciated.

REFERENCES

1. Alexander, W. D., Harrison, M. T., Harden, R. Mc. C., and Koutras, D. A. (1964): The effects of total fasting on thyroid function in man. *Metabolism,* 19:587–590.
2. Benedict, F. G. (1915): *A Study of Prolonged Fasting,* Publ. 203. Carnegie Institute, Washington, D.C.
3. Braverman, L. E., Ingbar, S. H., and Sterling, K. (1970): Conversion of thyroxine (T_4) to triiodothyronine (T_3) in athyreotic human subjects. *J. Clin. Invest.,* 49:855–864.
4. Braverman, L. E., Vagenakis, A. G., Downs, P., Foster, A. E., Sterling, K., and Ingbar, K. (1973): Effect of replacement doses of sodium thyroxine on the peripheral metabolism of thyroxine and triiodothyronine in man. *J. Clin. Invest.,* 52:1010–1017.
5. Braverman, L. E., Vagenakis, A. G., Foster, A. E., and Ingbar, S. H. (1971): Evaluation of a simplified technique for the specific measurement of serum thyroxine concentration. *J. Clin. Endocrinol. Metab.,* 32:497–502.
6. Bray, G. A. (1976): The obese patient. In: *Major Problems in Internal Medicine, Vol. 9,* edited by L. H. Smith, p. 331. W. B. Saunders Co., Philadelphia.
7. Bray, G. A., Fisher, D. A., and Chopra, I. J. (1976): Relation of thyroid hormones to body weight. *Lancet,* 1:1206–1208.
8. Burger, A., Nicod, P., Syter, P., Valloton, M., Vagenakis, A. G., and Braverman, L. E. (1976): Reduced active thyroid hormone levels in acute illness. *Lancet,* 1:653–657.
9. Burr, N. A., Black, C. G., Griffiths, R. S., and Hoffenberg, R. (1975): Serum T_3 and reverse T_3 after surgical operation. *Lancet,* 2:1277–1780.
10. Cahill, G. F., Jr. (1976): Starvation in man. *Clin. Endocrinol. Metab.,* 5:397–415.
11. Cavin, L. Rapoport, B. Hamond, M., and Cavalieri, R. R. (1976): Variable serum reverse T_3 and decreased T_3 concentrations in nonthyroidal systemic illness. *Clin. Res.,* 24:272A (abstract).
12. Chopra, I. J. (1976): An assessment of daily production and significance of thyroid secretion of 3,3′,5′-triiodothyronine (reverse T_3) in man. *J. Clin. Invest.,* 58:32–40.
13. Chopra, I. J., Chopra, U., Smith, S. R., Reza, M., and Solomon, P. H. (1975): Reciprocal changes in serum concentration of 3,3′5′ T_3 and 3,3′5 T_3 in systemic illness. *J. Clin. Endocrinol. Metab.,* 41:1043–1049.
14. Danforth, E., Jr., Tyzbir, E. D., Horton, E. S., Sims, E. A. H., Burger, A., Braverman, L. E., Vagenakis, A. G., and Ingbar, S. H. (1976): Reciprocal changes in serum triiodothyronine (T_3) and reverse (rT_3) induced by altering the carbohydrate content of the diet. *Clin. Res.,* 26:271 A (abstract).
15. Drenick, E. J. (1976): Weight reduction by prolonged fasting. In: *Obesity in Perspective, Vol. III, Part II,* edited by G. A. Bray. Fogarty International Center, Series on Preventive Medicine, Government Printing Office, Washington, D.C.
16. Nicod, P., Burger, A., Staeheli, V., and Valloton, M. B. (1976): A radioimmunoassay for 3,3′5′ triiodothyronine in unextracted serum: Method and clinical results. *J. Clin. Endocrinol. Metab.,* 42:823–829.
17. Nicod, P., Burger, A., Strauch, G., Vagenakis, A. G., and Braverman, L. E. (1976): The failure of physiologic doses of reverse T_3 to effect thyroid-pituitary function in man. *J. Clin. Endocrinol. Metab.,* 43:478–481.
18. Nicoloff, G. T., Low, J. C., Dussault, J. H., and Fisher, D. A. (1972): Simultaneous measurements of thyroxine and triiodothyronine peripheral turnover kinetics in man. *J. Clin. Invest.,* 51:473–480.
19. Nomura, S., Pittman, C. S., Chambers, J. B., Jr., Buck, M. W., and Shimuzu, T. (1975): Reduced peripheral conversion of thyroxine to triiodothyronine in patients with hepatic cirrhosis. *J. Clin. Invest.,* 56:643–652.
20. Reichlin, S., Bollinger, J., Nejard, J., and Sullivan, P. (1973): Tissue thyroid hormone concentration of rat and man determined by radioimmunoassay. Biologic significance. *Mt. Sinai J. Med. N.Y.,* 40:502–506.

21. Schatz, D. L., Sheppard, R. H., Palter, H. D., and Jaffri, M. H. (1967): Thyroid function studies in fasting obese subjects. *Metabolism,* 16:1075–1085.
22. Sims, E. A. H., Danforth, E. H., Jr., Horton, E. S., Bray, G. A., Glennon, J. A., and Salans, L. B. (1973): Endocrine and metabolic effects of experimental obesity in man. *Recent Prog. Horm. Res.,* 29:457–487.
23. Spaulding, S. W., Chopra, I. J., Sherwin, R. S., and Lyall, S. S. (1976): Effect of caloric restriction and dietary composition on serum T_3 and reverse T_3 in man. *J. Clin. Endocrinol. Metab.,* 42:197–200.
24. Surks, M. I., Schadlow, A. R., Stock, J. M., and Oppenheimer, J. H. (1973): Determination of iodothyronine absorption and conversion of L-thyroxine (T_4) to L-triiodothyronine (T_3) using turnover rate techniques. *J. Clin. Invest.,* 52:805–811.
25. Tait, J. F. (1963): Review: The use of isotopic steroids for the measurement of production rates in vivo. *J. Clin. Endocrinol. Metab.,* 23:1285–1297.
26. Vagenakis, A. G., Burger, A., Portnay, G. I., Rudolph, M., O'Brian, J. I., Azizi, F., Arky, R., Nicod, P., Ingbar, S. H., and Braverman, L. E. (1975): Diversion of peripheral thyroxine metabolism from activating to inactivating pathways during complete fasting. *J. Clin. Endocrinol. Metab.,* 41:191–194.
27. Verdy, M. (1968): Fasting in obese females: a study of thyroid function tests, serum proteins and electrolytes. *Can. Med. Assoc. J.,* 98:1031–1033.

Anorexia Nervosa, edited by
R. A. Vigersky. Raven Press,
New York © 1977.

Investigations Concerning Thyroxine Deiodinative Pathways in Patients with Anorexia Nervosa

Kenneth D. Burman, Robert A. Vigersky, D. Lynn Loriaux, Daniel Strum, Yin-Ying Djuh, Frances D. Wright, and Leonard Wartofsky

Endocrine-Metabolism Service, Kyle Metabolic Unit, Walter Reed Army Medical Center, Washington, D.C. 20012; and the National Institute of Child Health and Human Development, National Institutes of Health, Bethesda, Maryland 20014

INTRODUCTION

Included among the many signs and symptoms of the syndrome of anorexia nervosa are dry skin, low basal metabolic rate, bradycardia, and amenorrhea—findings that also frequently occur in hypothyroidism (36). Because of these several manifestations in common, studies have been performed to ascertain the state of thyroid function in patients with anorexia nervosa (22,23,36). Moshang et al. (23) and Miyai et al. (22) have observed that serum T4 concentrations may be within the normal range, but that anorexia nervosa patients as a group have T4 levels that are significantly lower than those of healthy adults; serum T3 concentrations were clearly decreased in both studies (22,23).

Conditions associated with this combination of slightly low or normal T4 levels and decreased T3 concentrations have been the subject of intensive study in the last several years (2,4,8,11,14,15,16,24,32). Using specific radioimmunoassays, investigators have demonstrated that T4 can be peripherally degraded either to 3,5,3′-triiodothyronine (T3), presumably the metabolically most active iodothyronine, or to 3,3′,5-triiodothyronine (reverse T3), a less-active metabolite (8). Although levels of both serum reverse T3 and T3 generally parallel alterations in serum T4 (e.g., thyrotoxicosis and hypothyroidism), several conditions, generally catabolic in nature, have been described in which T3 and reverse T3 concentrations vary reciprocally. Elevated levels of serum reverse T3 and decreased T3 levels have been observed in newborn infants (13,15) and in patients receiving corticosteroids (16), as well as in the sera of patients who are infected (37), fasted (35), or who have various types of acute or chronic illnesses (3,11). Because many similar metabolic alterations appear to occur in both fasting and anorexia nervosa (35,36), and since patients with anorexia nervosa demonstrate weight loss presumably secondary to decreased food intake, we decided to examine further the thyroxine deiodinative pathways in subjects with anorexia nervosa in order to gain greater insight into the mechanism by which these changes in reverse T3 and T3 occur.

MATERIALS AND METHODS

Serum T4, T3 (12), reverse T3 (6,24), 3,3′-diiodothyronine (7), growth hormone (21), and prolactin (20) concentrations were measured by specific radioimmunoassays.[1] Free T4 levels were determined by equilibrium dialysis (34) and thyrotropin-releasing hormone (TRH) stimulation tests were performed as previously described (36). All samples were collected after fasting for approximately 12 hr and were generally drawn at least 30 min following insertion of an indwelling catheter. All patients designated as having anorexia nervosa fulfilled the criteria of Feighner et al. (18), and none of these patients had been diagnosed as having other medical illnesses. One-tailed, unpaired *t*-tests were used to compare values obtained in patients with anorexia nervosa and control subjects. Portions of these results have been published previously (36).

RESULTS (TABLE 1)

Iodothyronines

In patients with anorexia nervosa, the mean (± SE) serum T4 and T3 levels were 5.6 ± 0.3 μg/dl ($N = 16$) and 72 ± 5 ng/dl ($N = 16$), respectively, values which were significantly lower ($p < 0.001$) than their respective concentrations in normal subjects. The mean (± SEM) free T4 level of 1.3 ± 0.07 ng/dl ($N = 13$) in patients with anorexia nervosa was not significantly different from the level of 1.5 ± 0.03 ng/dl determined in normal subjects.

In contrast, both the mean serum reverse T3 (58 ± 5 ng/dl; $N = 10$) and 3,3′T2 (33 ± 6 ng/dl; $N=6$) levels were increased relative to their values in euthyroid subjects. The elevation of 3,3′T2 was statistically significant ($p < 0.001$), but the elevation of reverse T3 failed to reach the 0.05 level ($p < 0.10$).

Prolactin and Growth Hormone

The mean (± SE) basal serum prolactin level of 15.5 ± 1.7 ng/ml ($N = 13$) in patients with anorexia nervosa was not significantly different from that of

[1]Growth hormone, prolactin, free T4, and several T4 and T3 measurements were performed at Bio-Science Laboratories, Van Nuys, California, where information concerning these assays was kindly provided.

TABLE 1. *Serum thyroid hormone parameters, prolactin, and growth hormone in patients with anorexia nervosa*

Patient	% Below ideal weight	T4 (μg/dl)	Free T4 (ng/dl)	T3 (ng/dl)	Reverse T3 (ng/dl)	3,3′T2 (ng/dl)	Prolactin (ng/ml)	Growth hormone (ng/ml)
1	45	4.1	1.3	54	68	—	15	180
2	38	4.0	1.3	27	49	—	<10	70
3	52	5.9	—	51	54	—	<10	360
4	49	6.6	1.7	60	76	44	<10	87
5	52	7	—	68	37	—	—	104
6	40	6.6	1.4	72	69	16	—	—
7	40	4.5	1.4	47	77	25	8.9	12
8	21	6.3	1.4	85	67	—	13	3
9	31	5.8	1.3	68	27	—	13.8	7
10	37	4.7	—	84	—	51	—	11
11	30	6.8	1.2	107	—	42	22.8	8.8
12	40	4.4	0.7	106	—	20	17.4	12.5
13	22	6.1	1.4	87	—	—	16.9	13.4
14	32	6.0	1.4	84	—	—	15.9	18.4
15	35	5.8	1.4	59	53	—	16.5	7
16	16	4.2	0.9	87	—	—	31.4	19
Mean	36	5.6	1.3	72	58	33	15.5	60.9
SE	3	0.3	0.07	5	5	6	1.7	25
N	16	16	13	16	10	6	13	15
Normal values								
Mean	—	8.5	1.5	156	49	17	16.2	10.4
SE	—	0.1	0.03	4	3	1	1.2	3.9
N	—	1000	50	47	29	18	21	10

16.2 ± 1.2 ng/ml ($N = 21$) observed in normal subjects. The mean (± SE) basal growth hormone level in patients with anorexia nervosa (60.9 ± 25 ng/ml; $N = 15$) was higher than in normal control subjects (10.4 ± 3.9 ng/ml), although this difference did not reach the 0.05 significance level.

TRH Stimulation Tests

When measured in the same three subjects with anorexia nervosa, the mean (± SE) serum T4 levels did not increase significantly from 5.6 ± 1.2 μg/dl basally to 5.9 ± 1.6 μg/dl at 120 min following TRH administration. In contrast, mean (± SE) serum T3 levels in three other patients increased from 52 ± 5 ng/dl basally to 102 ± 23 ng/dl 90 min following TRH. In other studies, the mean (± SE) T3 level in seven normal subjects increased from 153 ± 15 ng/dl basally to 214 ± 20 ng/dl at 90 min after injection of TRH. The mean (± SE) T4 concentration increased slightly from 6.5 ± 0.6 μg/dl to 6.9 ± 0.5 μg/dl during the same time interval. Thus, it appears that the percent increase in serum T3 levels at 90 min following TRH administration in patients with anorexia nervosa was not diminished compared to the observed increase in normal subjects.

DISCUSSION

The present report not only confirms earlier studies indicating that serum T3 levels are generally decreased in patients with anorexia nervosa (22,23), but, in addition, suggests that serum reverse T3 (24) and 3,3′T2 concentrations may be elevated in this disorder. Although kinetic studies are warranted to investigate these perturbations further (9,33), it appears that anorexia nervosa represents a condition in which T4 is preferentially degraded through relatively inactivating (reverse T3) rather than activating (T3) pathways (35). Although the mechanism by which these alterations occur is unknown, they presumably represent a homeostatic attempt at conserving energy. This theory, however, is largely dependent on the presumption that reverse T3 is inactive, or, at least, less active than T3. In fact, the degree of metabolic activity attributed to reverse T3 appears to depend on the system in which it is tested (10,25,27,28,29). For example, reverse T3 administration to human subjects does not affect their TSH responses to TRH (25). In contrast, incubation of reverse T3 in relatively larger doses *in vitro* with pituitary glands does appear to decrease the observed TSH response to TRH (10). Reverse T3 also appears metabolically active in other experiments as it is capable of increasing hepatic L-triiodothyronine aminotransferase activity (as are T3 and T4) (29), and, in addition, reverse T3 binds to nuclear receptors and may be capable of stimulating glucose consumption and growth hormone production by cultured pituitary cells (26). However, because the activities attributed to reverse T3 generally require greater quantities of reverse T3 and T3 for the same effect, it appears that reverse T3 is indeed less metabolically active than T3 (10,26,29).

Although both T3 and reverse T3 may be converted peripherally to 3,3′T2 (5,19,30–32,38), it appears that relatively more 3,3′T2 is derived from reverse T3 than from T3 (17). Because reverse T3 levels were elevated in subjects with anorexia nervosa, the finding of elevated 3,3′T2 levels in patients with anorexia nervosa is consistent with *in vitro* observations by Chopra et al. (17) and, in addition, indicates that the 5′ deiodinase enzyme system may be operative in situations where reverse T3 and T3 vary reciprocally. The elevated levels of serum 3,3′T2 reported herein are apparently at variance with the decreased levels in patients with anorexia nervosa reported by Burger (1). The explanation for this discrepancy is unknown but could relate to the different radioimmunoassay systems employed.

In addition to the above-mentioned abnormalities in thyroid hormone degradation and/or secretion, hypothalamic function may also be impaired in patients with anorexia nervosa (36). In this regard, Vigersky et al. (36) have demonstrated abnormal thermoregulation and delayed pituitary release of luteinizing hormone (LH) and follicle-stimulating hormone (FSH) to luteinizing hormone–releasing hormone administration. Furthermore, it has previously been reported that serum TSH responses to TRH administration in patients with anorexia nervosa did not appear quantitatively different from those in normal subjects, although the mean peak TSH response may be reached slightly later in subjects with anorexia nervosa (36). In the present study, we have determined that thyroid glands of patients with anorexia nervosa appear to respond normally to the rise in TSH evoked by TRH. By inference, therefore, it appears that physiologic elevations in reverse T3 do not interfere with TRH-induced TSH rises in these patients. This observation would be consistent with the recent report (25) that increased levels of reverse T3 due to reverse T3 administration in euthyroid subjects do not significantly alter their responses to TRH administration.

REFERENCES

1. Burger, A. (1976): Reduced active thyroid-hormone levels in acute illness. *Lancet,* 2:97.
2. Burger, A., Dinichert, D., Nicod, P., Jenny, M., Lemarchand-Beraud, T., and Vallotton, M. B. (1976): Effect of Amiodarone on serum triiodothyronine, reverse triiodothyronine, thyroxin, and thyrotropin. *J. Clin. Invest.,* 58:255–259.
3. Burger, A., Nicod, P., Suter, P., Vallotton, M. B., Vagenakis, A., and Braverman, L. (1976): Reduced active thyroid hormone levels in acute illness. *Lancet,* 1:653–655.
4. Burgi, H., Wimpfheimer, C., Burger, A., Zaunbauer, W., Rösler, H., and Lemarchand-Beraud, T. (1976): Changes of circulating thyroxine, triiodothyronine and reverse triiodothyronine after radiographic contrast agents. *J. Clin. Endocrinol. Metab.,* 43:1203–1210.
5. Burman, K. D., Dimond, R. C., McGuire, R. A., Earll, J. M., Strum, D., and Wartofsky, L. (1976): The effect of varying serum T4 concentrations on extrathyroidal production of T3, reverse T3, and 3,3′-diiodothyronine. *Clin. Res.,* 24:270A (abstract).

6. Burman, K. D., Read, J., Dimond, R. C., Strum, D., Wright, F. D., Patow, W., Earll, J. M., and Wartofsky, L. (1976): Measurements of 3,3′,5′-triiodothyronine (reverse T3), 3,3′-L-diiodothyronine, T3, and T4 in human amniotic fluid and in cord and maternal serum. *J. Clin. Endocrinol. Metab.*, 43:1351–1359.
7. Burman, K. D., Strum, D., Dimond, R. C., Djuh, Y.-Y., Wright, F. D., Earll, J. M., and Wartofsky, L. (1977): A radioimmunoassay for 3,3′-L-diiodothyronine. *J. Clin. Endocrinol. Metab.* (*in press*).
8. Chopra, I. J. (1974): A radioimmunoassay for measurement of 3,3′,5′-triiodothyronine (reverse T3). *J. Clin. Invest.*, 54:583–592.
9. Chopra, I. J. (1976): An assessment of daily production and significance of thyroidal secretion of 3,3′,5′-triiodothyronine (reverse T3) in man. *J. Clin. Invest.*, 58:32–40.
10. Chopra, I. J., Carlson, H. E., and Solomon, D. H. (1976): Comparison of TSH-suppressive effects of various thyroid hormones *in vitro*. *Clin. Res.*, 24:270A.
11. Chopra, I. J., Chopra, U., Smith, S. R., Reza, M., and Solomon, D. H. (1975): Reciprocal changes in serum concentration of 3,3′,5′-triiodothyronine (reverse T3) and 3,3′,5-triiodothyronine (T3) in systemic illnesses. *J. Clin. Endocrinol. Metab.*, 41:1043–1049.
12. Chopra, I. J., Ho, R. S., and Lam, R. (1972): An improved radioimmunoassay of triiodothyronine in serum: Its application to clinical and physiologic studies. *J. Lab. Clin. Med.*, 80:729–739.
13. Chopra, I. J., Sack, J., and Fisher, D. A. (1975*a*): 3,3′,5′-Triiodothyronine (reverse T3) and 3,3′,5-triiodothyronine (T3) in fetal and adult sheep: Studies of metabolic clearance rates, production rates, serum binding and thyroidal content relative to thyroxine. *Endocrinology*, 97:1080–1088.
14. Chopra, I. J., Sack, J., and Fisher, D. A. (1975*b*): Circulating 3,3′5′-triiodothyronine (reverse T3) in the human newborn. *J. Clin. Invest.*, 55:1137–1141.
15. Chopra, I. J., Sack, J., and Fisher, D. A. (1975*c*): Reverse T3 in the fetus and newborn. In: *Perinatal Thyroid Physiology and Disease, Vol. 3,* edited by D. A. Fisher and G. N. Burrow, pp. 33–40. Raven Press, New York.
16. Chopra, I. J., Williams, D. E., Orgiazzi, J., and Solomon, D. H. (1975): Opposite effects of dexamethasone on serum concentrations of 3,3′,5′-triiodothyronine (reverse T3) and 3,3′,5-triiodothyronine (T3). *J. Clin. Endocrinol. Metab.*, 41:911–920.
17. Chopra, I. J., Wu, S. Y., and Solomon, D. H. (1976): Extrathyroidal production of 3,3′-diiodothyronine (T2) *in vitro:* A major pathway of reverse T3 metabolism, a minor pathway for T3. *Endocrinology* [*Suppl.*], 98:102 (abstract).
18. Feighner, J. P., Robins, E., Guze, S. B., Woodruff, R. A., Jr., and Munoz, R. (1972): Diagnostic criteria for use in psychiatric research. *Arch. Gen. Psychiatry*, 26:57–63.
19. Flock, E. V., Bollman, J. L., and Grindlay, J. H. (1960): 3,3′-Diiodothyronine, a metabolite of 3,5,3′-triiodothyronine. *Mayo. Clin. Proc.*, 35:75–81.
20. Frantz, A. G., Kleinberg, D. L., and Noel, G. L. (1972): Studies on prolactin in man. *Recent Prog. Horm. Res.*, 28:527–590.
21. Glick, S. M., Roth, J., Yalow, R. S., and Berson, S. A. (1965): The regulation of growth hormone secretion. *Recent Prog. Horm. Res.*, 21:241–283.
22. Miyai, K., Yamamoto, T., Azukizawa, M., Ishibashi, K., and Kumahara, Y. (1975): Serum thyroid hormones and thyrotropin in anorexia nervosa. *J. Clin. Endocrinol. Metab.*, 40:334–338.
23. Moshang, T., Jr., Parks, J. S., Baker, L., Vaidya, V., Utiger, R. D., Bongiovanni, A. M., and Synder, P. J. (1975): Low serum triiodothyronine in patients with anorexia nervosa. *J. Clin. Endocrinol. Metab.*, 40:470–473.
24. Nicod, P., Burger, A., Staeheli, V., and Vallotton, M. B. (1976): A radioimmunoassay for 3,3′,5′-triiodo-L-thyronine in unextracted serum: Method and clinical results. *J. Clin. Endocrinol. Metab.*, 42:823–829.
25. Nicod, P., Burger, A., Strauch, G., Vagenakis, A. G., and Braverman, L. E. (1976): The failure of physiologic doses of reverse T3 to effect thyroid-pituitary function in man. *J. Clin. Endocrinol. Metab.*, 43:478–481.
26. Papavasiliou, S. S., Martial, J. A., Latham, K. R., and Baxter, J. D. (1976): Thyroid hormone-like actions of reverse T3 and 3,3′-diiodothyronine (3,3′T2). Program of the 52nd Annual Meeting of the American Thyroid Association, Inc., Toronto, Canada, T-18.
27. Pittman, C. S., and Pittman, J. A. (1974): Relation of chemical structure to the action and

metabolism of thyroactive substances, Section 7: Endocrinology. In: *Handbook of Physiology, Vol. III, Ed. 1,* edited by M. A. Greer and D. H. Solomon, pp. 233–253. Waverly Press, Baltimore.

28. Pittman, C. S., Shinohara, M., Thrasher, H., and McCraw, E. F. (1964): Effect of thyroxine analogues on the peripheral metabolism of thyroxine: The half-life and pattern of elimination. *Endocrinology,* 74:611–616.
29. Rivlin, R. S., and Huang, Y. P. (1976): Reverse T3 and cortisone as inducers of hepatic L-triiodothyronine aminotransferase. Program of the 52nd Annual Meeting of the American Thyroid Association, Inc., Toronto, Canada, T-18.
30. Roche, J., Michel, R., Jouan, P., and Wolf, W. (1956): The recovery of 3:5:3′-triiodothyroacetic acid and 3:3′-diiodothyronine from rat kidney after injection of 3:5:3′-triiodothyronine. *Endocrinology,* 59:425–432.
31. Roche, J., Michel, R., Nunez, J., and Jacquemin, C. (1959): On the metabolism of 3,3′-diiodothyronine and 3,3′5′-triiodothyronine. *Endocrinology,* 65:402–407.
32. Rudolph, M., Sakurada, T., Vagenakis, A., Fang, S., Braverman, L., and Ingbar, S. (1976): Demonstration of sequential monodeiodination as the major pathway of iodothyronine metabolism. *Clin. Res.,* 24:429A (abstract).
33. Stanbury, J. B., and Morris, M. L. (1957): The metabolism of 3:3′-diiodothyronine in man. *J. Clin. Endocrinol. Metab.,* 17:1324–1331.
34. Sterling, K., and Brenner, M. A. (1966): Free thyroxine in human serum: Simplified measurement with the aid of magnesium precipitation. *J. Clin. Invest.,* 45:153–163, 1966.
35. Vagenakis, A. G., Burger, A., Portnay, G. I., Rudolph, M., O'Brian, J. T., Azizi, F., Arky, R. A., Nicod, P., Ingbar, S. H., and Braverman, L. E. (1975): Diversion of peripheral thyroxine metabolism from activating to inactivating pathways during complete fasting. *J. Clin. Endocrinol. Metab.,* 41:191–194.
36. Vigersky, R. A., Loriaux, D. L., Andersen, A. E., and Lipsett, M. B. (1976): Anorexia nervosa: Behavioural and hypothalmic aspects. *Clin. Endocrinol. Metab.,* 5:517–535.
37. Wartofsky, L., Burman, K. D., Dimond, R. C., Noel, G. L., Frantz, A. G., and Earll, J. M. (1977): Studies on the nature of thyroidal suppression during acute falciparum malaria: Integrity of pituitary response to TRH and alterations in serum T3 and reverse T3. *J. Clin. Endocrinol. Metab.,* 44:85–90.
38. Wu, S. Y., Chopra, I. J., Nakamura, Y., Solomon, D. H., and Bennett, L. R. (1976): A radioimmunoassay for measurement of 3,3′-L-diiodothyronine (T2). *J. Clin. Endocrinol. Metab.,* 43:682–685.

Anorexia Nervosa, edited by
R. A. Vigersky. Raven Press,
New York © 1977.

Low Triiodothyronine Euthyroidism in Anorexia Nervosa

* Thomas Moshang, Jr., and ** Robert D. Utiger

* *Department of Pediatrics, Hahnemann Medical College, Philadelphia, Pennsylvania 19102; and ** Department of Medicine, University of Pennsylvania, School of Medicine, Philadelphia, Pennsylvania 19174*

INTRODUCTION

The endocrine aspects of anorexia nervosa (AN) have fascinated clinicians and endocrinologists for many years. Unlike the amenorrhea which is almost an integral part of the syndrome in females, the thyroid status of these patients has been tantalizingly enigmatic. There are many findings suggestive of hypothyroidism, such as low basal metabolic rates, constipation, dry skin, bradycardia, low pulse pressure, and elevated serum cholesterol and carotene levels (3,7). Yet many classic and almost pathognomonic signs of hypothyroidism, such as myxedema, resistant anemia, and delay in the relaxation phase of deep tendon reflexes, are not consistently observed. Serum concentrations of thyroxine (T4) and protein-bound iodine have been found to be normal or low normal (3,7,9,11,12). Thyrotropin (TSH) levels have been observed to be increased (1) but are generally regarded to be normal in AN (9,11,12). TSH responses to thyrotropin-releasing hormone (TRH) have been reported to be normal (9,11,12), although Aro et al. (1) reported delayed responses suggestive of hypothalamic hypothyroidism. Consistently, triiodothyronine (T3) levels have been noted to be low and in the range found in hypothyroid subjects (11,12). This chapter focuses on the implications of the low T3 levels noted in AN, using for comparative purposes data from patients with hypothalamic TSH and growth hormone deficiency.

MATERIALS AND METHODS

Patients

Nine female patients with AN, ages 9 to 18-2/12 years, were studied. The clinical data of the majority of these patients have been previously reported (12). All of the patients were anorectic and still losing weight when these studies were performed. The percent of weight loss ranged between 14.4 and 42.2%. One of the nine patients was only 9 years of age and had not yet attained menarche. The others had secondary amenorrhea of 5 to 12 months' duration.

The control group consisted of 15 children previously reported (16), who were free of organic and psychiatric disease except that all had short stature. Their results are comparable to the normal values reported by this laboratory for adults (21,22).

Six children with multiple pituitary deficiencies were classified as having idiopathic hypothalamic hypothyroidism on the basis of positive responses to TRH (6) and the lack of demonstrable intracranial disease. All of these children had clinical evidence of hypothyroidism. All six had growth hormone deficiency, and some had ACTH and gonadotropin deficiency as well.

Methods

Serum concentrations of T3 and TSH were determined by radioimmunoassay (8,15). Serum T4 concentrations were determined by competitive protein binding assay (13). The TRH test was performed by injection of 5 μg/kg of synthetic TRH in a single bolus intravenously, and serum TSH levels were determined at −10, 0, 10, 20, 30, 60, 90, 120, and 180 min.

RESULTS

Thyroid Function Tests in Anorexia Nervosa

The findings in the patients with AN are compared to the findings in normal children in Table 1. The normal ranges for the various tests in this laboratory are also included in this table. The T4 concentrations are generally lower in AN, but most of the determinations are within the normal range for this laboratory. Two of the patients had T4 concentrations in the hypothyroid range. The mean value of 7.1 μg/100 ml is significantly lower than the mean concentration of 9.5 μg/100 ml for the normal children ($p < 0.01$). The serum T3 concentrations in all but two of the AN patients were below the normal range, and the mean value of 56.1 ng/100 ml was markedly lower than the mean T3 concentration of 106 ng/100 ml for the normal children ($p < 0.001$). The basal TSH levels were not increased in any of the AN patients, and the mean basal TSH level was not significantly different from that of the control group.

The TRH test was performed in AN patients. Their individual responses and the mean response are compared to the mean TSH response to TRH of the control group in Fig. 1. There was no significant difference in the TSH values in AN and normal children at each time interval after intravenous

TABLE 1. *Comparison of thyroid function tests in anorexia nervosa patients and normal children*

Patients	T_4 (μg/100 ml)	T_3 (ng/100 ml)	TSH (μU/ml)
AN #1	7.8	56	1.5
AN #2	6.6	30	1.5
AN #3	6.5	36	3.8
AN #4	11.3	95	3.6
AN #5	6.4	45	4.0
AN #6	4.6	36	3.4
AN #7	7.4	76	1.5
AN #8	4.4	59	6.0
AN #9	8.7	72	—
Mean ± SEM	7.1 ± 0.7[a]	56.1 ± 7.7[b]	3.2 ± 0.6
15 normals			
Mean ± SEM	9.5 ± 0.3	106 ± 7.5	3.6 ± 0.4
Normal range	5.0–11.5	70–150	1.5–10

[a] p, compared to normals, <0.01.
[b] p, compared to normals, <0.001.

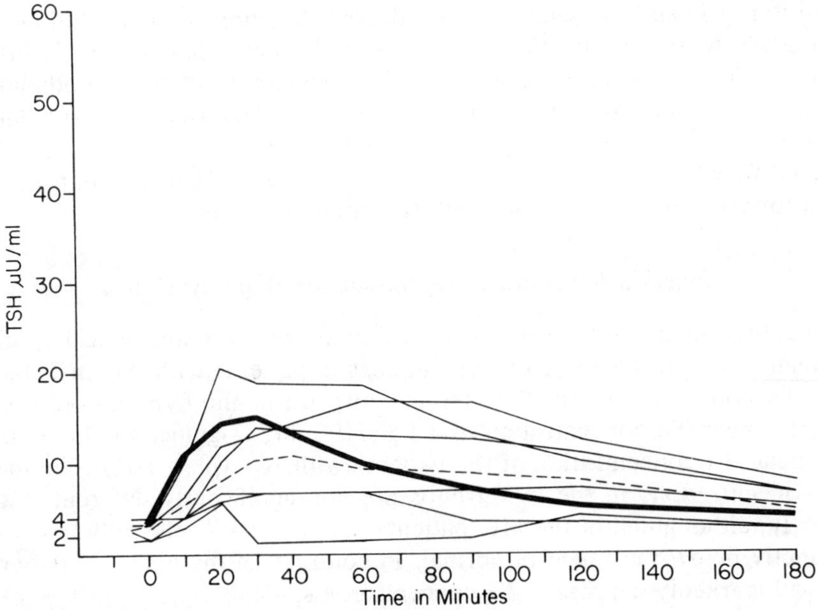

FIG. 1. The TRH test in patients with anorexia nervosa. (——) represents individual patient TSH responses to TRH. (----) represents mean TSH response to TRH in AN. (——) represents mean TSH response to TRH in 15 normal children.

TRH. The mean maximum incremental rise in TSH was 9 μU/ml in the AN patients, and this increase was not significantly different from the mean incremental rise of 12 μU/ml in normal children. Two of the AN patients did have a slight delay in response to TRH. However, the peak values, which were at 60 min, were only slightly greater than the responses at 30 min, and minor delayed responses in normal subjects have been observed in this laboratory.

These findings are similar to the findings reported by other investigators (9,11,12). There is general agreement that patients with AN have low or low-normal T4 concentrations, low T3 concentrations, and fairly normal TSH levels. Maximum incremental TSH responses to TRH in AN are similar to the maximum incremental rise noted in normals. However, a delayed response to TRH has been noted by several investigators (1,9, 11), and dysfunction of the hypothalamus has been suggested to be present in AN.

Various investigators (10,27) have suggested that not only do patients with AN have hypothalamic dysfunction, but perhaps a primary hypothalamic lesion of as yet undetermined cause may be the basis of the disease. Certainly psychic stress can alter hypothalamic function. In the classic studies of emotional deprivation dwarfism, Powell et al. (19,20) documented reversible abnormal hypothalamic dysfunction, including abnormalities of ACTH and growth hormone secretion. In AN, because of the severe inanition, it is still not clear to what degree the clinical manifestations are secondary to starvation, to psychic stress altering hypothalamic function, or to primary hypothalamic disease. The availability of the hypothalamic releasing hormone for thyrotropin permits the diagnosis of hypothalamic hypothyroidism in patients previously labeled as hypopituitary (6). The thyroid function tests in these patients, including TRH test responses, are used for comparative purposes with the findings in AN.

Anorexia Nervosa and Hypothalamic Hypothyroidism

The thyroid function tests in six children with hypothalamic hypothyroidism (HH) are compared to the findings in patients with AN in Table 2. The T4 concentrations in the HH patients are in the hypothyroid range, and the mean T4 concentration of 4.1 μg/100 ml is significantly lower than the mean T4 concentration of the patients with AN ($p < 0.01$). The mean T3 concentrations in the two groups are not significantly different. Interestingly, although all of the HH patients had low T3 levels, only two were distinctly below the range of normal. In contrast, of the nine AN patients, six had markedly depressed T3 concentrations.

These data are strongly suggestive that the low T3 levels are not due to decreased thyroid gland activity and certainly not due to hypothalamic dysfunction. These serum concentrations of T3 are similar to those levels observed in primary hypothyroidism, in which the T4 values are extremely

TABLE 2. *Comparison of thyroid function tests in anorexia nervosa patients and children with hypothalamic hypothyroidism*

Patients	T_4 (μg/100 ml)	T_3 (ng/100 ml)	TSH (μU/ml)
HH #1	3.8	69	4.3
HH #2	5.2	64	5.0
HH #3	4.3	54	7.0
HH #4	3.0	49	6.3
HH #5	4.2	60	4.1
HH #6	3.8	67	4.2
Mean ± SEM	4.1 ± 0.3[a]	60.5 ± 3.5[b]	5.2 ± 0.5[b]
9 AN patients			
Mean ± SEM	7.1 ± 0.7	56.1 ± 7.7	3.2 ± 0.6

[a] *p*, compared to AN, <0.01.
[b] *p*, compared to AN, ns

low (23). Inasmuch as 60 to 80% (or more) of the daily production of T3 is secondary to peripheral conversion of T4 to T3 (2), and the T4 levels in AN are significantly higher than those seen in primary or secondary hypothyroidism, these markedly low T3 values in AN cannot be adequately explained by absence of T3 secretion by the thyroid gland. These data are

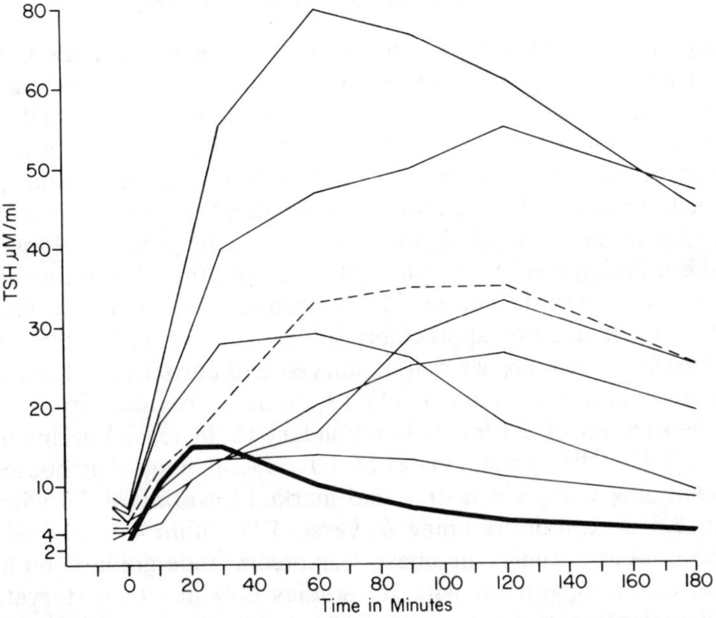

FIG. 2. The TRH test in patients with hypothalamic hypothyroidism and other pituitary hormone deficiencies. (——) represents individual patient TSH responses to TRH. (----) represents mean TSH response of the 6 patients to TRH. (▬▬) represents mean TSH response to TRH in 15 normal children.

suggestive that the low T3 levels in AN are secondary to decreased peripheral conversion of T4 to T3, a mechanism which appears operative in states of inanition which will be discussed below.

The low-normal T4 concentrations in AN might be explained by decreased thyroid gland activity secondary to hypothalamic dysfunction. In Fig. 2, the TSH responses to TRH in each of the six children with HH and their mean response are depicted. The mean response to TRH of the normal children is also illustrated. It is quite clear that the response to TRH in HH is markedly different from the response to TRH seen in AN (Fig. 1). The levels of TSH in HH at 30 min and subsequent time intervals after TRH are significantly higher than the levels found in normal subjects and AN patients.

Although these comparative data indicate that AN patients do not have HH, the possibility that a more subtle form of hypothalamic dysfunction exists (either primary or secondary to psychic stress) cannot be dismissed. However, an intriguing possibility is that the hypothalamic area regulating the pituitary-thyroid axis, i.e., the "thyrostat," is reset for lower levels of T4 and T3 during states of inanition. This decreased secretion of TRH during these circumstances would produce the minor delays in response to TRH noted by several investigators.

DISCUSSION AND CONCLUSIONS

The thyroid function tests in AN are similar to those findings reported in patients with chronic illness (4,25), in obese volunteers after acute but prolonged starvation (17,18,26), and in patients with protein-calorie malnutrition (5). Consistently, the T3 levels have been markedly depressed with some of the lowest values being reported in patients with protein-calorie malnutrition. Although some of the clinical findings suggestive of hypothyroidism noted in AN are also present in protein-calorie malnutrition, these findings are not necessarily seen in other debilitating illnesses or in acute starvation despite low T3 concentrations. Similar to findings in AN, TSH levels are not appreciably increased, and TSH responses and T3 responses to TRH are normal in starved and chronically ill individuals.

Acute starvation studies in man (17,18,26) have provided strong evidence that the depression of T3 levels is secondary to decreased peripheral conversion of T4 to T3. Vagenakis et al. (26) documented that obese volunteers undergoing complete fasting had marked lowering of T3 with an increase in 3,3′,5′-triiodothyronine (reverse T3) within 4 weeks of caloric deprivation. These studies in obese volunteers undergoing complete fast (17,18,26) are in agreement with rat studies (14) in which starvation decreased deiodination of thyroxine by 50% as compared to normally fed rats. Similar changes in T3 and reverse T3 have been reported by Chopra et al. (4) in systemic illnesses.

These lowered T3 levels have been ascribed to "defects" or "abnormalities" (4) of peripheral deiodination of T4 to T3. However, rather than an abnormality, a more teleological explanation is that the target cells for thyroid hormones have regulatory mechanisms based on metabolic needs for conversion of T4 to T3. This viewpoint would also encompass the findings of increased concentrations of reverse T3 and normal TSH levels in states of inanition. If the conversion of T4 to T3 at the cellular level is regulated by metabolic needs, then caloric deprivation, dietary content of hypocaloric diets, or debilitating illness would alter the cellular mechanisms regulating deiodination of T4 to decrease production of T3, enabling the target cell to protect itself from inappropriate metabolic activity due to excessive thyroid hormone stimulation. The increase in reverse T3, a much less calorigenic hormone, would be a reflection of the peripheral shunting of T4 toward reverse T3 and away from T3 (4,24,26). These subcellular mechanisms regulating T4 deiodination may also be an integral part of the pituitary thyrotrophs. The thyrotrophs would therefore not interpret the low levels of T3 as being insufficient for metabolic needs, explaining why TSH levels are not increased. This teleological hypothesis would also explain the variation in T4 and T3 values in individual patients, including those individuals with hypothyroid levels of T4 who nevertheless have normal TSH concentrations and normal responses to TRH. In those individuals, because of cellular metabolic needs, the "thyrostat" is set at a lower level, causing decreased secretion of TRH, TSH, and T4, but maintaining normal neuroendocrine feedback mechanisms.

This interpretation of the thyroid function tests in AN would maintain that AN patients are euthyroid. These patients may indeed be hypometabolic, as evidenced by hypothermia, bradycardia, and low pulse pressure. However, this hypometabolic state is probably not a result of abnormal hypothalamic function, decreased thyroid hormone secretion, or an inability to convert T4 to T3, but it is a homeostatic protective adjustment at the cellular level.

REFERENCES

1. Aro, A., Lamberg, B. A., and Pelkonen, R. (1975): Letter: Dysfunction of the hypothalamic axis in anorexia nervosa. *N. Engl. J. Med.*, 292:594.
2. Braverman, L. E., Ingbar, S. H., and Sterling, K. (1970): Conversion of thyroxine (T4) to triiodothyronine (T3) in athyreotic human subjects. *J. Clin. Invest.*, 49:855–864.
3. Bruch, H. (1965): Anorexia nervosa and its differential diagnosis. *J. Nerv. Ment. Dis.*, 141:555–566.
4. Chopra, I. J., Chopra, U., Smith, S. R., Reza, M., and Solomon, D. H. (1975): Reciprocal changes in serum concentrations of 3,3′,5′-triiodothyronine (reverse T3) and 3,3′,5-triiodothyronine (T3) in systemic illness. *J. Clin. Endocrinol. Metab.*, 41:1043–1049.
5. Chopra, I. J., and Smith, S. R. (1975): Circulating thyroid hormones and thyrotropin in adult patients with protein calorie malnutrition. *J. Clin. Endocrinol. Metab.*, 40:221–227.
6. Costom, B. H., Grumbach, M. M., and Kaplan, S. L. (1971): Effect of thyrotropin-releasing factor on serum thyroid-stimulating hormone. *J. Clin. Invest.*, 50:2219–2225.

7. Crisp, A. H. (1965): Clinical and therapeutic aspects of anorexia nervosa—a study of 30 cases. *J. Psychosom. Res.*, 9:67–78.
8. Lieblich, J., and Utiger, R. D. (1972): Triiodothyronine radioimmunoassay. *J. Clin Invest.*, 51:157–166.
9. Lundberg, P. O., Walinder, J., Werner, I., and Wide, L. (1972): Effects of thyrotropin-releasing hormone on plasma levels of TSH, FSH, LH and GH in anorexia nervosa *Eur. J. Clin. Invest.*, 2:150–153.
10. Mecklenberg, R. S., Loriaux, D. L., Thompson, R. H., Andersen, A. E., and Lipsett M. B. (1974): Hypothalamic dysfunction in patients with anorexia nervosa. *Medicine (Baltimore)*, 53:147–159.
11. Miyai, K., Yamamoto, T., Azukizawa, M., Ishibashi, K., and Kumahara, Y. (1975): Serum thyroid hormones and thyrotropin in anorexia nervosa. *J. Clin. Endocrinol. Metab.*, 40:334–338.
12. Moshang, T., Jr., Parks, J. S., Baker, L., Vaidya, V., Utiger, R. D., Bongiovanni, A. M., and Snyder, P. J. (1975): Low serum triiodothyronine in patients with anorexia nervosa. *J. Clin. Endocrinol. Metab.*, 40:470–473.
13. Murphy, B. E. P., and Pattee, C. J. (1964): Determination of thyroxine utilizing the property of protein-binding. *J. Clin. Endocrinol. Metab.*, 24:187–196.
14. Nathanielsz, P. W. (1970): The effect of diet and acute starvation on the deiodination of thyroxine and triiodothyronine in the thyroidectomized rat. *J. Physiol.*, 206:701–710.
15. Odell, W. D., Wilber, J. F., and Utiger, R. D. (1967): Studies of thyrotropin physiology by means of radioimmunoassay. *Recent Prog. Horm. Res.*, 23:47–78.
16. Parks, J. S., Snyder, P. J., Utiger, R. D., Moshang, T., Jr., and Bongiovanni, A. M. (1973): Thyrotropin and thyroidal responses to consecutive doses of thyrotropin-releasing hormone. *J. Clin. Endocrinol. Metab.*, 37:466–468.
17. Portnay, G. I., O'Brian, J. T., Bush, J., Vagenakis, A. G., Azizi, F., Arky, R. A., Ingbar, S. H., and Braverman, L. E. (1974): The effect of starvation on the concentration and binding of thyroxine and triiodothyronine in serum and the response to TRH. *J. Clin. Endocrinol. Metab.*, 39:191–194.
18. Portnay, G. I., O'Brian, J. T., Vagenakis, A. G., Rudolph, M., Arky, R., Ingbar, S. H., and Braverman, L. E. (1974): Abnormalities in triiodothyronine metabolism induced by starvation in man. *J. Clin. Invest.*, 53:61a (abstract).
19. Powell, G. F., Brasel, J. A., and Blizzard, R. M. (1967): Emotional deprivation and growth retardation simulating idiopathic hypopituitarism. I. Clinical evaluation of the syndrome. *N. Engl. J. Med.*, 276:1271–1278.
20. Powell, G. F., Brasel, J. A., Raiti, S., and Blizzard, R. M. (1967): Emotional deprivation and growth retardation simulating idiopathic hypopituitarism. II. Endocrinologic evaluation of the syndrome. *N. Engl. J. Med.*, 276:1279–1283.
21. Snyder, P. J., and Utiger, R. D. (1972*a*): Response to thyrotropin releasing hormone (TRH) in man. *J. Clin. Endocrinol. Metab.*, 34:380–385.
22. Snyder, P. J., and Utiger, R. D. (1972*b*): Response to thyrotropin-releasing hormone in females over forty. *J. Clin. Endocrinol. Metab.*, 34:1096–1098.
23. Snyder, P. J., and Utiger, R. D. (1972*c*): Inhibition of thyrotropin responses to thyrotropin-releasing hormone by small quantities of thyroid hormones. *J. Clin. Invest.*, 51:2077–2084.
24. Spalding, S. W., Chopra, I. J., Sherwin, R. S., and Lyall, S. S. (1976): Effect of caloric restriction and dietary composition on serum T3 and reverse T3 in man. *J. Clin. Endocrinol. Metab.*, 42:197–200.
25. Sullivan, P. R. C., Bollinger, J. A., and Reichlin, S. (1973): Selective deficiency of tissue triiodothyronine: a proposed mechanism of elevated free thyroxine in the euthyroid sick. *J. Clin. Invest.*, 52:83a (abstract).
26. Vagenakis, A. G., Burger, A., Portnay, G. I., Rudolph, M., O'Brian, J. T., Azizi, F., Arky, R. A., Nicod, P., Ingbar, S. H., and Braverman, L. E. (1975): Diversion of peripheral thyroxine metabolism from activating to inactivating pathways during complete fasting. *J. Clin. Endocrinol. Metab.*, 41:191–194.
27. Warren, M. P., and Vande Wiele, R. L. (1973): Clinical and metabolic features of anorexia nervosa. *Am. J. Obstet. Gynecol.*, 117:435–449.

Anorexia Nervosa, edited by
R. A. Vigersky. Raven Press,
New York © 1977.

Studies of Testosterone Metabolism in Anorexia Nervosa

† Robert M. Boyar and H. Leon Bradlow

Department of Oncology and Institute of Steroid Research, Montefiore Hospital and Medical Center, Bronx, New York 10467

INTRODUCTION

Anorexia nervosa is a disorder that occurs primarily in young women and is characterized by inappropriate hyperactivity in the presence of severe malnutrition. This combination is often helpful in distinguishing patients with this disorder from those with hypopituitarism and other significant organic disorders. Studies of thyroid function in patients with anorexia nervosa have shown low-normal plasma T4 levels, subnormal plasma T3 levels (2), and normal TSH levels (8). The significance of the isolated lowering of plasma T3 has not been established; however, it has been felt to represent a decrease in the peripheral deiodination of T4 to T3 with a reciprocal increase in the inactive form, reverse T3. This change to an inactive form of triiodothyronine may represent a protective mechanism during a catabolic state.

Studies of testosterone metabolism in patients with clinical hypothyroidism have shown a decrease in 5α-reductase activity so that the urinary metabolites of ^{14}C-testosterone show a preponderance of etiocholanolone at the expense of the 5α reduced compound, androsterone (4) (Fig. 1). To examine the significance of the low T3 levels in patients with anorexia nervosa, we measured the metabolism of testosterone to determine if the findings in this disorder were in any way similar to those found in patients with clinical hypothyroidism. We also measured testosterone metabolism during various degrees of recovery as well as after the acute administration of T3. The results of this study suggested that patients with anorexia nervosa have abnormalities that are similar to those of patients with classic hypothyroidism and that these changes can be reversed with acute T3 administration.

---

† Present address: Department of Internal Medicine, University of Texas Health Science Center, Dallas, Texas 75235.

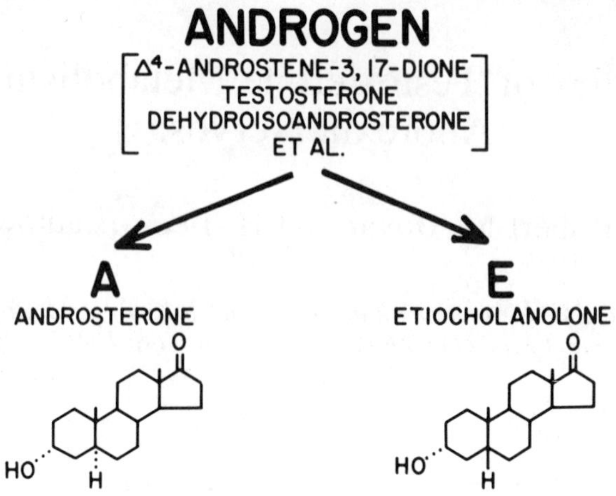

FIG. 1. Pathways of androgen metabolism.

METHODS

Patients

The 13 young women with anorexia nervosa (AN) were between 16 and 28 years of age. They had lost between 14 and 40.5% of their ideal body weight. They had no intercurrent illness and had no drug ingestion. The clinical characteristics of most of these patients have been reported previously.

Testosterone Metabolism

Testosterone-4-^{14}C or 1,2-^{3}H was obtained from New England Nuclear Corporation; its purity was established by paper chromatography in the system isooctane:methanol:water (10:8:2), and it was used without further purification. The hormone was dissolved in propylene glycol and administered as described previously (3). Urine collections, hydrolysis of the urinary conjugates, and isolation of the principal metabolites [androsterone (A) and etiocholanolone (E)] were carried out according to earlier published methods (3). The ratio of androsterone over etiocholanolone was used as an index of 5α-reductase activity.

Testosterone Metabolism after T3 Administration

Eleven patients with anorexia nervosa underwent control studies of testosterone metabolism. After the completion of these studies, 6 of the patients received 75 μg of triiodothyronine daily for 7 to 10 days at which time a repeat study of testosterone metabolism was carried out.

Thyroid Function

Plasma T4, T3, and TSH were measured by radioimmunoassay.

RESULTS

The mean $5\alpha/5\beta$ ratio from 4-^{14}C-testosterone was 0.42 in the AN patients compared to 0.70 in normal female subjects. The endogenous $5\alpha/5\beta$ ratio in the patient group was also reduced (0.44). The results for the individual subjects are summarized in Table 1. The response of 6 of the patients to the administration of exogenous triiodothyronine is summarized in Table 2. In each case the $5\alpha/5\beta$ ratio rose following treatment.

TABLE 1. *A/E ratios and plasma T3 in patients with anorexia nervosa in relapse*

Case	% Deviation from ideal weight	A/E ratio From ^{14}C-testosterone	A/E ratio Endogenous	T3
1	−15	0.36	0.34	109
2	−37	0.34	—	50
3	−17	0.39	0.24	63
4	−31	0.28	0.30	57
5	−43	0.33	0.45	62
6	−36	0.31	—	46
7	−35	0.35	—	70
8	−38	0.39	—	68
9	−14	0.77		96
10	−19	0.52		62
11	−35	0.58		82
Patient average		0.42 ± 0.04	0.44	
Average of normal young women		0.70 ± 0.03	0.80	

TABLE 2. *Effect of T3 therapy on the A/E ratios of patients with anorexia nervosa*

Patient	Control A/E ratio	Ratio after T3 therapy
4	0.28	0.59
6	0.31	0.82
7	0.35	1.21
9	0.77	1.01
10	0.52	1.54
11	0.58	1.38

TABLE 3. *A/E ratios and plasma T3 concentrations after weight gain associated with clinical remission*

Patient	% Below ideal weight	A/E ratio	Plasma T3 (ng/dl)
GE			
Relapse	31	0.28	57
Partial weight gain	22	0.39	101
Normal weight	0	0.54	148
SI			
Relapse	35	0.35	70
Partial weight gain	16	0.46	127
GR			
Relapse	43	0.33	62
Partial weight gain	25	0.59	—

In three subjects who recovered spontaneously, the $5\alpha/5\beta$ ratio increased as the patients gained weight and their T3 levels rose. The results for the individual patients are summarized in Table 3.

DISCUSSION

The metabolism of testosterone was assessed in patients with anorexia nervosa. The 5α:5β ratio in all patients was greatly diminished to about half that encountered in normal sex-matched controls. This was the result of a decrease in the 5α pathway and a concomitant increase in the 5β route. This is precisely the result one would find in hypothyroid patients with T3 levels like those in our AN patients. The finding of normal T4 and TSH and low plasma T3 in anoretic patients is similar to what is found in patients dying of chronic wasting disorders, a variety of chronic nonthyroidal diseases, liver disease, kidney disease, and acute and chronic starvation (9). Reichlin et al. (10) recently showed that patients dying of chronic wasting disorders with low plasma T3 levels before death also had low hepatic T3 levels compared with normal patients who died suddenly. These low levels of hepatic T3 may be the result of decreased T3 formation from T4 in the liver. These observations provide a rationale for suggesting a relationship between the low T3 levels in anorexia nervosa and the alterations in testosterone metabolism found in our patients.

The metabolism of testosterone is primarily reductive, involving a microsomal 5α-reductase leading to androsterone and a cytoplasmic 5β-reductase yielding etiocholanolone with the greatest part of this transformation occurring in the liver. Preliminary studies using simultaneous cutaneous application and intravenous administration suggest that the decrease in 5α-reductase activity is confined to the liver and is not apparent in cutaneous tissue. In our patients, the low hepatic T3 levels are most probably responsible for the decreased 5α-reductase activity. The finding that acute T3 administration resulted in a return of this abnormality to or toward normal lends further support to this hypothesis.

This shift in the metabolite pattern of testosterone could have physiologic consequences since the pharmacology of the alternative products is quite different. The 5β compounds have been shown to be pyrogenic (6) and porphyrinogenic (7), whereas the 5α compound has been shown to have hypocholesterolemic properties (5). What other properties these alternative compounds have is a matter of conjecture; however, it is conceivable that they may have effects beyond those mentioned above.

These results suggest that patients with anorexia nervosa have hypothyroid-like abnormalities of steroid metabolism. Studies of cortisol metabolism in these patients have shown an increase in the tetrahydrocortisol-tetrahydrocortisone ratio, also indicative of a hypothyroid state (1). The administration of T3 to these patients also caused an amelioration of these abnormalities to or toward normal. However, it must be noted that the metabolic fate of estradiol, which is primarily oxidative in nature, is not altered in the direction found in hypothyroidism but is shifted toward the pattern observed in hyperthyroidism (3a). Clearly, other biochemical changes present in these patients are responsible for the alteration of estradiol metabolism found in these anorexia nervosa patients. The results of these combined studies clearly establish that steroid metabolism is profoundly altered in anorexia nervosa and that the change occurs in those hormones whose metabolism is reductive in nature.

Therefore, summarizing the available data, one might suggest that the following sequence of events is responsible for the initiation and evolution of the steroid abnormalities in anorexia nervosa: (1) Unknown initiating event, probably psychiatric; (2) Avoidance of food and an insidious weight loss leading to subnormal plasma T3 concentration and (3) decreased 5α-reductase activity resulting in the hypothyroid-like abnormalities of androgen metabolism. The reversal of these steroid changes after acute T3 administration or clinical remission with its increase in endogenous plasma T3 suggests an association between T3 levels and the steroid abnormality but does not establish a cause and effect relationship. It is possible that the changes in both thyroxine and androgen metabolism reflect hepatic dysfunction caused by undernutrition and that they both serve a "protective hypometabolic" function in the face of a catabolic state.

ACKNOWLEDGMENTS

These studies were supported by NIH Grants CA07304, HL-14734, and RR-53. The technical assistance of Morris Kirschbaum and Hilda Denman is greatly appreciated.

REFERENCES

1. Boyar, R. M., Hellman, L. D., Roffwarg, H., Katz, J., Zumoff, B., O'Connor, J., Bradlow, H. L., Fukushima, D. K. (1977): Cortisol secretion and metabolism in anorexia nervosa. *New Engl. J. Med.,* 296:190–193.
2. Chopra, I. J., and Smith, S. R. (1975): Circulating thyroid hormones and thyrotropin in adult patients with protein-calorie malnutrition. *J. Clin. Endocrinol. Metab.,* 40:221–227.
3. Gallagher, T. F., Kappas, A., Hellman, L., Lipsett, M. B., Pearson, O. H., and West, C. D. (1958): Adrenocortical hyperfunction in "idiopathic" hirsutism and the Stein-Leventhal syndrome. *J. Clin. Invest.,* 37:794–799.

3a. Fishman, J., Boyar, R. M., and Hellman, L. (1975): Influence of body weight on estradiol metabolism in young women. *J. Clin. Endocrinol. Metab.,* 41:989–991.

4. Hellman, L., Bradlow, H. L., Zumoff, B., Fukushima, D. K., and Gallagher, T. F. (1959): Thyroid-androgen interrelations and the hypocholesteremic effect of androsterone. *J. Clin. Endocrinol. Metab.,* 19:936–948.
5. Hellman, L., Zumoff, B., Kessler, G., Kara, E., Rubin, I. L., and Rosenfeld, R. S. (1963): Reduction of serum cholesterol and lipids by ethyl chlorophenoxyisobutyrate. *J. Atherosclerosis Res.,* 3:454–466.
6. Kappas, A., Hellman, L., Fukushima, D. K., and Gallagher, T. F. (1957): The pyrogenic effect of etiocholanolone. *J. Clin. Endocrinol. Metab.,* 17:451–453.
7. Kappas, A., Bradlow, H. L., Gillette, P. V., and Gallagher, T. F. (1972): Studies in porphyria. *J. Exp. Med.,* 136:1043–1047.
8. Moshang, T., Parks, J. S., Baker, L., Vaidya, V., Utiger, R. D., Bongiovanni, A. M., and Snyder, P. J. (1975): Low serum triiodothyronine in patients with anorexia nervosa. *J. Clin. Endocrinol. Metab.,* 40:470–473.
9. Portnay, G. A., O'Brian, J. T., Vagenakis, A. G., Azizi, F., Arky, R. A., Ingbar, S. H., and Braverman, L. E. (1974): The effect of starvation on the concentration and binding of thyroxine and triiodothyronine in serum and on the response to TRH. *J. Clin. Endocrinol. Metab.,* 39:191–194.
10. Reichlin, S., Bollinger, J., Netad, I., and Sullivan, P. (1973): Tissue thyroid concentration of rat and man determined by radioimmunoassay: Biologic significance. *Mt. Sinai J. Med. N.Y.,* 40:502–510.

Anorexia Nervosa, edited by
R. A. Vigersky. Raven Press,
New York © 1977.

General Management of Anorexia Nervosa and Difficulties in Assessing the Efficacy of Treatment

G. F. M. Russell

Department of Psychiatry, Royal Free Hospital, London NW3 2QG, England

INTRODUCTION

All too often enthusiastic therapists publicize uncritically their favorite method of treatment, adducing support for its benefits from data that indicate that a number of patients with anorexia nervosa have, on average, gained X kg in weight over the course of Y weeks. An example of such a report appeared in the *Lancet* recently (13). Six patients had been given a course of amitriptyline (75 to 150 mg daily) and had apparently responded by gaining weight in amounts ranging from 2.8 to 16.9 kg. They had been under observation in hospital (as far as one can tell from the report) from 32 to 200 days. Not only did these workers deduce that the drug had been responsible for the beneficial changes in the patient, but they also proposed that it might have a specific effect on hypothalamic catecholamine function.

Clearly one should be cautious about accepting the efficacy of a drug without having recourse to the double-blind method. Even more important are the limitations of trying to assess the treatment of an illness so complex and so unpredictable as anorexia nervosa. The study referred to failed to take into account two basic facts about anorexia nervosa. First, the most immediately effective method of treatment is simply to admit the patient to hospital assuming that a basic level of care and understanding of the illness are available. Secondly, the criteria for a fundamental improvement in the course of the illness require a much more radical change in the patient than gain in weight over the course of a few weeks. This is not to minimize the importance of a substantial weight gain. By itself, however, it is not sufficient, especially if the appraisal is made too early. All too often, weight gained in hospital is relentlessly lost over the weeks or months following the patient's discharge. The outlook is brighter when it transpires that the patient can maintain a normal weight outside hospital: the longer this achievement lasts, the more promising the outlook is. Such a sustained progress is often accompanied by a return of the patient's mental state to normal, and there may also be a resumption of regular menstruation. Thus the criteria for a favorable course in anorexia nervosa, whether this occurs spontaneously or is induced by treatment, cannot be confined to a mere gain in weight, especially if this occurs within the protected environment of the hospital. The criteria must include maintenance of normal weight over a period of years, irrespective of the setting that the patient is in. Additional criteria are a return to mental health and a resumption of cyclical menstruation.

The aims of this chapter are: (a) to show how the patient's weight can be quickly restored to normal with comparative ease and without any "specific" method of treatment; and (b) to indicate the pitfalls that threaten an objective assessment of a given treatment if the investigator fails to base his appraisal on the eventual outcome of the illness or does not consider other variables that may influence the outcome.

SHORT-TERM TREATMENT AND ITS RESULTS

To show that body weight in emaciated patients can readily be restored to normal, it is appropriate to present two brief case reports that illustrate the short-term response to treatment. The important aspects of the treatment will then be described.

Case Studies

CASE 1

Patient M. P. (age 15 years 6 months) had begun losing weight and feeling depressed 6 months before her admission to hospital, but her menstrual periods had stopped 9 months before the weight loss. She attended an expensive boarding school where "all the girls were on diets." Her parents were prosperous and had high expectations of scholastic achievement from their daughter: she was indeed an intelligent girl. They appeared to allow their daughter to have some contacts with boys but at the same time were anxious that these contacts not escalate into a sexual relationship. The father's occupation kept him away from home for long periods. M. P. was admitted to the psychiatric ward of the Royal Free Hospital where she was given the full nursing care accorded to patients with anorexia nervosa. Figure 1 (*left*) shows an immediate gain in weight from a level of 37.5 kg on admission. The weight gain progressed steeply until she reached 50.5 kg on the 24th day. Thereafter the weight leveled off. During interviews the patient revealed her desire to sever the close emotional bonds with her parents, attend all-night parties, and fall in love with a virile young man. After discharge from hospital she had some difficulty in maintaining a normal weight but succeeded in doing so after 3 months when her weight had become steady at 51 kg and regular menstruation was resumed. She did not settle at school, however, and neglected her studies. She acted out her earlier fantasies of leading a "wild life" and had a quick succession of love affairs. Within a year of her admission she asked to be prescribed a contraceptive pill. She declined to follow advice given that she should discuss with her parents her intention to have a sexual relationship with her current boyfriend.

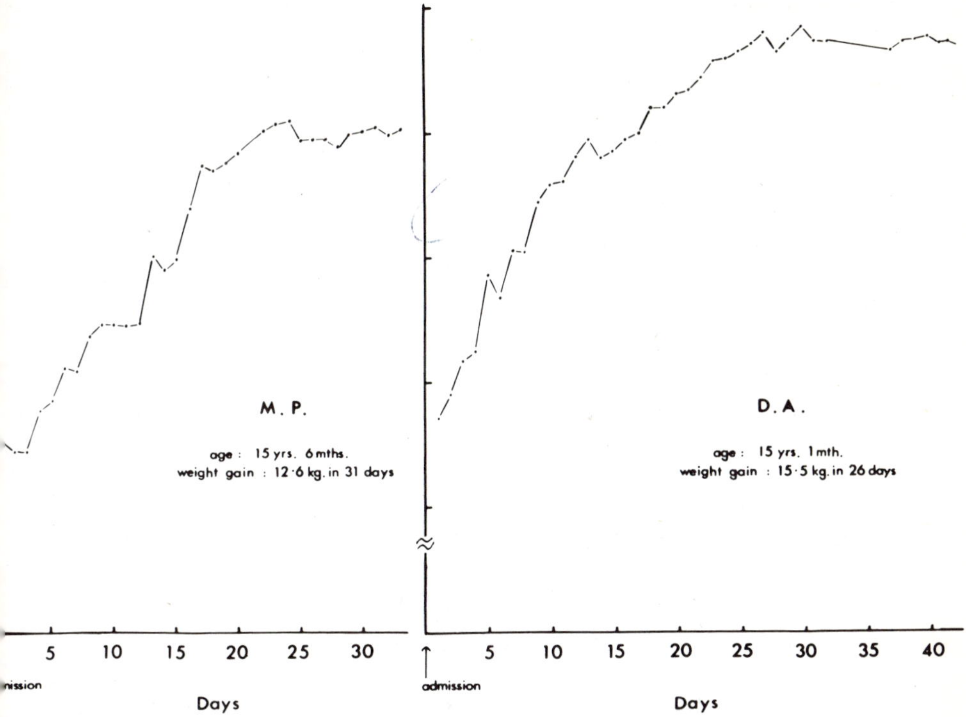

FIG. 1. Weight charts of 2 patients showing rapid gains in weight within 4 weeks.

CASE 2

Patient D. A. (age 15 years 1 month) had first been admitted to another hospital because of her marked loss of weight, amenorrhea, and depressive symptoms which had been present for almost 2 years. She failed to respond to treatment with antidepressants and gained no weight. She was then transferred to the psychiatric ward of the Royal Free Hospital. Figure 1 (*right*) shows a rapid gain in weight from 38.5 to 54.0 kg in 26 days, followed by its maintenance at a steady level. At the same time, the patient's mood returned to normal without antidepressant drugs having been needed. During exploratory interviews it was ascertained that her home life in general was satisfactory and that her parents were affectionate and sympathetic. However, they and the school teachers had not appreciated that the patient's intellectual level was a modest one (WISC IQ:85), and they had expected her to cope with a taxing scholastic course leading to GCE "O" level[1] examinations. The parents readily accepted the advice to modify the course of studies. The patient's menstrual periods returned at the end of her 2 months' stay in hospital, and

[1] General Certificate of Education at "ordinary" level—an examination taken by the more academic streams of schoolchildren aged 14 to 16 in England and Wales.

her subsequent progress has been completely satisfactory over the length of follow-up so far (1 year 6 months).

In summary, both patients responded rapidly to treatment aimed at restoring their weight to normal. This impressive short-term response is one that should be achieved in the majority of patients with anorexia nervosa and does not require any unusual form of treatment. But there is no guarantee that the initially good response will be followed by a permanent recovery. The omens were good in the second patient, but less favorable in the first. In a series of patients reported by the author, although many patients had an unpromising chronic illness, substantial weight gain was achieved in the majority (12). The mean weight of the patients on admission was 63% of "average body weight";[2] a mean of 84% was reached by the time of discharge. Yet it would be rash to predict the eventual prognosis from such results, and this subject will be returned to later in this chapter.

Treatment Regime

There is no specific method of treatment for anorexia nervosa. Reliance has to be put on a general management which has been found empirically to meet with success. The aims of treatment are:

1. to admit the patient to a psychiatric ward with good nursing facilities,
2. to induce the patient's weight to return to a normal "healthy" level (this is usually synonymous with the optimum weight before the onset of the illness),
3. to help resolve any psychological conflicts and remedy family and social problems in order to provide the best possible prospects for a sustained improvement leading to recovery,
4. in a few patients, to induce menstruation (e.g., with clomiphene) once a normal weight has been achieved.

Admission to a Psychiatric Unit

Only seldom can an emaciated patient with anorexia nervosa be expected to make satisfactory progress while remaining an outpatient. This should be stressed to the patient and her family; yet they may resist this advice. The doctor's skills should then be used to establish a good relationship with the patient so that she may be persuaded after two or three interviews to come into hospital voluntarily. On rare occasions, and especially when life is threatened, it may be necessary to admit her compulsorily, but this

[2] "Average body weight"—from data given in actuarial tables (Society of Actuaries: *Build and Blood Pressure Study,* Chicago, 1959) (7).

course of action should be avoided if possible because of the importance of maintaining a good relationship with a patient who may require several years of care and supervision.

Nursing Care Aimed at Inducing Weight Gain

The greater burden of responsibility for inpatient treatment should be given to the nurses caring for the patient. Members of the medical staff should indicate their high expectations in terms of restoring the patient's weight to normal and give their full support to the nurses whose confidence must be such as to enable them to apply a rigorous method of care consistently. Teamwork is of the essence. Nurses will become familiar with the clinical manifestations of anorexia nervosa and will be especially conversant with its psychopathology so as to understand the conflicts and distress experienced by their patient, and they will be able to predict the various forms of abnormal behavior that may be part of the illness (e.g., concealment of food, self-induced vomiting, or excessive exercise). The patient's case history is made available to the senior nurses to facilitate their appreciation of her individual problems and needs.

The key to the success of nursing care is the establishment of a relationship of trust between the patient and those nurses who will have the closest contact with her. Various examples may be given of the way this relationship is strengthened and used to persuade the patient to adopt healthier eating habits. The nurse conveys to the patient that she is aware of her fear of fatness and her difficulty in judging how much food she should eat. The nurse expresses her sympathy and offers to become responsible for her choice of food and its amount, saying "leave these decisions to me, I can promise that the amount of food chosen for you is what you need and I shall make sure that you do not become fat." The patient is encouraged to accept this agreement on trust, without stipulating a limit to the body weight that she should reach. If the subject of weight arises, the nurse indicates that concern about precise weights is a sign of persisting illness, and she is careful not to enter into a bargain with the patient over any weight level that might still be suggested as an upper limit. As the patient gains weight, she will probably express anxiety about becoming particularly fat in whatever region of the body causes her most sensitivity (especially the abdomen). Again, the nurse uses reassuring words such as "there is a tendency for the weight to go first to the tummy, but give yourself time and a chance for this weight to become generally distributed." This kind of reassurance may not stand up to scientific scrutiny but is often accepted by patients. It is important to compliment a patient on regaining her good looks as soon as her emaciation is corrected. She is encouraged to use cosmetics and restyle her hair, the nurse adding, "Your hair has been in a mess because you have been so undernourished: the unhealthy hair will gradually be replaced by healthy hair." It is important to obtain the parents' help to discard previous clothing that has been tailored to a shrunken body, and reward the patient with a new outfit of clothing that will accommodate a more shapely figure. It is wise for the parents to display some extravagance with these purchases because anorexic girls tend to be parsimonious and do not want to see their new clothing go to waste in the future.

It is also necessary for the patient's activities to be supervised so as to prevent her from discarding the food given to her. Thus it is essential for a number of weeks for the patient to remain confined to the ward and for the nurse to remain present at mealtimes until the whole meal has been consumed. She should preferably sit beside the patient and distract her from any anxieties that may persist when confronted with large helpings of food. It is also possible for a number of anorexic patients to be treated in the same room and to eat together so long as consistency and fairness are displayed toward them. There should be no undue emphasis on restrictions and supervision. Once the patient appreciates that the nurse is fully aware of her temptations to avoid food or induce vomiting, she is likely to abandon these deceptions and accept the need for cooperation.

Occasionally the nurses suspect that the patient is hiding food or purgatives; for example, if the patient's weight has remained static or if there is inexplicable diarrhea. It is then appropriate to search the patient's locker and her belongings, but care must be taken not to do this in an inquisitorial way. The nurse should say to her patient, "I know that you are really an honest and truthful person but I also know that your illness may compel you to do things which are not in your nature, especially when you become anxious about putting on weight." Following this explanation the nurse carries out her search in the presence of the patient. If a food hoard is discovered the nurse remains sympathetic and invites the patient to discuss the anxieties that led to the deception. If vomiting is suspected because of failure to gain weight or a lowered serum level of potassium, the patient is encouraged to admit that she vomits without necessarily being accused that the vomiting is self-induced. Vomiting may be difficult to control, but the best results are obtained by the nurse asking the patient to rest in bed under supervision for at least one hour after meals.

In other ways the patient should be restricted as little as possible: she should attend occupational therapy, study if she is still at school, and receive visitors. Visits should be deferred only when there is clear evidence that the parents (for example) rekindle the patient's anxieties or make her restless to return home. Even then the forbidding of parental visits should last no longer than 2 weeks. The nursing staff take advantage of the parents' visits to elicit their help in encouraging the patient to accept her increased weight and normal body size.

It has already been mentioned that the patient's weight provides the best index of progress and should be recorded each morning before breakfast.

Nurses will learn to equate food intake with expected increases in body weight: a surplus of 7,500 cal intake over energy expenditure leads on the average to a weight gain of 1 kg (15). Within 1 or 2 weeks the patient is asked to eat portions of food roughly equal to twice the intake of a normal adult (3,000 to 5,000 cal daily). Meals should be high in their content of carbohydrate and fat, and supplements of Complan®, Metrecal®, or Carnation Instant Breakfast® may be helpful. With such an intake of food, the positive balance in energy should amount to 1,500 to 3,000 cal daily. The corresponding gain in weight is 200 to 400 g daily, with a steeper rise during the early days of treatment caused by a selective body retention of water. Thus the weight charts should show curves similar to those shown in Fig. 1. Within a few weeks the patient's weight should be restored to normal. In a high proportion of patients the psychiatric symptoms diminish or disappear. In one series of severely ill patients, for example, it was found that in 60% of them eating had become unconstrained by the time they were due to leave hospital (12). Preoccupation with body size and shape is also likely to become reduced (17).

These results are obtained without resorting to any of the so-called specific methods. For example, antidepressants are usually found to be ineffective in the absence of a general regime leading to a gain in weight, whereas depressive symptoms disappear or are alleviated as a result of such a regime. Chlorpromazine has a small place in the treatment of a minority of patients who remain agitated after the first few days of admission: a moderate dose of the drug (up to 300 mg daily) will suffice. It will be clear that many of the features of the nursing treatment that has been described incorporate principles of psychotherapy and, to a lesser extent, those of behavior therapy. Certainly the treatment depends on close personal contact and the development of a personal relationship with therapeutic aims. In addition, the patient's doctor provides supportive psychotherapy amounting to approximately two 30-min interviews weekly. But it is doubtful if it could be said that the psychotherapy is specific in the sense of unravelling particular personal conflicts or providing specific interpretations. The treatment described is relatively new only in being administered primarily by nurses. Similar principles were put forward by Ryle (16) and Hurst (10), but they advised that a physician should be responsible for seeing that the patient consumes all her meals. Even William Gull's (9) advice in 1874 can be interpreted as having a similar basis: "the patients should be fed at regular intervals, and surrounded by persons who have more control over them, relations and friends being generally the worse attendants."

More recent methods extol some particular aspect of the treatment to which specific value is attached: chlorpromazine (4–6), behavior therapy (3,11), or psychotherapy (19). These reports all describe impressive short-term therapeutic benefits, but none that are clearly superior to the nursing regime that is described here and makes no claims to specificity. This treatment resembles most closely that of Groen and Feldman-Toledano (8), which was called "educational" and had as its theoretical basis the need for the physician and nurse to act as "substitute parents" for girls who had been deprived of love. Be that as it may, the nursing regime that has been outlined does not require any elaborate theoretical basis: it is based on the empirical observation that it succeeds in achieving the most important short-term aim of restoring weight to normal.

LONG-TERM OBSERVATIONS: EFFECT OF TREATMENT VERSUS NATURAL COURSE OF THE ILLNESS

The preceding section of this chapter has stressed that over a short period of time it is relatively easy to halt or even reverse the course of anorexia nervosa. After a few weeks of a basic nursing regime, it is possible to restore the patient's weight to normal. She will often declare with absolute sincerity that she has learned how dangerous it is to diet and that she will take care not to lose weight again. Yet experience shows that it is rash to accept such a startling improvement as evidence of recovery. In some patients recovery is indeed permanent. In many others, unfortunately, relapse with a progressive loss of weight and a return of the previous psychological disturbance occurs within a few weeks of leaving hospital. A second arrest of the illness can usually be achieved by readmitting the patient to hospital. This time recovery may last, but in a minority of patients the relapses are numerous and the illness extends over a course of years. For example, in one such patient it was possible to reverse the illness by inducing weight gains to normal on two of her three admissions to hospital. Figure 2 shows this patient's weight chart over 3 years: it is of interest that one spontaneous improvement occurred at the end of the first year, as well as the two remissions in hospital. Yet within 3 to 6 months of discharge on each occasion she had to be readmitted.

One of the mysteries of anorexia nervosa is the unpredictability of the prognosis in an individual patient. It seems impossible to forecast whether one admission to hospital will suffice, or whether several will be needed. Whereas a short-term improvement can be promised to most patients, the long-term course appears to be a function more of the individual patient's illness rather than the treatment she receives. In this chapter I shall hypothesize that, so far, no effective long-term treatment for patients with anorexia nervosa has been discovered. The illness runs its course and during this time the clinician does his utmost to support and protect his patient, readmitting her to hospital when her weight and health sink to a precariously low level. But both the patient and her therapist remain at the mercy of the natural course of the illness.

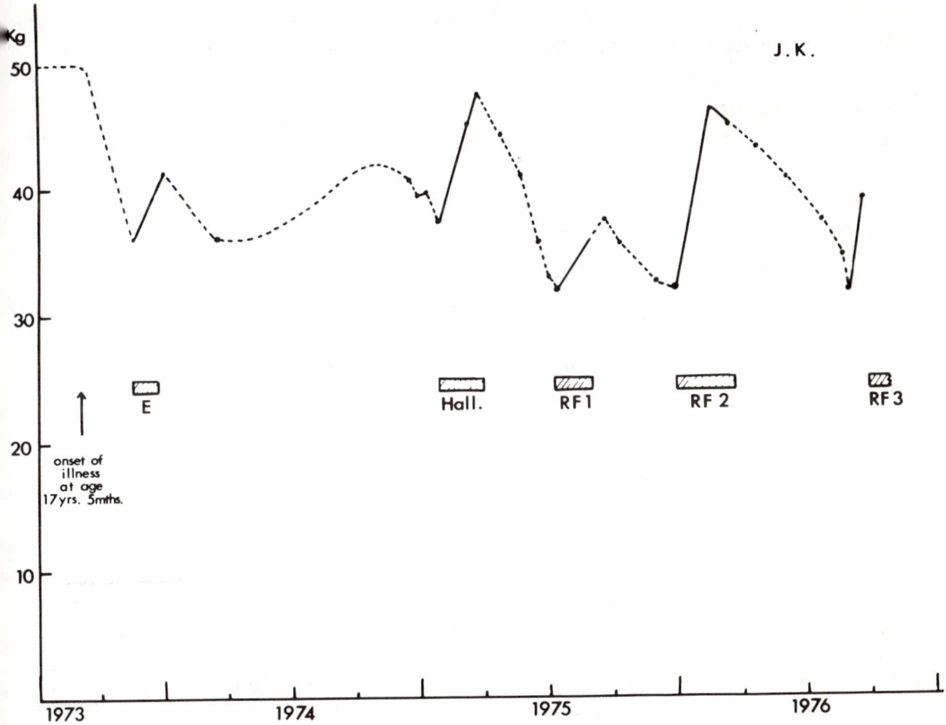

FIG. 2. Weight chart of a patient whose weight gain in hospital was not sustained in spite of four admissions. The patient had been readmitted at the time of writing. ▧, Hospital admissions:

RF 1, 2, and 3—Royal Free Hospital, London.
Hall.—Halliwick & Friern Hospital, London.
E—first admission, to another hospital.

Four-Year Follow-up Study

Because of the baffling uncertainties concerning the long-term prognosis, we conducted a follow-up study on 41 patients was conducted in the hope of identifying factors that modify the prognosis (12).

METHOD

The 41 patients included 3 males. Their ages ranged from 12.8 to 47 years (mean 21.5 years; SD ± 8.6 years). They all satisfied the strict diagnostic criteria for anorexia nervosa (2,14) and thus showed an inextricable combination of nutritional, psychiatric, and endocrine disturbances. It was decided to restrict the study to patients in whom the duration of the possible follow-up extended over 4 years or longer after the initial admission to hospital. (The follow-up ranged from 4 to 10 years.) I knew all the patients personally as I had been responsible for their care.[3] It was possible to trace all the patients at follow-up. In all, 34 patients had a personal interview; for the remainder of the patients, information was obtained by interview of a close relative (2 patients, including a patient who had died), by postal questionnaire completed by the patient (2), or by a relative (2). One patient had committed suicide. The outcome at follow-up was assessed from an amalgam of information given by the patient, her relatives, and any other sources that had been tapped. The patients were rated on their nutritional status (including body weight), menstrual function, mental state, sexual adjustment, and socioeconomic status. The ratings were based on the period of 6 months preceding the date of follow-up. These assessments were then compared with observations made on the patients at the time of their original admission so as to ascertain whether reliable predictors of outcome could be detected from the history, the mental state, or the immediate response to treatment.

RESULTS

Outcome

The results at follow-up can be most simply expressed in terms of the general outcome.

Good outcome. In 16 patients (39% of the series), body weight had been maintained at a normal level,[4] and in the 13 female patients within this group menstruation had been regular and cyclical. Only a few of the patients expressed psychological symptoms, and when present they consisted mainly of mild anxiety or depression.

Intermediate outcome. In 12 patients (27%) there were minor difficulties in maintaining a steady weight (including 2 obese patients), and menstruation had been sporadic or absent in over half this group. The psychological, sexual, and socioeconomic adjustment also tended to be less satisfactory.

Poor outcome. Eleven patients (29%) remained markedly underweight (mean weight was only 68% of "average body weight"). Menstruation was absent or sporadic in all these patients. Most patients experienced continuing and sometimes disabling depressive symptoms. Sexual adjustment was poor.

Death. There had been two deaths, one from suicide following a leukotomy performed elsewhere, and the other from status asthmaticus when the patient had been emaciated.

[3] The patients were all treated in the Metabolic Unit of the Maudsley Hospital, London.

[4] A normal body weight is defined as within 15% of the "average body weight" given in actuarial tables (7).

Predictions of Outcome

A comparison was made between the long-term outcome of a particular patient's illness and various aspects of her family background, premorbid personality, the illness itself, and her short-term response to treatment. The statistical significance of these comparisons was ascertained using two separate tests—the Wilcoxon-White ranking test (W-W) and the product-moment correlation.

It was disappointing that the clinical features of the illness itself yielded so few pointers to the nature of the eventual outcome. A very low weight on admission (under 60% "average body weight") was associated with a worse outcome according to only one of the two statistical procedures [P(W-W) < 0.02]. No statistically significant relationship was found between eventual outcome and the various initial psychological disturbances including the patient's fear of fatness, which is such a specific psychopathological feature. Neither was the occurrence of self-induced vomiting of ominous prognostic significance as had been thought by Theander (18) in his very thorough study. Not surprisingly, the duration of illness that the patient had endured before coming into the study was found to be relevant to the prognosis. If the patient had had a long illness before the time of admission, this was associated with a less favorable outcome. A more bewildering finding, and one already reported by Theander, is that a later age of onset of the illness was associated with a worse prognosis ($r = 0.53$, $p < 0.05$; the onset of the illness was measured from the onset of amenorrhea).

The family background also provided a predictor of poor outcome: the presence of a disturbed relationship between the patient and other members of the family before the onset of the illness [P(W-W) < 0.01; $r = 0.52$, $p < 0.05$]. Yet the presence of sibling rivalry was not significant; neither were other factors in the patient's background such as social class and educational achievement.

Premorbid personality difficulties were thought to be important because a clear association was found between a history of poor adjustment at school and a subsequent poor prognosis [P(W-W) < 0.01; $r = 0.51$, $p < 0.05$]. Yet no association was found with the presence of feeding difficulties in childhood, obesity preceding the illness, or the level of intelligence.

Most surprising of all was the lack of any prediction that could be made from the patient's initial response to treatment in hospital. It might have been thought that a patient who resisted strongly the treatment regime and responded less well to it would later be found to have had a worse outcome. This was not necessarily so. No prediction could be made from observations such as the degree of weight gain in hospital, the alleviation of psychological symptoms, the acceptance of the refeeding regime, the duration of stay in hospital, or even difficulty in maintaining the weight gained. The use of additional methods of treatment—antidepressants (in only nine patients), ECT (in five), or chlorpromazine (in seven)—was not found to influence long-term outcome either.

CONCLUSIONS

In the present study two-thirds of the patients had either recovered fully or shown considerable improvement by the time of the follow-up interview. Less than one-third of them remained incapacitated, and there had been two deaths (5% of the series). These results are not presented as being particularly good or bad. They are reported as the outcome of a series of patients who had received intensive treatment in hospital and a fair degree of outpatient care. Yet only a few of the patients were treated with chlorpromazine or antidepressants. None received intensive formal psychotherapy, but all were given supportive psychotherapy by the nursing and medical staff. If the general nursing treatment and the supportive psychotherapy that were given are considered nonspecific, the outcome can be seen to reflect the natural course of the illness, influenced only by the general care and management given to the patients. The study has the advantage that it included a large number of patients who had been chronically ill [nine (22%) patients had been ill for 7 years or longer]. Thus the series was weighted toward a poorer outcome because of the initial selection of patients. This study may therefore be taken as a base line showing the long-term natural outcome of anorexia nervosa, the patients being representative of a wide spectrum of severity of the illness, and the treatment given being of a nonspecific supportive type. Any new treatments that are introduced and claimed to be specific for anorexia nervosa should be compared with this base line.

In order to assess claims for new treatments for anorexia nervosa, it is necessary to assess the benefits in terms of an improvement in the long-term natural outcome. It has been shown how difficult it is to predict the eventual outcome in an individual patient, although a rough guide may be obtained from her age and the length of time she has already been ill. It must also be remembered that the average long-term outcome in a given series will depend on the ways in which the patients have been selected. This selection is not usually influenced so much by the treating physician as by the referring family doctor who will tend to treat the milder forms of the illness himself and refer the more severe forms to other physicians (or gynecologists). He will tend to refer those patients with disturbances of personality and severe psychological symptoms to a psychiatrist. It has also been shown that the psychiatrist working in a mental hospital is likely to receive more severe cases than one working in a general hospital (1).

It is therefore advisable to avoid comparing the outcome of different series of patients or trying to attribute differing results to the treatment that was chosen, because of the profound effects of patient selection. Instead, it is more reliable to contrast the effects of two or more treatments given to groups of comparable patients, the patients having been allocated at random from within the same unit and being cared for by the same therapeutic team. The criteria of success have to be based on the long-term outcome. There should indeed be a lapse of several years: even the minimum of 4 years chosen for the present study was probably too brief, for several patients were noted to have continued to improve right up to the time of the follow-up interview. The type of objective study recommended in this chapter presents a daunting prospect to a would-be investigator. Unless such a study is undertaken, however, it is wise to avoid coming to hasty conclusions regarding the merits of a treatment that has been assessed less stringently.

REFERENCES

1. Beck, J. C., and Brochner-Mortensen, K. (1954): Observations on the prognosis in anorexia nervosa. *Acta Med. Scand.,* 149:409–430.
2. Beumont, P. J. V., Beardwood, C. J., and Russell, G. F. M. (1972): The occurrence of the syndrome of anorexia nervosa in male subjects. *Psychol. Med.,* 2:216–231.
3. Blinder, B. J., Freeman, D. M. A., and Stunkard, A. J. (1970): Behavior therapy of anorexia nervosa: Effectiveness of activity as a reinforcer of weight gain. *Am. J. Psychiatry,* 126:1093–1098.
4. Crisp, A. H. (1966): A treatment regime for anorexia nervosa. *Br. J. Psychiatry,* 112:505–512.
5. Dally, P. J. (1967): Anorexia nervosa: Long-term follow-up and effects of treatment. *J. Psychosom. Res.,* 11:151–155.
6. Dally, P. J., and Sargant, W. (1966): Treatment and outcome in anorexia nervosa. *Br. Med. J.,* 2:793–795.
7. Geigy (1962): *Scientific Tables,* p. 623. Geigy Pharmaceuticals, Manchester.
8. Groen, J. J., and Feldman-Toledano, Z. (1966): Educative treatment of patients and parents in anorexia nervosa. *Br. J. Psychiatry,* 112:671–681.
9. Gull, W. W. (1874): Anorexia nervosa (apepsia hysterica, anorexia hysterica). *Trans. Clin. Soc. Lond.,* 7:22–28.
10. Hurst, A. (1939): Discussion on anorexia nervosa. *Proc. R. Soc. Med.,* 32:744–745.
11. Leitenberg, H., Agras, W. S., and Thomson, L. E. (1968): A sequential analysis of the effect of selective positive reinforcement in modifying anorexia nervosa. *Behav. Res. Ther.,* 6:211–218.
12. Morgan, H. G., and Russell, G. F. M. (1975): Value of family background and clinical features as predictors of long-term outcome in anorexia nervosa: Four year follow-up study of 41 patients. *Psychol. Med.,* 5:355–371.
13. Needleman, H. L., and Waber, D. (1976): Amitriptyline therapy in patients with anorexia nervosa. *Lancet,* 2:580.
14. Russell, G. F. M. (1965): Metabolic aspects of anorexia nervosa. *Proc. R. Soc. Med.,* 58:811–814.
15. Russell, G. F. M., and Mezey, A. G. (1962): An analysis of weight gain in patients with anorexia nervosa treated with high calorie diets. *Clin. Sci.,* 23:449–461.
16. Ryle, J. A. (1936): Anorexia nervosa. *Lancet,* 2:893.
17. Slade, P. D., and Russell, G. F. M. (1973): Awareness of body dimensions in anorexia nervosa: Cross-sectional and longitudinal studies. *Psychol. Med.,* 3:188–199.
18. Theander, S. (1970): Anorexia nervosa. A psychiatric investigation of 94 female cases. *Acta Psychiatr. Scand.* [*Suppl.*], 214.
19. Thomä, H. (1967): *Anorexia Nervosa,* translated by G. Brydone. International Universities Press, New York.

Anorexia Nervosa, edited by
R. A. Vigersky. Raven Press,
New York © 1977

Behavior Modification in Anorexia Nervosa: Research Foundations

Stewart Agras and Joellen Werne

Department of Psychiatry and Behavioral Sciences, Stanford University School of Medicine, and the Center for Advanced Study in the Behavioral Sciences, Stanford, California 94305

INTRODUCTION

One of the newest and perhaps most controversial (11) approaches to the treatment of anorexia nervosa is that based on the application of procedures derived from operant psychology. In this chapter, the research basis of this approach is reviewed and a typical therapeutic program described. As is usual with clinical research, the work began with case reports but, unlike almost every other therapeutic approach to anorexia nervosa, proceeded to controlled experiments.

UNCONTROLLED CASE STUDIES

The operant approach based on an impressive experimental literature documenting the effect of selective positive reinforcement (2,14) was first used in the treatment of anorexia nervosa by Bachrach et al. (6). Their patient, a 37-year-old woman, weighed 21.4 kg on admission, down from a stable adult weight of some 53.6 kg. The procedure used was social reinforcement which included attention, conversation, and praise made contingent on eating behavior. To enhance the efficacy of this procedure, the investigators used reinforcement deprivation, consisting of housing the patient in a hospital room devoid of the usual amenities of television, books, or frequent visits from the nursing and medical staff and relatives. Therapists then sat with the patient at every meal and conversed only when she ate. Later, other events such as going for walks or receiving visits from relatives were made contingent on satisfactory eating behavior. With this treatment, the patient gained weight to some 28.6 kg whereupon her weight leveled off perhaps due to vomiting. Reinforcement was then made contingent on weight gain rather than eating behavior. However, it is not clear what the effect of this change was since the patient was discharged shortly thereafter and treated as an outpatient. In hospital, she had gained weight at a rate of 0.12 kg/day. One year after discharge, her weight reached a high point of 40 kg.

An attempt to replicate this study was made by Leitenberg et al. (15), who reported that an extinction technique in which complaints and comments about eating difficulties were ignored led to no improvement over a 45-day period. Moreover, providing conversation and attention during meals contingent on eating was also unsuccessful, partly due to the artificiality of the situation. On the other hand, when weight gain was reinforced directly, a steady increase in both caloric intake and weight was observed, the patient almost regaining her preadmission weight in 45 days at a rate of 0.16 kg/day.

In all subsequent studies, weight gain has been directly reinforced, although some interesting variations have been reported. Blinder et al. (8) found that anorexic patients, long known to be overactive, in fact walk an average of 6.8 miles per day compared with 4.9 miles per day for women of normal weight. They therefore made access to physical activity contingent on weight gain, reporting marked success with three patients. In an interesting variation on this theme, these workers restricted the activity of their fourth patient by using chlorpromazine. Increments of drug dosage were removed dependent on weight gain, an example of the use of negative reinforcement in which paradigm a person works (eats) to remove an unpleasant event (chlorpromazine) from the environment. Two other patients in this series were treated with a simpler reinforcement schedule with only two target weights, the first allowing the patient out of bed and the second leading to discharge from hospital. Several other case reports (5,17) have confirmed the effectiveness of the reinforcement procedure in the treatment of anorexia nervosa, and two larger series (7,9) have been reported.

EXPERIMENTAL APPROACHES

Although a series of case reports of the successful use of a procedure might give rise to the belief that a new and effective therapy has been discovered, when viewed against the history of the treatment of this disorder, a more cautious assertion seems appropriate. Countless therapies ranging from the use of hormones and drugs to various psychotherapeutic procedures have been reported to be successful in the treatment of anorexia nervosa, although many of the successes described are limited to single cases or to small series. Nonetheless, successes from widely differing approaches raise the possibility that there are therapeutic procedures common to each approach and that the variation in results might be due to the unsystematic application of effective procedures. Based on the existing case studies, reinforcement was obviously the first variable to investigate experimentally.

The Effects of Reinforcement

In the first study of this issue, however, some rather puzzling results were obtained (15). The experiment was conducted within an inpatient clinical research unit with a 17-year-old girl who had been losing weight for over a year, and at the time of admission weighed 31.4 kg, some 11 kg below her usual weight. She was served 4,000 calories each day, distributed equally among four meals, and was not allowed to eat anything between meals so that an accurate record of caloric intake could be made. Meals lasted 30 min and were eaten alone in a special dining room, being served and removed without comment by the nursing staff. The patient was weighed on a metabolic scale at a standard time each day, the weight of the gown which she wore being subtracted to obtain true body weight.

Three experimental phases were held: base line, reinforcement, and base line, so that the effect of both adding and removing positive reinforcement on caloric intake and weight could be determined. During the base-line period, in order to have the patient attend to the process of recovery, she was given a careful therapeutic rationale and instructions, and asked to record the number of mouthfuls which she ate at each meal and to plot this number along with her daily weight on a graph kept on the wall of her room. Reinforcement consisted of praise and social attention for eating more, as measured by caloric intake and weight gain. In addition, pleasurable activities such as time out of her room and eventually off the unit (accompanied by a nurse) were made contingent on small weight increases (0.1 kg) over the previous high weight.

The introduction of reinforcement led to a dramatic increase in calories consumed each day, from about 1,900 cal during base line to 3,600 cal by the end of the reinforcement period with a corresponding increase in weight. However, when reinforcement was stopped, eating behavior and weight gain continued unchanged. This puzzling finding raised questions concerning the efficacy of selective positive reinforcement and suggested that another variable or variables might be partly responsible for the obtained therapeutic effect. Moreover, two replications of this experiment (4) with different patients showed similar results, as shown in Fig. 1. When reinforcement based on weight gain was introduced, caloric intake in one case (patient 2) and weight in the other (patient 1) showed gains over the corresponding measure in the base-line period. Yet removal of reinforcement in the second base-line condition did not affect either intake or weight gain, again suggesting that although positive reinforcement may have been responsible for the initiation of weight gain, another therapeutic variable (or variables) was probably responsible for the continued therapeutic progress.

A clue to the solution of this problem was suggested by what each of these patients said during the experiment. Once they realized that they

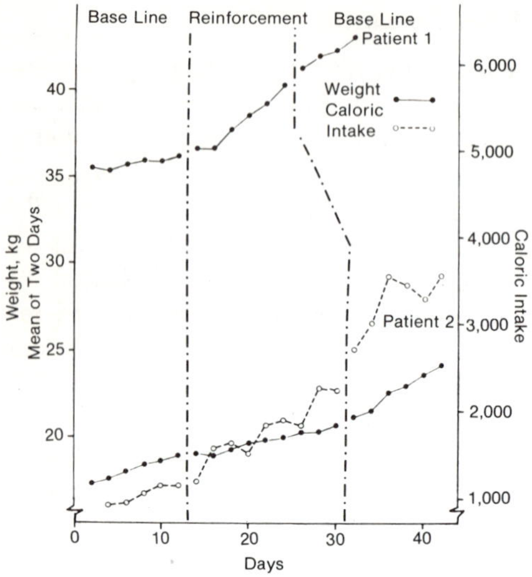

FIG. 1. Data from two single-case experiments examining the effect of reinforcing weight gain in anorexia nervosa. Caloric intake was not available for patient 1. (From ref. 4 with permission.)

could gain weight, they made it clear that they wished to leave hospital as soon as possible, and realized that to do this they had to gain weight. This wish to leave hospital was due to the rather strict requirements of the baseline and reinforcement conditions. Unlike their experience in previous hospitalizations, these patients found that privileges had to be earned, and without privileges the ward became a dull, not overly friendly place. This state of affairs is another example of negative reinforcement in which behavior (eating more and gaining weight) is directed toward decreasing the probability of occurrence of an unpleasant event (being in hospital).

To remove the effect of negative reinforcement, weight gain and leaving hospital were disconnected in the next series of experiments by contracting with the patient and her parents for a 12-week stay "for research purposes" whether or not the patient gained weight. With the exception of these initial instructions, the measures and procedures used were the same as for the first three cases. Four experimental phases—base line, reinforcement, nonreinforcement, and reinforcement—were held. During the nonreinforcement phase, privileges were given whether or not the patient gained weight. As can be seen in Fig. 2, both caloric intake and weight increased steadily during the application of positive reinforcement. However, in contrast to the three previous experiments, when reinforcement was removed in the third phase caloric intake dropped steadily and weight gain was much slowed. The reintroduction of reinforcement in the final phase led to further increases in both caloric intake and weight. Thus, removing the obscuring effect of negative reinforcement clarified the effects of adding and removing positive reinforcement, and it seems reasonable to conclude that both positive and negative reinforcement effectively encourage weight gain in the anorexic.

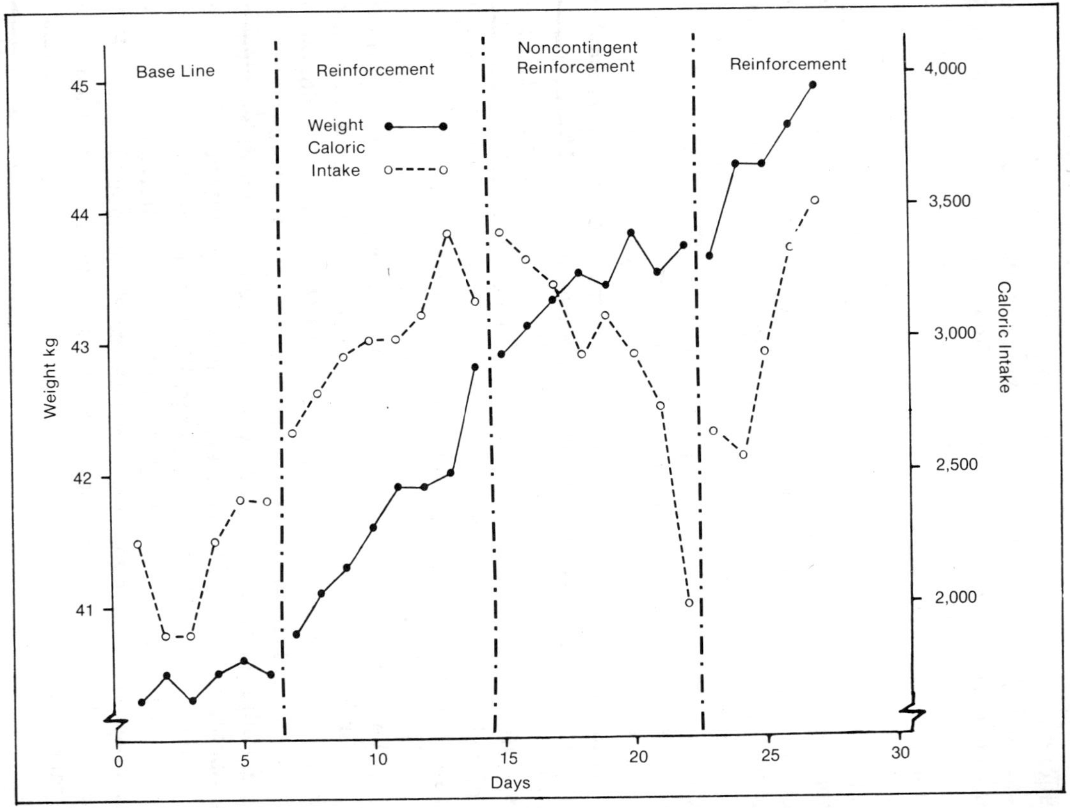

FIG. 2. Data from an experiment examining the effect of positive reinforcement in the absence of negative reinforcement. (From ref. 4 with permission.)

Schedules of Reinforcement

Various schedules of positive reinforcement are possible.[1] For example, in the research described above in which reinforcement for weight gain was available once each day, the schedule is a fixed-interval 1 day (FI1). However, different intervals can be chosen, e.g., FI1,2,3. In fact, several programs use an FI5 schedule. One such program is that of the University of Iowa in which reinforcement is given if weight gain during the preceding 5 days exceeds the previous weight reinforced by 0.5 kg. Larger weight gains lead to more reinforcement.

Since the programs at Stanford and Iowa are similar in other respects, the effects of the two different schedules of reinforcement could be examined by comparing two groups of seven patients, one from each center, matched for age of onset of anorexia nervosa. Two questions were asked: (a) would the immediate outcome of these two groups differ, and (b) would the patterns of weight gain be different? Thus, an FI1 schedule should lead to a more consistent weight gain (and eating pattern) than an FI5 schedule. In the latter case, based on the reinforcement literature, one would expect weight gain to be concentrated in the 2 or 3 days prior to reinforcement.

The overall weight gain at the end of 30 days of treatment was very similar for the two groups (6.94 kg at Stanford and 6.96 kg at Iowa). However, the number of days of positive weight gain was different (Stanford 22.7/30 and Iowa 18.6/30, $t = 2.26$, $df = 12$, $p = 0.04$). Since this suggested that the pattern of weight gain was different between the two centers, we examined whether the linear regressions of weight on time were the same at Stanford and Iowa. They may differ in slope, elevation, or in variances about the regression. The residual variance for the Stanford group was 16.34 and for the Iowa group 29.56. The test for homogeneity of the variances showed that the variances were indeed significantly different ($F = 1.81$; $df_1 = 48$, $df_2 = 46$; $p = 0.04$), with less variation in weight gain for the Stanford group.

These findings suggest that the two reinforcement schedules offer a variable opportunity to reinstate more normal eating patterns. The more variable pattern of the FI5 schedule is more like the eating behavior of many anorexics before treatment, namely, restricted intake interrupted by episodes of bingeing. The more steady weight gain encouraged by the FI1 schedule may then be a better management technique, likely to encourage more normal eating habits.

Informational Feedback

A closer inspection of Figs. 1 and 2 reveals that during the initial base-line period caloric intake and in most cases weight showed a tendency to in-

[1] The data reported in this section were obtained with the cooperation of Dr. Katherine Halmi of the Department of Psychiatry at the University of Iowa.

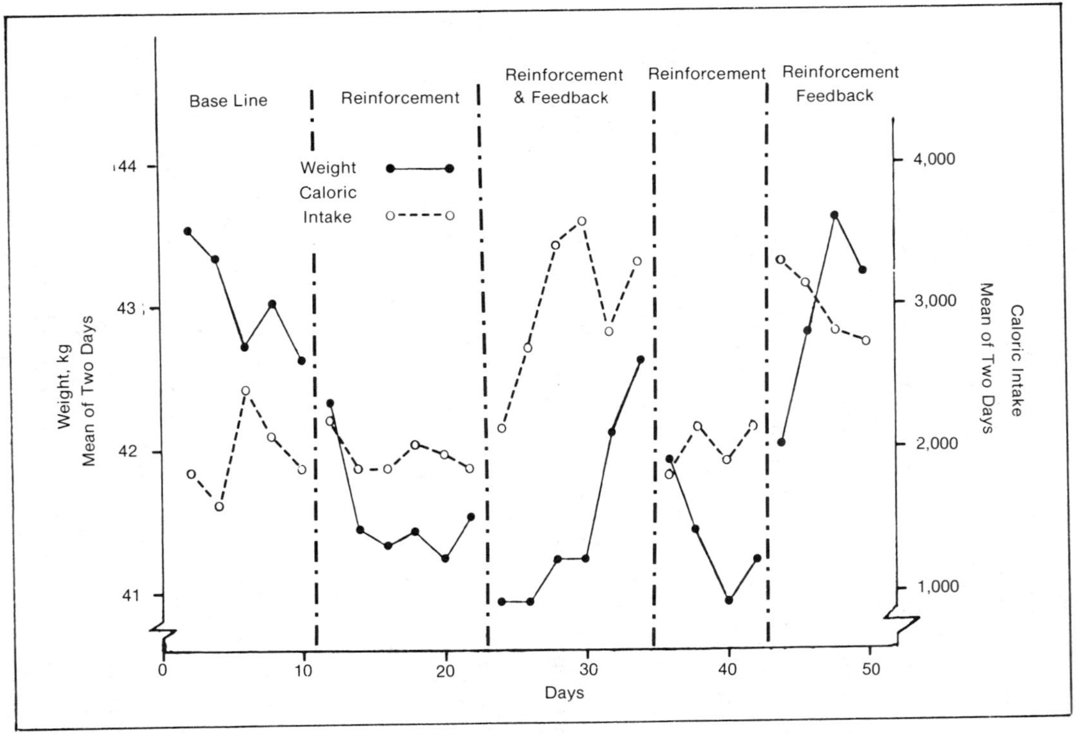

FIG. 3. Data from an experiment examining the effect of feedback on the eating behavior of a patient with anorexia nervosa. (From ref. 4 with permission.)

crease. This suggests the presence of an active therapeutic variable, and a consideration of the experimental literature on behavior change pointed to informational feedback as the most likely suspect. Feedback has been shown to play a part in the therapeutic modification of phobic behavior (16) as well as in the modification of heart rate and rhythm (10) and blood pressure (18). During the base-line condition in the previous experiments, the patient had been told her weight, had counted the number of mouthfuls eaten during each meal, and had been told her caloric intake after each meal, all of which provided information as to progress. The next series of experiments, then, were directed toward clarifying the effect of feedback and its interaction with positive reinforcement. As in the last experiment, the effect of negative reinforcement was nullified by contract.

A new base-line condition was arranged devoid of both feedback and reinforcement, although the patient continued to be served large meals of standard size to provide a measure of caloric intake. As can be seen in Fig. 3, caloric intake seemed stable under this condition and weight actually declined. When positive reinforcement was now added to the therapeutic regime, no effect was observed in the absence of feedback. However, once feedback was added to reinforcement, both caloric intake and weight showed large increases. A replication of this effect was shown in the subsequent two phases, and the entire effect was replicated in a subsequent experiment (4).

The findings of these six experiments taken together suggest that informational feedback by itself leads to small gains in caloric intake and weight, whereas reinforcement in the absence of feedback has no effect. Only a combination of the two leads to substantial gains.

Size of Meal

The final uninvestigated variable that might have a therapeutic effect is meal size, which was systematically varied in the next experiment while feedback and reinforcement were continued unchanged. During the first experimental phase, 6,000 cal were served, followed in the next phase by 3,000 cal, with a final return to 6,000 cal. At no point did the patient eat all the food offered her. A similar experiment was carried out by Elkin et al. (12), except that calories were varied from 4,500 to 3,000, to 4,500, and back to 3,000. The results of these experiments showed a striking similarity in that caloric intake was always lower by some 500 cal when small meals were being served.

Thus, we may conclude that four therapeutic procedures which modify weight and caloric intake in patients with anorexia nervosa have been identified, namely, positive and negative reinforcement, informational feedback, and large meals. Presumably there are other unidentified variables which may have a therapeutic effect. Nonetheless, the simple combination of four procedures sufficed to produce weight gains of approximately 0.2 kg/day with an average weight gain of 8.1 kg for the seven patients participating in the experiments.

FROM EXPERIMENT TO THERAPY

The aim of these experiments was to develop a therapeutic procedure to enhance the normalization of eating patterns and body weight in patients with anorexia nervosa. Naturally the transition from strictly controlled clinical research to the psychiatric clinic and ward involves embedding experimental therapeutic procedures within a richer and more complex therapeutic package, in this way adding procedures of unknown or uncertain effect. Thus, it seems reasonable to describe the clinical program for patients with anorexia nervosa which exists as part of a 20-bed psychiatric milieu ward at Stanford.

Treatment begins before hospitalization. During a short series of evaluation sessions, the principles of the treatment program are explained to the patient and its voluntary contractual nature emphasized. Some patients wish to attempt weight gain on an outpatient basis, in which case small weekly weight increments are set as a goal and, following a short trial, the patient's ability to gain weight is assessed. Once physician and patient agree that hospitalization is in order, a "target weight" is negotiated, with much importance being placed on agreement between physician and patient as to this and all ensuing goals. The target weight is understood to be the highest weight the patient will reach during hospitalization; and, because we stress compromise, this weight is often on the low side of "normal."

Once on the psychiatric unit, patients are instructed in the use of feedback as a tool for behavior change. They are asked to count the number of bites at each meal with a small hand counter and to keep a graph showing the cumulative total of bites for breakfast, lunch, dinner, and snacks. If an effort is made to eat a consistent yet heterogeneous diet, patients may effectively compare one day's intake with another throughout hospitalization. Adding a number of bites to each meal until sufficient intake is maintained to gain weight allows patients to predict the majority of their weight gains.

Patients may select from a menu any foods available in the hospital kitchen; however, the staff insists that they receive 5,000 cal divided into four meals a day, and the dietician (who is also part of the treatment team) may provide additional foods beyond those requested by the patient to construct a well-rounded diet. Patients are served their meals alone in their rooms and are asked to sit by their food for 45 min regardless of whether or not they eat. No attempt is made to observe their eating or to quantify the amount of food they consume. Patients are told that the staff will monitor their body weight and that it is the patient's responsibility to see that adequate daily weight gains are achieved. Daily weights are determined upon

gives anorexic responsibility indirectly

waking, usually postvoiding. Patients are weighed in nightclothes with a staff member present and the daily weights recorded and graphed for the patient to see.

Achievement of an explicit alliance between patient and staff is the first therapeutic task. After a base-line period of 3 to 4 days in hospital—which permits the patient to become used to the ward routine and to begin to feel comfortable with the community without the pressure or expectation of weight change—a contingency contract is negotiated which stipulates the exact nature of positive reinforcement for weight gain.

Weight gain of 0.2 kg or greater from the previous high weight leads to unlimited privileges which include full use of the ward's activities, groups, and day rooms, as well as the option for passes off the ward to visit neighboring shopping areas. Weight gain of 0.1 kg leads to full privileges from 7 A.M. until noon. For the remainder of the 24-hr period patients are asked to stay in their rooms and to minimize contact with the staff and other patients although they may move freely about the room, read or write, and leave the room once each nursing shift for a snack or shower. Patients are also asked not to accept phone calls or to see visitors, and to explain the nature of their restriction to others. A full day's restriction occurs when patients fail to gain or if they lose weight.

Bonus reinforcers are negotiated for set-weight criteria and are tailored to the interests and wishes of each individual, e.g., for one patient physical therapy when she reached 35 kg and a weekend pass home at 40 kg. For another patient attendance at a football game with her father at 43 kg and lunch and shopping with her mother at 45 kg. The contract is signed and witnessed, with copies going to the patient, family, nurses, therapists, and into the medical chart. At some point during hospitalization a discharge weight is negotiated which usually approximates the original goal weight. This provides a criterion for discharge and release from the negative reinforcement of being in the hospital.

The therapeutic milieu is considered a key factor in treatment. As noted elsewhere (3), the aims of direct behavior-change techniques and the milieu approach are quite compatible; thus Abroms (1) considers as the main aim of milieu therapy setting limits and teaching social skills, both of which are relevant to the treatment of most anorexics. Staff members convey their respect for and commitment to the patient and to what the contract concretely represents, i.e., the patient's wish to change, without functioning as "policemen" of an arbitrary or punitive system. This virtually eliminates battles over enforcement of room restriction or control struggles around eating, yet provides appropriate limit setting with the main responsibility for adherence residing with the patients themselves. A spirit of tolerance for minor infractions, with the "letter of the law" carrying less importance than the "spirit," is facilitated by weekly anorexia conferences in which a variety of issues are discussed—from presentation of new patients to dealing with the anxieties or frustrations of staff members. Training in interpersonal skills is provided through daily group therapy sessions and weekly planning sessions, the latter often emphasizing short-term goals and social skills immediately required (e.g., for job hunting or planning for return to school).

Individual therapy sessions begin with entrance into the program. As the medical status of patients improves, therapy can move from a more strictly supportive mode to a collaborative exploration of the patient's difficulties. Once weight gain is firmly established, family or couples therapy is added to clarify and change dysfunctional communication patterns. Specific interventions such as assertive training and relaxation techniques (13) are used where indicated.

During hospitalization, staff work closely with patients on a variety of problems: patient's fears of "blowing up like a balloon" or "looking fat in the mirror" and difficulties in expressing feelings and needs directly, as well as anxieties about goals and future plans. Weekly video sessions highlight the discrepancy between patients' views of themselves vis-à-vis other patients.

Eating continues to be a struggle; but, it is one in which patients are actively engaged in a way unique in their recent experience since they are responsible for keeping their records, imposing their restrictions when applicable, and taking the initiative when contract renegotiation seems appropriate. By the time of discharge, most patients have begun to experience a feeling of personal effectiveness conspicuously lacking prior to treatment. This embryonic sense of worth coupled with an acceptance of a more normal body size, while tentative and fragile at best, is a foundation on which patients continue to build following discharge.

THERAPEUTIC OUTCOME

Since behavioral research has been aimed at achieving satisfactory weight gain in the anorexic patient admitted to hospital, then the outcome of therapy based on the research must be measured by weight gain during hospitalization. Thus Brady and Rieger (9) reported a successful immediate outcome in 16 consecutive patients hospitalized for a median of 6 weeks and gaining at a rate of 0.9 kg/week, whereas Bhanji and Thompson (7) described the outcome for 11 patients treated for between 31 and 86 days who gained 1.7 kg/week. The first 25 patients treated within the Stanford program described above were all female, aged between 15 and 46 years ($\bar{x} = 26.0$ yr). The average length of hospitalization was 54 days, with a range from 12 to 113 days. Only 3 of the 25 patients did not gain weight and must be considered treatment failures, although all left in the first weeks of treatment. Including these 3 patients in the treatment results, we find that patients' weights increased from a mean of 38.7 kg to 46.0 kg for an average of 7.3 kg, a gain of some 20% in body weight at a rate of 0.15 kg/day. The effect of treatment on other problems of the patient with anorexia nervosa, such as abnormal patterns of eating, distorted body image, fear of gaining weight, and interpersonal difficulties, is at present unknown. However, significant changes in such behaviors might be expected given the systematic alteration of eating behavior as a consequence of feedback and reinforcement of weight gain, and the experience of negotiating and adhering to a therapeutic contract. A follow-up study of patients entering the Stanford program is in progress, but until it is complete, the broader and longer-term effects of the program must remain uncertain. The only published follow-up data of the treatment of anorexia nervosa with behavioral methods (7) was obtained by questionnaire and is so incomplete—with, for example, only 3 of 11 patients reporting their weight—that it is virtually useless as an indicator of outcome. However, a detailed follow-up of 29 patients treated in a behavioral program is presented in a subsequent chapter.

FUTURE DIRECTIONS

It appears that applied behavior analysis has made a contribution to our understanding of the control of weight gain in the patient with anorexia nervosa and a modest contribution to the treatment of the disorder. Much remains to be done before an effective therapy becomes a reality. First, other aspects of the pathological features of this puzzling ailment need to be defined in a precisely measurable way, and the effects of well-specified interventions tested experimentally, perhaps due to the rarity of the disorder, using the single-case experimental method exemplified in this chapter. As with weight gain, therapeutic components of immediate effect are likely to be isolated. Then methods to generalize these effects to life situations outside hospital and over long periods of time must be discovered. Automatic generalization cannot be expected from any therapeutic procedure. Finally, when a multifaceted therapeutic package based on the experimental analysis of each component is constructed, a long-term controlled comparison of effectiveness is in order.

ACKNOWLEDGMENTS

The bulk of the work described in this chapter was part of a collaborative effort involving many colleagues of whom we wish particularly to mention: Harold Leitenberg, Ph.D., of the University of Vermont; David Barlow, Ph.D., of Butler Hospital and Brown University; George Gulevich, M.D., of Stanford; and James M. Ferguson, M.D., of the University of California at La Jolla.

REFERENCES

1. Abroms, G. M. (1969): Defining milieu therapy. *Arch. Gen. Psychiatry,* 21:553–560.
2. Agras, W. S. (Ed.) (1972): *Behavior Modification: Principles and Clinical Applications.* Little, Brown & Co., Boston.
3. Agras, W. S. (1976): Behavior modification in the general hospital psychiatric unit. In: *Handbook of Behavior Modification and Therapy,* edited by H. Leitenberg. Prentice-Hall, Englewood Cliffs, N.J.
4. Agras, W. S., Barlow, D. H., Chapin, H. N., Abel, G. C., and Leitenberg, H. (1973): Behavior modification of anorexia nervosa. *Arch. Gen. Psychiatry,* 30:279–286.
5. Azarrod, J., and Stafford, R. L. (1969): Restoration of eating behavior in anorexia nervosa through operant conditioning and environmental manipulation. *Behav. Res. Ther.,* 7:165–171.
6. Bachrach, A. J., Erwin, W. J., and Mohr, J. P. (1965): The control of eating behavior in an anorexic by operant conditioning techniques. In: *Case Studies in Behavior Modification,* edited by L. P. Ullman and L. Krasner. Holt, Rinehart and Winston, New York.
7. Bhanji, S., and Thompson, J. (1974): Operant conditioning in the treatment of anorexia nervosa. *Br. J. Psychiatry,* 124:166–172.
8. Blinder, B. J., Freeman, D. M., and Stunkard, A. J. (1970): Behavior therapy of anorexia nervosa: Effectiveness of activity as a reinforcer of weight gain. *Am. J. Psychiatry,* 126: 1093–1098.
9. Brady, J. P., and Rieger, W. (1972): Behavioral treatment of anorexia nervosa. International Symposium on Behavior Modification, Minneapolis.
10. Brener, J., Kleinman, R. A., and Goesling, W. J. (1969): The effects of differential exposures to augmented sensory feedback on the control of heartrate. *Psychophysiology,* 5:510–516.
11. Bruch, H. (1974): Perils of behavior modification in the treatment of anorexia nervosa. *J.A.M.A.,* 230:1419–1422.
12. Elkin, T. E., Hersen, M., Eisler, R. M., and Williams, J. G. (1973): Modification of caloric intake in anorexia nervosa: An experimental analysis. *Psychol. Rep.,* 32:75–78.
13. Hallsten, E. A. (1965): Adolescent anorexia nervosa treated by desensitization. *Behav. Res. Ther.,* 3:87–91.
14. Leitenberg, H. (Ed.) (1976): *Handbook of Behavior Modification and Behavior Therapy.* Prentice Hall, Englewood Cliffs, N.J.
15. Leitenberg, H., Agras, W. S., and Thomson, L. (1968): A sequential analysis of the effect of selective positive reinforcement in modifying anorexia nervosa. *Behav. Res. Ther.,* 6:211–218.
16. Leitenberg, H., Agras, W. S., Thomson, L. E., and Wright, D. E. (1968): Feedback in behavior modification. *J. Appl. Behav. Anal.,* 1:131–137.
17. Liebman, R., Minuchin, S., and Baker, L. (1974): An integrated program for anorexia nervosa. *Am. J. Psychiatry,* 131:432–436.
18. Shapiro, D., Tursky, B., Gershon, E., and Stern, M. (1969): Effects of feedback and reinforcement on the control of human systolic blood pressure. *Science,* 163:583–585.

Anorexia Nervosa, edited by
R. A. Vigersky. Raven Press,
New York © 1977

Behavior Therapy: Extended Follow-up

Michael J. Pertschuk

Center for Behavioral Medicine, Department of Psychiatry, University of Pennsylvania, Hospital of the University of Pennsylvania, Philadelphia, Pennsylvania 19104

INTRODUCTION

The syndrome of anorexia nervosa is one of the few life-threatening diseases in psychiatry and as such has received attention from a variety of therapeutic schools with strikingly diverse approaches. Therapeutic interventions have included psychoanalysis (18), psychotherapy (6), family therapy (1,15), forced feeding (19), phenothiazine administration and bedrest (8), behavior modification (3,12), and combinations of these techniques (11,14). Even more remarkable than the range of these treatments is the fact that most have had some success at least in the short run. Weight gains during treatment have been reported between 1 and 2 kg/week (3,8,14,19).

Immediate success does not imply long-term cure. The ultimate goal for any treatment of anorexia nervosa must include maintenance of normal weight and eating habits over an extended period with a return to adequate functioning in daily life. From this larger perspective results often have been disappointing. Dally and Sargant (9) found that on 3-year follow-up patients treated with chlorpromazine and bedrest did not differ significantly in weight from patients who had received nonspecific therapy. Approximately one-third of both groups were markedly underweight. Browning and Miller (5), following 36 hospitalized anorectics treated by a variety of methods, could find no correlation between weight gained in the hospital and maintenance at follow-up. Similar findings were produced by Bhanji and Thompson's (2) review of 11 anorectics treated by behavior modification. Although 10 put on weight while in the hospital, only 3 of the 7 patients reached after a median follow-up of 3 years were at normal weight. More encouraging results were recently reported by Halmi et al. (13). In follow-up of 8 patients treated with behavior modification, all continued to gain weight after hospitalization, and all but 1 were judged to be functioning at least adequately. The study was limited, however, by the small number of subjects and the relatively brief average follow-up period of 7 months. In a larger series with longer follow-up, Minuchin et al. (16) also recorded a positive outcome. On an average of 2 years after treatment with family therapy, 21 of 25 anorectics were listed as recovered. The generalizations of these findings were limited by the fact that the population of Minuchin's group was younger (average age 13), with briefer duration of illness (7 months average) than is generally reported in the literature.

Long-term outcome in anorexia nervosa has been a special concern at the University of Pennsylvania. One of the first follow-up studies on behavioral treatment in anorexia came from our psychiatry department. The results were not encouraging. Following 15 patients an average of 2 years after in-hospital behavioral treatment, Brady and Rieger (3) noted two deaths and three failures to maintain weight. Although 10 were found to be at acceptable weight, only 5 were functioning well in daily life. Prior to Brady and Rieger's study, we viewed the hospital treatment of our anorectic patients as largely definitive. While in the hospital patients were placed on a behavioral contract in which various privileges were made contingent on weight gain. With this procedure, a number of patients returned to near-normal weight and all gained. It was assumed that progress made in the hospital would continue at home. The Brady and Rieger study indicated that this was not necessarily true, and since their report there has been a definite shift in how the hospitalization is used at the University of Pennsylvania.

Currently hospital treatment is considered as a first rather than the final stage in the anorectic's therapy. It is employed to help the patient gain some margin of safety in weight and to interrupt the often self-defeating behaviors and attitudes that the patients and their families have used in dealing with anorexia. It also serves as an opportunity to make appropriate referrals for subsequent outpatient treatment. The hospital stay is used to start the patients and their families on their way, it is not intended to be curative. With such limited goals hospitalizations have tended to be brief and continued treatment a necessity. In the following pages the immediate and long-term impact of such intervention is assessed.

CLINICAL POPULATIONS AND METHODS

Patient Sample

The charts of anorexia nervosa patients admitted to the University of Pennsylvania psychiatric service since March 1972 were reviewed. Patients admitted prior to March 1972 were excluded as their outcome had previously been reported by Brady and Rieger (3). In most cases the patients conformed to the criteria for the diagnosis of anorexia nervosa set forth by Feighner et al. (10). All patients had marked abnormalities in eating habits; none had a diagnosed medical condition that could account for anorexia and weight loss; all females were amenorrheic; many had a history of hyperactivity or vomiting. Most but not all met Feighner's criterion of 25% or more underweight. A total of 29 cases were identified. The

Patient	Sex	Adm. age (yr)	Illness length (months)	Adm. weight (kg)	% Standard weight[a]	Special symptoms[b]	Treatment: Behavioral	Treatment: Meds.	Treatment: Hyperaliment.	Days hosp.	Total gain (kg)	% Standard weight
1	F	19	18	38.1	76	V	+	P	–	45	7.3	91
2	F	26	72	39.0	65	LH	+	PA	–	13	4.7	73
3	F	14	8	33.8	67	H	–	–	+	20	7.0	80
4	F	18	36	37.2	67		–	–	–	14	4.5	75
5	F	26	36	33.1	68		+	–	–	20	–0.9	66
6	F	23	36	35.8	64		+	P	–	25	1.8	67
7	F	17	16	30.4	59		+	–	–	26	4.5	68
8	F	21	48	29.9	55		+	–	–	105	14.8	82
9	F	23	60	30.8	55		+	–	–	29	6.4	66
10	F	15	12	35.7	68		+	–	–	18	5.5	78
11	F	21	12	44.1	76		+	–	–	20	3.2	82
12	F	14	6	29.4	59		+	–	–	24	6.2	72
13	F	20	24	36.3	73	V	+	PA	–	64	6.8	86
14	F	29	120	31.3	61	V	+	–	–	21	2.3	71
15	F	14	12	26.8	56	H	+	–	–	40	7.2	71
16	F	14	6	34.5	72		+	–	–	29	4.4	82
17	F	20	60	32.7	59		+	A	–	72	5.9	69
18	F	26	36	29.5	49		+	A	+	62	6.8	61
19	M	19	12	52.2	69	H	+	–	–	26	8.8	81
20	F	17	6	41.2	76	V	+	–	–	29[c]	–0.1	76
21	M	20	9	45.4	65	H	+	–	–	21[c]	2.3	69
22	F	13	10	33.6	73		+	P	–	24[c]	5.4	85
23	F	22	18	40.6	81		+	–	–	7[c]	–0.5	81
24	F	20	12	36.7	66		+	–	–	32	5.7	76
25	F	18	12	30.8	60		+	–	–	70	9.5	79
26	F	16	16	42.2	79		+	–	–	24	7.2	93
27	F	20	24	43.5	78	V	+	–	–	40	7.1	90
28	F	34	156	34.5	63		+	P	–	35	4.8	72
29	F	23	9	45.8	74	LV	+	–	–	16[c]	–0.4	74

[a] For patients under 18 years of age, Average Weight for Height Table (17) used as reference for normal weight; for patients older than 18, normal weight references obtained from Fogarty International Center Conference on Obesity, Recommended Weight in Relation to Height (4).

[b] L, laxative abuse; A, antidepressant medication; H, hyperactivity; V, vomiting; P, phenothiazine.

[c] Discharged against medical advice.

author attempted to contact each patient by phone for follow-up evaluation. An immediate relative was interviewed if it was not possible to reach the patient. Information was successfully gathered on 27 of the 29 patients (Table 1).

TREATMENT PROCEDURES

The patients whose charts were reviewed were treated within the context of the psychiatric service of the Hospital of the University of Pennsylvania. This is an open, 34-bed unit run as a therapeutic community. Anorectics were included in the standard treatment modalities of the unit, i.e., group, occupational, and recreational therapy. For most of these patients special emphasis was placed on family therapy, which was usually conducted by a psychiatric resident and social worker. At one time phenothiazines had been administered occasionally, but more recently they were withheld as they appeared clinically ineffective. Antidepressants were used in cases with significant depression. With few exceptions anorectic patients were placed on a behavioral contract at some point during their hospitalization. The contracts drawn up by the patients with their physician typically required daily weight gain of 0.23 kg (0.5 lb) for access to specified activities or privileges. The exact contingencies varied from patient to patient. In some instances grounds, telephone, and visitor privileges were used as reinforcers. In more stringent contracts being allowed out of bed was made contingent on weight gain. Nutritional counseling was available. The treating staff in all cases had been instructed not to coach the patients in eating as it was considered the individual's responsibility to make the required daily weight gain. Two patients received intravenous hyperalimentation during their hospitalization, which was carried out on the medical service. Patients were transferred to psychiatry after hyperalimentation had been terminated.

FOLLOW-UP

Patients or immediate family members were contacted by telephone. They were informed that research was being conducted on treatment outcome in anorexia nervosa and their help was requested. Everyone contacted agreed to be interviewed. Information was gathered concerning the patients' present weight and eating habits, current menstrual history, family, social, and vocational functioning, psychiatric treatment following hospitalization, and attitudes about weight and food.

RESULTS

In Table 1 are listed patient demographic data and information on weight and symptoms during hospitalization. It is evident that the hospital treatment was generally effective in helping patients with their weight. In all, 25 of the 29 gained while in the hospital. Weight gain averaged 5.1 kg over an average stay of 32 days. Weight gain correlated with length of hospitalization ($r = 0.45$, $p < 0.001$) but was not significantly correlated with either the percent of standard weight at admission ($r = -0.18$, $p < 0.1$) or the duration of illness ($r = -0.03$, $p < 0.4$). The severity of illness in terms of weight or duration did not appear to influence treatment response in terms of weight gain.

Table 2 lists follow-up data. As a group the patients continued to improve. Discharged patients had averaged 24% below standard weight. At follow-up this had been reduced to 12%. Eleven patients were within 20% of normal weight at discharge. The number increased to eighteen at follow-up. Severity of anorexia in terms of duration of the illness and weight deficit prior to admission was uncorrelated with follow-up weight. A highly subjective rating of general functioning was made based on the telephone interviews: functioning was considered "good" if the patient appeared to be making satisfactory vocational, social, and family adjustments; "fair" if the patient expressed problems in one area; "poor" if the patient indicated difficulties in more than one. On this basis twelve patients were rated as having made a good adjustment, nine fair, and six poor. All patients rated as functioning poorly also had continued eating problems. Interestingly, a good adjustment did not necessarily imply resolution of the eating disorder. As one patient expressed it, although her weight was normal and her life was going well, she "still had a thing about food." Only two out of the twenty-seven could be said to be completely recovered in the sense of maintaining near-normal weight, functioning well, and eating normally.

Twelve patients had required rehospitalization, six for weight loss, four after suicide attempts, and two for depression. There were no deaths among the twenty-seven followed. Although weight generally increased, there was also an increase in the number of reported eating abnormalities other than food restriction. Bulimia, which had not been reported by any patient on admission, developed in ten patients on follow-up. In most cases this was accompanied by compulsive vomiting. No patient who had acknowledged vomiting as a problem at admission was found to have controlled it at follow-up.

Of major concern is how the outcome at follow-up relates to experience during hospitalization. Is improvement in the hospital predictive of long-term recovery? The answer appears to be no. The correlation between percent gained in the hospital and the percent weight gain at follow-up was nonsignificant ($r = -0.10$, $p = 0.23$). Of 21 patients who increased their percent of standard weight by five or more points in the hospital, only 10 did so during follow-up. All 5 who failed to gain while in the hospital had gained at follow-up.

TABLE 2. *Anorexia nervosa patients at follow-up*

Patient	Follow-up (months)	Rehospitalized	Menstruation	Special symptoms[a]	Follow-up weight	% Standard weight[b]	Adjustment
1	45	2	+	BV	50	92	Fair
2	39	1	—	LH	37.6	63	Poor
3	36	1	+	—	61.2	108	Good
4	33	2	+	BV	52.2	93	Fair
5	33	1	—	B	37.2	77	Fair
6	31	1	—	—	57.6	103	Fair
7	29	1	+	B	63.5	124	Good
8	29	—	—	—	43.1	79	Good
9	29	—	—	—	45.4	81	Good
10	28	—	+	BV	43.5	81	Good
11	27	1	+	V	54.4	94	Good
12	26	—	+	—	53.5	103	Good
13	25	—	—	BV	39.0	78	Fair
14	25	1	—	?	36.3	71	Poor
15	24	—	—	B	43.5	83	Good
16	24	—	?	—	49.6	94	Good
17	21	—	—	—	55.8	102	Good
18	17	1	—	—	37.2	62	Poor
19	15	—	NA	—	63.5	84	Fair
20	14	—	—	BVL, H	38.6	73	Poor
21	13	1	NA	—	55.3	80	Fair
22	11	—	+	—	56.7	115	Fair
23	10	1	—	BVL	50	98	Poor
24	10	—	+	—	45.8	82	Good
25	4	—	—	—	34.9	68	Poor
26	3	—	—	—	49.4	93	Good
27	3	—	—	BV	47.6	85	Fair
28	36	Unable to contact					
29	22	Unable to contact					

[a] B, bulimia; L, laxative abuse; H, hyperactivity; V, vomiting; ?, information not available.

[b] For patients under 18 years of age, Average Weight for Height Table (17) used as reference for normal weight; for patients older than 18, normal weight references obtained from Fogarty International Center Conference on Obesity Recommended Weight in Relation to Height (4).

DISCUSSION

The results indicate that the anorectic patients improved both during hospitalization and after discharge at least in terms of weight. Unfortunately, if there was a relationship between the conditions in hospital and at follow-up we could not find it. Hospitalization was intended as a first step in a treatment program. All the patients did, in fact, receive subsequent outpatient therapy. The type of therapy varied considerably as patients came from a wide geographic area and were referred back to local treatment resources. Halmi et al. (13) have suggested that the effectiveness of behavior therapy for anorexia in the hospital is maximized when it is continued after discharge. This was not the case for most of our patients, and discontinuity in treatment may have accounted for some discontinuity in progress.

Subsequent treatment also included rehospitalization for a disconcertingly large number of patients (12 of 27). Of these, 10 were readmitted within 6 months of discharge. More surprising than the number were the reasons for rehospitalization. Less than half required additional inpatient treatment for weight problems. Of the remainder, 4 patients made suicide attempts, and 2 were clinically depressed. Bruch (7) has suggested that depression and consequent suicide attempts are the result of behavioral intervention, "Its very efficiency increases the inner turmoil of patients who feel tricked into relinquishing control over their bodies and their lives." This is one interpretation of our findings; however, it does not explain why these particular patients and not all the behaviorally treated anorectics became depressed and suicidal. In reviewing the charts of these 6 rehospitalized for depression or suicide attempts, we found that 4 were depressed or suicidal at admission. The need for readmission may have stemmed from inadequate treatment of the affective problem rather than from effective treatment of weight.

It is of interest that normalization of eating patterns did not parallel normalization of weight. Most patients at follow-up continued to express an inordinate concern with food. Improvement in weight in some cases appeared to evolve from a balance of pathologic eating behaviors, e.g., bulimia and vomiting. In fact, 10 patients shifted from a pattern of food restriction to bulimia. As described above, the treatment program emphasized weight gain, and although information on nutrition was available, patients were generally left on their own concerning eating patterns. It is impossible to determine whether the failure to resolve pathologic eating behaviors was the result of our lack of focus on this area. The results suggest that greater concern about eating patterns might be in order.

What do our findings indicate regarding the role of the hospital for the anorectic? Clearly there are times when hospitalization is a necessity even if there is no long-term carry-over of improvement. Emergent situations resulting from cachexia or interfamily strife may require the immediate and dramatic intervention of hospitalization. In such cases, because continuation of improvement appears problematic, it would seem advisable, as Halmi et al. (13) suggest, to continue the specific interventions made in the hospital on an outpatient basis. When the situation is less critical, the difficulty in continuing at home progress made within the hospital may make hospitalization less advisable. Behavior, family, and individual therapy can all be conducted on an outpatient basis. Improvements made outside the hospital would, *a priori,* appear more likely to be maintained as they are occurring in the patient's daily environment. An alternative to brief or no hospitalization is, of course, long-term inpatient treatment. Our data did not speak directly to the effectiveness of extended hospitalization, although we found no significant correlation between length of time in the hospital and weight on follow-up. For some patients long stays may be necessary, but the realities of high hospital costs and the demands of third-party reimbursers will limit the number of cases in which this is a practical alternative.

Concerning the hospitalization itself, it is evident from the results that our interventions including behavior modification were successful in helping patients gain weight. Behavior modification has been described as "damaging" (7) in anorexia nervosa. Our findings do not support such a claim as most patients had improved at follow-up. Nor do our findings indicate that behavior modification is a panacea. Critics may be valid to the extent that behaviorally oriented therapists may tend to become fixated on the easily measurable; in the case of anorectics, on kilograms and percent of standard weight. This may have happened with some of our patients. The whole patient must be considered. It is quite feasible to combine behavioral treatment with other therapeutic modalities and this has been done frequently. Behavior modification and human concern are very compatible.

REFERENCES

1. Barcai, A. (1971): Family therapy in the treatment of anorexia nervosa. *Am. J. Psychiatry,* 128:284–290.
2. Bhanji, S., and Thompson, J. (1974): Operant conditioning in the treatment of anorexia nervosa: A review and retrospective study of 11 cases. *Br. J. Psychiatry,* 124:166–172.
3. Brady, J. P., and Rieger, W. (1975): Behavioral treatment of anorexia nervosa. In: *Applications of Behavior Modification,* edited by T. Thompson and W. S. Duckens, III. Academic Press, New York.
4. Bray, G. A. (Ed.) (1973): *Obesity in Perspective.* DHEW Publication No. (NIH) (75–708), Washington, D.C.
5. Browning, C. H., and Miller, S. I. (1968): Anorexia nervosa: A study in prognosis and management. *Am. J. Psychiatry,* 124:1128–1132.
6. Bruch, H. (1973): *Eating Disorders: Obesity, Anorexia Nervosa, and the Person Within.* Basic Books, New York.
7. Bruch, H. (1974): Perils of behavior modification in treatment of anorexia nervosa. *J.A.M.A.,* 230:1419–1422.
8. Dally, P., and Sargant, W. (1960): A new treatment of anorexia nervosa. *Br. Med. J.,* 1:793–795.
9. Dally, P., and Sargant, W. (1966): Treatment and outcome of anorexia nervosa. *Br. Med. J.,* 2:793–795.

10. Feighner, J. P., Robins, E., Guze, S. B., Woodruff, R. A., Jr., Winokur, G., and Munoz, R. (1972): Diagnostic criteria for use in psychiatric research. *Arch. Gen. Psychiatry,* 26:57–63.
11. Galdston, R. (1974): Mind over matter observations on 50 patients hospitalized with anorexia nervosa. *J. Am. Acad. Child Psychiatry,* 13:246–263.
12. Garfinkel, P. E., Kline, S. A., and Stancer, H. C. (1973): Treatment of anorexia nervosa using operant conditioning techniques. *J. Nerv. Ment. Dis.,* 157:428–433.
13. Halmi, K. A., Powers, P., and Cunningham, S. (1975): Treatment of anorexia nervosa with behavior modification. *Arch. Gen. Psychiatry,* 32:93–96.
14. Lucas, A. R., Duncan, J. W., and Piens, V. (1976): The treatment of anorexia nervosa. *Am. J. Psychiatry,* 133:1034–1038.
15. Minuchin, S. (1973): *Families and Family Therapy: A Structural Approach.* Harvard University Press, Boston.
16. Minuchin, S., Baker, L., Rosman, B. L., Liebman, R., Milman, L., and Todd, T. C. (1975): A conceptual model of psychosomatic illness in children. *Arch. Gen. Psychiatry,* 32: 1031–1038.
17. Robinson, C. H. (1972): *Normal and Therapeutic Nutrition.* Macmillan, New York.
18. Thoma, H. (1972): Treatment. *Adv. Psychosom. Med.,* 7:300–315.
19. Williams, E. (1958): Anorexia nervosa, a somatic disorder. *Br. Med. J.,* 2:190–193.

Anorexia Nervosa, edited by
R. A. Vigersky. Raven Press,
New York © 1977

The Outcome of Anorexia Nervosa: Significance of Clinical Features, Body Image, and Behavior Modification

Paul E. Garfinkel, Harvey Moldofsky, and David M. Garner

Clarke Institute of Psychiatry and University of Toronto, Toronto, Ontario, Canada M5T 1R8

INTRODUCTION

Because of the dangers of severe malnutrition, weight restoration is the immediate concern in treating many patients with anorexia nervosa. In this regard, behavioral modification techniques have been claimed to be instrumental in achieving rapid weight gain while avoiding the side effects of medical therapies (2–7,19,24,28,31,40).

However, Bruch (12) recently criticized behavioral techniques in anorexia nervosa as potentially dangerous. She claimed adverse psychological consequences in nine patients who relapsed after an initial weight gain with behavioristic treatment. By coercing them into eating in spite of intense fear, the treatment aggravated the patients' profound helplessness and ineffectiveness. Bruch's criticism is difficult to assess, however, given the selectivity of her cases and given the reported 25 to 50% (8,9,15,17,22,30) of patients with anorexia nervosa who have poor prognosis with traditional medical and psychiatric treatments. To date no studies have been reported on the long-term effects of behavior modification techniques versus other medical and psychological therapies in patients with anorexia nervosa.

Furthermore, in assessing prognosis most authors have focused on clinical features, personality functioning, and menstruation (8,9,11,15,17,20,22,30, 33,35,37,41,42). Recently a self-perceptual disturbance in patients with anorexia nervosa has been described (16,25,39). We also have found that anorexic patients overestimated their body sizes in comparison with control groups. Approximately one-half of these patients displayed such an overestimation. We hypothesized that such overestimation tendencies as well as clinical and treatment issues are related to clinical outcome.

The present investigation reports on the outcome of 42 patients with primary anorexia nervosa in terms of (a) clinical features, (b) self-perceptual disturbances, and (c) operant conditioning versus medical and psychologic therapies.

SUBJECTS AND METHODS

Subjects

Subjects consisted of all patients referred to the Clinical Investigation Unit (CIU), Clarke Institute of Psychiatry, who met the criteria of Feighner et al. (21) for primary anorexia nervosa. Only those patients for whom there was a follow-up period of greater than 1 year since the CIU treatment were included in the present study. A total of 42 patients, 40 female and 2 male, met these criteria. The duration of follow-up was 58.2 ± 3.9 months (mean $\pm$ SEM) from the onset of illness, and 31.7 ± 3.1 months from the time of treatment.

Methods

For each patient a chart review was conducted to assess clinical status at the time of first consultation. The following clinical-demographic factors were recorded: age, sex, age of onset of anorexia nervosa, percent weight loss, weight at time of CIU contact, percent of "average" weight for age and height (13), and number of previous hospitalizations. In addition, the

TABLE 1. *Global clinical score—criteria for assessing anorexia nervosa (on first CIU contact and on follow-up)*

I. Weight (% of average):	90–109% 0			
	110–119% 1			
	80– 89% 1			
	75– 79% 2			
	120–125% 2			
	<75% 3			
	>125% 3			
II. Eating habits:	Absent	Occasional	Moderate	Marked
a. Food faddishness	0	1	2	3
b. Vomiting	0	1	2	3
c. Bulimic episodes	0	1	2	3
d. Laxative abuse	0	1	2	3
III. Menses:				
Occurrence	0 (present)		1 (absent)	
Regularity	0 (yes)		1 (no)	
IV. Social adjustment:				
0, Relates well to male(s), peers, and family				
1, Relates well in 2 of the 3 above areas, but has difficulties in the third				
2, Relates well in only 1 of the 3 above areas				
3, Poor relations with peers and males and continuing problems with parents				
V. Educational and/or vocational adjustment:				
0, Attends school or work regularly and works efficiently				
1, Attendance is good, but work is below potential				
2, Frequent absences and/or poor performance				
3, Does not work or go to school				
VI. Total score (sum of I–V):				

presence and degree of each of the following were recorded on a 4-point scale (0-absent, 1-occasional, 2-moderate, 3-marked): food fads, bulimia, laxative abuse, and vomiting. Menstrual disturbances were also noted. The individual's social and educational/vocational adjustment were recorded for each patient along 4-point scales as outlined in Table 1.

On the basis of this information each subject received a global clinical score (Table 1) for the time of initial assessment (maximum score = 23).

Sainsbury and Krietman (36) have cautioned about errors involved in the analyses of hospital files. Since all the patients here had been under the care of the same three psychiatrists on the CIU and since the method of assessment was uniform, it was possible to minimize these errors.

METHOD OF TREATMENT

For the 42 patients, a variety of treatment methods were used. These included both inpatient and outpatient care, individual supportive psychotherapy, family therapy, operant conditioning, pharmacotherapies, and ECT. Each individual's treatments were obtained by reviewing the hospital files and by discussion with the patient's most recent physician/therapist. To be included in the operant conditioning group subjects had to have been treated in hospital, using a reward system for weight gain as described previously (24). Patients treated with operant conditioning were later treated by a variety of therapies—including family therapy, individual supportive psychotherapy, and pharmacotherapy. Family therapy was defined as present only when therapy considered the family as the unit of pathology (1) and not in the frequent supportive sessions with parents and relatives. Individual psychotherapy varied from regular weekly sessions over many months to brief supportive contacts. Decisions as to which treatments would be provided were determined clinically according to the considered needs of each individual.

MEASURES OF SELF-PERCEPTION

Of the 42 patients, 28 took part in objective measures of self-perception at the time of CIU assessment. These consisted of the individual estimating her "real" size and "ideal" size via a standardized slide photograph of herself (full length and in a two-piece bathing suit). This photograph was projected through an anamorphic lens capable of distorting her size by 20% in a direction of appearing thin or fat. Details of this test procedure have previously been described (25).

ASSESSMENT OF CLINICAL OUTCOME

For each patient assessment of clinical outcome was made through contact with her current physician/psychotherapist. Seventeen patients were being seen by one of the doctors from the CIU. The assessment was made using the global clinical scale (Table 1) previously described for assessment of initial clinical status. The lower the score on this scale, the better the outcome. Scores of 0 to 3 were defined as "excellent" outcome, 4 to 7 were "much improved," 8 to 11 were "symptomatic," and above 11 were "poor" outcome. In addition, the patient's current weight and return of menses were used as independent criteria of outcome.

The assessment of outcome was made by one of us (P.G.) who was blind to the individual's scores on body image tests.

STATISTICAL ANALYSIS

The statistical analysis was done by one-way analysis of variance, comparing the four outcome groups (excellent, much improved, symptomatic, and poor) for each of the relevant clinical, treatment, and self-perceptual measures. Group comparisons were done by Duncan's multiple range test (18). Comparisons of patients treated by operant conditioning with the remainder of the sample as well as comparisons of overestimators and underestimators of body size were analyzed by Student's *t*-test.

RESULTS

Characteristics of the Patients on Initial Assessment

CLINICAL FEATURES

At the time of our initial contact the mean age of the forty-two patients was 20.2 ± 0.8 years (range of 12 to 38). The age of onset of anorexia nervosa was 17.1 ± 0.4 (range 11 to 22). One patient was prepubertal. Seven patients were from 11 to 14 years at onset, twenty were 15 to 18, and fifteen were 19 to 22.

All patients had begun dieting at least 1 year prior to CIU assessment. Eleven began less than 2 years, twelve began from 2 to 4 years, thirteen from 4 to 6 years, and six more than 6 years before CIU assessment.

Nineteen patients had no previous hospitalizations. Eight had one prior hospitalization, and the remaining fifteen patients had from two to six hospital admissions.

The mean weight was 37.7 kg ± 1.0 (range 26 to 54 kg). The patients weighed 64.9% ± 1.4 (45 to 96%) of their "average" for sex, age, and height. One patient was between 90 and 110% of average; three were between 80 and 89%; four were 75 to 79%; and thirty-four were less than 75% of average.

All but one patient were noted to have food fads; in 62% these were "marked." Eight patients (19%) vomited at least occasionally (approximately once a month), and for six of these vomiting was a regular (at least four times per week) event. Twenty-six patients (62%) had bulimic episodes and seven (17%) abused laxatives.

Six patients had regular menses but the remainder were amenorrheic.

Only 2% related well to males, peers, and family; 17% related well in two of the three areas; and 69% related well in one of the areas. It was found that 12% related poorly in all three areas of social functioning.

Although 36% attended school or work regularly and worked efficiently, 24% attended regularly but worked below potential, 19% were either absent frequently or performed poorly in these areas, and 21% did not work or attend school.

The mean score on the global scale was 12.1 ± 0.5. On initial assessment none had total scores in the "excellent" (0 to 3) range; 1 was "much improved" (4 to 7), 17 were "symptomatic" (8 to 11), and 24 were "poor" (above 11).

SELF-PERCEPTION TESTS

The group as a whole slightly overestimated their sizes with a mean of $+0.47\% \pm 1.25$, but they exhibited a broad scatter of body estimation (−13.13 to +12.66). Thirteen persons were underestimators of their size and fifteen were overestimators.

In terms of ideal size estimates, the mean value of the group was $-2.31\% \pm 1.78$, but again there was a wide range (−20 to +20).

Methods of Treatment

Of the 42 patients, 26 (62%) were hospitalized as part of the CIU treatment whereas 16 (38%) were treated entirely as outpatients. In all, 31 (74%) received individual supportive psychotherapy and 9 (21%) pharmacotherapy (phenothiazines 4, benzodiazepines 2, tricyclic antidepressants 2, and cyproheptadine 1). Family therapy was the method of treating 5 (12%) patients. Electroconvulsive therapy was used for 2 (5%). Finally, 5 (12%) were seen for consultation-investigation only.

Operant conditioning was used as part of the hospital treatment for 17 (40%) patients. In subsequent analyses of operant conditioning these 17 patients were compared with the remaining 25 of the sample.

The duration of CIU treatment ranged from 2 to 36 months (m = 12.8, SEM = 1.4) combining both inpatient and active outpatient care.

Outcome of the Sample on Follow-Up

There was a significant correlation between the patients' weight and global scores on follow-up ($r = -0.44$, $p < 0.002$) and between return of menstruation and global scores ($r = -0.46$, $p < 0.002$).

On follow-up, 58% of the patients weighed between 80 and 120% of

TABLE 2. *Relationship between return of menses and weight on follow-up*

Follow-up weight (% average)	Menses Present	Menses Absent
90–125%	11	1
80–89%	6	8
<80%	2	11
Total	19	20

Chi-square = 14.83, df = 2, $p < 0.001$.

"average." One-quarter of the patients remained at weights of less than 75% of "average." Three patients (7%) had become obese.

The patients still showed food fads with 71% classified as either "moderate" or "marked." At least occasional episodes of vomiting were reported in 20%. One-half of the sample still had bulimic episodes, and 10% abused laxatives.

Of 39 patients (excluding the 2 males and 1 patient who died), 19 had a return of menses, and 17 had regular periods. The return of menses was found to be related to two variables. Patients with continued amenorrhea were ill for a shorter period of time (47.4 ± 5.5 months versus 70.1 ± 4.8; $p < 0.01$). In addition, the return of menses was highly correlated with the patient's follow-up weight ($r = 0.61$; $p < 0.001$). This relationship between return of menses and weight on follow-up is more clearly demonstrated in Table 2. From this table it is apparent that patients could be reasonably certain to resume menses only after their weight was up to 90% of "average."

On follow-up, 7% of the patients related well to males, peers, and family; 41% related well in two of the three areas; and 46% related well in one of the areas. It was found that 5% related poorly in all three areas of social functioning.

Although 49% attended school or work regularly and worked efficiently, 34% attended regularly but worked below potential, 7% were either absent frequently or performed poorly in these areas, and 10% did not work or attend school.

The mean follow-up global score was 8.4 ± 0.7. The outcome in 7 patients (16.7%) was "excellent;" 14 (33.3%) were "much improved"; 13 (31%) were "symptomatic;" and 8 (19%) were doing "poorly." Included in the last category is the patient who had died through suicide. Therefore, 50% of the group were doing very well on follow-up and 50% were not. On their global score, 37 patients showed some improvement, 2 were unchanged, and 3 were worse at follow-up than on initial assessment.

The group as a whole showed a 32% change in their global clinical scores from assessment to follow-up. It was found that 14 patients (33%) showed greater than a 50% change; 13 (31%) showed between 25 and 49% change;

TABLE 3. *Results of analysis of general clinical features in patients in the 4 outcome groups*

Outcome	*N*	Age ($m \pm SEM$)	Age of onset (years)	Duration of illness (months)	Weight on admission (kg)	% Weight loss	% Average weight	No. of previous hospitalizations[a]
Excellent	7	20.2 ± 3.3	15.7 ± 1.1	73.9 ± 8.8	33.0 ± 2.2	31.7 ± 2.5	61.9 ± 2.7	0.7 ± 0.4
Much improved	14	19.2 ± 1.1	16.8 ± 0.8	55.5 ± 6.1	38.3 ± 1.9	36.8 ± 2.3	63.5 ± 2.8	1.3 ± 0.5
Symptomatic	13	21.3 ± 1.3	18.1 ± 0.6	50.1 ± 7.8	40.7 ± 1.6	32.7 ± 2.6	70.3 ± 1.8	0.7 ± 0.3
Poor	8	20.1 ± 1.1	17.3 ± 0.9	63.0 ± 8.0	36.0 ± 1.7	35.4 ± 2.4	61.3 ± 3.0	2.4 ± 0.4

[a] $p < 0.05$.

10 (25%) showed between 1 and 24% change; and 5 (12%) showed no change or scored more poorly on follow-up.

Since their initial CIU assessment, 31 patients have not been rehospitalized; 7 have had one further hospitalization; and 3 have had more than one. Of the ten subsequent hospitalizations, eight have been for further episodes of weight loss and two for suicide attempts.

Factors Related to Outcome

CLINICAL FEATURES

Table 3 shows the results of some clinical data obtained on initial assessment, analyzed in terms of the four outcome groups. The four groups were very similar on these features, except that those patients with "poor" outcome had more hospitalizations prior to CIU assessment than did patients in the other three groups ($p < 0.05$; Duncan's test).

The analysis of relevant eating habits is presented in Table 4. The presence and degree of food fads did not differ among groups. However, the "poor" outcome group showed significantly more initial bulimia ($p < 0.01$) and vomiting ($p < 0.01$) than did either the "excellent" or "much improved" group. Although the presence of laxative abuse was not statistically different between the groups, none of the seven patients with excellent outcomes abused laxatives at the time of initial assessment.

The degree of initial social adjustment was not related to outcome (Table 5). The "poor" outcome group had significantly worse scores of educational/vocational adjustment than the other three groups ($p < 0.01$), and the "excellent" outcome group had better scores than the other three groups ($p < 0.01$).

The scores on the total initial global scale were higher for the "poor" outcome than for the others ($p < 0.01$) and lower for the "excellent" outcome group than for the others ($p < 0.01$).

Not unexpectedly, the patients with "poor" outcomes had more subsequent hospitalizations ($p < 0.01$) and episodes of further weight loss ($p < 0.05$) than those in the other three groups. Seven of the eight "poor" out-

TABLE 4. *Results of analysis of food-related clinical features in patients in the 4 outcome groups*

Outcome	N	Food fads	Vomiting[a]	Bulimia[a]	Laxative abuse
Excellent	7	2.3 ± 0.2	0.0	0.3 ± 0.2	0.0
Much improved	14	2.4 ± 0.2	0.2 ± 0.2	1.0 ± 0.3	0.1 ± 0.1
Symptomatic	13	2.9 ± 0.1	0.4 ± 0.3	1.4 ± 0.3	0.7 ± 0.3
Poor	8	2.6 ± 0.2	1.6 ± 0.5	2.3 ± 0.4	0.5 ± 0.4

[a] $p < 0.01$.

TABLE 5. *Results of comparisons among the 4 outcome groups on social adjustment, educational/vocational adjustment, and initial global scores*

Outcome	Social adjustment	Educational/vocational adjustment[a]	Initial global score[b]
Excellent	1.8 ± 0.1	0.3 ± 0.2	9.6 ± 0.5
Much improved	2.1 ± 0.2	1.2 ± 0.3	11.2 ± 0.7
Symptomatic	1.6 ± 0.2	1.2 ± 0.3	11.9 ± 0.6
Poor	2.1 ± 0.2	2.3 ± 0.4	16.4 ± 1.0

[a] $p < 0.01$.
[b] $p < 0.001$.

come patients had further hospitalizations. Only three patients in the rest of the sample had been rehospitalized.

SELF-PERCEPTION

The results of the patients' self-estimates for body size are presented in Table 6. Those with "poor" outcomes overestimated their sizes in comparison with the other three groups ($p < 0.01$).

All four patients with "excellent" outcomes who were tested underestimated their size, whereas all five with "poor" outcomes were overestimators. The one patient who died was a marked overestimator of her size.

The patients' self-estimates for body size were highly correlated with global clinical scores on follow-up ($r = 0.67$, $p < 0.001$) and final weight ($r = -0.68$, $p < 0.001$). That is, those with higher weights and lower global scores on follow-up had tended to underestimate their sizes.

Comparisons were made between those patients who overestimated body size ($N = 15$) versus those who underestimated ($N = 13$). The two groups were similar in terms of age, age of onset of anorexia nervosa, and percent weight loss. Overestimators had more prior hospitalizations (1.8 ± 0.5 versus 0.2 ± 0.2, $p < 0.01$). Overestimators scored higher on both initial (13.2 ± 0.8 versus 10.6 ± 0.6, $p < 0.05$) and final (11.3 ± 1.3 versus 6.1 ± 0.7, $p < 0.002$) global clinical scores. Although underestimators

TABLE 6. *Results of patients' self-estimates of body size in 4 outcome groups*

Group	*N*	m ± SEM[a]	Minimum	Maximum
Excellent	4	-7.7 ± 1.5	−10.5	−4.4
Much improved	8	-1.5 ± 2.0	−13.1	+5.6
Symptomatic	11	$+2.0 \pm 1.8$	−4.5	+12.7
Poor	5	$+6.9 \pm 1.5$	+3.6	+11.3

[a] $p < 0.002$.

showed considerable change in their global scores (42.1% ± 6.8), little change was seen in overestimators (12.7% ± 10.3, $p < 0.03$).

Ideal size estimates were very similar in all four groups.

METHODS OF TREATMENT

For most of the therapies statistical comparisons were not made because of small numbers in each cell. Statistical analyses of the data were made between operant conditioning versus other treatments, and the results of these are presented in Table 7.

Those patients treated in hospital with an operant conditioning program were significantly younger on CIU assessment ($p < 0.001$), younger at onset of anorexia nervosa ($p < 0.002$), and weighed less than their cohorts on assessment ($p < 0.001$). They were similar to other patients with anorexia nervosa on other clinical parameters. Of importance, they did not differ in self-perceptions of body size, personality features, or global scale on assessment.

At follow-up they again showed results similar to those of the remainder of the group on global score, percentage change in global score, and final weight. These results were not altered by analysis of covariance controlling for age, age of onset, or weight. Of the seven patients in the "excellent" outcome group, three were treated with operant conditioning; seven of fourteen "much improved," five of thirteen "symptomatic," and two of eight "poor" outcome patients were treated with operant conditioning.

Of the 17 patients treated with operant conditioning, 11 had not been rehospitalized, 3 had one further hospitalization, and 3 had more than one

TABLE 7. *Results of comparison between patients treated with operant conditioning vs other therapies*

	Patients treated with operant conditioning ($N = 17$)	Patients treated with other therapies ($N = 25$)	Level of statistical significance (Student's *t*-test)
Age (years)	17.3 ± 0.6	22.2 ± 1.1	$p < 0.001$
Age of onset (years)	15.6 ± 0.5	18.1 ± 0.5	$p < 0.002$
Initial weight (kg)	34.1 ± 0.8	40.2 ± 1.4	$p < 0.001$
No. of previous hospitalizations	1.2 ± 0.3	1.3 ± 0.3	ns
Duration of follow-up (onset)	57.1 ± 5.5	59.0 ± 5.5	ns
Self-estimates			
Real size (%)	+1.3 ± 1.7	−0.1 ± 1.7	ns
Ideal size (%)	−2.1 ± 3.1	−2.4 ± 2.2	ns
Global score on assessment	12.7 ± 0.6	11.8 ± 0.7	ns
Global score on follow-up	7.8 ± 0.9	8.8 ± 1.1	ns
Percent change in global score	39.4 ± 5.9	27.5 ± 7.5	ns

readmission. Only 4 of the remainder of the sample had been readmitted to hospital (however, of the latter, 16 had never been hospitalized).

DISCUSSION

Opinions have varied widely about the prognosis of anorexia nervosa. Gull (26) regarded the prognosis as "for the most part favorable." Hurst (28) felt that "a few straightforward conversations are sufficient to straighten out most mental tangles." On the other hand, others (30,43) have considered anorexia nervosa to be associated with a high mortality.

A number of methodological issues may have contributed to these divergent opinions. First, probably the major problem with earlier reports has been the lack of consistent diagnostic criteria for anorexia nervosa. As recently as 1960, anorexia nervosa was defined as weight loss of more than 25% due to any psychological cause (8), thus including many patients with weight loss secondary to a variety of primary disorders (e.g., schizophrenia). The arguments in favor of a separate syndrome of primary anorexia nervosa have recently been reviewed (10,34).

Second, the majority of prognostic studies have been retrospective in nature and as such dependent on the inherent deficiencies of medical records. Third, criteria for assessing outcome have varied. Restoration and maintenance of weight are frequently used indicators of improvement. However, some argue that weight gain is far less critical than improvement of intrapsychic and interpersonal conflicts (11,12,38). Other criteria of improvement have included menstrual regularity (17,37) and such ill-defined concepts as adequate sexual functioning (15,17), "normal" eating (14,15), and improved interpersonal relationships (15,32). These issues make comparisons among investigations difficult.

Nevertheless, the earlier reports are quite similar to our global ratings. Overall, 50% of our patients were doing quite well on follow-up with the remaining patients encountering varying degrees of difficulty, ranging from problems with peer and parental relationships and psychosexual adjustment to recurrent episodes of weight loss. Ten patients have required further hospitalization, two for attempted suicide. The one patient who died was treated with traditional medical therapies and later suicided.

The 2% mortality in the present study is rather low in comparison with the 5 to 25% reported earlier (22,30,33,37,41,42), but it is in agreement with the 2.8% found in Dally's (17) large series.

A number of investigators have identified clinical features that are said to have prognostic significance. Although early age of onset has been claimed to be related to good outcome (27,33,37,41), both Dally's study (17) and ours do not find age of onset to be important in determining outcome. In our study this may be because of the relatively older group seen; all but one patient was postpubertal. Furthermore, other clinical features such as degree of weight loss and food faddishness are not predictive of outcome in our study. However, some food-related habits on initial assessment may be important. We confirm other authors' (27,41) findings of both bulimia and vomiting to be significantly related to poor prognosis. Halmi et al. (27) have suggested that excessive use of laxatives is also a poor prognostic sign. Although frequency of laxative abuse was not significantly different among outcome groups in our study, no patients with excellent outcome abused laxatives.

The presence of good premorbid educational and vocational adjustment was significantly related to successful outcome. Several patients with defective career functioning reverted to the pattern of bulimia and weight fluctuation. In part this may have occurred when there was a failure of personal resources that necessitated return to support from the family. Seidensticker and Tzagournis (37) and Halmi et al. (27) have both reported favorable outcomes in patients with skilled and professional occupations.

The return of menses in anorexic patients has been unpredictable. Theander (41) observed that 76% of his surviving probands had recovered normal menses. In fact, 55% of those menstruating had borne children. Dally (17) reported 59% of his patients to be menstruating and felt the return of menses was related to weight restoration. Recently Frisch and MacArthur (23) have suggested a "critical weight" hypothesis for return of menstruation. They propose that normal menses will not resume unless the individual's body weight for height is above a critical level. Our results support this hypothesis for anorexic women. We suggest that an individual can be reasonably certain to resume menstruation when her weight is at least 90% of "average."

In the last 10 years, treatments derived from learning theory have grown in popularity. Prior to 1970, a few investigators (3,4,30) reported on an operant paradigm in treating patients with anorexia nervosa. Since 1970 there has been a steady stream of articles supporting the benefits of weight gain with this technique (2,5–7,19,24,28). Bruch (12) alone has been most antagonistic to these behavioral techniques claiming them to range between useless and harmful.

The proponents suggest such advantages of operant conditioning as rapid weight gain and the lack of possible adverse effects of somatic therapies. Also, when the positive contingencies are clearly defined at the commencement of treatment, the patient may feel responsibility for weight gain. An operant approach may also minimize confrontations with staff over eating. Unfortunately, most behaviorist studies have been without adequate control groups, of short follow-up, and have not focused on harmful sequelae. Blinder et al. (7), however, noted the suicide of a patient after weight gain. Bhanji and Thompson (5) recently shed some light on the long-term efficacy of operant management. Of their 11 patients, 10 gained weight readily. Follow-up was available on 7, of whom 3 had a poor outcome, 3 had achieved a fair adjustment, and 1 was in complete remission. Similarly, Halmi et al. (28) reported on the treatment of 8 patients using individualized positive reinforcement in hospital and after discharge. After an average period of 7 months' follow-up, 4 patients were rated as achieving "good" adjustment, 3 others maintained "adequate" stabilization, and 1 had only "fair" or marginal functioning. Despite the small samples, these results cast some doubt on the long-term effectiveness of the popular operant techniques.

Our follow-up study suggests that patients treated with behavior therapy were no different at outcome from those treated with somatic or alternate psychotherapies. Behavior modification, although not harmful, does not imply a better prognosis. Following operant conditioning patients have the same difficulties as others in regulation of eating and weight and interpersonal relationships. Behavior modification in no way prevents recurrence, for 6 of the 17 patients required repeat admission to hospital for weight loss.

One possible criticism of the present investigation is that the two groups, operant conditioning versus controls, were not similar on all parameters. The two groups were similar in terms of self-perception, personality, initial global score, and number of previous hospitalizations. However, those treated with operant conditioning were significantly lower in weight and younger at age of onset. Although degree of weight loss has not been a prognostic factor in previous outcome investigations, age of onset has in some (27,33,37,41), but not others (17). In our study, outcome results were not altered when weight, age, and age of onset were partialed out by analysis of covariance. A further deficiency may lie in the fact that our operant conditioning group was not "pure" because patients received a variety of psychotherapies after leaving hospital. Any differences between the two groups may have been neutralized by their posthospital experiences. Nevertheless, results from the current study suggest that behavior modification *per se* is not deleterious.

To summarize the role of behavioral modification, we can note that patients gain weight rapidly with this treatment and that, although not proving harmful, there is little evidence to suggest that it is superior to other conventional therapies. Not all patients with anorexia nervosa require or benefit from behavioral modification.

The present results indicate that most patients with anorexia nervosa improve. This is true regardless of the method of treatment employed. Similarly, some patients fare poorly after having received a variety of therapies. No one specific treatment whether behavioral, somatic, individual, or family psychotherapy has been shown to be superior in influencing outcome. An important finding in this regard was the objective determination of self-perceptual disturbances of body size. All patients with poor outcome who were tested were overestimators of body size. Not only were "overestimators" of body size more ill on follow-up, but they were also the group that showed less change in clinical status from the time of initial assessment. These results emphasize the importance of self-perceptual disturbances as prognostic indices in anorexia nervosa and also emphasize the need to delineate the factors involved in the disturbance in perception of one's size. For the anorexic patient this may reflect such phenomena as denial of illness and intolerance for one's body. Perhaps therapies directed to self-perception may be helpful to those patients experiencing only marginal improvement with conventional treatments.

ACKNOWLEDGMENTS

The authors acknowledge the assistance of Dr. Harvey Stancer, Mrs. D. Ratansi, Ms. Cathy Spegg, and the nursing staff of the Clinical Investigation Unit, Clarke Institute of Psychiatry.

REFERENCES

1. Ackerman, N. (1966): *Treating the Troubled Family.* Basic Books, New York.
2. Agras, W. S., Barlow, D. H., Chaplin, H. N., Abel, G. H., and Leitenberg, H. (1974): Behavior modification of anorexia nervosa. *Arch. Gen. Psychiatry,* 30:279–286.
3. Azerrad, J., and Stafford, R. L. (1969): Restoration of eating behavior in anorexia nervosa through operant conditioning and environmental manipulation. *Behav. Res. Ther.,* 7:165–171.
4. Bachrach, A. J., Erwin, W. J., and Mohr, J. P. (1965): The control of eating behavior in an anorexic by operant conditioning techniques. In: *Case Studies in Behavior Modification,* edited by L. P. Ullman and L. Krasner. Holt, Rinehart and Winston, New York.
5. Bhanji, S., and Thompson, J. (1974): Operant conditioning in the treatment of anorexia nervosa: A review and retrospective study of 11 cases. *Br. J. Psychiatry,* 124:166–172.
6. Bianco, F. J. (1972): Rapid treatment of two cases of anorexia nervosa. *J. Behav. Ther. Exp. Psychiatry,* 3:223–224.
7. Blinder, B. J., Freeman, D. M. A., and Stunkard, A. J. (1970): Behavior therapy of anorexia nervosa: Effectiveness of activity as a reinforcer of weight gain. *Am. J. Psychiatry,* 126:77–82.
8. Bliss, E. L., and Branch, E. H. H. (1960): *Anorexia Nervosa.* Hoeber, New York.
9. Browning, C. H., and Miller, S. I. (1968): Anorexia nervosa: A study in prognosis and management. *Am. J. Psychiatry,* 124:1128–1132.
10. Bruch, H. (1970): Changing approaches to anorexia nervosa. *Int. Psychiatr. Clin.,* 7:3–24.
11. Bruch, H. (1973): *Eating Disorders.* Basic Books, New York.
12. Bruch, H. (1974): Perils of behavior modification in treatment of anorexia nervosa. *J.A.M.A.,* 239:1418–1422.
13. Canadian Average Weights for Height, Age and Sex (Pamphlet) (1954), Nutrition Division of the Department of National Health and Welfare, Ottawa.
14. Crisp, A. H. (1965*a*): Clinical and therapeutic aspects of anorexia nervosa—a study of 30 cases. *J. Psychosom. Res.,* 9:67–77.
15. Crisp, A. H. (1965*b*): Some aspects of the evolution, presentation and follow-up of anorexia nervosa. *Proc. R. Soc. Med.,* 58:814–820.
16. Crisp, A. H., and Kalucy, R. S. (1974): Aspects of the perceptual disorder in anorexia nervosa. *Br. J. Med. Psychol.,* 47:349–361.
17. Dally, P. (1969): *Anorexia Nervosa.* Grune & Stratton, New York.
18. Duncan, D. B. (1955): Multiple range and multiple F tests. *Biometrics,* 11:1–42.

19. Elkin, M., Hersen, M., Eisler, R. M., and Williams, J. G. (1973): Modification of caloric intake in anorexia nervosa: An experimental analysis. *Psychol. Rep.*, 32:75–78.
20. Farquharson, R. F., and Hyland, H. H. (1966): Anorexia nervosa: The course of 15 patients treated from 20 to 30 years previously. *Can. Med. Assoc. J.*, 94:411–419.
21. Feighner, J. P., Robins, E., Guze, S. B., Woodruff, R. A., Jr., Winokur, G., and Munoz, R. (1972): Diagnostic criteria for use in psychiatric research. *Arch. Gen. Psychiatry*, 26:57–63.
22. Frazier, S. H. (1965): Anorexia. *Dis. Nerv. Syst.*, 26:155–159.
23. Frisch, R. E., and McArthur, J. W. (1974): Menstrual cycles: Fatness as a determinant of minimum weight for height necessary for their maintenance or onset. *Science*, 185:949–951.
24. Garfinkel, P. E., Kline, S. A., and Stancer, H. C. (1973): Treatment of anorexia nervosa using operant conditioning techniques. *J. Nerv. Ment. Dis.*, 157:428–433.
25. Garner, D. M., Garfinkel, P. E., Stancer, H. C., and Moldofsky, H. (1976): Body image disturbances in anorexia nervosa and obesity. *Psychosom. Med.*, 38:327–336.
26. Gull, W. W. (1874): Anorexia nervosa. Translation. *Clin. Soc. Lond.*, 7:22–28.
27. Halmi, K., Broadland, G., and Loney, J. (1973): Prognosis in anorexia nervosa. *Ann. Intern. Med.*, 78:907–909.
28. Halmi, J. A., Powers, P., and Cunningham, S. (1975): Treatment of anorexia nervosa with behavior modification. *Arch. Gen. Psychiatry*, 32:93–96.
29. Hurst, A. (1939): Discussion on anorexia nervosa. *Proc. Roy. Soc. Med.*, 32:744–745.
30. Kay, D. W. K., and Leigh, D. (1954): The natural history, treatment and prognosis of anorexia nervosa, based on a study of 38 patients. *J. Ment. Sci.*, 100:411–431.
31. Leitenburg, H., Agras, W. S., and Thomson, L. E. (1968): A sequential analysis of the effect of selective positive reinforcement in modifying anorexia nervosa. *Behav. Res. Ther.*, 6:211–218.
32. Morgan, H. G., and Russell, G. F. M. (1975): Value of family background and clinical features as predictors of long-term outcome in anorexia nervosa: Four-year follow-up study of 41 patients. *Psychol. Med.*, 5:355–371.
33. Rowland, C. F. (1970): Anorexia nervosa—a survey of the literature and review of thirty cases. *Int. Psychiatr. Clin.*, 7:37–137.
34. Russell, G. F. M. (1970): Anorexia nervosa: Its identity as an illness and its treatment. In: *Modern Trends in Psychological Medicine*, 2, edited by J. H. Price. Butterworths, London.
35. Russell, G. F. (1973): The management of anorexia nervosa. Symposium on Anorexia Nervosa and Obesity presented at the meeting of the Royal College of Physicians. Publication #42, Edinburgh.
36. Sainsbury, P., and Kreitman, N. (1963): *Methods of Psychiatric Research. An Introduction for Clinical Psychiatrists.* Oxford University Press, London.
37. Seidensticker, J. F., and Tzagournis, M. (1968): Anorexia nervosa—clinical features and long term follow-up. *J. Chronic Dis.*, 21:361–367.
38. Selvini, M. P. (1970): Anorexia nervosa. In: *The World Biennial of Psychiatry and Psychotherapy*, edited by S. Arieti. Basic Books, New York.
39. Slade, P. D., and Russell, G. F. M. (1973): Awareness of body dimensions in anorexia nervosa: Cross-sectional and longitudinal studies. *Psychol. Med.*, 3:188–199.
40. Stunkard, A. (1972): New therapies for the eating disorders: Behavior modification of obesity and anorexia nervosa. *Arch. Gen. Psychiatry*, 26:391–398.
41. Theander, S. (1970): Anorexia nervosa: A psychiatric investigation of 94 female patients. *Acta Psychiatr. Scand.* [*Suppl.*], 214.
42. Thoma, H. (1967): *Anorexia Nervosa*, translated by G. Brydone. International Universities Press, New York.
43. Williams, E. (1958): Anorexia nervosa: A somatic disorder. *Br. Med. J.*, 2:190–195.

Anorexia Nervosa, edited by
R. A. Vigersky. Raven Press,
New York © 1977

Anorexia Nervosa: Clinical and Metabolic Observations in a Successful Treatment Plan

Joseph A. Silverman

Department of Pediatrics, Columbia University College of Physicians and Surgeons, and Babies Hospital, The Children's Medical and Surgical Center of New York at the Columbia-Presbyterian Medical Center, New York, New York 10032

INTRODUCTION

In July 1684, an 18-year-old English girl developed amenorrhea apparently from "a multitude of cares and passions of her mind." Subsequently her appetite began to abate, and her digestion deteriorated. Over the next 2 years, she lost more weight and developed fainting spells.

Two years later, in the "last degree of a marasmus," she sought help from Dr. Richard Morton. Shocked by her appearance, he described her as follows: "I do not remember that I did ever in all my practice see one, that was conversant with the living so much wasted with the greatest degree of a consumption (like a skeleton only clad with skin), yet there was no fever, but on the contrary a coldness of the whole body; no cough, or difficulty of breathing, nor an appearance of any other distemper of the lungs or of any other entrail. . . . Only her appetite was diminished and her digestion uneasy, with fainting fits which did frequently return upon her." Morton treated her with salts, waters, and tinctures; however, she would not cooperate and lost more weight. About 3 months later, she died during a fainting fit.

In his text, he described this girl in a chapter on so-called nervous consumptions. He properly concluded that this disease, now misnamed anorexia nervosa, "does almost always proceed from sadness and anxious cares" (5). Morton thus is responsible for describing the first case of anorexia nervosa in the medical literature. More importantly, about 160 years before the birth of Freud, he correctly stated that the etiology was psychiatric.

Today, 290 years after this young woman's death, we are still attempting to understand this puzzling illness. To study this disease, investigators organized a program 10 years ago in New York City at Babies Hospital, the pediatric wing of the Columbia-Presbyterian Medical Center. A special unit was set up in which children with anorexia nervosa could be treated in hospital. Over the past decade, 65 anorexic patients were admitted to this unit by a pair of physicians, one a psychiatrist-psychoanalyst, the other a pediatrician. After discharge from the hospital, the patients were treated regularly in follow-up by these same doctors. No substitute, ancillary, or intermediary personnel were used in the treatment of our patients. Presented herewith are data derived from our study.

MEDICAL HISTORIES

The histories in all of our patients were surprisingly similar (Table 1). In each case, the patient was somewhat overweight and was chided or teased by parents, relatives, teachers, or peers. A systematic program of strict food avoidance resulted, which culminated in considerable weight loss. Subsequent cachexia, bizarre behavior, and metabolic changes ensued. Early weight loss was often ignored or not noted by the family. Those parents who were concerned and reported such losses to their physicians often received reassurance that their children were healthy. Only after the onset of frank cachexia or markedly aberrant behavior were the patients referred to me. In addition to weight loss and behavioral problems, amenorrhea was the universal presenting symptom of the post-menarchic female.

TABLE 1. *Historical data of 65 patients with anorexia nervosa*

A.	Sex: female, 59; male, 6
B.	Race: Caucasian, 64; Oriental, 1
C.	Religion: Jewish, 27; Roman Catholic, 22; Protestant, 15; none, 1
D.	Social class: upper, 16; middle, 45; lower, 4
E.	Residence: suburban, 54; urban, 10; rural, 1
F.	Family history of emotional illness: 32 (49%)
G.	Age at onset of anorexia nervosa: 9–20 years
H.	Age of presentation: 10–21 years
I.	Interval between onset and presentation: 2–30 months
J.	Intellectual ability: average, 60 (IQ 90–110); superior, 4 (IQ 110–130); below average, 1 (IQ under 90)
K.	Educational level of parents: college, 104[a]; high school, 22; primary school, 2
L.	Psychiatric aberration: behavioral disorder, 44; neurosis, 2; schizophrenia, 19
M.	Menarche prior to onset of illness: 43 of 59
N.	Amenorrhea: 100% of those who had reached menarche
O.	Constipation: 100%

[a] Patients 1 and 65 are sisters.

A typical patient is a teen-age girl who is depressed, weepy, hostile, frequently agitated, and in seemingly constant motion. She usually wears heavy sweaters and slacks not only to mask her emaciation, but also to keep warm. In addition to feelings of perpetual chilliness, all complain of severe constipation, some having bowel movements fortnightly or even once monthly (8).

PSYCHIATRIC ABERRATIONS

The characteristic pattern in all patients is overwhelming envy, greed, selfishness, narcissism, and a great desire to control the family and environment, by a strong-willed, compulsive child. Usually the parents state that the patient in the past had been a so-called model child, rarely causing the family any anxiety. Prior to the onset of her illness, the patient was usually cooperative, agreeable, and easy to get along with. At the time of hospitalization, most of the patients are acutely depressed. Schizophrenic behavior, which is rare in the pediatric patient with anorexia nervosa, is more commonly seen in the afflicted adult. However, over the past decade, we have seen an increasing number of schizophrenics, most of whom are in their teens (8).

INTELLECTUAL ABILITY

Typically the patients with anorexia nervosa are described as bright or even brilliant students. Often they are regarded by their teachers as intellectually outstanding. However, in our group, detailed psychometric evaluation revealed that this is not the case. Nearly all of our anorexics were found to have average intelligence. Almost universally, they were "overachievers" who compulsively studied many hours daily to acquire and maintain high marks (8). [Of historical interest is Morton's note (5) about his first patient whom he described as studying continually, night and day.]

PHYSICAL FINDINGS

Skin changes are the commonest physical abnormality noted in the anorexic (Table 2). The skin appears dark and dirty; texture is rough and resembles fine sandpaper; desquamation is common. Generalized hirsutism is frequent and consists of long, silken, lanugo-like hairs extensively found

TABLE 2. *Abnormalities noted on physical examination of 65 patients with anorexia nervosa*

Abnormality	No. affected	% Affected
A. Skin (hairiness, scaliness, dirtiness, desquamation)	57	88
B. Hypothermia (rectal temperatures <96.6°F)	55	85
C. Bradycardia (<60 beats per min)	52	80
D. Cachexia	47	72
E. Bradypnea (<14 breaths per min)	43	66
F. Hypotension (systolic pressures below 70 mm Hg)	34	52
G. Heart murmurs	25	38
H. Peripheral edema	15	23

over the trunk, extremities, and sometimes on the face. Loss of scalp hair is commonly noted.

Hypothermia occurs with rectal basal temperatures of 93.6 to 96.6°F. This is usually accompanied by bradycardia and bradypnea. Heart rates below 60 beats per minute and respiratory rates of 14 per minute or less occurred in 80 and 66% of our patients, respectively.

Cachexia was noted in 72% of our patients. A markedly skeletal appearance with tissue wasting and absence of buttocks is common. However, in those cases in which knowledgeable referring physicians made early diagnoses, cachexia was not seen.

Hypotension with systolic blood pressures of 70 mm Hg or below was noted in 52% of patients. In addition, transitory, functional, systolic heart murmurs were detected in 38%. Transitory unexplained peripheral pitting edema was noted in 23% of our patients.

All of the physical abnormalities described above are secondary to starvation and have been experimentally duplicated and reported in other studies (3). All of these abnormalities reverted to normal as patients recovered.

PHYSIOLOGIC AND METABOLIC ABNORMALITIES

Laboratory testing was performed in our patients to evaluate the effects of starvation on various physiologic and metabolic functions. The variety of

TABLE 3. *Abnormalities noted in laboratory tests of 65 patients with anorexia nervosa*

Abnormality	No. abnormal	% Abnormal
A. LH decrease	47	72
B. EKG	45	69
C. FSH decrease	44	68
D. Hypoplasia of bone marrow	43	66
E. Oral glucose tolerance test	41	63
F. Hypercarotenemia (normal: 50–150 μg%)	39	60
G. Hypovitaminosis A (normal: 50–150 μg%)	39	60
H. Plasma glucocorticoids (absence of diurnal variation)	38	58
I. Elevation of blood urea nitrogen (normal: 5–20 mg/100 ml)	29	45
J. Leukopenia (normal: >5,000 WBC/mm^3)	23	35
K. Decrease in xylose excretion (normal: 20–25% recovered in 5-hr urine)	23	35
L. Decrease in serum thyroxine iodine (normal: 3.2–6.4 μg%)	21	32
M. Decrease in serum triiodothyronine (T_3RIA) (normal: 110–230 ng/100 ml)	14[a]	60

[a] Of 23 tested.

different types of abnormalities found is summarized in Table 3. It should be noted that most of the laboratory aberrations described below are similar to those found in starvation produced either experimentally or in famines, wars, prisons, and concentration camps (1,3).

Electrocardiographic (EKG) Abnormalities

In 69% of our patients, grossly aberrant EKG patterns were seen. Abnormalities included sinus bradycardia, extremely low voltage, and low or inverted T waves in all standard leads except aVr and in all V leads. The greater the degree of wasting and cachexia, the more pronounced were the EKG abnormalities.

Endocrinologic Abnormalities

Evaluation of endocrine function included study of (a) pituitary function [follicle-stimulating hormone (FSH) and luteinizing hormone (LH)]; (b) thyroid function (thyroxine iodine, triiodothyronine, free thyroxine, and thyroxine-binding globulin); and (c) adrenal cortical function (plasma glucocorticoids, urinary ketosteroids, and urinary ketogenic steroids). Noteworthy in our data are gross abnormalities seen in levels of LH, FSH, glucocorticoids, triiodothyronine, and thyroxine iodine. In general, levels of free thyroxine, thyroxine-binding globulin, and urinary ketosteroids and ketogenic steroids were normal.

Very low and often undetectable levels of LH and FSH were noted in 72 and 68%, respectively, of our patients.

The usual diurnal variation of plasma glucocorticoids was absent in 58% of our patients.

Decreases in triiodothyronine levels were noted in 14 of 23 patients tested (or 60%). Thyroxine iodine levels were decreased in 32% of our patients.

Abnormalities of Hematopoiesis

Bone marrow hypoplasia and peripheral leukopenia were noted in 66 and 35%, respectively, of our patients. Similar findings have been described elsewhere (6).

Oral Glucose Tolerance Tests

In 41 of our patients (63%), abnormalities were detected. Approximately one-half had so-called diabetic curves; "flat-curves" were noted in the other half.

Hypercarotenemia and Hypovitaminosis A

Marked increases in serum carotene and very low serum levels of vitamin A were found in 60% of our patients (2,7).

Elevations of Blood Urea Nitrogen

Levels as high as 65 mg/100 ml occurred in 45% of our patients.

Xylose Excretion

Small amounts of xylose were recovered in the urine of 35% of our patients.

With recovery from starvation, most of the above-mentioned laboratory aberrations quickly return to normal. FSH and LH values, however, are exceptions; often, 6 to 12 months ensue before they reach normal ranges. In addition, amenorrhea may persist long after return of FSH and LH to so-called normal levels.

It is noteworthy that certain organ systems seem to function quite well despite the very severe semistarvation found in some of our patients. Table 4 demonstrates those determinations which were normal in this group.

TABLE 4. *Consistently normal laboratory data in 65 patients with anorexia nervosa*

A.	Plasma electrolytes (Na^+, K^+, Cl^-)
B.	Plasma total calcium and inorganic phosphorus
C.	Plasma proteins
D.	Plasma immunoglobulins (IgG, IgA, IgM)
E.	Blood acid-base equilibrium

DISCUSSION

Since Morton's account about his first patient, the medical literature has abounded with descriptive articles about anorexia nervosa. Over the past 290 years we have come to understand more and more about the metabolic changes which occur in starvation. However, one wonders how deeply we have scratched the surface of this entity. As our psychiatrist colleagues have plumbed the depths of the unconscious of these troubled patients, they have uncovered much. However, as their analysis unfolds, it seems obvious that there are few common denominators to explain the cause of the disease. Those of us who deal with the nonpsychiatric metabolic aspects of the disease have fared no better. Although we have described much, we understand little.

For example, although it is logical and perhaps even correct to ascribe marrow hypoplasia and leukopenia to malnutrition of the hematopoietic system, the explanation is insufficient. It is proper to ascribe amenorrhea to marked decreases in FSH and LH, but why do up to 50% of anorexics stop menstruating very early in their disease, and certainly long before significant weight loss occurs? Why do many anorexics in recovery states, with normal weights and normal gonadotropin levels, fail to menstruate? How does one explain the hypercarotenemia found in 60% of these patients? What is the source of the carotene? Are the thyroxine and triiodothyronine levels truly or spuriously low? What is the explanation for these low levels?

What causes the peripheral pitting edema seen in 23% of our patients? In no case was there evidence of the usual causes of edema, i.e., cardiac, renal, or hepatic disease or serum protein decrease. Is such fluid accumulation secondary to a combination of capillary permeability and prolonged standing? Why is xylose excretion so low? Is it due to atrophy of the small intestine secondary to malnutrition? Are biopsies and studies indicated? The mechanisms for the explanation of these problems remain to be described.

With the correction of nutrition and recovery of body weight, we know that most if not all of the abnormal laboratory data quickly revert to normal. If medications can be found to accelerate release of hormones such as FSH, LH, T4, or T3, or to stimulate hematopoiesis, or to decrease carotene levels, etc., can they, or more importantly, should they be used? Further studies and many patient years will be necessary before we have answers that will stand the test of time.

CLINICAL INPATIENT MANAGEMENT

All of our patients are admitted to a general medical ward at our institution. We believe that this milieu with its emotionally healthier patients and their parents is more salubrious to the patient with anorexia nervosa than is a psychiatric unit. In our ward, we attempt to create a protective nonpunitive environment free of the many stresses which have previously distracted and diverted our patients. The child is permitted limited contact with her parents, who may visit briefly on Sundays. She is also allowed to make a very short telephone call to them once nightly. It is our belief that a small amount of parent-child interaction (and its resultant problems) is beneficial to the treatment situation. The patient is relieved of decision making (particularly selection of food and clothing) and the struggles involved therein.

Although patients with anorexia nervosa have a seemingly omnipotent wish to dominate, they actually feel quite helpless. We provide them with total care. We recognize that they are sick and cannot take care of themselves. Until they can do so, we make all of their decisions. The patients are not permitted to act in a manipulative way toward the hospital staff which has been trained to parry such maneuvers.

In essence, it is our wish to create a situation in which reasonable and responsible adults completely take over the management of the child's life and affairs. We attempt to create for the patient a "realistic regression" in which she can concentrate her efforts on getting better.

Each child is supplied on admission with hospital garb. The patient is allowed neither clothing, possessions, nor privacy. She is placed in an individual cubicle in our large ward. Strict rules about fluid intake must be followed. The patient is told that the hospital requires her to drink a minimum of 1 liter/day of calorie-containing fluid, i.e., milk. Failure to comply with this regulation results in at least 3 days of make-up intravenous fluid therapy. We emphasize that the intravenous therapy is a hospital regulation for non-drinkers and is not to be construed as punishment. We make it clear to the patient on admission that her illness is serious and potentially fatal. We declare our intention of preventing disaster by maintaining adequate fluid intake.

We review with each patient all the metabolic abnormalities that have been uncovered in her work-up. We emphasize that in our experience all such abnormalities will either correct themselves or be corrected by us with her cooperation.

On the day of admission the child begins intensive psychiatric treatment. She is seen four times weekly by a fully trained, certified psychiatrist/psychoanalyst. The parents are also treated once weekly by the same psychiatrist. This routine continues throughout the hospital course and after discharge.

Under this regimen, patients cooperate quickly. After 24 hr of hospitalization, most children were drinking the required daily liter of fluids. After 1 week as inpatients, most were eating a standard diet of 2,500 cal/day.

In our experience, hospitalization is required for an average of 3 months. By this time, the children have corrected nearly all of their metabolic abnormalities and have made a sufficient start in their psychotherapy. At this point, eating and drinking habits are usually normal. The children are then released and followed medically and psychiatrically as outpatients. Since our hospital contains a unit which is part of the municipal school system, our patients receive daily individualized tutoring. As a result, upon release from the hospital, all have been able to return to their original classes at their own schools.

MORBIDITY AND MORTALITY

Case fatality rates in the range of 10 to 15% have been cited in the literature (4). In our series of 65 patients, there were no deaths.

Morbidity in our group of patients studied over almost 10 years was invariably psychiatric in nature and not physical. In each case it was related either to severe emotional disease on the part of the patient (i.e., schizophrenia) or to "sabotage" of our treatment program on the part of the parents, who, because of their own psychopathology, undermined the therapeutic regimen. As a result of such psychiatric morbidity, 9 of our 65 patients required more than one period of hospitalization.

CONCLUSION

This chapter has presented historical and clinical data noted in 65 anorexic patients studied over the past 10 years. Although much information has been gathered in the evaluation of this bizarre illness, more important questions are raised which reflect our lack of knowledge.

ACKNOWLEDGMENT

The author wishes to thank Kathryn F. Prescott, M.D., psychiatrist, who treated our patient group with great wisdom, compassion, and skill.

REFERENCES

1. Brozek, J., Wells, A., and Keys, A. (1946): Medical aspects of semistarvation in Leningrad (siege 1941–1942). *Am. Rev. Soviet Med.*, 4:70–86.
2. Dally, P. J. (1959): Carotenaemia occurring in a case of anorexia nervosa. *Br. Med. J.*, 5133:1333.
3. Keys, A., Brozek, J., Henschel, A., Mickelson, O., and Taylor, H. L. (1950): *The Biology of Human Starvation, Vols. 1 and 2.* University of Minnesota Press, Minneapolis.
4. Langford, W. S. (1972): In: *Pediatrics, 15 Ed.*, edited by H. L. Barnett and A. H. Einhorn, pp. 270–273. Appleton-Century-Crofts, New York.
5. Morton, R. (1694): *Phthisiologia: or a Treatise of Consumptions,* (English translation). Smith and Walford, London.
6. Pearson, H. A. (1967): Marrow hypoplasia in anorexia nervosa. *J. Pediatr.*, 71:211–215.
7. Pops, M. A., and Schwabe, A. D. (1968): Hypercarotenemia in anorexia nervosa. *J.A.M.A.*, 205:533–534.
8. Silverman, J. A. (1974): Anorexia nervosa: Clinical observations in a successful treatment plan. *J. Pediatr.*, 84(1):68–73.

Anorexia Nervosa, edited by
R. A. Vigersky. Raven Press,
New York © 1977

A Family Approach to Anorexia Nervosa: Study, Treatment, and Outcome

Bernice L. Rosman, Salvador Minuchin, Lester Baker, and Ronald Liebman

Philadelphia Child Guidance Clinic and Children's Hospital of Philadelphia, Philadelphia, Pennsylvania 19104

INTRODUCTION

In scientific explorations, significant phenomena emerge in relation to a given point of view. It is not only the interpretation of events which differs from one worker to another, but the very selection of events to be studied and the methods of study as well. This is particularly the case when a shift is occurring to novel conceptual models. The different kinds of data which result inevitably continue to reinforce and to shape the underlying conceptualizations in a given direction.

So it has been in the study of anorexia nervosa. Most of the studies of anorectics have been undertaken from a particular vantage point: that the pathology of anorexia is localized within the identified patient—moreover, that this pathology is related to earlier traumatic events in the life of the child which have left their marks in the form of distorted ego development or dysfunctional habits. Starting from this conceptual position, studies are "naturally" done by evaluating the individual person in therapy, testing, or experimental sessions. The information gathered has to do with the experience or personality of the individual patient during the anorectic period, although it may involve a reconstruction of the etiologically significant events through her eyes. The work of Bruch, for example, describes the sense of hopelessness and of being controlled that all of these children experience, as well as their ideations about food. Interpretations of symptomatic behavior may be developed out of observations of these children in the artificial context of the relationship with the therapist, or of the anorectic in a test situation. The information derived from such studies of the identified patient can be information only about her; this is also true of formulations about the anorectic's interpersonal relationships with mother or significant others.

However, since we approached anorexia nervosa from a different point of view—namely, that of locating the problem right in the system of familial relationships in which the patient is engaged—a different set of information needed to be collected, a different methodology needed to be employed.

Our first opportunities to collect important information about the anorectic in the family context came about in family therapy sessions. During these interviews the therapists were able to observe the patient, parents, and siblings together in interaction, to examine family members' responses to interventions which "tested" the strength or direction of certain interactive patterns, and to follow sequences of interactive events over a period of time. Following from the therapeutic assumption that interventions must be made in the interpersonal system and not the intrapersonal system, the field of observation had been opened up and new kinds of data emerged, some of them rather startling to see at first hand. For example, a girl who had hitherto presented as a helpless, hopeless person who felt dominated and invaded by her mother could be seen tyrannically manipulating her intimidated parents; a father whose dearest wish was to see his child eat and grow healthy again might be seen undercutting his wife's efforts in this direction.

Anorectic children were not the only psychosomatic patients engaged in these new kinds of therapeutic studies. "Brittle" diabetics and intractable asthmatics whose pediatricians had judged them to be psychosomatic (that is, their symptoms were exacerbated due to emotional stress) were being studied and treated in a similar way in a family therapy context. Comparisons of the observations across different symptomatologies crystallized in a set of formulations about the organization and functioning of these families, which we now call the conceptual model of the psychosomatogenic family. It was felt by the family clinicians that these generalizations about the families were consistent across the families and nonspecific with respect to the specific type of symptom. That is, there was not a diabetic "type," an asthma "type," or an anorectic "type" of family. What was proposed was a model for a type of family whose organization predisposed or supported somatic symptoms as an expression of emotional distress; further, that the somatic symptom bearer was not merely the recipient or expressor of emotional stress in the family but, in a dysfunctional kind of way, was the reliever of such stress.

TRANSACTIONAL CHARACTERISTICS OF THE PSYCHOSOMATIC FAMILY

Four characteristics of family functioning—enmeshment, overprotectiveness, rigidity, and lack of conflict resolution—could be observed in a family's behavior during family therapy sessions and later in the course of family interaction testing and family diagnostic interviews. Although none alone seemed sufficient, the cluster of these transactional patterns was felt to be characteristic of a family process that encourages somatization.

These, then, were the general structural and functional characteristics identified as typical of families with psychosomatic children. Although descriptive of a stress-inducing family context for a vulnerable child, the identification of these characteristics alone would have been inadequate as an "explanation" for the etiology and/or maintenance of the child's symptom from a family system point of view. A final concept, a fifth characteristic was needed to close the gap—to move from a linear model to an open systems or circular model. From a transactional point of view, the patient's symptom behavior acquired new significance as a regulator of the family system. More specifically, it had become apparent that the key factor supporting the symptom was the *child's involvement in parental conflict in such a way so as to detour, avoid, or suppress it.*

Within the psychosomatic type of family context, the symptomatic child was involved in parental conflict in particular ways. Parents unable to deal with each other directly might unite in protective concern over their sick child. A marital conflict might be transformed into a parental conflict over the patient and her management. The child might be recruited into taking sides by the parents, or might intrude herself as a mediator or helper.

The effectiveness of the symptom bearer in regulating the internal stability of the family seemed to reinforce both the continuation of the symptom and the peculiar aspects of the family organization in which it emerged.

A graphic representation of the open systems model of psychosomatic illness may be seen in Table 1. Note that there is no "beginning" or "end" point, that the system can be activated at any number of points, and has feedback mechanisms operative at several points. The highlights of this system are the ways in which child and other family members mutually regulate

TABLE 1. *Open systems model of psychosomatic disease*

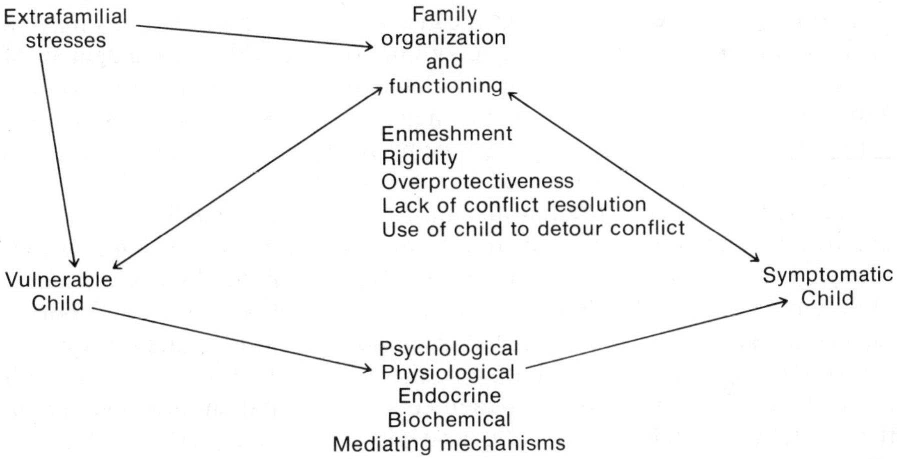

each other according to certain well-established family "rules" (family characteristics) and the transactional significance of the symptom behavior as part of this system.

TREATMENT APPROACH

With this theoretical framework we approached the work with the anorexia nervosa patients. This work can be characterized at three levels—an ecological model, a family systems model, and a specific family model.

The ecological model (4) implies a recognition that the behavior of individuals is shaped by the social context in which they exist, that this context changes over time and in response to external forces unrelated directly to the individual, and that the contextual elements impinge on and interact with the set of individual characteristics of the person. To produce change one can tackle the individual, the context, or the nature of their interaction, but it is necessary to know the relationship of all the elements involved.

The family systems model goes beyond this by specifying that the parts of the social context—in this case the collection of individual family members, as well as the structured units of two (dyads) we call parent-child, spouse-spouse, sibling-sibling, etc. within it—are so interconnected that changes in one part of the system (individual or dyad) both influence and are influenced by the other parts. Symptoms, psychological and/or somatic, are behaviors of individuals in this system which influence and are influenced by the network of relationships. Furthermore, homeostatic mechanisms operative in all families but which are exaggerated in dysfunctional families operate so that the symptom maintains the patterns of relationships within the family in some tolerable balance, and the pattern of relationship operates in such a way as to maintain the symptom. There is no single cause or effect—the whole pattern is both cause and effect. Interventions may be made at any point in the system according to the intervener's judgment of feasibility and effectiveness. Once this happens, however, the entire system must be considered and supported as new, more adaptive patterns emerge.

Finally, as mentioned before, a specific family model of psychosomatic illness in children was developed which identified (a) certain characteristics of the family context (enmeshment, rigidity, lack of conflict resolution, and overprotectiveness) and (b) the "economic" principle, which powered the symptom-maintaining system—the involvement of the child as a detourer of parental conflict who thereby protects the system. We will not elaborate further on this model here as it has been developed more fully elsewhere (5). It has been, however, definitive in shaping our treatment planning both in the goals of treatment (family oriented as well as patient oriented) and in the creation of specific therapeutic strategies and techniques.

TREATMENT PROGRAM

Inpatient Treatment

Inpatient treatment is deemphasized in a program such as ours. Slightly more than half of the patients reported here were admitted to a pediatric medical unit for a brief period of from 1 to 4 weeks. This is usually done for medical evaluation, to restore some of the most physically debilitated patients, and in some cases to test the effects of disengagement of the patient from the family (3). A higher proportion of the cases hospitalized were those treated in the earlier years of our program; currently we are more likely to begin treatment on an outpatient basis except when medical needs for care or differential diagnosis require inpatient admission. While in the hospital patients are placed on a behavioral paradigm in which participation in activities is made contingent on weight gain. This procedure may be as useful in facilitating management in reducing confrontations about eating as it is in reversing the eating behavior of the patients. We have found that the initiation of family therapy even while the patient is still in the hospital is successful in promoting normal behavior and weight gain (6).

Family Therapy

Family therapy begins in all cases with conjoint family sessions including patient, parents, and siblings. (Other relatives may be involved if they are part of the household and family system.) A typical first session will be held around lunch so that the observations may be made of the transactional patterns around the symptom, the ways in which family members are organized around the illness and reinforce it. The therapist is able to intervene directly into this system in the session and also to prescribe interactional "tasks" to be carried out at home which will begin to change the patterns of dysfunctional relationships. During the early stages of treatment therapeutic efforts are primarily directed toward symptom removal, not arbitrarily, but by using the resources of the family. This is important to improve the health of the patient, to reduce the family's preoccupation with the illness, and to relieve the patient of the burden of being the symptom bearer for the rest of the family. Symptom relief under such conditions when the family members experience themselves as movers in the treatment enhances motivation to continue therapy. Intermediate and final stages of the outpatient sessions focus on broader and yet more specific issues within the family. These include the marital problems of the parent couple, parenting problems within the family, individual problems of patient and siblings with each other or peers, etc. Modalities of treatment become more diverse during these stages, and therapists may employ couple therapy, individual psychotherapy, behavioral techniques, and other methods, as well as conjoint sessions. All treatment is conducted within a family frame of reference, however, with the constant awareness that changes in single family members or within dyads such as spouse couple or parent-child will affect and be affected by other family members. Therapists focus on the here-and-now experience of the family members and deploy their interventions so as to provide these people with new experiences of themselves and of each other as competent and individuated.

A study of the goals of treatment for the 53 cases reported here as formulated by the 16 different family therapists who treated them indicated a strong developmental trend. Although all therapists were concerned about disengaging the family, blocking the detouring of family conflicts through the child, reducing overprotectiveness and rigidity, and improving conflict resolution, there were age- or developmental stage–specific aims around which these strategies were organized. For the preadolescent patients, therapists were concerned about increasing parental effectiveness and strengthening the parental coalition. For midadolescent patients, the most numerous, the aims were to enhance autonomy and individuation of the patient and to prevent intrusion into the parent couple's domain by the children; for the older adolescents and young adults the aims were to effect successful separation from the family (college, job, and/or independent life). Complementing these different aims were differentiated uses of therapeutic techniques within the family framework [for a fuller discussion of these aims and strategies see 7].

PATIENT SAMPLE AND OUTCOME

The population reported on here, 53 cases, is essentially a pediatric population with a little stretch at the top to include the older adolescent and young adult group. One-quarter of the group (13) were preadolescents ranging in age from 9 to 12. The adolescents aged 13 to 16 represented 60% (31) of the patients seen, whereas the remaining 15% (9) fell in the age range 17 to 21. Male patients, 11% of the group, were similar to the females in diagnostic characteristics and course of treatment. Weight loss at time of admission ranged from 20 to 50% with a median of 30%. In addition to weight loss, the patients exhibited the pathogenic signs of anorexia nervosa: amenorrhea, denial of hunger, hyperactivity, delusional body image, and fear of fatness. Forty percent of the patients had been treated prior to referral to us, with individual treatment. About 20% had been previously hospitalized. All cases diagnosed as anorectic at Children's Hospital of Philadelphia within a 3-year period were referred to us for treatment with, as we shall see, a very low attrition. Approximately 20% of the cases were additional private referrals. The median interval between onset and beginning family treatment was 6 months (range 1 month to 3 years). The

TABLE 2. *Outcome results*

Category		No. of cases	Percent
	Pediatric assessment		
Recovered	Eating patterns normal, body weight stabilized within normal limits for height and age	43	86
Fair	Gained weight, still shows effects of illness (borderline, obesity, vomiting occasional)	4	8
Unimproved	Little or no change	3	6
	Clinical assessment		
Recovered	Satisfactory adjustment in family, as participant in school or at work, and in social and peer relationships	44	88
Fair	Adjustment in one or another of these areas unsatisfactory	3	6
Unimproved	Unable to function even at borderline levels and/or shows disturbances of behavior, thought, and affect	3	6

median course of treatment was 6 months. Three cases dropped out after two to three sessions (attrition of 6%). Follow-up evaluations were conducted at regular intervals. For the reported sample, follow-up times range from 3 months to 4 years (median 1 year after termination of treatment) and 25% have been followed for at least 2 years. Table 2 indicates the outcome results, based both on pediatric assessment of the anorexia and on a clinical assessment of psychosocial functioning in relation to home, school, and social adjustment.

Bruch (2) has suggested that it is relatively easy to treat younger patients successfully and that our dramatic outcomes are less significant on that account. That this is not necessarily the case is indicated by the rather mediocre outcomes for youngsters reported by Warren (8), Blitzer et al. (1), and even among Dr. Bruch's reported cases in the young adolescent age range (1973). We found that of the three unsuccessful outcomes in our sample, one occurred in each of our age groups, and the three fair outcomes clustered in the midadolescent group. Duration of illness before treatment was somewhat more important; two of the three dropouts from treatment and five of the seven unsuccessful or fair outcomes had been sick 1 year or longer prior to referral. These findings indicate the importance of preventing chronicity and the dangers of retaining patients in unsuccessful treatment situations while the symptom becomes more crystallized and the family more tightly organized around it.

There are many different conceptualizations concerning the cause and treatment of anorexia. For the most part, however, all agree that anorexia is an illness "inside" the anorectic patient. The abnormality is localized in the hypothalamus, the endocrine/metabolic system, or the early mother-child relationship.

We have put the locus of disease at the interphase between the anorectic patient and other family members. The open system model allows (indeed, prescribes) a different approach to the treatment of the anorectic and his family. This approach has been effective in 88% of our cases. It consists of family treatment of approximately 6 months' duration. Brief periods of hospitalization are employed when necessary. The anorectic symptomatology disappears 2 to 8 weeks after the beginning of treatment.

These results are a challenge to the sense of hopelessness that has accompanied follow-up studies on the anorectic patient. Without any doubt, when anorexia nervosa patients are treated within a year of the beginning of the illness with an open systems approach in the context of their family, they can be cured in a short period of time.

REFERENCES

1. Blitzer, J. R., Rollins, N., and Blackwell, A. (1961): Children who starve themselves: Anorexia nervosa. *Psychosom. Med.,* 23:369–383.
2. Bruch, H. (1973): *Eating Disorders.* Basic Books, New York.
3. Liebman, R., Minuchin, S., and Baker, L. (1974): An integrated treatment program for anorexia nervosa. *Am. J. Psychiatry,* 131:432–436.
4. Minuchin, S. (1970): The use of an ecological framework in the treatment of a child. In: *The Child and His Family,* edited by I. Anthony and C. Kaupernik, pp. 41–57. John Wiley & Sons, New York.
5. Minuchin, S., Baker, L., Rosman, B., Liebman, R., Milman, L, and Todd, T. (1975): A conceptual model of psychosomatic illness in children. *Arch. Gen. Psychiatry,* 32:1031–1038.
6. Rosman, B., Minuchin, S., and Liebman, R. (1975): Family lunch session: An introduction to family therapy in anorexia nervosa. *Am. J. Orthopsychiatry,* 45: 846–853.
7. Rosman, B., Minuchin, S., Liebman, R., and Baker, L. (1976): Input and outcome of family therapy in anorexia nervosa. *Successful Psychotherapy.* Brunner/Mazel, New York.
8. Warren, W. (1968): A study of anorexia nervosa in young girls. *J. Child Psychol. Psychiatry,* 9:27–40.

Anorexia Nervosa, edited by
R. A. Vigersky. Raven Press,
New York © 1977

The Effect of Cyproheptadine in Anorexia Nervosa: A Double-Blind Trial

Robert A. Vigersky and D. Lynn Loriaux

Reproduction Research Branch, National Institutes of Child Health and Human Development, National Institutes of Health, Bethesda, Maryland 20014

INTRODUCTION

Anorexia nervosa is an illness occurring predominantly in young women and characterized by weight loss, abnormal ideation about food and body image, secondary amenorrhea, and absence of other medical or psychiatric disease (6).

Studies in lower animals have long suggested that the hypothalamus controls eating behavior. Numerous recent studies have shed some light on the pathophysiology of anorexia nervosa. For instance, it has been shown that patients with anorexia nervosa have dysfunction of the hypothalamus (15). Others (3,7) have shown that serotoninergic pathways within the hypothalamus are involved in feeding behavior. These observations and those of Lavenstein et al. (8) showing that an antiserotoninergic drug, cyproheptadine, caused weight gain in children receiving the drug for asthma stimulated several investigators to use cyproheptadine to promote weight gain in underweight patients (2,5,8–10). The results have been generally successful. There have been no large studies on the effect of this drug in anorexia nervosa. We report here a double-blind study with cyproheptadine in a group of 24 patients with anorexia nervosa.

METHODS

Patients

All candidates for this study were admitted to a metabolic ward for complete medical and psychiatric evaluation. Most patients had been previously diagnosed as having anorexia nervosa by their referring physician. Psychopharmacologically active medications were discontinued at least 30 days prior to patient evaluation. The diagnosis was confirmed in each patient according to the criteria of Feighner et al. (6). Organic illness was ruled out by complete physical examination, hemogram, renal and liver function tests, urinalysis, X-rays of skull, sella turcica, and chest, electroencephalogram, electrocardiogram, and visual field measurements. A total of 26 consecutive patients, 25 women and 1 man, were then entered into the study. Before completion of the drug trial 2 women withdrew from the study, and the results reported below are on 24 patients.

Endocrine Testing

All studies were begun at 8 A.M. with the patients fasting. Growth hormone (GH), prolactin (PRL), luteinizing hormone (LH), follicle-stimulating hormone (FSH), free thyroxine (fT_4), and triiodothyronine (T_3) were determined as previously described (16). Normal values (mean $\pm$ SD) for plasma GH were 10.4 $\pm$ 12.2 ng/ml ($N = 10$) and for PRL were 16.4 $\pm$ 5.5 ng/ml ($N = 21$). In 7 regularly cycling women in the early follicular phase of the menstrual cycle (days 2 to 5), plasma LH was 7.9 $\pm$ 4.4 mIU/ml and plasma FSH was 15.3 $\pm$ 2.7 mIU/ml. Normal fT_4 was 1.5 $\pm$ 0.2 ng/dl ($N = 50$) and T_3 was 156 $\pm$ 30.0 ng/100 ml ($N = 47$). TSH was not detectable in 37 of 48 normal subjects and was less than 7.6 μU/ml in 11.

One or more provocative tests of GH release or suppression were performed in each patient. Arginine hydrochloride, 0.5 mg/kg, was infused intravenously over 30 min; regular insulin, 0.1 U/kg, was administered intravenously over 15 sec; L-DOPA, 500 mg, was administered orally. Pulse and blood pressure were monitored every 15 min during the insulin tolerance test.

Plasma TSH and PRL were measured at 0, 10, 20, 30, 45, 60, 120, and 180 min after the administration of 500 μg of thyrotropin-releasing hormone (TRH) given intravenously over 15 sec. Plasma LH and FSH were measured at -40, -30, -20, -10, 0, 5, 15, 30, 45, 60, 120, and 180 min after 10 μg of luteinizing hormone–releasing hormone (LHRH) given intravenously over 15 sec.

Drug Trial

Base-line weight was the mean of at least three determinations made at over a minimum of 2 weeks prior to beginning the drug trial. Upon discharge, patients were given either drug or placebo on a double-blind basis in a coded 4 mg capsule to be taken three times a day before meals for 8 weeks. Patients then were weighed weekly. After 8 weeks, the code was broken and their final weight recorded. Weight change was the difference between the mean base-line weight and final weight.

RESULTS

Thirteen patients received cyproheptadine and eleven patients received placebo during the study period. There were no side effects or adverse

TABLE 1. *Clinical data of drug vs placebo groups*

	N	Age (years)	Initial weight (kg)	% Below IBW	Duration of disease	Marital status (S/M)	Method of weight loss[a] (% of subjects) A	D	V	E
Drug	13	28.9 ± 3.4[b]	34.9 ± 2.0	33.9 ± 3.7	8.9 ± 2.4[c]	10/3	62	38	38	15
Placebo	11	19.4 ± 1.3	33.6 ± 1.5	37.8 ± 1.8	2.7 ± 0.6	11/0	91	9	9	36

[a] A, abstinence; D, drugs; V, vomiting; E, exercise.
[b] Mean ± SEM; $p < 0.05$.
[c] $p < 0.02$.

TABLE 2. *Results of double-blind administration of cyproheptadine to patients with anorexia nervosa*

	Patients (*N*)	Responders (*N*)	% Responders
Drug	13	4	31
Placebo	11	2	18

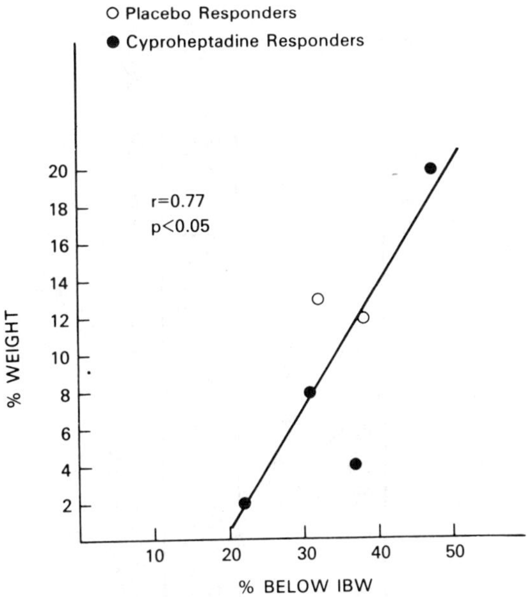

FIG. 1. Linear regression analysis of the severity of weight loss (% below IBW) vs the percent weight gain while receiving drug or placebo.

TABLE 3. *Clinical data of patients receiving cyproheptadine*

	Patients (N)	Age (years)	Initial weight (kg)	% Below IBW	Duration of disease	Marital status (S/M)	Method of weight loss[a] (% of patients)				Pulse	Blood pressure
							A	D	V	E		
Responders	4	22.7 ± 5.3[b]	36.3 ± 3.0	33.8 ± 4.9	5.2 ± 3.3	3/1	75	50	25	0	65 ± 2.2	85/54
Nonresponders	9	28.7 ± 4.3	35.3 ± 2.5	34.0 ± 5.1	10.5 ± 3.2	8/1	44	33	56	22	60.3 ± 2.5	92/57

[a] A, abstinence; D, diuretics; V, vomiting; E, exercise.
[b] Mean ± SEM.

TABLE 4. *Thyroid, prolactin, and growth hormone responses in patients receiving cyproheptadine*

	Responders ($N = 4$)	Nonresponders ($N = 9$)
Free T_4 (ng/dl)	1.4 ± 0.1[a]	1.4 ± 0.1
T_3 (ng/100 ml)	69.7 ± 9.6	97.0 ± 12.7
TSH (μU/ml)	3.3 ± 1.1	2.7 ± 0.6
% TSH response to TRH	378 ± 13	402 ± 93
Time of peak TSH after TRH (min)	38 ± 8	45 ± 5
Basal prolactin (ng/ml)	15.2 ± 0.9	20.7 ± 5.1
% PRL suppression with L-DOPA	63 ± 2	54 ± 11
% PRL rise with CPZ	466 ± 120	242± 49
% PRL rise with TRF	508 ± 223	411 ± 93
Time of peak PRL after TRF (min)	23 ± 8	40 ± 7
Basal GH (ng/ml)	54.2 ± 41.7	82.7 ± 41.4
% Rise to arginine	181 ± 91	1,625 ± 1,235
% Rise to insulin	67 ± 28	245 ± 91
% Rise to L-DOPA	352 ± 125	313 ± 135

[a] Mean ± SEM.

reactions to the drug. The clinical data for the two groups are shown in Table 1. The groups were not distinguishable on the basis of weight loss (percent below ideal body weight, IBW). However, the group that received the drug was significantly older ($p < 0.05$) and had been ill significantly longer ($p < 0.02$) than the placebo group. In addition, the methods employed to lose and maintain a low weight by each group were different. The use of drugs, diuretics, and/or laxatives, was more prevalent in the group receiving cyproheptadine, whereas exercise and abstinence were more common in the placebo group.

The results of the double-blind trial are shown in Table 2. Four patients (31%) who received cyproheptadine and two patients (18%) who received placebo had an increase in weight over 2 months. This difference in response is not statistically significant. The remaining patients did not gain weight or continued to lose weight. The weight gains in the four patients on drug were 2, 4, 8, and 20%, and in the placebo responders were 12 and 13%.

TABLE 5. *Responses to insulin-induced hypoglycemia in patients receiving cyproheptadine*

	Patients (N)	Basal blood glucose (mg/100 ml)	% Below basal glucose at nadir	% Below basal glucose at 90 min	% GH rise after insulin
Responders	4	69.5 ± 4.0[a]	72 ± 11	13 ± 9	67 ± 28
Nonresponders	9	64.9 ± 8.4	61 ± 4	33 ± 7	245 ± 91

[a] Mean ± SEM.

TABLE 6. *Gonadotropin response in patients receiving cyproheptadine*

	Patients (N)	Basal LH (mIU/ml)	% LH rise after LHRH	Time of peak LH after LHRH (min)	Basal FSH (mIU/ml)	% FSH rise after LHRH	Time of peak FSH after LHRH (min)
Responders	4	5.1 ± 0.42[a]	283 ± 103	53 ± 4	5.8 ± 1.6	138 ± 42	90 ± 16
Nonresponders	9	4.1 ± 0.6	330 ± 96	36 ± 6	6.1 ± 1.2	371 ± 115	109 ± 14

[a] Mean ± SEM.

The correlation of the weight gain to the severity of the disease is shown in Fig. 1. There is a significant correlation between the percent below IBW and the percent increase in weight in all patients (drug plus placebo) responding with a weight gain ($r = 0.77, p < 0.05$).

Clinical parameters of those patients responding to cyproheptadine ($N = 4$) and those not responding ($N = 9$) were compared (Table 3). These groups differed only in the method of achieving and maintaining weight loss. When the endocrine parameters of the two groups were compared, there was no significant difference in thyroid, gonadotropin, growth hormone, prolactin, or glucose indices (Tables 4 through 6). Similarly, there was no difference in either clinical or endocrine parameters when comparing all patients who gained weight ($N = 6$) to those who did not ($N = 18$).

DISCUSSION

The results of this study indicate that cyproheptadine did not promote weight gain in significantly more patients than did a placebo. Although our findings do not support those of several investigators who have found that cyproheptadine promoted weight gain in patients with a variety of illnesses such as irritable bowel syndrome (9) and asthma (2,5,8) and in otherwise healthy but chronically underweight subjects (11–14), patients with anorexia nervosa differ considerably from these groups since the "relentless pursuit of thinness" (4) is responsible for their weight loss. Benady (1) has reported successful treatment of anorexia nervosa with cyproheptadine in a single case, but to our knowledge, no double-blind study of the effect of cyproheptadine has previously been performed.

The reason for the failure of cyproheptadine to promote weight gain is not clear. The group receiving the drug was older and had a longer duration of disease compared to the placebo group and, thus, may have been more refractory to treatment. Moreover, although there was no difference in the pretreatment endocrine parameters between those who responded to the drug and those who did not, only one of the responding patients (25%) but five of the nonresponding patients (56%) were chronic vomiters. Thus, possible explanations for the failure of the drug in those not responding include its lack of absorption or abnormal metabolism in these patients. Because of the outpatient design and the lack of a suitable marker for compliance of the patients in taking the medication, the drug's absorption and metabolism could not be evaluated. It might be predicted that there would be low compliance in patients who are preoccupied with maintaining a low body weight and often do so in a surreptitious manner. Furthermore, since vomiting was a method of maintaining this low weight, the degree of drug absorption might have been highly variable. In light of these observations, the greater percentage of responders in the drug group could be more significant.

There was no apparent difference in any endocrine parameters in those who responded to drug compared to those who did not. Similarly, if all patients who gained weight (drug responders and placebo responders, $N = 6$) during the study period were compared to those who did not, there were no predictors of who would respond.

Since the data suggest that the drug group was weighted with more severely affected patients and there were more (though not statistically significant) responders in this group, we would recommend further trial of cyproheptadine on a double-blind basis either alone or in combination with other treatment modalities.

ACKNOWLEDGMENTS

We would like to thank Dr. Morton Rosenberg and Merck Sharp & Dohme for kindly supplying the cyproheptadine and matching placebo tablets.

REFERENCES

1. Benady, D. R. (1970): Cyproheptadine hydrochloride (Periactin) and anorexia nervosa: A case report. *Br. J. Psychiatry,* 117:681–682.
2. Bergen, S. S. (1964): Appetite stimulating properties of cyproheptadine. *Am. J. Dis. Child.,* 108:270–273.
3. Bruch, H. (1973): *Eating Disorders.* Basic Books, New York.
4. Chakrabarty, A. S., Pillai, R. V., Anand, B. K., and Singh, B. (1967): Effect of cyproheptadine on the electrical activity of the hypothalamic feeding centers. *Brain Res.,* 6:561–569.
5. Drash, A., Elliot, J., Langs, H., Lavenstein, A. F., and Cooke, R. E. (1966): Effect of cyproheptadine on carbohydrate metabolism. *Clin. Pharmacol. Ther.,* 7:340–346.
6. Feighner, J. P., Robins, E., Guze, S. B., Woodruff, R. A., Jr., Winokur, G., and Munoz, R. (1972): Diagnostic criteria for use in psychiatric research. *Arch. Gen. Psychiatry,* 26: 57–63.
7. Ghosh, M. N., and Parvathy, S. (1973): The effect of cyproheptadine on water and food intake and on body weight in the fasted adult and weanling rats. *Br. J. Pharmacol.,* 48: 328P–329P.
8. Lavenstein, A. F., Dacaney, E. P., Lasagna, L., and Van Metre, T. E. (1962): Effect of cyproheptadine on asthmatic children. *J.A.M.A.,* 180:912–916.
9. Mainguet, P. (1972): Effect of cyproheptadine on anorexia and loss of weight in adults. *Practitioner,* 208:797–800.
10. Noble, R. E. (1969): Effect of cyproheptadine on appetite and weight gain in adults. *J.A.M.A.,* 209:2054–2055.
11. Pawlowski, G. T. (1975): Cyproheptadine: Weight-gain and appetite stimulation in essential anorexia patients. *Curr. Ther. Res.,* 18:673–678.
12. Penfold, J. L. (1971): Effect of cyproheptadine and a multivitamin preparation on appetite stimulation, weight gain and linear growth. *Med. J. Aust.,* 1:307–310.
13. Silbert, M. V. (1971): The weight gain effect of Periactin in anorexic patients. *S. Afr. Med. J.,* 45:374–377.
14. Silverstone, T., and Schuyler, D. (1975): The effect of cyproheptadine on hunger, caloric intake and body weight in man. *Psychopharmacologia,* 40:335–340.
15. Vigersky, R. A., Loriaux, D. L., Andersen, A. E., and Lipsett, M. B. (1976): Anorexia nervosa: Behavioural and hypothalamic aspects. *Clin. Endocrinol. Metab.,* 5:517–535.
16. Vigersky, R. A., Loriaux, D. L., Andersen, A. E., Mecklenburg, R. S., and Vaitukaitis, J. L. (1977): Delayed pituitary response to LRF and TRF in patients with anorexia nervosa and with secondary amenorrhea associated with simple weight loss. *J. Clin. Endocrinol. Metab.,* 43:893–900.

Anorexia Nervosa, edited by
R. A. Vigersky. Raven Press,
New York © 1977

The Use of Amitriptyline in Anorexia Nervosa

Herbert L. Needleman and Deborah Waber

*Department of Psychiatry, Children's Hospital Medical Center,
Boston, Massachusetts 02115*

INTRODUCTION

The pathogenesis of the anorexia nervosa syndrome remains unclear and choice of therapy in debate. In addition to food aversion, weight loss, and amenorrhea, many patients display signs of motor and speech retardation and express feelings of sadness. This suggests to us that a tricyclic antidepressant, amitriptyline, might be of benefit in the management of the syndrome. We report here the results of a clinical trial of this drug in six consecutive patients with anorexia nervosa in an inpatient pediatric setting.

METHODS

The patients were five young women between the ages of 11 and 17 years, and one 16-year-old male. All had severe aversion to food, cold extremities, and weight loss greater than 20%. The duration of illness was between 3 and 13 months. All of the females were amenorrheic. After the patients were admitted to the pediatric ward, routine base-line studies were obtained, and the patients begun on oral amitriptyline in individually determined dose. In general, the drug was started at a low level and increased in 20- to 25-mg increments. The daily dose varied between 75 and 150 mg. Patients consulted with a dietician daily, were asked to keep a diet diary, and encouraged, but not coerced, to increase their intake of food. No systematic psychotherapy or behavior modification was employed.

RESULTS

Results are summarized in Fig. 1 and Table 1. All patients began to gain weight between the 6th and 12th day of drug treatment. The change in weight was always preceded by a rather striking brightening of mood, increased warmth of extremities, and noticeable improvement in social relationships. At the same time, eating behavior was noted by the ward staff to be different, and attitudes toward food were reported by the patients as changed. Patients frequently made such statements as: "I don't think

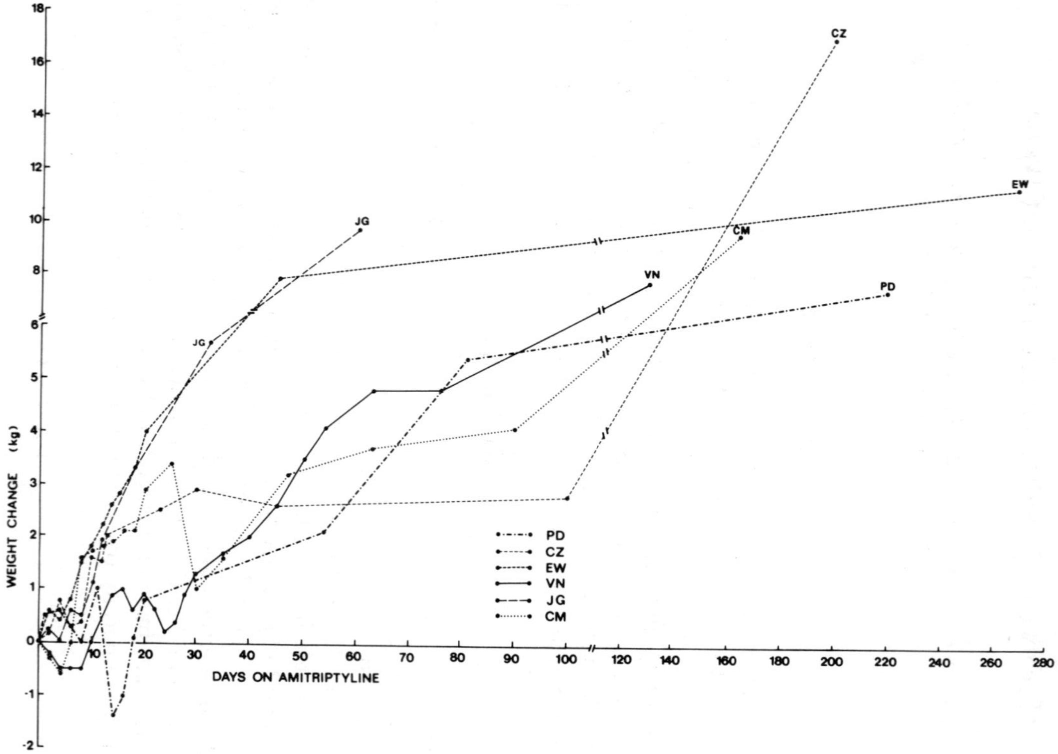

FIG. 1. Results of amitriptyline therapy in 6 patients with anorexia nervosa.

TABLE 1. *Clinical data on 6 patients with anorexia nervosa treated with amitriptyline*

Patient	Duration of illness (months)	Initial weight (kg)	Pre-drug weight (kg)	Loss kg (%)	Maximum weight gain
CZ	8	59.1	39.7	21.4 (36%)	2.8 kg/100 days 9.6 kg/175 days 16.9 kg/200 days
EW	13	40.0	28.2	11.8 (29%)	11.7 kg/80 days 11.35 kg/270 days
JG	6	61.4	48.5	13.9 (23%)	5.7 kg/32 days 9.6 kg/68 days
CM	7	53.2	32.5	20.7 (39%)	4.1 kg/93 days 9.5 kg/165 days
PD	3	54.6	42.6	12.0 (22%)	5.8 kg/120 days 7.4 kg/220 days
VN	12	27.7	22.0	5.7 (21%)	4.8 kg/76 days 7.7 kg/130 days

about food as much," or "Eating is not as big a deal," or "Food tastes good." Time taken to select menus and eat meals shortened noticeably.

Four of the patients in this study were noted on admission to have slow speech, immobility of the lower face, rigidity of the shoulders, and a small gait. These behaviors were noticeable enough to suggest a Parkinsonian-like movement disorder. The motor behavior improved after drug administration, concomitant with weight gain.

Three patients had intercurrent illnesses while on medication that led to temporary weight loss. One (PD) had a febrile illness with abdominal pain, vomiting, anorexia, and rapid weight loss. After recovery from this illness and discharge, she continued to gain weight. At 220 days after onset of drug therapy, she had gained 7.4 kg (13.5% of the initial weight). Two patients (VN and CM) had brief bouts of diarrhea, which occurred while other patients on the ward had gastroenteritis. One of these (CM) was taken off amitriptyline when the diarrhea began. After 20 days off drug she began to decrease her intake, appear sad, and withdraw from friends. The drug was restarted, and after 14 days she again began to gain weight and seek out her friends.

Three patients (EW, CZ, and JG) discontinued medication after discharge and continued to gain weight. The other patients have been continued on amitriptyline and also continued to gain weight.

DISCUSSION

The rather prompt response of patients given amitriptyline raises a number of questions for consideration.

Is this sample representative of the clinical syndrome of anorexia nervosa? The patients reported here were not a selected sample, but were consecutive admissions to the pediatric division. The diagnosis was first made by the attending physician and confirmed by the psychiatric consultant. All of the patients demonstrated motor and speech retardation, expressed feelings of sadness, and displayed compulsive behavior patterns. The length of illness ranged from 3 to 13 months; no long-term patients were treated in this study. This sample may then represent relatively recent cases of anorexia in which depressive symptomatology predominates.

Were factors other than the drug responsible for their improvement? Undoubtedly, hospitalization and removal from the family struggles had an impact on these patients. The patients were treated on a general pediatric ward, in contact with patients with a variety of medical illnesses. Unlimited family visiting was allowed; the milieu was generally supportive and nonrestrictive; and discussions of intrapsychic or familial conflict were avoided.

Significant stress between parents and patient were noted in many but not all of the families. As the patients' physical, emotional, and behavioral status improved, the quality of parent-offspring interaction often became less tense and more supportive. This suggests to us that much of the familial distress often occurs as an effect rather than a cause of the syndrome.

Patients were allowed free activity, given dietary counseling, but allowed to choose their own menus. Although weight gain or increased caloric intake was greeted with approval, we attempted to minimize the amount of attention given to this. Two of the patients had previous admissions to other hospitals and one had been in psychotherapy for 6 months prior to amitriptyline therapy. During this time their condition continued to decline.

Was the drug effect due to nonspecific appetite stimulation, or did it reflect a more specific impact on the disease? Although weight gain was the outcome variable given closest attention, changes in mood, sociability, and motor behavior were equally noticeable and often preceded the change in eating. It was often possible to predict when a patient would begin to gain weight by observing increased mobility of the face and trunk, speed and length of gait, and increased interest in other patients.

A number of studies have demonstrated evidence of hypothalamic dysfunction in patients with anorexia nervosa (1–6), and some investigators have suggested that central neurotransmitter function is disturbed.

Johanson and Knorr (3) remarked on the similarity of behavior between anorectic patients and those with Parkinson's disease, noting that some display rigid, obsessive-compulsive, often stereotyped behavior. They treated six patients with levodopa and found improvement in four. This report suggests that central dopamine dysfunction could be a factor in anorexia nervosa.

Although other factors attendant to hospitalization of our patients may have influenced the course of their illness, the prompt improvement in temperature regulation, motor behavior, speech, and appetite after 6 to 12 days of amitriptyline suggests that a more specific effect of this drug on hypothalamic catecholamine function might account for these combined changes.

We are currently studying, under double-blind conditions, a group of anorectic patients to identify the relative contribution of amitriptyline to outcome as measured by a number of physical, physiological, and behavioral indices.

REFERENCES

1. Barry, V. C., and Klawans, H. L. (1976): On the role of dopamine in the pathophysiology of anorexia nervosa. *J. Neural Transm.*, 38:107–122.
2. Boyar, R. M., Katz, J., Finkelstein, J. W., Kapen, S., Weiner, H., Weitzman, E. D., and Hellman, L. (1974): Anorexia nervosa; immaturity of the 24-hour luteinizing hormone secretion pattern. *N. Engl. J. Med.*, 291:861–865.
3. Johanson, A. J., and Knorr, N. J. (1974): Treatment of anorexia nervosa by levodopa. *Lancet*, 1:591.

4. Mawson, A. R. (1974): Anorexia nervosa and the regulation of intake: A review. *Psychol. Med.,* 4:289–308.
5. Mecklenburg, R. S., Loriaux, D. L., Thompson, R. H. et al. (1974): Hypothalamic dysfunction in patients with anorexia nervosa. *Medicine* (*Baltimore*), 53:147–159.
6. Wakeling, A., and Russell, G. F. M. (1970): Disturbances in the regulation of body temperature in anorexia nervosa. *Psychol. Med.,* 1:30–39.

Anorexia Nervosa, edited by
R. A. Vigersky. Raven Press,
New York © 1977

L-DOPA as Treatment for Anorexia Nervosa

Ann J. Johanson and Norman J. Knorr

Departments of Pediatrics and Psychiatry, University of Virginia Medical School, Charlottesville, Virginia 22904

INTRODUCTION

Anorexia nervosa is a disorder predominantly of adolescent girls occurring with variable frequency (3), significant morbidity, and occasional mortality. The incidence has reportedly increased significantly in recent years (9) and resulted in a proliferation of information regarding therapeutic approaches (2,8) and associated endocrine abnormalities (6,7), among other aspects of the disorder. The constant features of severe weight loss, anorexia (which is sometimes obscured by hyperphagia or apparently normal eating behavior in association with surreptitious vomiting), oligo- or amenorrhea (in females), and refractoriness to therapeutic attempts are associated with variable but frequent concomitants of disturbed family dynamics, obsessional-compulsive personality, exceptional school performance, and abnormal endocrine function.

Hypothalamic dysfunction in anorexia nervosa has been well documented by Mecklenburg et al. (6) as evidenced by impaired thermoregulation, partial diabetes insipidus, and insulin sensitivity. The observed endocrine abnormalities, i.e., depressed gonadotropins and gonadal steroid levels, abnormally low T_3 levels (7), and occasionally elevated growth hormone and prolactin levels (6) are also of hypothalamic origin since responses to hypothalamic releasing hormones are normal or consistent with lack of stimulation, and the abnormalities revert to normal in most instances with restoration of normal weight.

Many and varied therapeutic approaches have met with frustratingly poor results and occasional disastrous consequences (1). Classic approaches have been psychotherapeutic and more recently behavior modification. Drugs selected to treat isolated associated symptomatology, e.g., depression with phenothiazines or anorexia with cyproheptadine, have helped some patients.

Our interest in a therapeutic trial of 3,4-L-dihydroxydopamine (L-DOPA), the immediate precursor of dopamine, was occasioned by several observations. Individuals with anorexia nervosa frequently have rigid, obsessive-compulsive, stereotyped behavior that involves eating and movement and the development of rituals. Although hyperactivity has been described in some with anorexia nervosa, our experience has been more often that weakness and inactivity predominate. These features are reminiscent of similar manifestations of Parkinson's disease, which results from destruction of the dopaminergic nigrostriatal tracts. L-DOPA treatment of parkinsonism has been greatly successful. Additional related evidence for the suggestion that brain dopamine deficiency may exist in anorexia nervosa has been obtained by selective destruction of the nigrostriatal dopamine tracts in rats by the intracerebral injection of 6-hydroxydopamine with resultant adipsia and aphagia (11). Hyperactivity was observed as an early phenomenon, followed later by hypokinesia, as the rats were sustained artificially. It therefore seemed possible to us that with evidence of hypothalamic disturbance and these observations, brain dopamine metabolism may be impaired, and attempted restoration by L-DOPA was a logical approach.

STUDIES AND RESULTS

We have treated in the Clinical Research Center nine individuals (eight females, one male) 13 to 22 years old with low doses of L-DOPA for periods of 16 to 27 days. Total treatment periods have been up to 4 months. Family constellation and relevant characteristics of the patients are seen in Table 1. More anorexic patients were first children than might be expected. Obvious parental discord was not frequent. All but one patient were very good students. Most, contrary to many reports, were weak and relatively inactive, presumably consequent to their marked weight loss.

Pertinent laboratory data are shown in Table 2. One girl had a questionable parietal focus on EEG. Other EEGs performed were interpreted as normal. All skull X-rays were normal. Serum cholesterols were normal. Serum T_4 as T_4 iodine or by the Murphy-Pattee method was normal in most cases. Serum T_3 by radioimmunoassay on the one occasion it was performed was decreased. Urinary 17-OH steroid excretion in response to metyrapone was normal. Maximal growth hormone responses to pharmacologic stimuli were very high except in two individuals, one of whom was subsequently shown to have hypopituitarism with growth hormone deficiency (4). Integrated concentrations (ICs) of growth hormone (10) in two patients were high. ICs of prolactin in the same two patients were consistent with normal isolated values. Serum or urine gonadotropins were in the very low normal adult or hypogonadotropic range (5).

The dose of and response to L-DOPA are shown in Table 3. Prior to receiving L-DOPA, three patients were given a placebo for 6 to 8 days during which time there was insignificant (<0.5 kg) weight gain, or weight loss. All patients at the time of treatment with placebo or L-DOPA had been water and electrolyte repleted so that weight changes were not a reflection of rehydration. The initial dose given was 200 to 500 mg/day, and this was incrementally increased to final doses of 1 to 3 g/day.

TABLE 1. *Patient characteristics*

Patient	Sex	Age at treatment (years)	Sib rank	Parents' relationship	School performance	Menarche	Activity
1	F	13	—[a]	—	—	—	Increased
2	F	21	2/2	Intact	Very good	11	Decreased
3	F	13	1/2	Intact	Very good	$12^{2}/_{12}$	Increased
4	F	17	1/5	F. on welfare	Average	14	Normal
5	F	13	2/2	Intact	Excellent	None	Normal
6	F	22	1/1 (twin)	Divorced	Excellent	—	Decreased
7	F	$14^{8}/_{12}$	2/4	M. nurse; F. truck driver	Excellent	$12^{1}/_{2}$	Increased
8	F	21	1/3	Both professional	Excellent	14	Decreased
9	M	$15^{3}/_{12}$	1/2	Divorced	Excellent	—	Decreased

[a] Information not available.

TABLE 2. *Endocrine and other laboratory studies*

Patient	EEG	Skull X-ray	Cholesterol (mg/dl)	T_4 (μg/dl)	Urinary 17-OH steroid response to metyrapone	Growth hormone (ng/ml) maximum	Prolactin (ng/ml) IC[a]	FSH (mIU/ml)	LH (mIU/ml)
1	—[b]	—	—	—	—	—	—	—	—
2	Normal	Normal	—	3.2 (4–8)	Normal	21	—	5.5	2
3	Normal	Normal	—	10.5 (5–14) T_3 38% (25–35%)	Normal	29	—	1.5	1
4	Normal	Normal	260	15 (5–14)	Normal	21	—	5.5	2
5	Left parietal focus	Normal	182	8.6 (5–14)	Normal	3	—	1.5	1
6	—	Normal	185	7.3 (5–14) T_3 30% (25–35%)	Normal	>40	—	—	—
7	—	Normal	158	4.9 (5–14) T_3 29% (25–35%)	—	25 (IC)	12	1	4
8	Normal	—	—	—	—	5.3	—	5 IU/d (urine)	2 IU/d (urine)
9		Normal	199	8.8 (4–12) T_3 94 (110–230)	Normal	8 (IC)	16	1.2	4

[a] IC, integrated concentration.
[b] Data not available.

TABLE 3. *Response to L-DOPA therapy*

Patient	Age at treatment (years)	Maximum weight:age	Pretreatment weight (lb)	Dose L-DOPA (g)	Response	Outcome
1	13	92:	58	0.2–0.6	↑ 5.5 kg/21 d	Normal weight after 1 year; well after 3 years
2	21	130:18	79	0.2–1.2	↑ 4.1 kg/27 d	Menses 2.5 years after initial weight gain; normal weight for height
3	13	105:12$^{5}/_{12}$	63	0.2–1.2	↑ 3 kg/21 d	Menses 5 months after weight gain; normal weight 3 years later
4	17	130:14	75	0.2–1.2	↑ 5.3 kg/24 d	Remains underweight, amenorrheic, withdrawn from society
5	13	84:9$^{1}/_{2}$	60	0.2–1.0	No change	Recovered normal pituitary function at 15$^{9}/_{12}$; +12 cm in 1 year; stage 3 sex development; normal gonadotropins
6	22	150:15	64	0.4–3.0	↓ 1 kg/18 d	Remains anorexic, underweight, amenorrheic
7	14$^{8}/_{12}$	115:13$^{8}/_{12}$	71	1.0	↑ 0.7 kg/14 d	Gained 65 lb in 1 year; menses 10 months
8	21	105:16(?)	76	0.5–1.5	↑ 1 kg/18 d	Remains markedly underweight, amenorrheic
9	15$^{3}/_{12}$	162:13	95	0.5–1.5	↑ 3.5 kg/19 d	+25 lb in 6 months; normal weight 1 year later

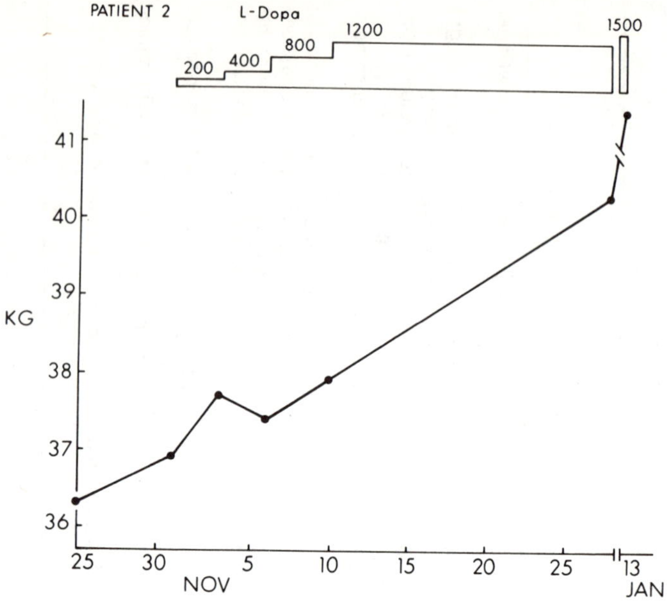

FIG. 1. Weight response of patient 2 to L-DOPA.

Five of the nine patients experienced weight gain of 3 to 5.5 kg in 19 to 27 days in the hospital. Four continued to gain weight taking L-DOPA after leaving the hospital (Fig. 1). One patient, following discharge, reverted to weight loss, presumably while taking L-DOPA, which she soon arbitrarily

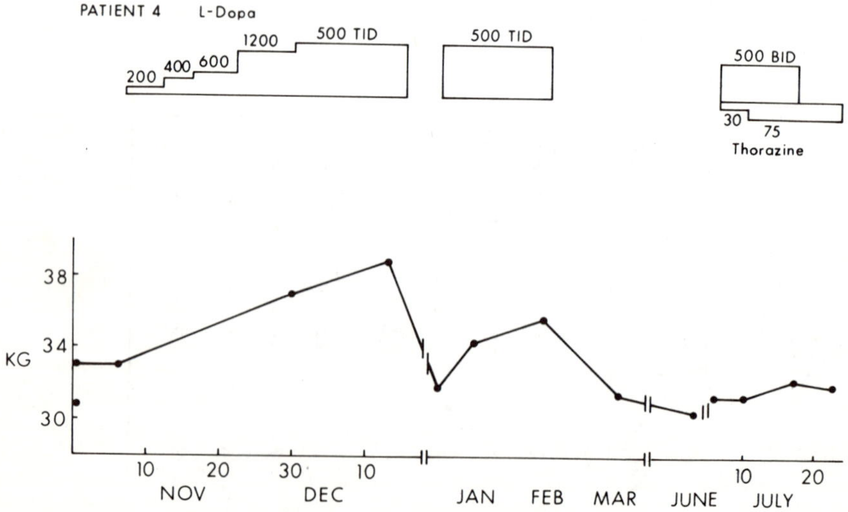

FIG. 2. Weight response of patient 4 to L-DOPA.

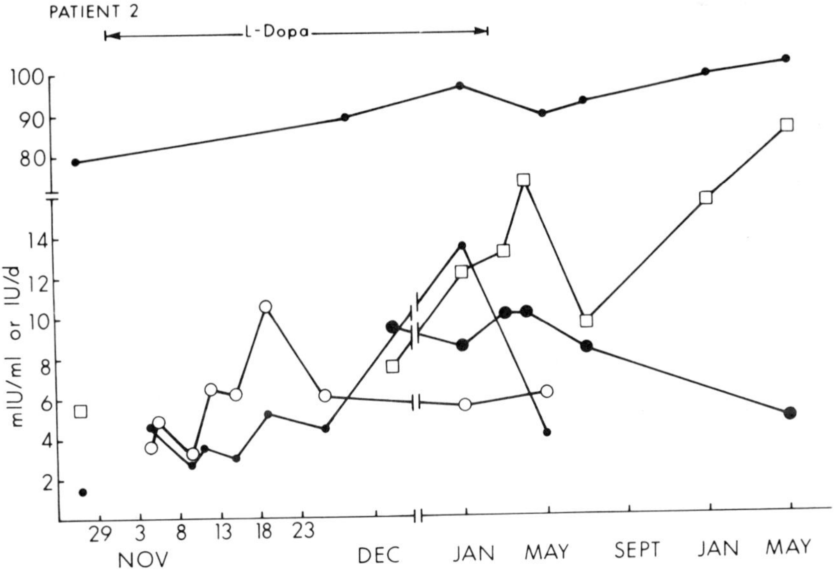

FIG. 3. Gonadotropin levels and weight changes in patient 2. □ serum FSH; ● serum LH; ○ urine FSH; • urine LH.

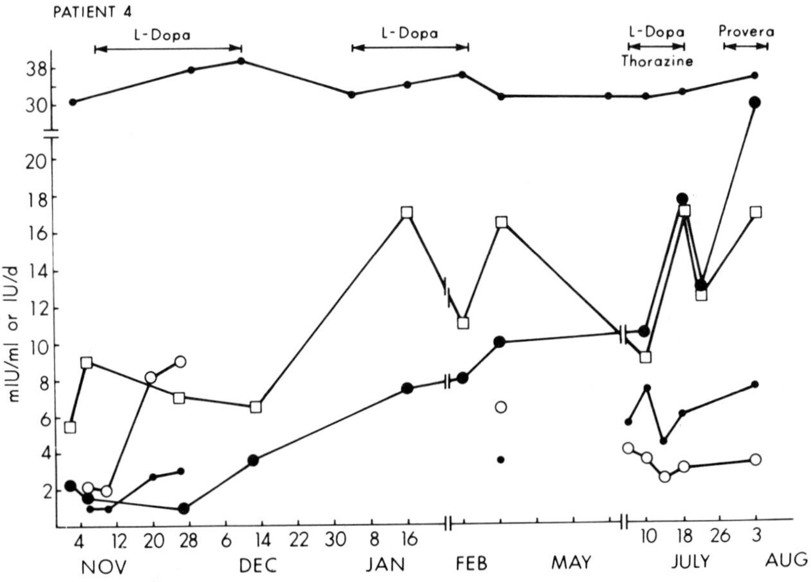

FIG. 4. Gonadotropin levels and weight changes in patient 4. □ serum FSH; ● serum LH; ○ urine FSH; • urine LH.

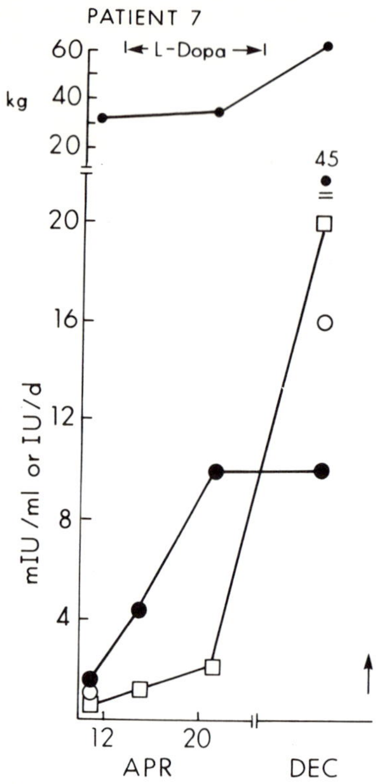

FIG. 5. Gonadotropin levels and weight changes in patient 7. □ serum FSH; ● serum LH: ○ urine FSH; • urine LH. Arrow indicates menses.

discontinued (Fig. 2). When L-DOPA was resumed while she was an outpatient, there was once more a significant (4 kg) weight gain only to be followed by weight loss when it was once again discontinued.

Four patients failed to respond with significant weight gain (<1 kg). One, after transfer to a psychiatric facility and treatment with psychotherapy, behavior modification, and behavior-modifying drugs, progressively gained weight (Fig. 4). One patient, who was very underweight for her age, was not underweight for her abnormally short stature which had followed acute weight loss of several years previously. She subsequently responded to cyproheptadine and later oxandrolone with significant weight gain and statural growth. Growth hormone responses to multiple stimuli which had been abnormally low also became normal (4). When last seen, two patients who did not respond were unchanged in their pathologic state of anorexia with incapacitating weight loss.

Serum and urine gonadotropin levels were observed relative to weight change and L-DOPA administration. All patients had abnormally low serum and urine gonadotropins when treatment with L-DOPA was initiated. Levels of both LH and FSH seemed unaffected by L-DOPA administration but rose in general relationship to weight gain. (Figs. 3 through 5). In two patients, menses resumed when their weights attained 50 and 64 kg, respectively, and following documented serum LH rises approaching midcycle peak levels (5) (Fig. 5).

DISCUSSION

In this uncontrolled study, five of nine adolescents and young adults with anorexia nervosa who were treated with L-DOPA responded with significant weight gain. One later relapsed to her former state of anorexia and weight loss. Two nonresponders subsequently responded to other forms of treatment and two remained, at last knowledge of their condition, unchanged from their state of inanition. Since the patients were treated with L-DOPA in an environment considerably different from the one prior to hospitalization, factors relative to psychological aspects of emotional support, rewards, and punishment (real or as viewed by the patient) akin to some behavior modification programs could not be completely controlled. An attempt to evaluate the drug therapy exclusive of environment was made with three patients who received placebo prior to L-DOPA. These individuals did not respond significantly, but one did not respond to L-DOPA either. These observations with L-DOPA therapy remain, then, inadequately tested in a controlled manner.

Several patients commented spontaneously that they "felt better" while taking L-DOPA and one elected to take L-DOPA on going home after having been off the medication in the hospital for several days. The nature of "feeling better" involved a modestly improved appetite and general sense of improved well-being. Most patients noted no similar feelings either spontaneously or when questioned.

There were no adverse effects. The drug was well tolerated. Black urine was observed in several taking L-DOPA, and several girls late in the course of therapy noted significant hair loss. It was difficult to attribute the latter to L-DOPA rather than to reestablishment of an improved nutritional status.

If one can make an analogy to the adipsia, aphagia, and decreased activity of rats that have had their nigrostriatal dopamine pathways destroyed and use the evidence obtained from numerous studies of deficient hypothalamic function, one might be persuaded that these patients could be deficient in brain dopamine. L-DOPA then would be logical treatment. In contrast to the very high doses that have been used in treating parkinsonism, we used very low doses of L-DOPA. It is possible that some of the nonresponse to L-DOPA was a result of inadequate dose.

In a disease with the considerable morbidity and even mortality of anorexia nervosa, one is often faced with a dilemma of choosing from numerous therapeutic courses that are moderately successful. L-DOPA may be one such course. We believe it can be used safely and with better-than-average possibility of success.

ACKNOWLEDGMENTS

Supported by U.S.P.H.S. Grant RR 847. Expert secretarial assistance was provided by Miss Emmy Behrens.

REFERENCES

1. Bruch, H. (1971): Death in anorexia nervosa. *Psychosom. Med.,* 33:135–144.
2. Bruch, H. (1973): *Eating Disorders: Obesity, Anorexia Nervosa and the Person Within.* Basic Books, New York.
3. Halmi, K. A. (1974): Anorexia nervosa: Demographic and clinical features in 94 cases. *Psychosom. Med.,* 36:18–26.
4. Huseman, C., and Johanson, A. J. (1975): Growth hormone deficiency in anorexia nervosa. *J. Pediatr.,* 87:946–948.
5. Johanson, A. J. (1971): FSH and LH in serum and urine of normal children and adults and in endocrine disorders. In: *Proceedings of the VII Pan American Congress of Endocrinology,* Sao Paulo, 1970, ICS 238. Excerpta Medica, Amsterdam.
6. Mecklenburg, R. S., Loriaux, D. L., Thompson, R. H., Andersen, A. E., and Lipsett, M. B. (1974): Hypothalamic dysfunction in patients with anorexia nervosa. *Medicine* (*Baltimore*), 53:147–159.
7. Moshang, T., Parks, J. S., Baker, L., Vaidya, V., Utiger, R. D., Bongiovanni, A. M., and Snyder, P. J. (1975): Low serum triiodothyronine in patients with anorexia nervosa. *J. Clin. Endocrinol. Metab.,* 40:470–473.
8. Silverman, J. A. (1974): Anorexia nervosa: Clinical observations in a successful treatment plan. *J. Pediatr.,* 84:68–73.
9. Theander, S. (1970): Anorexia nervosa. *Acta Psychiatr. Scand.* [*Suppl.*], 214:1–194.
10. Thompson, R., Rodriguez, A., Kowarski, A., Migeon, C. J., and Blizzard, R. M. (1972): Integrated concentrations of growth hormone correlated with plasma testosterone and bone age in preadolescent and adolescent males. *J. Clin. Endocrinol.,* 35:334–336.
11. Ungerstedt, U. (1971): Adipsia and aphagia after 6-hydroxydopamine induced degeneration of the nigro-striatal dopamine system. *Acta Physiol. Scand.* [*Suppl.*], 360:95–122.

Anorexia Nervosa, edited by
R. A. Vigersky. Raven Press,
New York © 1977

Preliminary Report on Metoclopramide in Anorexia Nervosa

H. Moldofsky, N. Jeuniewic, and P. E. Garfinkel

Clarke Institute of Psychiatry, Toronto, Ontario, Canada M5T 1R8

INTRODUCTION

Patients suffering from anorexia nervosa often complain of flatulent dyspepsia. Their symptoms may include postprandial epigastric discomfort, fullness, and bloating with inability to finish a meal. They may experience eructation with temporary relief, regurgitation of sour fluid to the mouth with heartburn, nausea, and vomiting (which may or may not be self-induced). The discomfort has been suggested to be related to delayed gastric emptying.

Metoclopramide is a potent antiemetic (6). It increases lower esophageal sphincter tone, increases the strength of gastric antral contractions, hastens gastric emptying (1,2,7,8), relaxes duodenal cap (4), and prevents pyloric regurgitation (5). The drug has been found to be of benefit in flatulent dyspepsia in association with delayed gastric emptying in subacute and chronic gastritis, or after such surgical procedures as cholecystectomy, vagotomy, and pyloroplasty (5). We hypothesized that metoclopramide would be effective in alleviating flatulent dyspepsia in patients with anorexia nervosa.

METHOD

Patients fulfilling criteria for anorexia nervosa (3) and admitted for treatment to the Clinical Investigation Unit at the Clarke Institute of Psychiatry were assessed by questionnaire for the presence of flatulent dyspepsia. After signing an informed consent they entered a 4-week double-blind placebo-controlled study of metoclopramide (Maxeran®) 10 mg t.i.d. p.c. Placebo and drug were given in randomized order, each over a 2-week period. After each meal the patients rated their symptom state on a 10-cm analogue scale. The symptoms include belching, fullness, tightness of clothing over abdomen, burning discomfort in upper abdomen and chest, regurgitation of bitter fluid to the mouth, and nausea. Vomiting and inability to finish the prescribed meal were rated as present or absent. Patients were interviewed daily to detect the emergence of untoward effects. Every 2 weeks the following blood tests were carried out: Hb, WBC and differential, blood smear, ESR, serum electrolytes, creatinine, direct and total bilirubin, SGOT, alkaline phosphatase, and serum T3 and T4.

RESULTS

To date five anorexic patients (four female and one male) have participated in this study. One patient who dropped out of the study while receiving the drug described major depressive symptoms. The depression remitted soon after discontinuing metoclopramide. Another patient refused to continue in the study after switching from drug to placebo. She had experienced a rapid return to dyspeptic symptoms after having had a remission on medication. Two had experienced dramatic relief. The one patient who had higher total dyspeptic scores had become agitated and depressed and dropped out of the study. Of interest, all subjects described greater ability to finish their meals. In follow-up (3 to 6 months) three patients have continued with the medication and experience symptom relief. A sixth patient who did not participate in the study has remained free of dyspeptic symptoms for the 10-month period on metoclopramide 10 mg at bedtime. Initially she had become depressed on 30 mg/day but was free of depressive symptoms on 10 mg daily.

CONCLUSIONS

Preliminary results favor metoclopramide having a beneficial influence on the symptoms of flatulent dyspepsia in anorexia nervosa. In 2 patients a major untoward effect was depression, which remitted with discontinuation of the drug.

As a cautionary note, metoclopramide has been recently reported to have potent effects on stimulating prolactin secretion (6,9) so that its long-term effects on neuroendocrine functioning, return of menstruation, and fertility in anorexic patients are unknown.

REFERENCES

1. Banke, L. (1969): Research in the action of metoclopramide in the gastrointestinal tract. VIII International Gastroenterology Congress, Prague, 1968. In: *Modern Gastroenterology,* edited by O. Grecor and O. Riedl, pp. 571–572. F. K. Schattauer, Stuttgart.
2. Connell, A. M., and George, J. D. (1969): Effect of metoclopramide on gastric function in man. *Gut,* 10:678–680.
3. Feighner, P., Robins, E., Guze, S. B., Woodruff, R. A., Jr., Winokur, G., and Munoz, R. (1972): Diagnostic criteria for use in psychiatric research. *Arch. Gen. Psychiatry,* 26:57–63.
4. Jacoby, H. I., and Brodie, D. A. (1967): Gastrointestinal actions of metoclopramide. An experimental study. *Gastroenterology,* 52:676–684.
5. Johnson, A. G. (1971): Controlled trial of metoclopramide in the treatment of flatulent dyspepsia. *Br. Med. J.,* 2:25–26.

6. Judd, S. J., Lazarus, S., and Smythe, G. (1976): Prolactin secretion by metoclopramide in man. *J. Clin. Endocrinol. Metab.,* 43:313–317.
7. Justin-Besancon, L., and Laville, C. (1964): Action anti-émétique du metaclopramide vis-à-vis de l'apomorphine et de l'hydergine. *C. R. Soc. Biol.* (*Paris*), 158:723–727.
8. Kreel, L. (1970): The use of oral metoclopramide in the barium meal and follow through examination. *Br. J. Radiol.,* 43:31–34.
9. Sowers, J. R., McCallum, R. W., Hershman, J. M., Carlson, H. E., Sturdevant, R. A. L., and Meyer, N. (1976): Comparison of metoclopramide with other dynamic tests of prolactin secretion. *J. Clin. Endocrinol. Metab.,* 43:679–681.

Anorexia Nervosa, edited by
R. A. Vigersky. Raven Press
New York © 1977

The Use of Diphenylhydantoin in Compulsive Eating Disorders: Further Studies

*Richard S. Green and **John H. Rau

*Departments of *Psychiatry and **Psychology, Long Island Jewish-Hillside Medical Center, Glen Oaks, N.Y. 11004; *Stony Brook Medical College, Stony Brook, N.Y. 11794; and *Department of Psychiatry, Cornell Medical College, New York, New York 10021*

INTRODUCTION

In our clinical experience, anorexia nervosa is not a unitary disease, but is a heterogeneous syndrome. Bliss and Branch (1), King (5), Bruch (2), and Feighner (3) have differentiated two groups diagnostically: viz., primary and secondary anorexia nervosa. Even among patients who would be reliably characterized as having anorexia nervosa, there is considerable variation as to symptoms and cause. Thus, there is substantial reason to question the utility of maintaining the diagnosis. It is interesting that anorexia nervosa is one of the few psychiatric syndromes in which the end result, that is, severe weight loss, is predominantly responsible for the diagnosis. Elsewhere in psychiatry, classification proceeds on a different basis. Should we consider suicide attempters or wrist cutters as a diagnostic group, or should we consider their behaviors as symptoms which can occur among various diagnostic entities?

The difficulty with a unitary diagnosis of anorexia nervosa arises if one asks whether a patient can be so diagnosed after a return to near-normal weight by such devices as tube feeding or behavior modification. That is, if the person met Bruch's (2) criteria of relentless pursuit of thinness, distorted body image, and sense of ineffectiveness but was of normal weight, would we consider her as having "anorexia nervosa"?

In a previous publication (6), we considered the possibility of looking at the various aspects of the syndrome from the point of view of eating behavior or subjective eating experience, in addition to outcome. It had been reported in the literature that approximately 25% of the patients with so-called anorexia nervosa have episodes of binge eating, whereas the remainder do not. The patients who are losing weight by not eating would seem to be in a separate behavioral category from those patients who are losing weight while eating compulsively at times and throwing up or using laxatives to prevent absorption of food. We had become interested in trying to understand the symptom of compulsive binge eating, and this chapter is an analysis of this group of patients. As with many symptoms, we feel that binge eating too is a heterogeneous symptom, which has a variety of etiologies.

METHODS

Our original paper (4) discussed the possible neurophysiological element in compulsive eating and its treatment by diphenylhydantoin. Further study of an additional 31 patients has led us to conclude that although the neurophysiological element is still clearly present in some patients, it is not in others. In these other patients, eating seems to have a different quality that can be related to attempts to deal with internal feeling states, primarily depression and anger; or else in some way it is a substitute for sexual activity.

In those patients who would ordinarily be diagnosed as having anorexia nervosa who are also compulsive eaters, it might be postulated that the relentless pursuit of thinness may really be an obesity phobia. The patients feel that they must control their weight and that extreme emaciation is a way of overcontrol; at the same time, it provides assurance that if their controls are temporarily disrupted, they will not become fat. We might compare this to a person who is afraid of poverty and is constantly accumulating money in the bank as an insurance policy. It has struck us in following these patients how, over time, they set various weight goals for themselves which they have to achieve, first 90 pounds, then 85, then 80, 75, 70, and so on down the line, as a way of assuring themselves that if they did gain some weight, they would not become obese.

All of the 31 patients we report on were studied: (a) with an extensive structured interview and an electroencephalogram (which included sleep, drowsy, and awake recordings); (b) with a check list of accompanying neurological soft signs (including rage attacks, headaches, abdominal pains, paresthesias, and feelings of depersonalization); (c) for evidence of other "compulsive behavior"; and (d) with psychological tests (MMPI, analogy test, and figure drawings).

PATIENT GROUPS

As we studied these patients, it became quite apparent that the term "compulsive eating" or "eating binges" meant different things to different people, and that it was important to delineate what was actually going on in the individual patient rather than accept on face value their description of their being compulsive eaters. Four groups of patients were delineated.

The first group of patients were constantly eating; they had been unable to control their food intake and had been referred to various physicians for diets. These patients were usually overweight and described themselves as compulsive eaters, meaning they could not go on a diet and lose weight.

They seemed to feel that the eating was not their responsibility. They did not get pleasure out of eating and were aware of what they were eating and when they were eating. Apart from their eating, these people would receive various characterological diagnoses. They complained of not being able to control their appetite because they felt hungry or needed to fill their stomachs. In the past, such patients were treated with amphetamines and other anorexics. The history was usually of losing weight and then regaining it.

The second group of patients described episodes during which they stuffed themselves with food. They felt they had to do this to relieve severe emotional states. On careful examination, this would be related to an episode of rejection, in which they felt lonely and unhappy; the food was a source of comfort to them. They usually ate something they enjoyed and were well aware of the sensations of pleasure. Some talked about eating when they felt angry and humiliated, and said that food was somehow their way of getting back at the world. Further analysis revealed that they were also making up for feelings of hurt and rejection.

The third group of patients characterized themselves as "sneak eaters," in that food was treated as "forbidden fruit." They usually ate at night and hid it from the family. These patients equated this with masturbatory experiences when they were younger, which they were now able to control, but the food and the pleasure in eating seemed to replace the masturbation. These first three groups we titled (for want of a better name) "pseudo-compulsive eaters."

The fourth group we called "true compulsive eaters." They were characterized in the following manner: their eating episodes were irregular, unpredictable, and ego-dystonic, wherein excessively large quantities of food were consumed "against the eaters' will." By ego-dystonic, we mean that the patients felt that their eating was unwanted and unacceptable, alien to their concept of themselves, and not within their control. It should be noted that the eating episode itself was considered unwanted and alien, rather than that they had postprandial guilt which many overeaters have. In addition, the patients usually reported some type of aura preceding and feelings of mild depersonalization during the eating episodes. They stated that they did not even taste the food, derived no pleasure from it, and felt compelled just to shove it into their mouths. There was no searching for any special type of food. Anything that was available was eaten. For example, some patients had taken food out of garbage cans. One of our patients, a nurse, had eaten food that came from a patient's tray on the unit, even though she knew it might have been infected.

The compulsion was so strong that patients risked their lives by traveling alone in the streets of Manhattan in search of all-night food stores where they might have something to eat. They also reported that as soon as they walked into the store, they took food off the shelf, opened it, and started eating while they gathered more food into their baskets. Many of these patients reported the abrupt cessation of the eating episode, followed by a strong desire to go to sleep. Several patients stated that if they were awakened from their sleep, they had a short period of disorientation. We indicated in our previous publications that these "true compulsive eating episodes" were described by some patients as "eating attacks." In fact, they appeared to us to be similar to a type of epileptic seizure.

We offered patients in each of the four groups an opportunity to try diphenylhydantoin to determine whether it might be of some assistance in controlling their behavior. This was done in order to see if the medication was an anorexic which would indiscriminately be of assistance to all patients who consider themselves compulsive eaters. A complete informed consent was signed by all the patients. Some of them refused to take the drug because of the possible side effects.

The group of 31 patients presented a wide-ranging group of psychiatric syndromes, including obsessive-compulsive neurosis, hysterical personality, borderline personality, schizophrenia, and passive-dependent personality.

RESULTS

The preliminary results indicated the following:

1. Of the 31 patients, 14 had abnormal electroencephalograms.
2. Seventeen patients had normal electroencephalograms.
3. Seven patients were categorized as having "true compulsive eating disorders." The other twenty-four patients had "pseudo-compulsive eating disorders." Of the seven true compulsive eaters, five had abnormal electroencephalograms and two did not. Of the pseudo-compulsive eaters, seven had abnormal electroencephalograms and fifteen did not.
4. Twenty-six patients were treated with diphenylhydantoin, 100 mg q.i.d. Nine patients responded positively, but seventeen either failed to respond or had an inadequate trial with the medicine. Of the twelve patients with abnormal electroencephalograms, six patients had a positive response to the medication. Of the fourteen patients with normal electroencephalograms, three patients had positive responses and eleven patients had negative responses.
5. In the true compulsive eating group, six of the seven patients had a definitive positive response to the medication. Their episodes of compulsive eating had greatly diminished or had stopped completely, and they were able to maintain a normal diet the remainder of the time. Among these six patients, two were extremely thin and would be diagnosed as having anorexia nervosa. They both had an overwhelming desire to remain thin and were inducing vomiting after each compulsive eating episode. They were literally starving themselves in between these episodes. In regard to their body image, it is of interest that they reported to us initially that they felt they looked fine. We then asked them if they saw a picture of themselves with their heads blocked off, would they comment about the figure if it belonged to someone other than themselves? They both laughingly said they thought

that person would look very thin. They despaired of their inability to control their eating, were obsessed with thoughts of food, felt it dominated their lives. They were constantly in dread of the attacks occurring, and were fearful that if something happened and they no longer were able to induce vomiting, they would become extremely obese.

One of these two women responded to medication with a cessation of her compulsive eating and a gradual return to normal weight as she became certain over a period of 8 months that she could control her weight and no longer needed to remain extremely thin.

The second emaciated patient in the group had an inadequate trial on diphenylhydantoin. This patient was given medication, and she reported a week later that she might have had a response to the medication but insisted on stopping it (allegedly because her analyst felt it was interfering with his treatment). We do not have any follow-up on her.

6. Three pseudo-compulsive eaters in the second group had positive responses to diphenylhydantoin. Two of them had abnormal EEGs and one had a normal EEG.

7. In four patients who were good responders to the medication (including one patient with a normal EEG), double-blind studies were done using the patients as their own controls. A placebo medication was prepared by our pharmacy using code numbers that were known only to the pharmacists. The patients were treated with either diphenylhydantoin or the placebo for 30 days at a time for 4 months. For 2 months the patients received the placebo, and the other 2 months they received active medication. The patients kept a record of the number of compulsive eating episodes they experienced, their weight, etc. In all four patients diphenylhydantoin was clearly the effective medication. It is of interest to note that when the patients returned 4 months later, they were sure which medication was the placebo and which was diphenylhydantoin, not only by their eating episodes but by other symptoms that were absent with the medication and present during the placebo period.

DISCUSSION

Anorexia nervosa is a syndrome. It is a description of signs and symptoms that appear together rather than an illness based on etiological factors, such as the infectious diseases or other illnesses in which we see pathological entities, as in the carcinomas or blood dyscrasias. On this assumption, it is our impression that this group of patients presenting with the syndrome of marked weight loss, relentless pursuit of thinness, distorted body image and feeling of ineffectiveness, hyperactivity, and amenorrhea actually have a variety of different disturbances. Some are intrapsychic, some interpersonal, and some neurophysiological.

We are trying to study one phenomenon that some members of this group present, namely, episodic compulsive eating. As of this date (in addition to the study group), we have encountered seven patients who have been diagnosed as having anorexia nervosa, who in addition to exhibiting the above-described signs and symptoms were also compulsive eaters. Of this group of seven, five were true episodic compulsive eaters. They had abnormal EEGs, and four of the five had other types of compulsive behavior (three of them compulsive stealing and one compulsive house cleaning). They had responded to treatment of their compulsive eating behavior with diphenylhydantoin, 100 mg q.i.d.; and subsequently on follow-up ranging from 6 months to 3 years, they regained their normal weight. They no longer feel they have to maintain an emaciated appearance. They also feel they are in control of their lives.

The mechanism of action of diphenylhydantoin is unknown. It is thought to act by preventing the spread of excessive neuronal discharges from one or more existing sites to other locations. However, the information obtained from the EEG tracings does not necessarily shed light on the locus in the central nervous system that may influence the onset of the cessation of an eating episode. Several possible methods by which such neurological dysregulation could affect eating and how the medication is effective suggest themselves. First, diphenylhydantoin may inhibit the appetite center and prevent a discharge in that area of the hypothalamus; second, perhaps the medication actually reduces the excitability of the nervous system in general and decreases general impulsive, compulsive activity. This is certainly possible since patients report that they are able to think better and their thoughts do not race as fast. Moreover, as has been noted, there is a cessation of other compulsive symptoms, such as kleptomania.

The third possibility, which has to be explored, is that diphenylhydantoin has some actual metabolic effect. We have noted in several patients with true compulsive eating that there tends to be a very flat glucose tolerance curve with a 1-hr postprandial blood sugar never rising above 130 mg/100 ml. This will have to be explored further.

REFERENCES

1. Bliss, E. L., and Branch, C. H. (1960): *Anorexia Nervosa: Its History, Psychology and Biology.* Paul B. Hoeber, Harper & Row, New York.
2. Bruch, H. (1973): *Eating Disorders: Obesity, Anorexia Nervosa and the Person Within.* Basic Books, New York.
3. Feighner, J. P., Robins, E., Guze, B., Woodruff, R. A., Jr., Winokur, G., and Munoz, R. (1972): Diagnostic criteria for use in psychiatric research. *Arch. Gen. Psychiatry,* 26:57–63.
4. Green, R., and Rau, J. (1974): Treatment of compulsive eating disturbances with anticonvulsant medication. *Am. J. Psychiatry,* 131:428–432.
5. King, A. (1963): Primary and secondary anorexia nervosa syndromes. *Br. J. Psychiatry,* 109:470–479.
6. Rau, J., and Green, R. (1975): Compulsive eating: A neuropsychologic approach to certain eating disorders. *Compr. Psychiatry,* 16:223–231.

Anorexia Nervosa, edited by
R. A. Vigersky. Raven Press,
New York © 1977

Conclusions

Robert A. Vigersky and *Arnold E. Andersen

*Reproduction Research Branch, National Institute of Child Health and Human Development, National Institutes of Health, Bethesda, Maryland 20014; and *Henry Phipps Psychiatric Clinic, The Johns Hopkins Hospital, Baltimore, Maryland 21205*

The cause of anorexia nervosa remains unclear despite the intensive worldwide investigative efforts of which the chapters in this book represent only a small part. A number of crucial issues raised in this volume need reiteration here.

1. A number of different criteria for the diagnosis of anorexia nervosa have been used, all of which are syndromic in nature. These criteria must be precisely stated in each communication in order to allow valid interstudy comparisons. Just as important is the definition of patient selection and the psychiatric and medical status of the patient at the time of entry into a study. For instance, abstainers and bulimic-vomiters may represent different entities, and, therefore, lumping them into one group for study or treatment may not be valid.

2. It should be recognized that patients referred to a particular center with special interest in anorexia nervosa may be a preselected group—early or late in their disease, untreated or treatment failures, and type of presenting symptom—depending on the location and interest of that center. Thus, only randomization of patients to different treatment modalities within a center is a valid test of any treatment's efficacy.

3. It is still unclear how much of what we see, both medically and psychiatrically, is a reflection of the effects of starvation *per se*. What we study may be a complicated mixture of what is specific for the disease and what is a more general effect of inanition.

4. Short-term weight gain can be achieved by a variety of methods, suggesting a nonspecific but as yet unidentified effect. Such short-term weight gain is probably necessary but not sufficient for long-term cure.

5. Endocrine-metabolic studies suggest that there is hypothalamic *dysfunction* but not necessarily hypothalamic *disease* in anorexia nervosa. Such abnormalities may be secondary to starvation itself and, although of great interest, do not differentiate primary from secondary processes.

6. Endocrinologically, anorexia patients appear to have a reversal of puberty. These changes appear to be related to weight (or fatness). This relationship is not absolutely clear, however, because menses after occur at a significantly higher weight than did menarche.

7. There is a virtual absence of the disorder in lower socioeconomic groups and it rarely occurs in men.

It is clear that the following among others need to be accomplished in the near future if we are to bring our understanding of anorexia nervosa from infancy to adulthood:

1. A true estimate of incidence and prevalence of this disorder in the United States.
2. A study of the gross and microscopic abnormalities of the cerebral cortex and hypothalamus in these patients.
3. A comparison of patients with anorexia nervosa and those who suffer from protein-calorie malnutrition with modern psychologic, hypothalamic, and endocrine testing.
4. Randomization of patients *within* a treatment center to different treatment modalities.
5. Double-blind protocols for the investigation of drug effects.
6. Further studies on factors affecting long- and short-term prognosis.
7. Hypothalamic-endocrine studies on long-term recovery patients.
8. Intracenter multidisciplinary approaches to large groups of patients.
9. A better understanding of the natural history of the disease and to what extent short-term therapy modifies it.
10. The measurement of weight and fatness with an accuracy comparable to that of the endocrine-metabolic parameters to which they are compared.
11. The development of measures which would accurately reflect the true thyroid and metabolic status of patients with anorexia nervosa.

Subject Index